# SHORTER
# CHRISTIAN PRAYER

# SHORTER
# CHRISTIAN PRAYER

### The Four-Week Psalter
### of the Liturgy of the Hours
### Containing

### MORNING PRAYER
### AND
### EVENING PRAYER

### With Selections for the Entire Year

Approved for Use
in the Dioceses of the United States of America

## CATHOLIC BOOK PUBLISHING CO.
New York
1988

Concordat Cum Originali:

John A. Gurrieri, Executive Director
Bishops' Committee on the Liturgy,
National Conference of Catholic Bishops

Taken from *The Liturgy of the Hours,* a translation of *Liturgia Horarum,* approved by the National Conference of Catholic Bishops for use in the Dioceses of the United States of America, October 21, 1974. Confirmed by the decree of the Congregation for Divine Worship, December 6, 1974 (Prot N. 2253/74).

Also approved for use in The Antilles, Bangladesh, Burma, the Pacific CEPAC (Fiji Islands, Rarotonga, Samoa and Tokelau, Tonga), Ghana, India, New Zealand, Pakistan, Papua New Guinea and the Solomons, The Philippines, Zimbabwe, South Africa, Sri Lanka, Tanzania, Uganda.

Published by Authority of the Bishops' Committee on the Liturgy, National Conference of Catholic Bishops.

For music and poetry, see acknowledgments on page 670.

(T-408)

© 1988 by *Catholic Book Publishing Co., N.Y.*
Printed in Korea
1 2 3 4 5 6 7 8 9 10 11 12 13 14 15

# CONTENTS

5

## 6      Contents

# PREFACE

In the Holy Spirit Christ carries out through the Church "the work of human redemption and God's perfect glorification," not only when the Eucharist is celebrated and the sacraments are administered but also in other ways, and especially when *The Liturgy of the Hours* is celebrated. In it Christ himself is present, in the assembled community, in the proclamation of God's word, "in the prayer and song of the Church."

The sanctification of human beings is accomplished, and worship offered to God, in *The Liturgy of the Hours* in an exchange or dialogue between God and human beings in which "God speaks to his people ... and his people reply to him in song and prayer."

Those taking part in *The Liturgy of the Hours* have access to holiness of the richest kind through the lifegiving word of God, to which it gives such great importance. The readings are drawn from Sacred Scripture, God's words in the psalms are sung in his presence, and the intercessions, prayers, and hymns are steeped in the inspired language of Scripture.

*The Liturgy of the Hours* is the prayer of the entire Church. The Liturgical renewal of Vatican II has endeavored to make it accessible to all Catholics by a simplification of structure. The Church desires that wherever possible at least the celebration of Morning Prayer and Evening Prayer in public worship services should be encouraged.

*The Liturgy of the Hours,* distributed over various periods of each day, is intended to sanctify time and work. It is also a perfect means for putting into practice the word of Jesus "about the necessity of praying always without growing weary"

(Luke 18:1). Contact with the riches of this liturgical prayer, which is pervaded by Sacred Scripture, will give Christians authentic spiritual food, encourage them to do good, and unite them closer to the Church of God throughout the world.

This shorter edition of *Christian Prayer* (which is the one-volume edition of *The Liturgy of the Hours*) has been drawn up precisely for this purpose. It presents a selection of material for Morning Prayer and Evening Prayer in a format that is easier for the lay person to use than the complete *Christian Prayer* or the four-volume *Liturgy of the Hours*.

It contains the complete Four-Week Psalter; material from the Proper of Seasons and the Proper of Saints; Night Prayer; Office for the Dead; Memorial of the Blessed Virgin; and the complete series of hymns found in the regular edition of *Christian Prayer*. The whole volume is printed in two colors on Bible paper and is a very handy pocket-size Office Book.

Thus, this *Shorter Christian Prayer* is ideal for parish use as well as private use. It may also be of help to clergy who are traveling or otherwise unable to utilize the complete edition of *The Liturgy of the Hours*.

It is the firm hope of the publishers that this aid will serve to nourish the spirit of prayer and to make *The Liturgy of the Hours* truly the prayer of the whole Church of God.

# INTRODUCTION

## From the General Instruction of the Liturgy of the Hours

[1.]* Public and common prayer by the people of God is rightly considered to be among the primary duties of the Church. From the very beginning those who were baptized "devoted themselves to the teaching of the apostles and to the community, to the breaking of the bread and to the prayers" (Acts 2:42). The Acts of the Apostles give frequent testimony to the fact that the Christian community prayed with one accord.[1]

The witness of the early Church teaches us that individual Christians devoted themselves to prayer at fixed times. Then, in different places, the custom soon grew of assigning special times to common prayer, for example, the last hour of the day, when evening draws on and the lamp is lighted, or the first hour, when night draws to a close with the rising of the daystar.

In the course of time other hours came to be sanctified by common prayer. These were seen by the Fathers as foreshadowed in the Acts of the Apostles. There we read of the disciples gathered together at the third hour.[2] The prince of the apostles "went up on the housetop to pray, about the sixth hour" (10:9); "Peter and John were going up to the temple at the hour of prayer, the ninth hour" (3:1); "about midnight Paul and Silas were praying and singing hymns to God" (16:25).

[2.] This kind of common prayer gradually took shape in the form of an ordered round of Hours. This Liturgy of the Hours or Divine Office, enriched by readings, is principally a prayer of praise and petition. In fact, it is the prayer of the Church with Christ and to Christ.

* The numbers in brackets correspond to those in the General Instruction of the Liturgy of the Hours.

---

[1] See Acts 1:14; 4:24; 12:5, 12; see Ephesians 5:19-21.    [2] See Acts 2:1-15.

## The *Commandment To Pray*

[5.] Jesus has commanded us to do as he did. On many occasions he said: "Pray," "ask," "seek,"[30] "in my name."[31] He gave us a formula of prayer in what is known as the Lord's Prayer.[32] He taught us that prayer is necessary,[33] that it should be humble,[34] vigilant,[35] persevering, confident in the Father's goodness,[36] single-minded and in conformity with God's nature.[37]

The apostles have handed on to us, scattered throughout their letters, many prayers, especially of praise and thanksgiving. They warn us that we must be urgent and persevering[41] in prayer offered to God[40] in the Holy Spirit[38] through Christ.[39] They tell us of its sure power in sanctifying[42] and speak of the prayer of praise,[43] of thanksgiving,[44] of petition[45] and of intercession on behalf of all.[46]

## *Christ's Prayer Continued by the Church*

[6.] Since man depends wholly on God, he must recognize and express this sovereignty of the Creator, as the devout people of every age have done by means of prayer.

Prayer directed to God must be linked with Christ, the Lord of all, the one mediator[47] through whom alone we have access to God.[48]

[30] Matthew 5:44; 7:7; 26:41; Mark 13:33; 14:38; Luke 6:28; 10:2; 11:9; 22:40, 46.
[31] John 14:13ff; 15:16; 16:23ff, 26.
[32] Matthew 6:9-13; Luke 11:2-4.
[33] Luke 18:1.
[34] Luke 18:9-14.
[35] Luke 21:36; Mark 13:33.
[36] Luke 11:5-13; 18:1-8; John 14:13; 16:23.
[37] Matthew 6:5-8; 23:14; Luke 20:47; John 4:23.
[38] Romans 8:15, 26; 1 Corinthians 12:3; Galatians 4:6; Jude 20.
[39] 2 Corinthians 1:20; Colossians 3:17.
[40] Hebrews 13:15.
[41] Romans 12:12; 1 Corinthians 7:5; Ephesians 6:18; Colossians 4:2; 1 Thessalonians 5:17; 1 Timothy 5:5; 1 Peter 4:7.
[42] 1 Timothy 4:5; James 5:15ff; 1 John 3:22; 5:14ff.
[43] Ephesians 5:19ff; Hebrews 13:15; Revelation 19:5.
[44] Colossians 3:17; Philippians 4:6; 1 Thessalonians 5:17; 1 Timothy 2:1.
[45] Romans 8:26; Philippians 4:6.
[46] Romans 15:30; 1 Timothy 2:1ff; Ephesians 6:18; 1 Thessalonians 5:25; James 5:14, 16.
[47] 1 Timothy 2:5; Hebrews 8:6; 9:15; 12:24.
[48] Romans 5:2; Ephesians 2:18; 3:12.

The excellence of Christian prayer lies in this, that it shares in the very love of the only-begotten Son for the Father and in that prayer which the Son put into words in his earthly life and which still continues unceasingly in the name of the whole human race and for its salvation, throughout the universal Church and in all its members.

### The Action of the Holy Spirit

[8.] The unity of the Church at prayer is brought about by the Holy Spirit, who is the same in Christ,[52] in the whole Church, and in every baptized person. It is this Spirit who "helps us in our weakness" and "intercedes for us with longings too deep for words" (Romans 8:26). As the Spirit of the Son, he gives us "the spirit of adopted sonship, by which we cry out: Abba, Father" (Romans 8:15; see Galatians 4:6; 1 Corinthians 12:3; Ephesians 5:18; Jude 20). There can be no Christian prayer without the action of the Holy Spirit who unites the whole Church and leads it through the Son to the Father.

### Prayer as Community Prayer

[9.] It follows that the example and precept of our Lord and the apostles in regard to constant and persevering prayer are not to be seen as a purely legal regulation. They belong to the very essence of the Church itself. The Church is a community, and it must express its nature as a community in its prayer as well as in other ways. Hence, when the community of the faithful is first mentioned in the Acts of the Apostles, it is seen as a community gathered together at prayer "with the women and Mary, the Mother of Jesus, and his brothers" (Acts 1:14). "There was one heart and soul in the company of those who believed" (Acts 4:32). Their oneness in spirit was founded on the word of God, on the brotherly communion, on the prayer and on the Eucharist.[53]

---

[52] See Luke 10:21.    [53] See Acts 2:42 (Greek).

Though prayer in one's room behind closed doors[54] is always necessary and to be encouraged[55] and is performed by the members of the Church through Christ in the Holy Spirit, yet there is a special excellence in the prayer of the community. Christ himself has said: "Where two or three are gathered together in my name, I am there in their midst" (Matthew 18:20).

## The Consecration of Time

[10.] Christ has taught us the necessity of praying at all times without losing heart (Luke 18:1). The Church has been faithful in obeying this instruction; it never ceases to offer prayer, and makes this exhortation its own: "Through him (Jesus) let us offer to God an unceasing sacrifice of praise" (Hebrews 15:15). The Church satisfies this requirement not only by the celebration of the Eucharist but in other ways also, especially through the Liturgy of the Hours, which is distinguished from other liturgical actions by the fact that it consecrates to God the whole cycle of day and night, as it has done from early Christian times.[56]

[11.] Since the purpose of the Liturgy of the Hours includes the sanctification of the day and of the whole range of human activity, its structure has been revised in such a way that, as far as possible, each Hour might be celebrated once more at the proper time and account taken of the circumstances of life today.[57]

Hence, "in order that the day may be truly sanctified and the Hours themselves recited with spiritual profit, it is preferable that they should be recited at the hour nearest to the one indicated by each canonical Hour."[58]

---

[54] See Matthew 6:6.
[55] See Second Vatican Council, constitution *Sacrosanctum Concilium*, no. 12.
[56] See *ibid.*, no. 83-84.
[57] See *ibid.*, no. 88.
[58] *Ibid.*, no. 94.

# THE CELEBRATION OF THE HOURS

## Introduction to the Hours

Morning Prayer begins with the Invitatory:

Lord, open my lips. And my mouth will proclaim your praise.

The invitatory psalm (95, 100, 67 or 24) with its antiphon follows.

The antiphon may be said first and then repeated after each strophe of the psalm.

The Glory to the Father concludes the invitatory psalm.

Evening Prayer and Night Prayer begin with the verse:

God, come to my assistance. Lord, make haste to help me. Glory to the Father. Alleluia.

The Alleluia is omitted during Lent.

## Morning and Evening Prayer

Introduction as above

Hymn — from the Four-Week Psalter or from the Proper of Seasons

Morning Prayer: psalm, O.T. canticle, psalm, with their antiphons

Evening Prayer: two psalms and N.T. canticle, with their antiphons

Reading

Responsory

Gospel Canticle (of Mary or Zechariah) with its antiphon

Intercessions

Lord's Prayer

Concluding Prayer (without Let us pray and with long conclusion) is proper except on weekdays in Ordinary Time

If a priest or deacon is presiding, he blesses and dismisses the people; otherwise the hour concludes with: May the Lord bless us . . . .

## Night Prayer

Introduction as above
Examination of conscience
Hymn
Psalmody
Reading
Responsory
Gospel Canticle (of Simeon) with its antiphon
Prayer from the Psalter
May the all-powerful Lord. . . .
Marian Antiphon

# THE CYCLE OF THE FOUR-WEEK PSALTER

Begin Week I on:

    First Sunday of Advent

    Monday after the Baptism of the Lord

    First Sunday of Lent

    Easter Sunday

On the Monday after Pentecost, use the Week indicated below:

| | |
|---|---|
| 2004 – Week 1 | 2010 – Week 4 |
| 2005 – Week 3 | 2011 – Week 3 |
| 2006 – Week 1 | 2012 – Week 4 |
| 2007 – Week 4 | 2013 – Week 3 |
| 2008 – Week 2 | 2014 – Week 2 |
| 2009 – Week 1 | 2015 – Week 4 |

**ORDINARY**

# MORNING PRAYER

## Introduction

Lord, open my lips.
—And my mouth will proclaim your praise.

## Invitatory (Antiphon and Psalm)

Psalm 95 with its antiphon is said. For Psalm 95, Psalms 100, 67, or 24 may be substituted.

In individual recitation, the antiphon may be said only at the beginning of the psalm; it need not be repeated after each strophe.

Ordinary Time: Weeks I and III

Sunday
Come, let us sing to the Lord, and shout with joy to the Rock who saves us.

Monday
Let us approach the Lord with praise and thanksgiving.

Tuesday
Come, let us worship our mighty King and Lord.

Wednesday
Come, let us worship before the Lord, our maker.

Thursday
Come, let us worship the Lord, for he is our God.

Friday
Come, let us give thanks to the Lord, for his great love is without end.

Saturday
Come, let us worship God who holds the world and its wonders in his creating hand.

## Ordinary Time: Weeks II and IV

**Sunday**

Come, worship the Lord, for we are his people, the flock he shepherds, alleluia.

**Monday**

Come, let us sing joyful songs to the Lord.

**Tuesday**

Come, let us worship the Lord, our mighty God.

**Wednesday**

Cry out with joy to the Lord, all the earth, serve the Lord with gladness.

**Thursday**

Come into the Lord's presence singing for joy.

**Friday**

Come, let us praise the Lord; in him is our delight.

**Saturday**

Let us listen to the voice of God; let us enter into his rest.

## Advent Season

**To Dec. 16**

Come, let us worship the Lord, the King who is to come.

**Dec. 17-23**

The Lord is close at hand; come, let us worship him.

**Dec. 24**

Today you will know the Lord is coming, and in the morning you will see his glory.

## Christmas Season

**Before Epiphany**

Christ is born for us; come, let us adore him.

**Holy Family**

Come, let us worship Christ, the Son of God, who was obedient to Mary and Joseph.

Jan. 1

Let us celebrate the motherhood of the Virgin Mary;
let us worship her Son, Christ the Lord.

After Epiphany

Christ has appeared to us; come, let us adore him.

Baptism of the Lord

Come, let us worship Christ, the beloved Son in
whom the Father was well pleased.

Lenten Season

Lent/Holy Week

Come, let us worship Christ the Lord, who for our
sake endured temptation and suffering.

Lent

Today if you hear the voice of the Lord, harden not
your hearts.

Good Friday

Come, let us worship Christ, the Son of God, who
redeemed us with his blood.

Holy Saturday

Though sinless, the Lord has been put to death.
The world is in mourning as for an only son.

Easter Season

To Ascension

The Lord is risen, alleluia.

Ascension

Alleluia, come, let us worship Christ the Lord as he
ascends into heaven, alleluia.

To Pentecost

Come, let us adore Christ the Lord who promised
to send the Holy Spirit on his people, alleluia.

## Pentecost
Alleluia, the Spirit of the Lord has filled the whole world; come, let us worship him, alleluia.

## Solemnities or Feasts

### Corpus Christi
Come, let us adore Christ the Lord, the bread of life.

### Sacred Heart
Come, let us worship Jesus, whose heart was wounded for love.

### Presentation of the Lord
Come, let us worship the Lord of creation; he enters his holy temple.

### Saint Joseph
Let us praise Christ the Lord as we celebrate the feast of Saint Joseph (alleluia).

### Annunciation
The Word was made flesh; come, let us worship him (alleluia).

### Birth of John the Baptist
Come, let us worship the Lord, the Lamb of God, proclaimed by John.

### Peter and Paul
Come, let us worship the Lord, the king of apostles.

### Transfiguration
Come, let us worship the King of glory, exalted on high.

### Assumption
Come, let us worship the King of kings; on this day his Virgin Mother was taken up to heaven.

**Triumph of the Cross**
Come, let us worship the King who was lifted up on the cross for our sake.

**All Saints**
Come, let us worship God whose praises are sung in the assembly of the saints.

**All Souls**
Come, let us worship the Lord; all things live for him.

**Dedication of Saint John Lateran**
Come, let us worship Christ, the Bridegroom of his Church (alleluia).

or

Come, let us worship Christ, who has shown his love for the Church (alleluia).

**Immaculate Conception**
Come, let us celebrate the Immaculate Conception of the Virgin Mary; let us worship her Son, Christ the Lord.

**BVM on Saturday**
Come, let us worship Christ, the Son of Mary.

or

Let us sing to the Lord as we keep this day in memory of the Blessed Virgin Mary.

## Invitatory Psalm

Psalm 95

A call to praise God

*Encourage each other daily while it is still today* (Hebrews 3:13).

(The antiphon is recited and then repeated)

Come, let us sing to the Lord
    and shout with joy to the Rock who saves us.—

Let us approach him with praise and thanksgiving
and sing joyful songs to the Lord.

(Antiphon repeated)

The Lord is God, the mighty God,
the great king over all the gods.
He holds in his hands the depths of the earth
and the highest mountains as well.
He made the sea; it belongs to him,
the dry land, too, for it was formed by his hands.

(Antiphon repeated)

Come, then, let us bow down and worship,
bending the knee before the Lord, our maker.
For he is our God and we are his people,
the flock he shepherds.

(Antiphon repeated)

Today, listen to the voice of the Lord:
Do not grow stubborn, as your fathers did
in the wilderness,
when at Meriba and Massah
they challenged me and provoked me,
Although they had seen all of my works.

(Antiphon repeated)

Forty years I endured that generation.
I said, "They are a people whose hearts go astray
and they do not know my ways."
So I swore in my anger,
"They shall not enter into my rest."

(Antiphon repeated)

Glory to the Father, and to the Son, and to the Holy
Spirit:
as it was in the beginning, is now, and will be for
ever. Amen.

(Antiphon repeated)

## Alternative Invitatory Psalms

In place of psalm 95 one of the following three psalms may be said. And if the substituted psalm occurs in the Office, psalm 95 may be said in its place.

### Psalm 100

Joyful song on entering God's temple

*The Lord calls his ransomed people to sing songs of victory* (Saint Athanasius).

Cry out with joy to the Lord, all the earth.
Serve the Lord with gladness.
Come before him, singing for joy.

Know that he, the Lord, is God.
He made us, we belong to him,
we are his people, the sheep of his flock.

Go within his gates, giving thanks.
Enter his courts with songs of praise.
Give thanks to him and bless his name.

Indeed, how good is the Lord,
eternal his merciful love.
He is faithful from age to age.

### Psalm 67

People of all nations will worship the Lord

*You must know that God is offering his salvation to all the world* (Acts 28:28).

O God, be gracious and bless us
and let your face shed its light upon us.
So will your ways be known upon earth
and all nations learn your saving help.

Let the peoples praise you, O God;
let all the peoples praise you.—

Let the nations be glad and exult
for you rule the world with justice.

With fairness you rule the peoples,
you guide the nations on earth.

Let the peoples praise you, O God;
let all the peoples praise you.

The earth has yielded its fruit
for God, our God, has blessed us.
May God still give us his blessing
till the ends of the earth revere him.

## Psalm 24

### The Lord's entry into his temple

*Christ opened heaven for us in the manhood he
assumed* (Saint Irenaeus).

The Lord's is the earth and its fullness,
the world and all its peoples.
It is he who set it on the seas;
on the waters he made it firm.

Who shall climb the mountain of the Lord?
Who shall stand in his holy place?
The man with clean hands and pure heart,
who desires not worthless things,
who has not sworn so as to deceive his neighbor.

He shall receive blessings from the Lord
and reward from the God who saves him.
Such are the men who seek him,
seek the face of the God of Jacob.

O gates, lift high your heads;
grow higher, ancient doors.
Let him enter, the king of glory!

Who is the king of glory?
The Lord, the mighty, the valiant,
the Lord, the valiant in war.

O gates, lift high your heads;
grow higher, ancient doors.
Let him enter, the king of glory!

Who is he, the king of glory?
He, the Lord of armies,
he is the king of glory.

## HYMN

Then the appropriate hymn is said.

## PSALMODY

The psalmody follows the hymn and consists of
one morning psalm, an Old Testament canticle
and another psalm of praise, together with the appropriate antiphons.

For the Sunday and weekday offices, the psalms,
canticle, and antiphons are taken from the current week of the Psalter.

During Advent, Christmas, Lent, and Easter the
antiphons are taken from the Proper of Seasons.

## READING

For the Sunday and weekday offices, the reading
is given in the Psalter.

During Advent, Christmas, Lent, and Easter the
reading is taken from the Proper of Seasons.

## RESPONSE TO THE WORD OF GOD

A period of silence may be observed after the
reading or homily.

Next a responsorial song or the responsory given
after the reading follows.

Other suitable songs may be substituted provided
they have been approved by the conference of
bishops.

GOSPEL CANTICLE (of Zechariah)         Luke 1:68-79

The following gospel canticle with the appropriate antiphon is then said.

For the Sunday office, the antiphon is taken from the Proper of Seasons; for the weekday office, from the Psalter.

During Advent, Christmas, Lent and Easter the antiphon is taken from the Proper of Seasons.

On solemnities and feasts the antiphon is taken from the Proper of Seasons or the Proper of Saints.

### The Messiah and his forerunner

Blessed be the Lord, the God of Israel;
he has come to his people and set them free.

He has raised up for us a mighty savior,
born of the house of his servant David.

Through his holy prophets he promised of old
   that he would save us from our enemies,
   from the hands of all who hate us.

He promised to show mercy to our fathers
and to remember his holy covenant.

This was the oath he swore to our father Abraham:
to set us free from the hands of our enemies,
free to worship him without fear,
holy and righteous in his sight
   all the days of our life.

You, my child, shall be called the prophet of the Most High;
for you will go before the Lord to prepare his way,
to give his people knowledge of salvation
by the forgiveness of their sins.

In the tender compassion of our God
the dawn from on high shall break upon us,
to shine on those who dwell in darkness and the
    shadow of death,
and to guide our feet into the way of peace.

The **Glory to the Father** is said at the end of the
canticles, unless otherwise noted.

The antiphon is repeated as usual.

INTERCESSIONS

The intercessions follow the canticle.

For the Sunday and weekday offices, the intercessions are found in the Psalter.

During Advent, Christmas, Lent and Easter the intercessions are taken from the Proper of Seasons.

All then say the **Lord's Prayer.** It may be preceded
by a brief invitation:

Now let us offer together the prayer our Lord Jesus
Christ taught us:

Now let us pray as Christ the Lord has taught us:

With longing for the coming of God's kingdom, let
us offer our prayer to the Father:

Gathering our prayers and praises into one, let us
offer the prayer Christ himself taught us:

Let us make our prayers and praise complete by offering the Lord's prayer:

Let us conclude our prayers with the Lord's prayer:

Let us again offer our praise to God and pray in the
words of Christ:

If the intercessions are addressed to Christ:

Remember us, Lord, when you come to your kingdom and teach us how to pray:

And now let us pray with confidence as Christ our Lord asked:

And now let us pray as the Lord told us:

We pattern our prayer on the prayer of Christ our Lord, and say:

Now let us offer the prayer Christ has given us as the model for all prayer:

The Lord's Prayer

Our Father . . .

### CONCLUDING PRAYER

The concluding prayer, without the invitation **Let us pray,** is added immediately after the **Lord's Prayer.**

For the weekday offices, the concluding prayer is taken from the current week of the Psalter; in all other offices it is taken from the Proper.

During Advent, Christmas, Lent and Easter the prayer is taken from the Proper of Seasons.

### CONCLUSION

If a priest or deacon presides, he dismisses the people:

The Lord be with you.
— And also with you.

May almighty God bless you,
the Father, and the Son, and the Holy Spirit.
— Amen.

Another form of the blessing may be used, as at Mass.

Then he adds:

Go in peace.
— Thanks be to God.

In the absence of a priest or deacon and in individual recitation, Morning Prayer concludes:

May the Lord bless us,
protect us from all evil
and bring us to everlasting life.
— Amen.

## EVENING PRAYER

God, come to my assistance.
— Lord, make haste to help me.

Glory to the Father, and to the Son, and to the Holy
    Spirit:
as it was in the beginning, is now, and will be for
    ever. Amen. Alleluia.

HYMN

Then the appropriate hymn is said.

PSALMODY

The psalmody follows the hymn and consists of two
psalms or parts of psalms, and a New Testament
canticle, together with the appropriate antiphons.

For the Sunday and weekday offices, the psalms,
canticle and antiphons are taken from the current
week of the Psalter.

During Advent, Christmas, Lent, and Easter the antiphons are taken from the Proper of Seasons.

READING

For the Sunday and weekday offices, the reading
is given in the Psalter.

During Advent, Christmas, Lent and Easter the reading is taken from the Proper of Seasons.

RESPONSE TO THE WORD OF GOD

A period of silence may be observed after the reading or homily.

Next a responsorial song or the responsory given after the reading follows.

Other suitable songs may be substituted, provided they have been approved by the conference of bishops.

GOSPEL CANTICLE (of Mary)                    Luke 1:46-55

The following gospel canticle with the appropriate antiphon is then said.

For the Sunday office, the antiphon is taken from the Proper of Seasons; for the weekday office, from the Psalter.

During Advent, Christmas, Lent and Easter the antiphon is taken from the Proper of Seasons.

On solemnities and feasts the antiphon is taken from the Proper of Seasons or the Proper of Saints.

The soul rejoices in the Lord

My soul proclaims the greatness of the Lord,
my spirit rejoices in God my Savior
for he has looked with favor on his lowly servant.

From this day all generations will call me blessed:
the Almighty has done great things for me,
and holy is his Name.

He has mercy on those who fear him
in every generation.

He has shown the strength of his arm,
he has scattered the proud in their conceit.

He has cast down the mighty from their thrones,
and has lifted up the lowly.

He has filled the hungry with good things,
and the rich he has sent away empty.

He has come to the help of his servant Israel
for he has remembered his promise of mercy,
the promise he made to our fathers,
to Abraham and his children for ever.

The **Glory to the Father** is said at the end of the canticles, unless otherwise noted.

The antiphon is repeated as usual.

INTERCESSIONS

The intercessions follow the canticle.

For the Sunday and weekday offices, the intercessions are found in the Psalter.

During Advent, Christmas, Lent and Easter the intercessions are taken from the Proper of Seasons.

All then say the **Lord's Prayer**. It may be preceded by a brief invitation:

Now let us offer together the prayer our Lord Jesus Christ has taught us:

Now let us pray as Christ the Lord has taught us:

With longing for the coming of God's kingdom, let us offer our prayer to the Father:

Gathering our prayers and praises into one, let us offer the prayer Christ himself taught us:

Let us make our prayers and praise complete by offering the Lord's prayer:

Let us conclude our prayers with the Lord's prayer:

Let us again offer our praise to God and pray in the words of Christ:

If the intercessions are addressed to Christ:

Remember us, Lord, when you come to your kingdom and teach us how to pray:

And now let us pray with confidence as Christ our Lord asked:

And now let us pray as the Lord told us:

We pattern our prayer on the prayer of Christ our Lord, and say:

Now let us offer the prayer Christ has given as the model for all prayer:

The Lord's Prayer

Our Father. . . .

CONCLUDING PRAYER

The concluding prayer, without the invitation **Let us pray,** is added immediately after the **Lord's Prayer.**

For the weekday offices, the concluding prayer is taken from the current week of the Psalter; in all other offices it is taken from the Proper.

During Advent, Christmas, Lent and Easter the prayer is taken from the Proper of Seasons.

CONCLUSION

If a priest or deacon presides, he dismisses the people:

**The Lord be with you.**
**— And also with you.**

**May almighty God bless you,**
**the Father, and the Son, and the Holy Spirit.**
**— Amen.**

Another form of the blessing may be used, as at Mass.

Then he adds:

Go in peace.
— Thanks be to God.

In the absence of a priest or deacon and in individual recitation, Evening Prayer concludes:

May the Lord bless us,
protect us from all evil
and bring us to everlasting life.
— Amen.

# THE FOUR-WEEK PSALTER

The four-week cycle of the Psalter is so arranged in conjunction with the liturgical year that the first week of the cycle coincides with the First Sunday of Advent, the First Sunday of Lent and the first week of Ordinary Time. On Ash Wednesday and the following three days, the psalms are taken from Week IV of the Psalter. After the Octave of Easter, Week II of the Psalter is resumed on Monday of the Second Week of Easter.

Proper antiphons for Advent, Lent, Christmas and Easter are taken from the Proper of Seasons.

The red dash (—) indicates that the strophe continues on the next page.

# WEEK I

## SUNDAY

### Evening Prayer I

God, come to my assistance. Glory to the Father. As it was in the beginning. Alleluia.

HYMN, no. **32** or **184**. Outside Ordinary Time, see Guide, **578**.

PSALMODY

Ant. 1  Like burning incense, Lord, let my prayer rise up to you.

> Advent: Proclaim the good news among the nations: Our God will come to save us.

> Lent, 1st Sunday: Lord God, we ask you to receive us and be pleased with the sacrifice we offer you this day with humble and contrite hearts.

> Lent, 5th Sunday: I shall place my law in their hearts; I shall be their God, and they will be my people.

> Easter, 5th Sunday: Like the evening offering my hands rise up in prayer to you, O Lord, alleluia.

Psalm 141:1-9

A prayer when in danger

*An angel stood before the face of God, thurible in hand. The fragrant incense soaring aloft was the prayer of God's people on earth* (Revelation 8:4).

I have called to you, Lord; hasten to help me!
Hear my voice when I cry to you. —

37

Let my prayer arise before you like incense,
the raising of my hands like an evening oblation.

Set, O Lord, a guard over my mouth;
keep watch at the door of my lips!
Do not turn my heart to things that are wrong,
to evil deeds with men who are sinners.

Never allow me to share in their feasting.
If a good man strikes or reproves me it is kindness;
but let the oil of the wicked not anoint my head.
Let my prayer be ever against their malice.

Their princes were thrown down by the side of
the rock:
then they understood that my words were kind.
As a millstone is shattered to pieces on the
ground,
so their bones were strewn at the mouth of the
grave.

To you, Lord God, my eyes are turned:
in you I take refuge; spare my soul!
From the trap they have laid for me keep me safe:
keep me from the snares of those who do evil.

Glory to the Father, and to the Son, and to the
Holy Spirit:
as it was in the beginning, is now, and will be
for ever. Amen.

All psalms and canticles are concluded with the
Glory to the Father unless otherwise indicated.

Psalm-prayer

Lord, from the rising of the sun to its setting
your name is worthy of all praise. Let our prayer
come like incense before you. May the lifting up of
our hands be as an evening sacrifice acceptable to
you, Lord our God.

Ant. 2  **You are my refuge, Lord; you are all that I desire in life.**

Advent: Know that the Lord is coming and with him all his saints; that day will dawn with a wonderful light, alleluia.

Lent, 1st Sunday: Call upon the Lord and he will hear you; cry out and he will answer: Here I am.

Lent, 5th Sunday: I count everything as loss but this: the surpassing worth of knowing Christ Jesus my Lord.

Easter, 5th Sunday: You have led me forth from my prison, that I may give praise to your name, alleluia.

## Psalm 142

### You, Lord, are my refuge

*What is written in this psalm was fulfilled in our Lord's passion* (Saint Hilary).

With all my voice I cry to the Lord,
with all my voice I entreat the Lord.
I pour out my troubles before him;
I tell him all my distress
while my spirit faints within me.
But you, O Lord, know my path.

On the way where I shall walk
they have hidden a snare to entrap me.
Look on my right and see:
there is not one who takes my part.
I have no means of escape,
not one who cares for my soul.

I cry to you, O Lord.
I have said: "You are my refuge,
all I have left in the land of the living."
Listen then to my cry
for I am in the depths of distress.

Rescue me from those who pursue me
for they are stronger than I.

Bring my soul out of this prison
and then I shall praise your name.
Around me the just will assemble
because of your goodness to me.

Psalm-prayer

Lord, we humbly ask for your goodness. May you
help us to hope in you, and give us a share with
your chosen ones in the land of the living.

Ant. 3  The Lord Jesus humbled himself, and God
exalted him for ever.

Advent: The Lord will come with mighty power; all mortal eyes shall see him.

Lent, 1st Sunday: Christ died for our sins, the innocent
for the guilty to bring us back to God. In the body he
was put to death, but in the spirit he was raised to
life.

Lent, 5th Sunday: Although he was the Son of God,
Christ learned obedience through suffering.

Easter, 5th Sunday: The Son of God learned obedience
through suffering and became for all who obey him
the source of eternal salvation, alleluia.

Canticle          Philippians 2:6-11

Christ, God's holy servant

Though he was in the form of God,
Jesus did not deem equality with God
something to be grasped at.

Rather, he emptied himself
and took the form of a slave,
being born in the likeness of men.

He was known to be of human estate,
and it was thus that he humbled himself,
obediently accepting even death,
death on a cross!

Because of this,
God highly exalted him
and bestowed on him the name
above every other name,

So that at Jesus' name
every knee must bend
in the heavens, on the earth,
and under the earth,
and every tongue proclaim
to the glory of God the Father:
JESUS CHRIST IS LORD!

READING                    Romans 11:25, 30-36

I do not want you to be unaware of this mystery, brothers, so that you will not become wise [in] your own estimation: Just as you once disobeyed God but have now received mercy because of their disobedience, so they have now disobeyed in order that, by virtue of the mercy shown to you, they too may [now] receive mercy. For God delivered all to disobedience, that he might have mercy upon all.

Oh, the depth of the riches and wisdom and knowledge of God! How inscrutable are his judgments and how unsearchable his ways!

"For who has known the mind of the Lord
  or who has been his counselor?"

"Or who has given him anything
  that he may be repaid?"

For from him and through him and for him are all things. To him be glory forever. Amen.

RESPONSORY

Our hearts are filled with wonder as we contemplate your works, O Lord.
— Our hearts are filled with wonder as we contemplate your works, O Lord.

We praise the wisdom which wrought them all,
— as we contemplate your works, O Lord.

Glory to the Father . . .
— Our hearts are filled with wonder as we contemplate your works, O Lord.

CANTICLE OF MARY, antiphon as in the Proper of Seasons.

INTERCESSIONS

We give glory to the one God—Father, Son and Holy Spirit—and in our weakness we pray:
*Lord, be with your people.*
Holy Lord, Father all-powerful, let justice spring up on the earth,
— then your people will dwell in the beauty of peace.
Let every nation come into your kingdom,
— so that all peoples will be saved.
Let married couples live in your peace,
— and grow in mutual love.
Reward all who have done good to us, Lord,
— and grant them eternal life.
Look with compassion on victims of hatred and war,
— grant them heavenly peace.

Our Father . . .

Concluding prayer, as in the Proper of Seasons.

Conclusion, as in the Ordinary, 29.

## Invitatory
Lord, open my lips.

Ant. Come, let us sing to the Lord, and shout with joy to the Rock who saves us, alleluia.

Invitatory psalm, 22.

## Morning Prayer

The following verse and response are omitted when the hour begins with the invitatory.

God, come to my assistance. Glory to the Father.
As it was in the beginning. Alleluia.

HYMN, no. 1 or 151. Outside Ordinary Time, see
Guide, 578.

PSALMODY

Ant. 1  As morning breaks I look to you, O God, to
be my strength this day, alleluia.

Advent: On that day sweet wine will flow from the mountains, milk and honey from the hills, alleluia.

Lent, 1st Sunday: I will praise you all my life, O Lord; in
your name I will lift up my hands.

Lent, 5th Sunday: My God, you have become my help.

Easter, 5th Sunday: Whoever thirsts will drink freely of
life-giving water, alleluia.

Psalm 63:2-9

A soul thirsting for God

*Whoever has left the darkness of sin, yearns for God.*

O God, you are my God, for you I long;
for you my soul is thirsting.
My body pines for you
like a dry, weary land without water.
So I gaze on you in the sanctuary
to see your strength and your glory.

For your love is better than life,
my lips will speak your praise.
So I will bless you all my life,
in your name I will lift up my hands.
My soul shall be filled as with a banquet,
my mouth shall praise you with joy.

On my bed I remember you.
On you I muse through the night
for you have been my help;
in the shadow of your wings I rejoice.
My soul clings to you;
your right hand holds me fast.

Psalm-prayer

Father, creator of unfailing light, give that same light to those who call to you. May our lips praise you; our lives proclaim your goodness; our works give you honor, and our voices celebrate you for ever.

Ant. 2 **From the midst of the flames the three young men cried out with one voice: Blessed be God, alleluia.**

Advent: The mountains and hills will sing praise to God; all the trees of the forest will clap their hands, for he is coming, the Lord of a kingdom that lasts for ever, alleluia.

Lent, 1st Sunday: Sing a hymn of praise to our God; praise him above all for ever.

Lent, 5th Sunday: Free us by your wonderful works; deliver us from the power of death.

Easter, 5th Sunday: Worship the Lord who made the heavens and the earth, springs of water and the mighty sea, alleluia.

Canticle        Daniel 3:57-88, 56

Let all creatures praise the Lord

*All you servants of the Lord, sing praise to him* (Revelation 19:5).

Bless the Lord, all you works of the Lord.
Praise and exalt him above all forever.
Angels of the Lord, bless the Lord.
You heavens, bless the Lord.
All you waters above the heavens, bless the Lord.
All you hosts of the Lord, bless the Lord.
Sun and moon, bless the Lord.
Stars of heaven, bless the Lord.

Every shower and dew, bless the Lord.
All you winds, bless the Lord.
Fire and heat, bless the Lord.
Cold and chill, bless the Lord. —

Dew and rain, bless the Lord.
Frost and chill, bless the Lord.
Ice and snow, bless the Lord.
Nights and days, bless the Lord.
Light and darkness, bless the Lord.
Lightnings and clouds, bless the Lord.

Let the earth bless the Lord.
Praise and exalt him above all forever.
Mountains and hills, bless the Lord.
Everything growing from the earth, bless the
    Lord.
You springs, bless the Lord.
Seas and rivers, bless the Lord.
You dolphins and all water creatures, bless the
    Lord.
All you birds of the air, bless the Lord.
All you beasts, wild and tame, bless the Lord.
You sons of men, bless the Lord.

O Israel, bless the Lord.
Praise and exalt him above all forever.
Priests of the Lord, bless the Lord.
Servants of the Lord, bless the Lord.
Spirits and souls of the just, bless the Lord.
Holy men of humble heart, bless the Lord.
Hananiah, Azariah, Mishael, bless the Lord.
Praise and exalt him above all forever.

Let us bless the Father, and the Son, and the
    Holy Spirit.
Let us praise and exalt him above all forever.
Blessed are you, Lord, in the firmament of
    heaven.
Praiseworthy and glorious and exalted above
    all forever.

At the end of the canticle the Glory to the Father
is not said.

Ant. 3  Let the people of Zion rejoice in their King,
        alleluia.

Advent: A great prophet will come to Jerusalem; of that people he will make a new creation.

Lent, 1st Sunday: The Lord delights in his people; he honors the humble with victory.

Lent, 5th Sunday: The hour has come for the Son of Man to be glorified.

Easter, 5th Sunday: The saints will rejoice in glory, alleluia.

## Psalm 149

### The joy of God's holy people

*Let the sons of the Church, the children of the new people, rejoice in Christ, their King* (Hesychius).

Sing a new song to the Lord,
his praise in the assembly of the faithful.
Let Israel rejoice in its maker,
let Zion's sons exult in their king.
Let them praise his name with dancing
and make music with timbrel and harp.

For the Lord takes delight in his people.
He crowns the poor with salvation.
Let the faithful rejoice in their glory,
shout for joy and take their rest.
Let the praise of God be on their lips
and a two-edged sword in their hand,

to deal out vengeance to the nations
and punishment on all the peoples;
to bind their kings in chains
and their nobles in fetters of iron;
to carry out the sentence pre-ordained;
this honor is for all his faithful.

Psalm-prayer

Let Israel rejoice in you, Lord, and acknowledge you as creator and redeemer. We put our trust in your faithfulness and proclaim the wonderful truths of salvation. May your loving kindness embrace us now and for ever.

READING                                    Revelation 7:9-12

I had a vision of a great multitude, which no one could count, from every nation, race, people, and tongue. They stood before the throne and before the Lamb, wearing white robes and holding palm branches in their hands. They cried out in a loud voice:

"Salvation comes from our God, who is seated on
      the throne,
   and from the Lamb."

All the angels stood around the throne and around the elders and the four living creatures. They prostrated themselves before the throne, worshiped God, and exclaimed:

"Amen. Blessing and glory, wisdom and thanks-
      giving,
   honor, power, and might
   be to our God forever and ever. Amen."

RESPONSORY

Christ, Son of the living God, have mercy on us.
— Christ, Son of the living God, have mercy on us.

You are seated at the right hand of the Father,
— have mercy on us.

Glory to the Father . . .
— Christ, Son of . . .

CANTICLE OF ZECHARIAH, antiphon as in the Proper of Seasons.

INTERCESSIONS

Christ is the sun that never sets, the true light that shines on every man. Let us call out to him in praise:
   Lord, you are our life and our salvation.
Creator of the stars, we thank you for your gift, the first rays of the dawn,
— and we commemorate your resurrection.

May your Holy Spirit teach us to do your will today,
— and may your Wisdom guide us always.

Each Sunday give us the joy of gathering as your
    people,
— around the table of your word and your body.

From our hearts we thank you,
— for your countless blessings.

Our Father . . .

Concluding prayer, as in the Proper of Seasons.

Conclusion, as in the Ordinary, 29.

## Evening Prayer II

God, come to my assistance. Glory to the Father. As
it was in the beginning. Alleluia.

HYMN, no. 33 or 182. Outside Ordinary Time, see
Guide, 578.

PSALMODY

Ant. 1  The Lord will stretch forth his mighty scepter
        from Zion, and he will reign for ever, alleluia.

   Advent: Rejoice, daughter of Zion; shout for joy, daughter
   of Jerusalem, alleluia.

   Lent, 1st Sunday: Worship your Lord and God; serve him
   alone.

   Lent, 5th Sunday: As the serpent was lifted up in the
   desert, so the Son of Man must be lifted up.

   Easter, 5th Sunday: The Lord has risen and is seated at
   the right hand of God, alleluia.

Psalm 110:1-5, 7

The Messiah, king and priest

*Christ's reign will last until all his enemies are
made subject to him* (1 Corinthians 15:25).

   The Lord's revelation to my Master:
   "Sit on my right:
   your foes I will put beneath your feet."

The Lord will wield from Zion
your scepter of power:
rule in the midst of all your foes.

A prince from the day of your birth
on the holy mountains;
from the womb before the dawn I begot you.

The Lord has sworn an oath he will not change.
"You are a priest for ever,
a priest like Melchizedek of old."

The Master standing at your right hand
will shatter kings in the day of his great wrath.

He shall drink from the stream by the wayside
and therefore he shall lift up his head.

Psalm-prayer

Father, we ask you to give us victory and peace.
In Jesus Christ, our Lord and King, we are already
seated at your right hand. We look forward to praising you in the fellowship of all your saints in our
heavenly homeland.

Ant. 2  The earth is shaken to its depths before the
glory of your face.

Advent: Christ our King will come to us, the Lamb of
God foretold by John.

Lent, 1st Sunday: This is the time when you can win
God's favor; the day when you can be saved.

Lent, 5th Sunday: The Lord of hosts protects us and
sets us free; he guides and saves his people.

Easter, 5th Sunday: He has rescued us from the power of
darkness and has brought us into the kingdom of his
Son, alleluia.

## Psalm 114

The Israelites are delivered from the bondage of Egypt

*You too left Egypt when, at baptism, you renounced that world which is at enmity with God* (Saint Augustine).

When Israel came forth from Egypt,
Jacob's sons from an alien people,
Judah became the Lord's temple,
Israel became his kingdom.

The sea fled at the sight:
the Jordan turned back on its course,
the mountains leapt like rams
and the hills like yearling sheep.

Why was it, sea, that you fled,
that you turned back, Jordan, on your course?
Mountains, that you leapt like rams,
hills, like yearling sheep?

Tremble, O earth, before the Lord,
in the presence of the God of Jacob,
who turns the rock into a pool
and flint into a spring of water.

Psalm-prayer

Almighty God, ever-living mystery of unity and trinity, you gave life to the new Israel by birth from water and the Spirit, and made it a chosen race, a royal priesthood, a people set apart as your eternal possession. May all those you have called to walk in the splendor of the new light render you fitting service and adoration.

Ant. 3 All power is yours, Lord God, our mighty King, alleluia.

Advent: I am coming soon, says the Lord; I will give to everyone the reward his deeds deserve.

Easter, 5th Sunday: Alleluia, our God is king; glory and
    praise to him, alleluia.

The following canticle is said with the **Alleluia**
when Evening Prayer is sung; when the office is
recited, the **Alleluia** may be said at the beginning
and end of each strophe.

Canticle  See Revelation 19:1-7

The wedding of the Lamb

Alleluia.
Salvation, glory, and power to our God:
(℟. **Alleluia**.)
his judgments are honest and true.
℟. **Alleluia** (alleluia).

Alleluia.
Sing praise to our God, all you his servants,
(℟. **Alleluia**.)
all who worship him reverently, great and small.
℟. **Alleluia** (alleluia).

Alleluia.
The Lord our all-powerful God is King;
(℟. **Alleluia**.)
let us rejoice, sing praise, and give him glory.
℟. **Alleluia** (alleluia).

Alleluia.
The wedding feast of the Lamb has begun,
(℟. **Alleluia**.)
and his bride is prepared to welcome him.
℟. **Alleluia** (alleluia).

## Lent

Lent, 1st Sunday: Now we must go up to Jerusalem,
    where all that has been written about the Son of Man
    will be fulfilled.

Lent, 5th Sunday: **He was pierced for our offenses and burdened with our sins. By his wounds we are healed.**

Canticle                    1 Peter 2:21-24

The willing acceptance of his passion by Christ,
the servant of God

Christ suffered for you,
and left you an example
to have you follow in his footsteps.

He did no wrong;
no deceit was found in his mouth.
When he was insulted,
he returned no insult.

When he was made to suffer,
he did not counter with threats.
Instead he delivered himself up
to the One who judges justly.

In his own body
he brought your sins to the cross,
so that all of us, dead to sin,
could live in accord with God's will.

By his wounds you were healed.

READING                    2 Corinthians 1:3-7

Blessed be the God and Father of our Lord Jesus Christ, the Father of compassion and God of all encouragement, who encourages us in our every affliction, so that we may be able to encourage those who are in any affliction with the encouragement

with which we ourselves are encouraged by God.
For as Christ's sufferings overflow to us, so
through Christ does our encouragement also overflow. If we are afflicted, it is for your encouragement and salvation; if we are encouraged, it is for
your encouragement, which enables you to endure
the same sufferings that we suffer. Our hope for
you is firm, for we know that as you share in the
sufferings, you also share in the encouragement.

RESPONSORY

The whole creation proclaims the greatness of your
   glory.
— The whole creation proclaims the greatness of
   your glory.
Eternal ages praise
— the greatness of your glory.
Glory to the Father . . .
— The whole creation . . .

CANTICLE OF MARY, antiphon as in the Proper of
Seasons.

INTERCESSIONS

Christ the Lord is our head; we are his members. In
   joy let us call out to him:
   *Lord, may your kingdom come.*
Christ our Savior, make your Church a more vivid
   symbol of the unity of all mankind,
— make it more effectively the sacrament of salvation for all peoples.
Through your presence, guide the college of bishops
   in union with the Pope,
— give them the gifts of unity, love and peace.
Bind all Christians more closely to yourself, their
   divine Head,
— lead them to proclaim your kingdom by the witness of their lives.

Grant peace to the world,
— let every land flourish in justice and security.
Grant to the dead the glory of resurrection,
— and give us a share in their happiness.

Our Father . . .

Concluding prayer, as in the Proper of Seasons.

Conclusion, as in the Ordinary, 29.

# MONDAY, WEEK I

## Invitatory

Lord, open my lips.

Ant. Let us approach the Lord with praise and thanksgiving.

Invitatory psalm, 22.

## Morning Prayer

The following verse and response are omitted when the hour begins with the invitatory.

God, come to my assistance. Glory to the Father. As it was in the beginning. Alleluia.

HYMN, no. 2 or 132. Outside Ordinary Time, see Guide, 578

PSALMODY

Ant. 1 I lift up my heart to you, O Lord, and you will hear my morning prayer.

Easter: All those who love your name will rejoice in you, alleluia.

Psalm 5:2-10, 12-13

A morning prayer asking for help

*Those who welcome the Word as the guest of their hearts will have abiding joy.*

To my words give ear, O Lord,
give heed to my groaning.
Attend to the sound of my cries,
my King and my God.

It is you whom I invoke, O Lord.
In the morning you hear me;
in the morning I offer you my prayer,
watching and waiting.

You are no God who loves evil;
no sinner is your guest.
The boastful shall not stand their ground
before your face.

You hate all who do evil:
you destroy all who lie.
The deceitful and bloodthirsty man
the Lord detests.

But I through the greatness of your love
have access to your house.
I bow down before your holy temple,
filled with awe.

Lead me, Lord, in your justice,
because of those who lie in wait;
make clear your way before me.

No truth can be found in their mouths,
their heart is all mischief,
their throat a wide-open grave,
all honey their speech.

All those you protect shall be glad
and ring out their joy.
You shelter them; in you they rejoice,
those who love your name.

It is you who bless the just man, Lord:
you surround him with favor as with a shield.

Psalm-prayer

Lord, all justice and all goodness come from you;
you hate evil and abhor lies. Lead us, your servants, in the path of your justice, so that all who
hope in you may rejoice with the Church and in
Christ.

Ant. 2 We praise your glorious name, O Lord, our
God.

Easter: Yours is the kingdom, Lord, and yours the primacy
over all the rulers of the earth, alleluia.

Canticle 1 Chronicles 29:10-13

Glory and honor are due to God alone

*Blessed be the God and Father of our Lord Jesus
Christ* (Ephesians 1:3).

Blessed may you be, O Lord,
God of Israel our father,
from eternity to eternity.

Yours, O Lord, are grandeur and power,
majesty, splendor, and glory.

For all in heaven and on earth is yours;
yours, O Lord, is the sovereignty:
you are exalted as head over all.

Riches and honor are from you,
and you have dominion over all.
In your hands are power and might;
it is yours to give grandeur and strength to all.

Therefore, our God, we give you thanks
and praise the majesty of your name.

Ant. 3 Adore the Lord in his holy court.

Easter: The Lord is enthroned as king for ever, alleluia.

## Psalm 29

A tribute of praise to the Word of God

*The Father's voice proclaimed: "This is my beloved Son"* (Matthew 3:17).

O give the Lord, you sons of God,
give the Lord glory and power;
give the Lord the glory of his name.
Adore the Lord in his holy court.

The Lord's voice resounding on the waters,
the Lord on the immensity of waters;
the voice of the Lord, full of power,
the voice of the Lord, full of splendor.

The Lord's voice shattering the cedars,
the Lord shatters the cedars of Lebanon;
he makes Lebanon leap like a calf
and Sirion like a young wild-ox.

The Lord's voice flashes flames of fire.

The Lord's voice shaking the wilderness,
the Lord shakes the wilderness of Kadesh;
the Lord's voice rending the oak tree
and stripping the forest bare.

The God of glory thunders.
In his temple they all cry: "Glory!"
The Lord sat enthroned over the flood;
the Lord sits as king for ever.

The Lord will give strength to his people,
the Lord will bless his people with peace.

Psalm-prayer

You live for ever, Lord and King. All things of the earth justly sing your glory and honor. Strengthen your people against evil, that we may rejoice in your peace and trust in your eternal promise.

READING                                 2 Thessalonians 3:10b-13

If anyone is unwilling to work, neither should that one eat. We hear that some are conducting themselves among you in a disorderly way, by not keeping busy but minding the business of others. Such people we instruct and urge in the Lord Jesus Christ to work quietly and to eat their own food. But you, brothers, do not be remiss in doing good.

RESPONSORY

Blessed be the Lord our God,
blessed from age to age.
— Blessed be the Lord our God,
blessed from age to age.

His marvelous works are beyond compare,
— blessed from age to age.

Glory to the Father . . .
— Blessed be the . . .

CANTICLE OF ZECHARIAH

Ant. Blessed be the Lord our God.

INTERCESSIONS

We esteem Christ above all men, for he was filled with grace and the Holy Spirit. In faith let us implore him:
    Give us your Spirit, Lord.
Grant us a peaceful day,
— when evening comes we will praise you with joy and purity of heart.
Let your splendor rest upon us today,
— direct the work of our hands.
May your face shine upon us and keep us in peace,
— may your strong arm protect us.
Look kindly on all who put their trust in our prayers,
— fill them with every bodily and spiritual grace.

Our Father . . .

CONCLUDING PRAYER

Father,
may everything we do
begin with your inspiration
and continue with your saving help.
Let our work always find its origin in you
and through you reach completion.

We ask this through our Lord Jesus Christ, your Son,
who lives and reigns with you and the Holy Spirit,
one God, for ever and ever.

Conclusion, as in the Ordinary, 29.

## Evening Prayer

God, come to my assistance. Glory to the Father.
As it was in the beginning. Alleluia.

HYMN, no. 34 or 47. Outside Ordinary Time, see
Guide, 578.

PSALMODY

Ant. 1 The Lord looks tenderly on those who are
poor.

Easter: Have courage; I have overcome the world, alleluia.

### Psalm 11

God is the unfailing support of the just

*Blessed are those who hunger and thirst for jus-*
*tice; they shall be satisfied* (Matthew 5:6).

In the Lord I have taken my refuge.
How can you say to my soul:
"Fly like a bird to its mountain.

See the wicked bracing their bow;
they are fixing their arrows on the string
to shoot upright men in the dark.
Foundations once destroyed, what can the just
do?"

The Lord is in his holy temple,
the Lord, whose throne is in heaven.
His eyes look down on the world;
his gaze tests mortal men.

The Lord tests the just and the wicked:
the lover of violence he hates.
He sends fire and brimstone on the wicked;
he sends a scorching wind as their lot.

The Lord is just and loves justice:
the upright shall see his face.

## Psalm-prayer

Lord God, you search the hearts of all, both the good and the wicked. May those who are in danger for love of you, find security in you now, and, in the day of judgment, may they rejoice in seeing you face to face.

Ant. 2  Blessed are the pure of heart, for they shall see God.

Easter: He shall sojourn in your tent; he shall dwell on your holy mountain, alleluia.

## Psalm 15

Who is worthy to stand in God's presence?

*You have come to Mount Zion, to the city of the living God* (Hebrews 12:22).

Lord, who shall be admitted to your tent
and dwell on your holy mountain?

He who walks without fault;
he who acts with justice
and speaks the truth from his heart;
he who does not slander with his tongue;

he who does no wrong to his brother,
who casts no slur on his neighbor,
who holds the godless in disdain,
but honors those who fear the Lord;

he who keeps his pledge, come what may;
who takes no interest on a loan
and accepts no bribes against the innocent.
Such a man will stand firm for ever.

Psalm-prayer

Make our lives blameless, Lord. Help us to do what
is right and to speak what is true, that we may dwell
in your tent and find rest on your holy mountain.

Ant. 3  God chose us in his Son to be his adopted
children.

Easter: When I am lifted up from the earth I shall draw
all people to myself, alleluia.

Canticle          Ephesians 1:3-10

God our Savior

Praised be the God and Father
of our Lord Jesus Christ,
who has bestowed on us in Christ
every spiritual blessing in the heavens.

God chose us in him
before the world began
to be holy
and blameless in his sight,
to be full of love.

He predestined us
to be his adopted sons through Jesus Christ,
such was his will and pleasure,
that all might praise the glorious favor
he has bestowed on us in his beloved.

In him and through his blood, we have been redeemed,
and our sins forgiven,
so immeasurably generous
is God's favor to us.

God has given us the wisdom
to understand fully the mystery,
the plan he was pleased
to decree in Christ.

A plan to be carried out
in Christ, in the fullness of time,
to bring all things into one in him,
in the heavens and on earth.

READING                         Colossians 1:9b-13

May you be filled with the knowledge of his will
through all spiritual wisdom and understanding to
live in a manner worthy of the Lord, so as to be
fully pleasing, in every good work bearing fruit and
growing in the knowledge of God, strengthened
with every power, in accord with his glorious might,
for all endurance and patience, with joy giving
thanks to the Father, who has made you fit to share
in the inheritance of the holy ones in light. He delivered us from the power of darkness and trans-
ferred us to the kingdom of his beloved Son.

RESPONSORY

Lord, you alone can heal me, for I have grieved you
    by my sins.
— Lord, you alone can heal me, for I have grieved
    you by my sins.
Once more I say: O Lord, have mercy on me,
— for I have grieved you by my sins.
Glory to the Father . . .
— Lord, you alone . . .

CANTICLE OF MARY

Ant. My soul proclaims the greatness of the Lord, for
     he has looked with favor on his lowly servant.

INTERCESSIONS

God has made an everlasting covenant with his people, and he never ceases to bless them. Grateful for these gifts, we confidently direct our prayer to him:
*Lord, bless your people.*
Save your people, Lord,
— and bless your inheritance.
Gather into one body all who bear the name of Christian,
— that the world may believe in Christ whom you have sent.
Give our friends and our loved ones a share in divine life,
— let them be symbols of Christ before men.
Show your love to those who are suffering,
— open their eyes to the vision of your revelation.
Be compassionate to those who have died,
— welcome them into the company of the faithful departed.

Our Father . . .

CONCLUDING PRAYER

Father,
may this evening pledge of our service to you
bring you glory and praise.
For our salvation you looked with favor
on the lowliness of the Virgin Mary;
lead us to the fullness of the salvation
you have prepared for us.

We ask this through our Lord Jesus Christ, your Son,
who lives and reigns with you and the Holy Spirit,
one God, for ever and ever.

Conclusion, as in the Ordinary, 29.

# TUESDAY, WEEK I

## Invitatory

Lord, open my lips.

Ant. Come, let us worship our mighty King and Lord.

Invitatory psalm, 22.

## Morning Prayer

The following verse and response are omitted when the hour begins with the invitatory.

God, come to my assistance. Glory to the Father. As it was in the beginning. Alleluia.

HYMN, no. 3 or 91. Outside Ordinary Time, see Guide, 578.

PSALMODY

Ant. 1 The man whose deeds are blameless and whose heart is pure will climb the mountain of the Lord.

Easter: The one who came down from heaven has ascended above all the heavens, alleluia.

When psalm 24 is the invitatory psalm, psalm 95, 22, is used as the first psalm of Morning Prayer.

### Psalm 24

The Lord's entry into his temple

*Christ opened heaven for us in the manhood he assumed* (Saint Irenaeus).

The Lord's is the earth and its fullness,
the world and all its peoples.
It is he who set it on the seas;
on the waters he made it firm.

Who shall climb the mountain of the Lord?
Who shall stand in his holy place? —

The man with clean hands and pure heart,
who desires not worthless things,
who has not sworn so as to deceive his neighbor.

He shall receive blessings from the Lord
and reward from the God who saves him.
Such are the men who seek him,
seek the face of the God of Jacob.

O gates, lift high your heads;
grow higher, ancient doors.
Let him enter, the king of glory!

Who is the king of glory?
The Lord, the mighty, the valiant,
the Lord, the valiant in war.

O gates, lift high your heads;
grow higher, ancient doors.
Let him enter, the king of glory!

Who is he, the king of glory?
He, the Lord of armies,
he is the king of glory.

Psalm-prayer

King of glory, Lord of power and might, cleanse our hearts from all sin, preserve the innocence of our hands, and keep our minds from vanity, so that we may deserve your blessing in your holy place.

Ant. 2 Praise the eternal King in all your deeds.

Easter: Keep this day as a festival day and give praise to the Lord, alleluia.

Canticle Tobit 13:1-8

God afflicts but only to heal

*Blessed be the God and Father of our Lord Jesus Christ, who in his great love for us has brought us to a new birth* (1 Peter 1:3).

Blessed be God who lives forever,
because his kingdom lasts for all ages.

For he scourges and then has mercy;
he casts down to the depths of the nether world,
and he brings up from the great abyss.
No one can escape his hand.

Praise him, you Israelites, before the Gentiles,
for though he has scattered you among them,
he has shown you his greatness even there.

Exalt him before every living being,
because he is the Lord our God,
our Father and God forever.

He scourged you for your iniquities,
but will again have mercy on you all.
He will gather you from all the Gentiles
among whom you have been scattered.

When you turn back to him with all your heart,
to do what is right before him,
then he will turn back to you,
and no longer hide his face from you.

So now consider what he has done for you,
and praise him with full voice.
Bless the Lord of righteousness,
and exalt the King of the ages.

In the land of my exile I praise him,
and show his power and majesty to a sinful na-
      tion.
"Turn back, you sinners! do the right before him:
perhaps he may look with favor upon you
and show you mercy.

"As for me, I exalt my God,
and my spirit rejoices in the King of heaven.
Let all men speak of his majesty,
and sing his praises in Jerusalem."

Ant. 3  **The loyal heart must praise the Lord.**
Easter: The mercy of the Lord fills the earth, alleluia.

### Psalm 33
Song of praise for God's continual care
*Through the Word all things were made* (John 1:3).

Ring out your joy to the Lord, O you just;
for praise is fitting for loyal hearts.

Give thanks to the Lord upon the harp,
with a ten-stringed lute sing him songs.
O sing him a song that is new,
play loudly, with all your skill.

For the word of the Lord is faithful
and all his works to be trusted.
The Lord loves justice and right
and fills the earth with his love.

By his word the heavens were made,
by the breath of his mouth all the stars.
He collects the waves of the ocean;
he stores up the depths of the sea.

Let all the earth fear the Lord,
all who live in the world revere him.
He spoke; and it came to be.
He commanded; it sprang into being.

He frustrates the designs of the nations,
he defeats the plans of the peoples.
His own designs shall stand for ever,
the plans of his heart from age to age.

They are happy, whose God is the Lord,
the people he has chosen as his own.
From the heavens the Lord looks forth,
he sees all the children of men.

From the place where he dwells he gazes
on all the dwellers on the earth, —

he who shapes the hearts of them all
and considers all their deeds.

A king is not saved by his army,
nor a warrior preserved by his strength.
A vain hope for safety is the horse;
despite its power it cannot save.

The Lord looks on those who revere him,
on those who hope in his love,
to rescue their souls from death,
to keep them alive in famine.

Our soul is waiting for the Lord.
The Lord is our help and our shield.
In him do our hearts find joy.
We trust in his holy name.

May your love be upon us, O Lord,
as we place all our hope in you.

Psalm-prayer

Nourish your people, Lord, for we hunger for
your word. Rescue us from the death of sin and fill
us with your mercy, that we may share your presence and the joys of all the saints.

READING                                Romans 13:11-14

You know the time; it is the hour now for you to
awake from sleep. For our salvation is nearer now
than when we first believed; the night is advanced,
the day is at hand. Let us then throw off the works
of darkness [and] put on the armor of light; let us
conduct ourselves properly as in the day, not in orgies and drunkenness, not in promiscuity and licentiousness, not in rivalry and jealousy. But put
on the Lord Jesus Christ, and make no provision
for the desires of the flesh.

RESPONSORY

My God stands by me, all my trust is in him.
— My God stands by me, all my trust is in him.

I find my refuge in him, and I am truly free;
— all my trust is in him.

Glory to the Father . . .
— My God stands . . .

CANTICLE OF ZECHARIAH

Ant. God has raised up for us a mighty Savior, as he promised through the words of his holy prophets.

INTERCESSIONS

Beloved brothers and sisters, we share a heavenly calling under Christ, our high priest. Let us praise him with shouts of joy:
*Lord, our God and our Savior.*
Almighty King, through baptism you conferred on us a royal priesthood,
— inspire us to offer you a continual sacrifice of praise.
Help us to keep your commandments,
— that through the power of the Holy Spirit we may live in you and you in us.
Give us your eternal wisdom,
— to be with us today and to guide us.
May our companions today be free of sorrow,
— and filled with joy.

Our Father . . .

CONCLUDING PRAYER

God our Father,
hear our morning prayer
and let the radiance of your love
scatter the gloom of our hearts.
The light of heaven's love has restored us to life:
free us from the desires that belong to darkness.

We ask this through our Lord Jesus Christ, your Son, who lives and reigns with you and the Holy Spirit, one God, for ever and ever.

Conclusion, as in the Ordinary, 29.

# Evening Prayer

God, come to my assistance. Glory to the Father. As it was in the beginning. Alleluia.

HYMN, no. 35 or 46. Outside Ordinary Time, see Guide, 578.

PSALMODY

Ant. 1 God has crowned his Christ with victory.

Easter: Now the reign of our God has begun and power is given to Christ, his anointed, alleluia.

## Psalm 20

### A prayer for the king's victory

*Whoever calls upon the name of the Lord will be saved* (Acts 2: 21).

May the Lord answer in time of trial;
may the name of Jacob's God protect you.

May he send you help from his shrine
and give you support from Zion.
May he remember all your offerings
and receive your sacrifice with favor.

May he give you your heart's desire
and fulfill every one of your plans.
May we ring out our joy at your victory
and rejoice in the name of our God.
May the Lord grant all your prayers.

I am sure now that the Lord
will give victory to his anointed,
will reply from his holy heaven
with the mighty victory of his hand.

Some trust in chariots or horses,
but we in the name of the Lord.
They will collapse and fall,
but we shall hold and stand firm.

Give victory to the king, O Lord,
give answer on the day we call.

Psalm-prayer

Lord, you accepted the perfect sacrifice of your
Son upon the cross. Hear us during times of trouble and protect us by the power of his name, that
we who share his struggle on earth may merit a
share in his victory.

Ant. 2   We celebrate your mighty works with songs
of praise, O Lord.

Easter: You have assumed the authority that is yours;
you have established your kingdom, alleluia.

Psalm 21:2-8, 14

Thanksgiving for the king's victory

*He accepted life that he might rise and live for ever*
(Saint Hilary).

O Lord, your strength gives joy to the king;
how your saving help makes him glad!
You have granted him his heart's desire;
you have not refused the prayer of his lips.

You came to meet him with the blessings of
success,
you have set on his head a crown of pure gold.
He asked you for life and this you have given,
days that will last from age to age.

Your saving help has given him glory.
You have laid upon him majesty and splendor,
you have granted your blessings to him for ever.
You have made him rejoice with the joy of your
presence.

The king has put his trust in the Lord:
through the mercy of the Most High he shall
    stand firm.
O Lord, arise in your strength;
we shall sing and praise your power.

Psalm-prayer

Father, you have given us life on this earth and have
met us with the grace of redemption. Bestow your
greatest blessing on us, the fullness of eternal life.

Ant. 3 Lord, you have made us a kingdom and
        priests for God our Father.

Easter: Let all creation serve you, for all things came
    into being at your word, alleluia.

Canticle                    Revelation 4:11; 5:9, 10, 12

Redemption hymn

O Lord our God, you are worthy
to receive glory and honor and power.

For you have created all things;
by your will they came to be and were made.

Worthy are you, O Lord,
to receive the scroll and break open its seals.

For you were slain;
with your blood you purchased for God
men of every race and tongue,
of every people and nation.

You made of them a kingdom,
and priests to serve our God,
and they shall reign on the earth.

Worthy is the Lamb that was slain
to receive power and riches,
wisdom and strength,
honor and glory and praise.

READING                                           1 John 3:1-3

See what love the Father has bestowed on us that
we may be called the children of God. Yet so we are.
The reason the world does not know us is that it
did not know him. Beloved, we are God's children
now; what we shall be has not yet been revealed.
We do know that when it is revealed we shall be
like him, for we shall see him as he is. Everyone
who has this hope based on him makes himself
pure, as he is pure.

RESPONSORY

Through all eternity, O Lord, your promise stands
  unshaken.
— Through all eternity, O Lord, your promise
  stands unshaken.
Your faithfulness will never fail;
— your promise stands unshaken.
Glory to the Father . . .
— Through all eternity . . .

CANTICLE OF MARY

Ant. My spirit rejoices in God my Savior.

INTERCESSIONS

Let us praise Christ the Lord, who lives among us,
  the people he redeemed, and let us say:
    Lord, hear our prayer.
Lord, king and ruler of nations, be with all your
  people and their governments,
— inspire them to pursue the good of all according
  to your law.
You made captive our captivity,
— to our brothers who are enduring bodily or spiritual chains, grant the freedom of the sons of God.

May our young people be concerned with remaining
   blameless in your sight,
— and may they generously follow your call.
May our children imitate your example,
— and grow in wisdom and grace.
Accept our dead brothers and sisters into your
   eternal kingdom,
— where we hope to reign with you.

Our Father . . .

CONCLUDING PRAYER

Almighty God,
we give you thanks
for bringing us safely
to this evening hour.
May this lifting up of our hands in prayer
be a sacrifice pleasing in your sight.

We ask this through our Lord Jesus Christ, your Son,
who lives and reigns with you and the Holy Spirit,
one God, for ever and ever.

Conclusion, as in the Ordinary, 29.


# WEDNESDAY, WEEK I

### Invitatory

Lord, open my lips.

Ant. Come, let us worship before the Lord, our
    maker.

Invitatory psalm, 22.

### Morning Prayer

The following verse and response are omitted
when the hour begins with the invitatory.

God, come to my assistance. Glory to the Father.
As it was in the beginning. Alleluia.

HYMN, no. 4 or 5. Outside Ordinary Time, see
Guide, 578.

PSALMODY

Ant. 1  O Lord, in your light we see light itself.

Easter: You, O Lord, are the source of life, alleluia.

Psalm 36

The malice of sinners and God's goodness

*No follower of mine wanders in the dark; he shall
have the light of life* (John 8:12).

Sin speaks to the sinner
in the depths of his heart.
There is no fear of God
before his eyes.

He so flatters himself in his mind
that he knows not his guilt.
In his mouth are mischief and deceit.
All wisdom is gone.

He plots the defeat of goodness
as he lies on his bed.
He has set his foot on evil ways,
he clings to what is evil.

Your love, Lord, reaches to heaven;
your truth to the skies.
Your justice is like God's mountain,
your judgments like the deep.

To both man and beast you give protection.
O Lord, how precious is your love.
My God, the sons of men
find refuge in the shelter of your wings.

They feast on the riches of your house;
they drink from the stream of your delight.
In you is the source of life
and in your light we see light.

Keep on loving those who know you,
doing justice for upright hearts.
Let the foot of the proud not crush me
nor the hand of the wicked cast me out.

See how the evil-doers fall!
Flung down, they shall never arise.

Psalm-prayer

Lord, you are the source of unfailing light. Give
us true knowledge of your mercy so that we may re-
nounce our pride and be filled with the riches of
your house.

Ant. 2  O God, you are great and glorious; we marvel at your power.

Easter: You sent forth your Spirit, O Lord, and all things
were created, alleluia.

Canticle  Judith 16:2-3a, 13-15

God who created the world takes care of his people

*They were singing a new song* (Revelation 5:9).

Strike up the instruments,
a song to my God with timbrels,
chant to the Lord with cymbals.
Sing to him a new song,
exalt and acclaim his name.

A new hymn I will sing to my God.
O Lord, great are you and glorious,
wonderful in power and unsurpassable.

Let your every creature serve you;
for you spoke, and they were made,
you sent forth your spirit, and they were created;
no one can resist your word.

The mountains to their bases, and the seas,
are shaken;
the rocks, like wax, melt before your glance. —

But to those who fear you,
   you are very merciful.

Ant. 3  Exult in God's presence with hymns of
   praise.

Easter: God is King over all the earth; make music for
   him with all your skill, alleluia.

## Psalm 47
### The Lord Jesus is King of all

*He is seated at the right hand of the Father, and
his kingdom will have no end.*

All peoples, clap your hands,
   cry to God with shouts of joy!
For the Lord, the Most High, we must fear,
   great king over all the earth.

He subdues peoples under us
   and nations under our feet.
Our inheritance, our glory, is from him,
   given to Jacob out of love.

God goes up with shouts of joy;
   the Lord goes up with trumpet blast.
Sing praise for God, sing praise,
   sing praise to our king, sing praise.

God is king of all the earth.
   Sing praise with all your skill.
God is king over the nations;
   God reigns on his holy throne.

The princes of the peoples are assembled
   with the people of Abraham's God.
The rulers of the earth belong to God,
   to God who reigns over all.

### Psalm-prayer

God, King of all peoples and all ages, it is your
victory we celebrate as we sing with all the skill at

our command. Help us always to overcome evil by good, that we may rejoice in your triumph for ever.

READING                          Tobit 4:15a, 16a, 18a, 19

Do to no one what you yourself dislike. Give to the hungry some of your bread, and to the naked some of your clothing. Seek counsel from every wise man. At all times bless the Lord God, and ask him to make all your paths straight and to grant success to all your endeavors and plans.

RESPONSORY

Incline my heart according to your will, O God.
— Incline my heart according to your will, O God.

Speed my steps along your path,
— according to your will, O God.

Glory to the Father . . .
— Incline my heart . . .

CANTICLE OF ZECHARIAH

Ant. Show us your mercy, Lord; remember your holy covenant.

INTERCESSIONS

Let us give thanks to Christ and offer him continual praise, for he sanctifies us and calls us his brothers:
    *Lord, help your brothers to grow in holiness.*
With single-minded devotion we dedicate the beginnings of this day to the honor of your resurrection,
— may we make the whole day pleasing to you by our works of holiness.
As a sign of your love, you renew each day for the sake of our well-being and happiness,
— renew us daily for the sake of your glory.
Teach us today to recognize your presence in all men,
— especially in the poor and in those who mourn.
Grant that we may live today in peace with all men,
— never rendering evil for evil.

Our Father . . .

CONCLUDING PRAYER

God our Savior,
hear our morning prayer:
help us to follow the light
and live the truth.
In you we have been born again
as sons and daughters of light:
may we be your witnesses before all the world.

We ask this through our Lord Jesus Christ, your Son,
who lives and reigns with you and the Holy Spirit,
one God, for ever and ever.

Conclusion, as in the Ordinary, 29.

## Evening Prayer

God, come to my assistance. Glory to the Father.
As it was in the beginning. Alleluia.

HYMN, no. 36 or 45. Outside Ordinary Time, see
Guide, 578.

PSALMODY

Ant. 1 The Lord is my light and my help; whom
shall I fear?

Easter: With his right hand God has raised him up as
king and savior, alleluia.

### Psalm 27

God stands by us in dangers

*God now truly dwells with me* (Revelation 21:3).

I

The Lord is my light and my help;
whom shall I fear?
The Lord is the stronghold of my life;
before whom shall I shrink?

When evil-doers draw near
to devour my flesh,—

it is they, my enemies and foes,
who stumble and fall.

Though an army encamp against me
my heart would not fear.
Though war break out against me
even then would I trust.

There is one thing I ask of the Lord,
for this I long,
to live in the house of the Lord,
all the days of my life,
to savor the sweetness of the Lord,
to behold his temple.

For there he keeps me safe in his tent
in the day of evil.
He hides me in the shelter of his tent,
on a rock he sets me safe.

And now my head shall be raised
above my foes who surround me
and I shall offer within his tent
a sacrifice of joy.

I will sing and make music for the Lord.

Ant. 2  I long to look on you, O Lord; do not turn
        your face from me.

Easter: I believe that I shall see the goodness of the Lord
        in the land of the living, alleluia.

II

*Some rose to present lies and false evidence
against Jesus (Mark 14:57).*

O Lord, hear my voice when I call;
have mercy and answer.
Of you my heart has spoken:
"Seek his face."

It is your face, O Lord, that I seek;
hide not your face.
Dismiss not your servant in anger;
you have been my help.

Do not abandon or forsake me,
O God my help!
Though father and mother forsake me,
the Lord will receive me.

Instruct me, Lord, in your way;
on an even path lead me.
When they lie in ambush protect me
from my enemy's greed.
False witnesses rise against me,
breathing out fury.

I am sure I shall see the Lord's goodness
in the land of the living.
Hope in him, hold firm and take heart.
Hope in the Lord!

Psalm-prayer

Father, you protect and strengthen those who hope
in you; you heard the cry of your Son and kept him
safe in your tent in the day of evil. Grant that your
servants who seek your face in times of trouble may
see your goodness in the land of the living.

Ant. 3  He is the first-born of all creation; in every
way the primacy is his.

Easter: From him, through him, and in him all things
exist: glory to him for ever, alleluia.

Canticle    Colossians 1:12-20
Christ the first-born of all creation and the
first-born from the dead

Let us give thanks to the Father
for having made you worthy —

to share the lot of the saints
in light.

He rescued us
from the power of darkness
and brought us
into the kingdom of his beloved Son.
Through him we have redemption,
the forgiveness of our sins.

He is the image of the invisible God,
the first-born of all creatures.
In him everything in heaven and on earth was
    created,
things visible and invisible.

All were created through him;
all were created for him.
He is before all else that is.
In him everything continues in being.

It is he who is head of the body, the church!
he who is the beginning,
the first-born of the dead,
so that primacy may be his in everything.

It pleased God to make absolute fullness reside
    in him
and, by means of him, to reconcile everything
    in his person,
both on earth and in the heavens,
making peace through the blood of his cross.

READING                                           James I:19-25

Know this, my dear brothers: everyone should be
quick to hear, slow to speak, slow to wrath, for the
wrath of a man does not accomplish the righteousness of God. Therefore, put away all filth and evil
excess and humbly welcome the word that has
been planted in you and is able to save your souls.

Be doers of the word and not hearers only, deluding yourselves. For if anyone is a hearer of the word and not a doer, he is like a man who looks at his own face in a mirror. He sees himself, then goes off and promptly forgets what he looked like. But the one who peers into the perfect law of freedom and perseveres, and is not a hearer who forgets but a doer who acts, such a one shall be blessed in what he does.

RESPONSORY

Claim me once more as your own, Lord, and have
    mercy on me.
— Claim me once more as your own, Lord, and have
    mercy on me.
Do not abandon me with the wicked;
— have mercy on me.
Glory to the Father . . .
— Claim me once . . .

CANTICLE OF MARY

Ant. The Almighty has done great things for me,
    and holy is his Name.

INTERCESSIONS

In all that we do, let the name of the Lord be
    praised, for he surrounds his chosen people with
    boundless love. Let our prayer rise up to him:
    Lord, show us your love.
Remember your Church, Lord,
— keep her from every evil and let her grow to the
    fullness of your love.
Let the nations recognize you as the one true God,
— and Jesus your Son, as the Messiah whom you
    sent.
Grant prosperity to our neighbors,
— give them life and happiness for ever.

Console those who are burdened with oppressive
   work and daily hardships,
— preserve the dignity of workers.
Open wide the doors of your compassion to those
   who have died today,
— and in your mercy receive them into your kingdom.

Our Father . . .

Lord,
watch over us by day and by night.
In the midst of life's countless changes
strengthen us with your never-changing love.

We ask this through our Lord Jesus Christ, your Son,
who lives and reigns with you and the Holy Spirit,
one God, for ever and ever.

Conclusion, as in the Ordinary, 29.


# THURSDAY, WEEK I

## Invitatory

Lord, open my lips.

Ant. Come, let us worship the Lord, for he is our
   God.

Invitatory psalm, 22.

## Morning Prayer

The following verse and response are omitted
when the hour begins with the invitatory.

God, come to my assistance. Glory to the Father.
As it was in the beginning. Alleluia.

HYMN, no. 6 or 82. Outside Ordinary Time, see
Guide, 578.

PSALMODY

Ant. 1 Awake, lyre and harp, with praise let us
   awake the dawn.

Easter: Be exalted, O God, high above the heavens, alleluia.

## Psalm 57

### Morning prayer in affliction

*This psalm tells of our Lord's passion* (Saint Augustine).

Have mercy on me, God, have mercy
for in you my soul has taken refuge.
In the shadow of your wings I take refuge
till the storms of destruction pass by.

I call to God the Most High,
to God who has always been my help.
May he send from heaven and save me
and shame those who assail me.

May God send his truth and his love.

My soul lies down among lions,
who would devour the sons of men.
Their teeth are spears and arrows,
their tongue a sharpened sword.

O God, arise above the heavens;
may your glory shine on earth!

They laid a snare for my steps,
my soul was bowed down.
They dug a pit in my path
but fell in it themselves.

My heart is ready, O God,
my heart is ready.
I will sing, I will sing your praise.
Awake, my soul,
awake, lyre and harp,
I will awake the dawn.

I will thank you, Lord, among the peoples,
among the nations I will praise you —

for your love reaches to the heavens
and your truth to the skies.

O God, arise above the heavens;
may your glory shine on earth!

Psalm-prayer

Lord, send your mercy and your truth to rescue us
from the snares of the devil, and we will praise you
among the peoples and proclaim you to the nations,
happy to be known as companions of your Son.

Ant. 2  My people, says the Lord, will be filled with
my blessings.

Easter: The Lord has ransomed his people, alleluia.

Canticle     Jeremiah 31:10-14

The happiness of a people who have been redeemed

*Jesus was to die . . . to gather God's scattered children into one fold* (John 11:51, 52).

Hear the word of the Lord, O nations,
proclaim it on distant coasts, and say:
He who scattered Israel, now gathers them together,
he guards them as a shepherd his flock.

The Lord shall ransom Jacob,
he shall redeem him from the hand of his conqueror.
Shouting, they shall mount the heights of Zion,
they shall come streaming to the Lord's blessings:
the grain, the wine, and the oil,
the sheep and the oxen;
they themselves shall be like watered gardens,
never again shall they languish.

Then the virgins shall make merry and dance,
and young men and old as well.—

I will turn their mourning into joy,
I will console and gladden them after their sorrows.
I will lavish choice portions upon the priests,
and my people shall be filled with my blessings,
says the Lord.

Ant. 3  The Lord is great and worthy to be praised
in the city of our God.

Easter: Such is our God, he will be our guide for ever, alleluia.

## Psalm 48

Thanksgiving for the people's deliverance

*He took me up a high mountain and showed me Jerusalem, God's holy city* (Revelation 21:10).

The Lord is great and worthy to be praised
in the city of our God.
His holy mountain rises in beauty,
the joy of all the earth.

Mount Zion, true pole of the earth,
the Great King's city!
God, in the midst of its citadels,
has shown himself its stronghold.

For the kings assembled together,
together they advanced.
They saw; at once they were astounded;
dismayed, they fled in fear.

A trembling seized them there,
like the pangs of birth.
By the east wind you have destroyed
the ships of Tarshish.

As we have heard, so we have seen
in the city of our God,
in the city of the Lord of hosts
which God upholds for ever.

O God, we ponder your love
within your temple.
Your praise, O God, like your name
reaches to the ends of the earth.

With justice your right hand is filled.
Mount Zion rejoices;
the people of Judah rejoice
at the sight of your judgments.

Walk through Zion, walk all round it;
count the number of its towers.
Review all its ramparts,
examine its castles,

that you may tell the next generation
that such is our God,
our God for ever and always.
It is he who leads us.

## Psalm-prayer

Father, the body of your risen Son is the temple
not made by human hands and the defending wall
of the new Jerusalem. May this holy city, built of
living stones, shine with spiritual radiance and witness to your greatness in the sight of all nations.

READING                                    Isaiah 66:1-2

Thus says the Lord:
The heavens are my throne,
    and the earth is my footstool.
What kind of house can you build for me;
    what is to be my resting place?
My hand made all these things
    when all of them came to be, says the Lord.
This is the one whom I approve:
    the lowly and afflicted man who trembles at my
    word.

RESPONSORY

From the depths of my heart I cry to you; hear me,
O Lord.
— From the depths of my heart I cry to you; hear
me, O Lord.

I will do what you desire;
— hear me, O Lord.

Glory to the Father . . .
— From the depths . . .

CANTICLE OF ZECHARIAH

Ant. Let us serve the Lord in holiness, and he will
save us from our enemies.

INTERCESSIONS

The Lord Jesus Christ has given us the light of another day. In return we thank him as we cry out:
*Lord, bless us and bring us close to you.*
You offered yourself in sacrifice for our sins,
— accept our intentions and our work today.
You bring us joy by the light of another day,
— let the morning star rise in our hearts.
Give us strength to be patient with those we meet
today,
— and so imitate you.
Make us aware of your mercy this morning, Lord,
— and let your strength be our delight.

Our Father . . .

CONCLUDING PRAYER

All-powerful and ever-living God,
at morning, noon, and evening we pray:
cast out from our hearts the darkness of sin
and bring us to the light of your truth,
Jesus Christ, who lives and reigns with you and the
Holy Spirit,
one God, for ever and ever.

Conclusion, as in the Ordinary, 29.

## Evening Prayer

God, come to my assistance. Glory to the Father.
As it was in the beginning. Alleluia.

HYMN, no. 37 or 44. Outside Ordinary Time, see
Guide, 578.

PSALMODY

Ant. 1  I cried to you, Lord, and you healed me; I
        will praise you for ever.

Easter: You have turned my mourning into joy, alleluia.

### Psalm 30

Thanksgiving for deliverance from death

*Christ, risen in glory, gives continual thanks to
his Father* (Cassian).

I will praise you, Lord, you have rescued me
and have not let my enemies rejoice over me.

O Lord, I cried to you for help
and you, my God, have healed me.
O Lord, you have raised my soul from the dead,
restored me to life from those who sink into
    the grave.

Sing psalms to the Lord, you who love him,
give thanks to his holy name.
His anger lasts a moment; his favor through life.
At night there are tears, but joy comes with dawn.

I said to myself in my good fortune:
"Nothing will ever disturb me."
Your favor had set me on a mountain fastness,
then you hid your face and I was put to confu-
    sion.

To you, Lord, I cried,
to my God I made appeal:—

"What profit would my death be, my going to
    the grave?
Can dust give you praise or proclaim your truth?"

The Lord listened and had pity.
The Lord came to my help.
For me you have changed my mourning into
    dancing,
you removed my sackcloth and clothed me
    with joy.
So my soul sings psalms to you unceasingly.
O Lord my God, I will thank you for ever.

Psalm-prayer

God our Father, glorious in giving life, and even
more glorious in restoring it, when his last night on
earth came, your Son shed tears of blood, but dawn
brought incomparable gladness. Do not turn away
from us, or we shall fall back into dust, but rather
turn our mourning into joy by raising us up with
Christ.

Ant. 2  The one who is sinless in the eyes of God is
          blessed indeed.

Easter: We have been reconciled to God by the death of
        his Son, alleluia.

Psalm 32

They are happy whose sins are forgiven

*David speaks of the happiness of the man who is
holy in God's eyes not because of his own worth,
but because God has justified him* (Romans 4:6).

Happy the man whose offense is forgiven,
whose sin is remitted.
O happy the man to whom the Lord
imputes no guilt,
in whose spirit is no guile.

I kept it secret and my frame was wasted.
I groaned all the day long —

for night and day your hand
was heavy upon me.
Indeed, my strength was dried up
as by the summer's heat.

But now I have acknowledged my sins;
my guilt I did not hide.
I said: "I will confess
my offense to the Lord."
And you, Lord, have forgiven
the guilt of my sin.

So let every good man pray to you
in the time of need.
The floods of water may reach high
but him they shall not reach.
You are my hiding place, O Lord;
you save me from distress.
You surround me with cries of deliverance.

I will instruct you and teach you
the way you should go;
I will give you counsel
with my eye upon you.

Be not like horse and mule, unintelligent,
needing bridle and bit,
else they will not approach you.
Many sorrows has the wicked
but he who trusts in the Lord,
loving mercy surrounds him.

Rejoice, rejoice in the Lord,
exult, you just!
O come, ring out your joy,
all you upright of heart.

Psalm-prayer

You desired, Lord, to keep from us your indignation and so did not spare Jesus Christ, who was

wounded for our sins. We are your prodigal children, but confessing our sins we come back to you. Embrace us that we may rejoice in your mercy together with Christ your beloved Son.

Ant. 3 The Father has given Christ all power, honor, and kingship; all people will obey him.

Easter: Lord, who is your equal in power? Who is like you, majestic in holiness? alleluia.

Canticle                    Revelation 11:17-18; 12:10b-12a
                   The judgment of God

We praise you, the Lord God Almighty,
who is and who was.
You have assumed your great power,
you have begun your reign.

The nations have raged in anger,
but then came your day of wrath
and the moment to judge the dead:
the time to reward your servants the prophets
and the holy ones who revere you,
the great and the small alike.

Now have salvation and power come,
the reign of our God and the authority
of his Anointed One.
For the accuser of our brothers is cast out,
who night and day accused them before God.

They defeated him by the blood of the Lamb
and by the word of their testimony;
love for life did not deter them from death.
So rejoice, you heavens,
and you that dwell therein!

READING                                          1 Peter 1:6-9

In this you rejoice, although now for a little while you may have to suffer through various trials, so that

the genuineness of your faith, more precious than
gold that is perishable even though tested by fire,
may prove to be for praise, glory, and honor at the
revelation of Jesus Christ. Although you have not
seen him you love him; even though you do not see
him now yet believe in him, you rejoice with an in-
describable and glorious joy, as you attain the goal
of [your] faith, the salvation of your souls.

RESPONSORY

The Lord has given us food, bread of the finest
    wheat.
— The Lord has given us food, bread of the finest
    wheat.

Honey from the rock to our heart's content,
— bread of the finest wheat.

Glory to the Father . . .
— The Lord has . . .

CANTICLE OF MARY

Ant. God has cast down the mighty from their
      thrones, and has lifted up the lowly.

INTERCESSIONS

Our hope is in God, who gives us help. Let us call
    upon him, and say:
    Look kindly on your children, Lord.
Lord, our God, you made an eternal covenant with
    your people,
— keep us ever mindful of your mighty deeds.
Let your ordained ministers grow toward perfect love,
— and preserve your faithful people in unity by the
    bond of peace.
Be with us in our work of building the earthly city,
— that in building we may not labor in vain.
Send workers into your vineyard,
— and glorify your name among the nations.

Welcome into the company of your saints our relatives and benefactors who have died,
— may we share their happiness one day.

Our Father . . .

CONCLUDING PRAYER

Father,
you illumine the night
and bring the dawn to scatter darkness.
Let us pass this night in safety,
free from Satan's power,
and rise when morning comes
to give you thanks and praise.

We ask this through our Lord Jesus Christ, your
Son,
who lives and reigns with you and the Holy Spirit,
one God, for ever and ever.

Conclusion, as in the Ordinary, 29.

# FRIDAY, WEEK I

## Invitatory

Lord, open my lips.

Ant. Come, let us give thanks to the Lord, for his
great love is without end.

Invitatory psalm, 22.

## Morning Prayer

The following verse and response are omitted
when the hour begins with the invitatory.

God, come to my assistance. Glory to the Father.
As it was in the beginning. Alleluia.

HYMN, no. 7 or 20. Outside Ordinary Time, see
Guide, 578.

Ant. 1    Lord, you will accept the true sacrifice of-
          fered on your altar.

Easter: Remember me, Lord God, when you come into
your kingdom, alleluia.

### Psalm 51

#### O God, have mercy on me

*Your inmost being must be renewed, and you must
put on the new man* (Ephesians 4:23-24).

Have mercy on me, God, in your kindness.
In your compassion blot out my offense.
O wash me more and more from my guilt
and cleanse me from my sin.

My offenses truly I know them;
my sin is always before me.
Against you, you alone, have I sinned;
what is evil in your sight I have done.

That you may be justified when you give sentence
and be without reproach when you judge.
O see, in guilt I was born,
a sinner was I conceived.

Indeed you love truth in the heart;
then in the secret of my heart teach me wisdom.
O purify me, then I shall be clean;
O wash me, I shall be whiter than snow.

Make me hear rejoicing and gladness,
that the bones you have crushed may revive.
From my sins turn away your face
and blot out all my guilt.

A pure heart create for me, O God,
put a steadfast spirit within me.
Do not cast me away from your presence,
nor deprive me of your holy spirit.

Give me again the joy of your help;
with a spirit of fervor sustain me,
that I may teach transgressors your ways
and sinners may return to you.

O rescue me, God, my helper,
and my tongue shall ring out your goodness.
O Lord, open my lips
and my mouth shall declare your praise.

For in sacrifice you take no delight,
burnt offering from me you would refuse,
my sacrifice, a contrite spirit.
A humbled, contrite heart you will not spurn.

In your goodness, show favor to Zion:
rebuild the walls of Jerusalem.
Then you will be pleased with lawful sacrifice,
holocausts offered on your altar.

Psalm-prayer

Father, he who knew no sin was made sin for us,
to save us and restore us to your friendship. Look
upon our contrite heart and afflicted spirit and heal
our troubled conscience, so that in the joy and
strength of the Holy Spirit we may proclaim your
praise and glory before all the nations.

Ant. 2  All the descendants of Israel will glory in
the Lord's gift of victory.

Easter: Truly you are a hidden God, the God of Israel,
the Savior, alleluia.

Canticle          Isaiah 45:15-25

People of all nations will become disciples
of the Lord

*Every knee shall bend at the name of Jesus*
(Philippians 2:10).

Truly with you God is hidden,
the God of Israel, the savior! —

Those are put to shame and disgrace
who vent their anger against him.
Those go in disgrace
who carve images.

Israel, you are saved by the Lord, saved forever!
You shall never be put to shame or disgrace
in future ages.

For thus says the Lord,
the creator of the heavens,
who is God,
the designer and maker of the earth
who established it,
not creating it to be a waste,
but designing it to be lived in:

I am the Lord, and there is no other.
I have not spoken from hiding
nor from some dark place of the earth.
And I have not said to the descendants of Jacob,
"Look for me in an empty waste."
I, the Lord, promise justice,
I foretell what is right.

Come and assemble, gather together,
you fugitives from among the Gentiles!
They are without knowledge who bear wooden
    idols
and pray to gods that cannot save.

Come here and declare
in counsel together:
Who announced this from the beginning
and foretold it from of old?
Was it not I, the Lord,
besides whom there is no other God?
There is no just and saving God but me.

Turn to me and be safe,
all you ends of the earth,
for I am God; there is no other!

By myself I swear,
uttering my just decree
and my unalterable word:

To me every knee shall bend;
by me every tongue shall swear,
saying, "Only in the Lord
are just deeds and power.

Before him in shame shall come
all who vent their anger against him.
In the Lord shall be the vindication and the glory
of all the descendants of Israel.'

Ant. 3  Let us go into God's presence singing for joy.

Easter: Serve the Lord with gladness, alleluia.

When psalm 100 is the invitatory psalm, psalm 95,
22, is used as the third psalm at Morning Prayer.

### Psalm 100

The joyful song of those entering God's Temple

*The Lord calls his ransomed people to sing songs
of victory* (Saint Athanasius).

Cry out with joy to the Lord, all the earth.
Serve the Lord with gladness.
Come before him, singing for joy.

Know that he, the Lord, is God.
He made us, we belong to him,
we are his people, the sheep of his flock.

Go within his gates, giving thanks.
Enter his courts with songs of praise.
Give thanks to him and bless his name.

Indeed, how good is the Lord,
eternal his merciful love.
He is faithful from age to age.

Psalm-prayer

With joy and gladness we cry out to you, Lord, and ask you: open our hearts to sing your praises and announce your goodness and truth.

READING                                    Ephesians 4:29-32

No foul language should come out of your mouths, but only such as is good for needed edification, that it may impart grace to those who hear. And do not grieve the holy Spirit of God, with which you were sealed for the day of redemption. All bitterness, fury, anger, shouting, and reviling must be removed from you, along with all malice. [And] be kind to one another, compassionate, forgiving one another as God has forgiven you in Christ.

RESPONSORY

At daybreak, be merciful to me.
— At daybreak, be merciful to me.

Make known to me the path that I must walk.
— Be merciful to me.

Glory to the Father . . .
— At daybreak, be . . .

CANTICLE OF ZECHARIAH

Ant. The Lord has come to his people and set them free.

INTERCESSIONS

Through his cross the Lord Jesus brought salvation to the human race. We adore him and in faith we call out to him:
*Lord, pour out your mercy upon us.*
Christ, Rising Sun, warm us with your rays,
— and restrain us from every evil impulse.
Keep guard over our thoughts, words, and actions,
— and make us pleasing in your sight this day.
Turn your gaze from our sinfulness,
— and cleanse us from our iniquities.

Through your cross and resurrection,
— fill us with the consolation of the Spirit.

Our Father . . .

CONCLUDING PRAYER

God our Father,
you conquer the darkness of ignorance
by the light of your Word.
Strengthen within our hearts
the faith you have given us;
let not temptation ever quench the fire
that your love has kindled within us.

We ask this through our Lord Jesus Christ, your Son,
who lives and reigns with you and the Holy Spirit,
one God, for ever and ever.

Conclusion, as in the Ordinary, 29.

# Evening Prayer

God, come to my assistance. Glory to the Father.
As it was in the beginning. Alleluia.

HYMN, no. 38 or 42. Outside Ordinary Time, see
Guide, 578.

PSALMODY

Ant. 1 Lord, lay your healing hand upon me, for I
have sinned.

Easter: Christ became poor for our sake, that we might
become rich, alleluia.

## Psalm 41

### Prayer of a sick person

*One of you will betray me, yes, one who eats with me*
(Mark 14:18).

Happy the man who considers the poor and the
weak.
The Lord will save him in the day of evil,
will guard him, give him life, make him happy
in the land —

and will not give him up to the will of his foes.
The Lord will help him on his bed of pain,
he will bring him back from sickness to health.

As for me, I said: "Lord, have mercy on me,
heal my soul for I have sinned against you."
My foes are speaking evil against me.
"How long before he dies and his name be for-
    gotten?"
They come to visit me and speak empty words,
their hearts full of malice, they spread it abroad.

My enemies whisper together against me.
They all weigh up the evil which is on me:
"Some deadly thing has fastened upon him,
he will not rise again from where he lies."
Thus even my friend, in whom I trusted,
who ate my bread, has turned against me.

But you, O Lord, have mercy on me.
Let me rise once more and I will repay them.
By this I shall know that you are my friend,
if my foes do not shout in triumph over me.
If you uphold me I shall be unharmed
and set in your presence for evermore.

Blessed be the Lord, the God of Israel
from age to age. Amen. Amen.

Psalm-prayer

Lord Jesus, healer of soul and body, you said:
Blessed are the merciful, they will obtain mercy.
Teach us to come to the aid of the needy in a spirit
of brotherly love, that we in turn may be received
and strengthened by you.

Ant. 2 The mighty Lord is with us; the God of
        Jacob is our stronghold.

Easter: The streams of the river gladden the city of God,
    alleluia.

## Psalm 46

### God our refuge and strength

*He shall be called Emmanuel, which means: God-with-us* (Matthew 1:23).

God is for us a refuge and strength,
a helper close at hand, in time of distress:
so we shall not fear though the earth should
   rock,
though the mountains fall into the depths of the
   sea,
even though its waters rage and foam,
even though the mountains be shaken by its
   waves.

The Lord of hosts is with us:
the God of Jacob is our stronghold.

The waters of a river give joy to God's city,
the holy place where the Most High dwells.
God is within, it cannot be shaken;
God will help it at the dawning of the day.
Nations are in tumult, kingdoms are shaken:
he lifts his voice, the earth shrinks away.

The Lord of hosts is with us:
the God of Jacob is our stronghold.

Come, consider the works of the Lord,
the redoubtable deeds he has done on the earth.
He puts an end to wars over all the earth;
the bow he breaks, the spear he snaps.
He burns the shields with fire.
"Be still and know that I am God,
supreme among the nations, supreme on the
   earth!"

The Lord of hosts is with us:
the God of Jacob is our stronghold.

### Psalm-prayer

All-powerful Father, the refuge and strength of
your people, you protect in adversity and defend in
prosperity those who put their trust in you. May

they persevere in seeking your will and find their
way to you through obedience.

Ant. 3 **All nations will come and worship before
you, O Lord.**

Easter: Let us sing to the Lord, glorious in his triumph,
alleluia.

Canticle          Revelation 15:3-4

Hymn of adoration

Mighty and wonderful are your works,
  Lord God Almighty!
Righteous and true are your ways,
  O King of the nations!

Who would dare refuse you honor,
  or the glory due your name, O Lord?

Since you alone are holy,
  all nations shall come
  and worship in your presence.
  Your mighty deeds are clearly seen.

READING                           Romans 15:1-6

We who are strong ought to put up with the failings
of the weak and not to please ourselves; let each of
us please our neighbor for the good, for building up.
For Christ did not please himself; but, as it is written,
"The insults of those who insult you fall upon me."
For whatever was written previously was written for
our instruction, that by endurance and by the encouragement of the scriptures we might have hope.
May the God of endurance and encouragement grant
you to think in harmony with one another, in keeping with Christ Jesus, that with one accord you may
with one voice glorify the God and Father of our Lord
Jesus Christ.

RESPONSORY

Christ loved us and washed away our sins, in his
  own blood.

— Christ loved us and washed away our sins, in his own blood.

He made us a nation of kings and priests,
— in his own blood.

Glory to the Father . . .
— Christ loved us . . .

CANTICLE OF MARY

Ant. The Lord has come to the help of his servants, for he has remembered his promise of mercy.

INTERCESSIONS

Blessed be God, who hears the prayers of the needy, and fills the hungry with good things. Let us pray to him in confidence:
*Lord, show us your mercy.*

Merciful Father, upon the cross Jesus offered you the perfect evening sacrifice,
— we pray now for all the suffering members of his Church.

Release those in bondage, give sight to the blind,
— shelter the widow and the orphan.

Clothe your faithful people in the armor of salvation,
— and shield them from the deceptions of the devil.

Let your merciful presence be with us, Lord, at the hour of our death,
— may we be found faithful and leave this world in your peace.

Lead the departed into the light of your dwelling place,
— that they may gaze upon you for all eternity.

Our Father . . .

CONCLUDING PRAYER

God our Father,
help us to follow the example
of your Son's patience in suffering.
By sharing the burden he carries,

may we come to share his glory
in the kingdom where he lives with you and the
   Holy Spirit,
one God, for ever and ever.

Conclusion, as in the Ordinary, 29.

## SATURDAY, WEEK I

### Invitatory

Lord, open my lips.

Ant. Come, let us worship God who holds the world
   and its wonders in his creating hand.

Invitatory psalm, 22.

### Morning Prayer

The following verse and response are omitted
when the hour begins with the invitatory.

God, come to my assistance. Glory to the Father.
As it was in the beginning. Alleluia.

Hymn, no. 8 or 19. Outside Ordinary Time, see
Guide, 578.

Psalmody

Ant. 1 Dawn finds me ready to welcome you, my
   God.

Easter: Lord, in your love, give me life, alleluia.

Psalm 119:145-152

XIX (Koph)

I call with all my heart; Lord, hear me,
I will keep your commands.
I call upon you, save me
and I will do your will.

I rise before dawn and cry for help,
I hope in your word.
My eyes watch through the night
to ponder your promise.

In your love hear my voice, O Lord;
give me life by your decrees.
Those who harm me unjustly draw near:
they are far from your law.

But you, O Lord, are close:
your commands are truth.
Long have I known that your will
is established for ever.

Psalm-prayer

Save us by the power of your hand, Father, for
our enemies have ignored your words. May the fire
of your word consume our sins, and its brightness
illumine our hearts.

Ant. 2  The Lord is my strength, and I shall sing
his praise, for he has become my savior.

Easter: Those who were victorious sang the hymn of
Moses, the servant of God, and the hymn of the Lamb,
alleluia.

Canticle                            Exodus 15:1-4a, 8-13, 17-18

Hymn of victory after the crossing of the Red Sea

*Those who had conquered the beast were singing the
song of Moses, God's servant* (see Revelation 15:2-3).

I will sing to the Lord, for he is gloriously tri-
    umphant;
horse and chariot he has cast into the sea.

My strength and my courage is the Lord,
and he has been my savior.
He is my God, I praise him;
the God of my father, I extol him.

The Lord is a warrior,
Lord is his name!
Pharaoh's chariots and army he hurled into the
    sea.—

At a breath of your anger the waters piled up,
the flowing waters stood like a mound,
the flood waters congealed in the midst of the
    sea.

The enemy boasted, "I will pursue and overtake
    them;
I will divide the spoils and have my fill of them;
I will draw my sword; my hand shall despoil
    them!"
When your wind blew, the sea covered them;
like lead they sank in the mighty waters.

Who is like to you among the gods, O Lord?
Who is like to you, magnificent in holiness?
O terrible in renown, worker of wonders,
when you stretched out your right hand, the
    earth swallowed them!

In your mercy you led the people you redeemed;
in your strength you guided them to your holy
    dwelling.

And you brought them in and planted them on
    the mountain of your inheritance—
the place where you made your seat, O Lord,
the sanctuary, O Lord, which your hands es-
    tablished.
The Lord shall reign forever and ever.

Ant. 3  O praise the Lord, all you nations.

Easter: Strong and steadfast is his love for us, alleluia.

Psalm 117

Praise for God's loving compassion

*I affirm that . . . the Gentile peoples are to praise
God because of his mercy* (Romans 15:8-9).

O praise the Lord, all you nations,
acclaim him, all you peoples!

Strong is his love for us;
he is faithful for ever.

## Psalm-prayer

God our Father, may all nations and peoples praise you. May Jesus, who is called faithful and true and who lives with you eternally, possess our hearts for ever.

READING                    2 Peter 1:10-11

Brothers, be all the more eager to make your call and election firm, for, in doing so, you will never stumble. For, in this way, entry into the eternal kingdom of our Lord and savior Jesus Christ will be richly provided for you.

## RESPONSORY

I cry to you, O Lord, for you are my refuge.
— I cry to you, O Lord, for you are my refuge.

You are all I desire in the land of the living;
— for you are my refuge.

Glory to the Father . . .
— I cry to . . .

## CANTICLE OF ZECHARIAH

Ant. Lord, shine on those who dwell in darkness and the shadow of death.

## INTERCESSIONS

Let us all praise Christ. In order to become our faithful and merciful high priest before the Father's throne, he chose to become one of us, a brother in all things. In prayer we ask of him:
*Lord, share with us the treasure of your love.*
Sun of Justice, you filled us with light at our baptism,
— we dedicate this day to you.
At every hour of the day, we give you glory,
— in all our deeds, we offer you praise.

Mary, your mother, was obedient to your word,
— direct our lives in accordance with that word.
Our lives are surrounded with passing things; set our
    hearts on things of heaven,
— so that through faith, hope and charity we may
    come to enjoy the vision of your glory.

Our Father . . .

CONCLUDING PRAYER

Lord,
free us from the dark night of death.
Let the light of resurrection
dawn within our hearts
to bring us to the radiance of eternal life.

We ask this through our Lord Jesus Christ, your
Son,
who lives and reigns with you and the Holy Spirit,
one God, for ever and ever.

Conclusion, as in the Ordinary, 29.

# WEEK II

## SUNDAY

### Evening Prayer I

God, come to my assistance. Glory to the Father. As it was in the beginning. Alleluia.

Hymn, no. 39 or 33. Outside Ordinary Time, see Guide, 578.

Psalmody

Ant. 1  Your word, O Lord, is the lantern to light our way, alleluia.

Advent: New city of Zion, let your heart sing for joy; see how humbly your King comes to save you.

Lent, 2nd Sunday: Jesus took Peter, James and his brother John and led them up a high mountain. There he was transfigured before them.

Lent, Passion (Palm) Sunday: Day after day I sat teaching you in the temple and you did not lay hands on me. Now you come to scourge me and lead me to the cross.

Easter, 6th Sunday: The man of truth welcomes the light, alleluia.

Psalm 119:105-112

XIV (Nun)

A meditation on God's law

*This is my commandment: that you should love one another* (John 15:12).

Your word is a lamp for my steps
and a light for my path.
I have sworn and have made up my mind
to obey your decrees.

111

Lord, I am deeply afflicted:
by your word give me life.
Accept, Lord, the homage of my lips
and teach me your decrees.

Though I carry my life in my hands,
I remember your law.
Though the wicked try to ensnare me
I do not stray from your precepts.

Your will is my heritage for ever,
the joy of my heart.
I set myself to carry out your will
in fullness, for ever.

Psalm-prayer

Let your Word, Father, be a lamp for our feet and
a light to our path, so that we may understand what
you wish to teach us and follow the path your light
marks out for us.

Ant. 2   When I see your face, O Lord, I shall know
the fullness of joy, alleluia.

Advent: Have courage, all of you, lost and fearful; take
heart and say: Our God will come to save us, alleluia.

Lent, 2nd Sunday: His face was radiant as the sun, and
his clothing white as snow.

Lent, Passion (Palm) Sunday: The Lord God is my help;
no shame can harm me.

Easter, 6th Sunday: God freed Jesus from the pangs of
death, and raised him up to life, alleluia.

Psalm 16

The Lord himself is my heritage

*The Father raised up Jesus, freeing him from the
grip of death* (Acts 2:24).

Preserve me, God, I take refuge in you.
I say to the Lord: "You are my God.
My happiness lies in you alone."

He has put into my heart a marvelous love
for the faithful ones who dwell in his land.
Those who choose other gods increase their
    sorrows.
Never will I offer their offerings of blood.
Never will I take their name upon my lips.

O Lord, it is you who are my portion and cup;
it is you yourself who are my prize.
The lot marked out for me is my delight:
welcome indeed the heritage that falls to me!

I will bless the Lord who gives me counsel,
who even at night directs my heart.
I keep the Lord ever in my sight:
since he is at my right hand, I shall stand firm.

And so my heart rejoices, my soul is glad;
even my body shall rest in safety.
For you will not leave my soul among the dead,
nor let your beloved know decay.

You will show me the path of life,
the fullness of joy in your presence,
at your right hand happiness for ever.

Psalm-prayer

Lord Jesus, uphold those who hope in you and
give us your counsel, so that we may know the joy
of your resurrection and deserve to be among the
saints at your right hand.

Ant. 3  Let everything in heaven and on earth bend
        the knee at the name of Jesus, alleluia.

Advent: The law was given to Moses, but grace and truth
    come through Jesus Christ.

Lent, 2nd Sunday: Moses and Elijah were speaking to
    him of the death he would endure in Jerusalem.

Lent, Passion (Palm) Sunday: The Lord Jesus humbled
himself by showing obedience even when this meant
death, death on the cross.

Easter, 6th Sunday: Was it not necessary for Christ to
suffer and so enter into his glory? alleluia.

Canticle       Philippians 2:6-11

### Christ, God's holy servant

Though he was in the form of God,
Jesus did not deem equality with God
something to be grasped at.

Rather, he emptied himself
and took the form of a slave,
being born in the likeness of men.

He was known to be of human estate,
and it was thus that he humbled himself,
obediently accepting even death,
death on a cross!

Because of this,
God highly exalted him
and bestowed on him the name
above every other name,

So that at Jesus' name
every knee must bend
in the heavens, on the earth,
and under the earth,
and every tongue proclaim
to the glory of God the Father:
JESUS CHRIST IS LORD!

READING                           Colossians 1:2b-6a

Grace to you and peace from God our Father. We
always give thanks to God, the Father of our Lord
Jesus Christ, when we pray for you, for we have
heard of your faith in Christ Jesus and the love that
you have for all the holy ones because of the hope
reserved for you in heaven. Of this you have already

heard through the word of truth, the gospel, that has come to you. Just as in the whole world it is bearing fruit and growing, so also among you, from the day you heard it and came to know the grace of God in truth.

RESPONSORY

From the rising of the sun to its setting,
may the name of the Lord be praised.
— From the rising of the sun to its setting,
may the name of the Lord be praised.

His splendor reaches far beyond the heavens;
— may the name of the Lord be praised.

Glory to the Father . . .
— From the rising . . .

CANTICLE OF MARY, antiphon as in the Proper of Seasons.

INTERCESSIONS

God aids and protects the people he has chosen for his inheritance. Let us give thanks to him and proclaim his goodness:
*Lord, we trust in you.*
We pray for N., our Pope, and N., our bishop,
— protect them and in your goodness make them holy.
May the sick feel their companionship with the suffering Christ,
— and know that they will enjoy his eternal consolation.
In your goodness have compassion on the homeless,
— help them to find proper housing.
In your goodness give and preserve the fruits of the earth,
— so that each day there may be bread enough for all.

(or:

Graciously protect our nation from evil,
— that it may prosper in your peace.)

Lord, you attend the dying with great mercy,
— grant them an eternal dwelling.

Our Father . . .

Concluding prayer, as in the Proper of Seasons.

Conclusion, as in the Ordinary, 29.

## Invitatory

Lord, open my lips.

Ant. Come, worship the Lord, for we are his people,
the flock he shepherds, alleluia.

Invitatory psalm, 22.

## Morning Prayer

The following verse and response are omitted
when the hour begins with the invitatory.

God, come to my assistance. Glory to the Father.
As it was in the beginning. Alleluia.

HYMN, no. 9 or 131. Outside Ordinary Time, see
Guide, 578.

PSALMODY

Ant. 1  Blessed is he who comes in the name of the
Lord, alleluia.

Advent: Zion is our mighty citadel, our saving Lord its wall
and its defense; throw open the gates, for our God is
here among us, alleluia.

Lent, 2nd Sunday: The right hand of the Lord has shown
its power; the right hand of the Lord has raised me up.

Lent, Passion (Palm) Sunday: The great crowd that had
gathered for the feast cried out to the Lord: Blessed is
he who comes in the name of the Lord. Hosanna in the
highest.

Easter, 6th Sunday: This is the day which the Lord has
made, alleluia.

## Psalm 118

### Song of joy for salvation

*This Jesus is the stone which, rejected by you builders, has become the chief stone supporting all the rest* (Acts 4:11).

Give thanks to the Lord for he is good,
for his love endures for ever.

Let the sons of Israel say:
"His love endures for ever."
Let the sons of Aaron say:
"His love endures for ever."
Let those who fear the Lord say:
"His love endures for ever."

I called to the Lord in my distress;
he answered and freed me.
The Lord is at my side; I do not fear.
What can man do against me?
The Lord is at my side as my helper:
I shall look down on my foes.

It is better to take refuge in the Lord
than to trust in men:
it is better to take refuge in the Lord
than to trust in princes.

The nations all encompassed me;
in the Lord's name I crushed them.
They compassed me, compassed me about;
in the Lord's name I crushed them.
They compassed me about like bees;
they blazed like a fire among thorns.
In the Lord's name I crushed them.

I was hard-pressed and was falling
but the Lord came to help me.
The Lord is my strength and my song;
he is my savior.
There are shouts of joy and victory
in the tents of the just.

The Lord's right hand has triumphed;
his right hand raised me.
The Lord's right hand has triumphed;
I shall not die, I shall live
and recount his deeds.
I was punished, I was punished by the Lord,
but not doomed to die.

Open to me the gates of holiness:
I will enter and give thanks.
This is the Lord's own gate
where the just may enter.
I will thank you for you have answered
and you are my savior.

The stone which the builders rejected
has become the corner stone.
This is the work of the Lord,
a marvel in our eyes.
This day was made by the Lord;
we rejoice and are glad.

O Lord, grant us salvation;
O Lord, grant success.
Blessed in the name of the Lord
is he who comes.
We bless you from the house of the Lord;
the Lord God is our light.

Go forward in procession with branches
even to the altar.
You are my God, I thank you.

My God, I praise you.
Give thanks to the Lord for he is good;
for his love endures for ever.

Psalm-prayer

Lord God, you have given us the great day of rejoicing: Jesus Christ, the stone rejected by the

builders, has become the cornerstone of the Church, our spiritual home. Shed upon your Church the rays of your glory, that it may be seen as the gate of salvation open to all nations. Let cries of joy and exultation ring out from its tents, to celebrate the wonder of Christ's resurrection.

Ant. 2  Let us sing a hymn of praise to our God, alleluia.

Advent: Come to the waters, all you who thirst; seek the Lord while he can be found, alleluia.

Lent, 2nd Sunday: Let us sing the hymn of the three young men which they sang in the fiery furnace, giving praise to God.

Lent, Passion (Palm) Sunday: God grant that with the angels and the children we may be faithful, and sing with them to the conqueror of death: Hosanna in the highest.

Easter, 6th Sunday: Blessed are you, Lord our God, in the firmament of heaven. You are worthy of praise for ever, alleluia.

### Canticle          Daniel 3:52-57

Let all creatures praise the Lord

*The Creator . . . is blessed for ever* (Romans 1:25).

Blessed are you, O Lord, the God of our fathers,
praiseworthy and exalted above all forever.

And blessed is your holy and glorious name,
praiseworthy and exalted above all for all ages.

Blessed are you in the temple of your holy glory,
praiseworthy and glorious above all forever.

Blessed are you on the throne of your kingdom,
praiseworthy and exalted above all forever.

Blessed are you who look into the depths
from your throne upon the cherubim,
praiseworthy and exalted above all forever.

Blessed are you in the firmament of heaven,
praiseworthy and glorious forever.

Bless the Lord, all you works of the Lord,
praise and exalt him above all forever.

Ant. 3 **Praise the Lord for his infinite greatness,
alleluia.**

Advent: Our God will come with great power to enlighten
the eyes of his servants, alleluia.

Lent, 2nd Sunday: Praise the Lord in his heavenly power.

Lent, Passion (Palm) Sunday: Blessed is he who comes
in the name of the Lord; peace in heaven and glory in
the highest.

Easter, 6th Sunday: Worship God who is seated upon the
throne; sing to him in praise: Amen, alleluia.

## Psalm 150

### Praise the Lord

*Let mind and heart be in your song: this is to glorify God with your whole self* (Hesychius).

Praise God in his holy place,
praise him in his mighty heavens.
Praise him for his powerful deeds,
praise his surpassing greatness.

O praise him with sound of trumpet,
praise him with lute and harp.
Praise him with timbrel and dance,
praise him with strings and pipes.

O praise him with resounding cymbals,
praise him with clashing of cymbals.
Let everything that lives and that breathes
give praise to the Lord.

Psalm-prayer

Lord God, maker of heaven and earth and of all
created things, you make your just ones holy and
you justify sinners who confess your name. Hear
us as we humbly pray to you: give us eternal joy
with your saints.

READING                                    Ezekiel 36:25-28

I will sprinkle clean water upon you to cleanse
you from all your impurities, and from all your
idols I will cleanse you. I will give you a new heart
and place a new spirit within you, taking from your
bodies your stony hearts and giving you natural
hearts. I will put my spirit within you and make you
live by my statutes, careful to observe my decrees.
You shall live in the land I gave your fathers; you
shall be my people, and I will be your God.

RESPONSORY

We give thanks to you, O God, as we call upon your
   name.
— We give thanks to you, O God, as we call upon
   your name.

We cry aloud how marvelous you are,
— as we call upon your name.

Glory to the Father . . .
— We give thanks . . .

CANTICLE OF ZECHARIAH, antiphon as in the Proper
of Seasons.

INTERCESSIONS

Let us give thanks to our Savior who came into this
   world as God's presence among us. Let us call
   upon him:
   *Christ, King of Glory, be our light and our joy.*
Lord Jesus, you are the rising Sun, the firstfruits of
   the future resurrection,

— grant that we may not sit in the shadow of death
but walk in the light of life.
Show us your goodness, present in every creature,
— that we may contemplate your glory everywhere.
Do not allow us to be overcome by evil today,
— but grant that we may overcome evil through the
power of good.
You were baptized in the Jordan and anointed by
the Holy Spirit,
— grant that we may this day give thanks to your
Holy Spirit.

Our Father . . .

Concluding prayer, as in the Proper of Seasons.

Conclusion, as in the Ordinary, 29.

## Evening Prayer II

God, come to my assistance. Glory to the Father.
As it was in the beginning. Alleluia.

HYMN, no. 40 or 32. Outside Ordinary Time, see
Guide, 578.

PSALMODY

Ant. 1  Christ our Lord is a priest for ever, like
Melchizedek of old, alleluia.

Advent: The Lord will come on the clouds of heaven with
great power and might, alleluia.

Lent, 2nd Sunday: In holy splendor the Lord will send
forth your mighty scepter from Zion.

Lent, Passion (Palm) Sunday: Christ was scourged and
treated with contempt, but God's right hand has
raised him up.

Easter, 6th Sunday: God raised up Christ from the dead
and gave him a place at his right hand in heaven, alleluia.

## Psalm 110:1-5, 7

### The Messiah, king and priest

*Christ's reign will last until all his enemies are made subject to him* (1 Corinthians 15:25).

The Lord's revelation to my Master:
"Sit on my right:
your foes I will put beneath your feet."

The Lord will wield from Zion
your scepter of power:
rule in the midst of all your foes.

A prince from the day of your birth
on the holy mountains;
from the womb before the dawn I begot you.

The Lord has sworn an oath he will not change.
"You are a priest for ever,
a priest like Melchizedek of old."

The Master standing at your right hand
will shatter kings in the day of his great wrath.

He shall drink from the stream by the wayside
and therefore he shall lift up his head.

Psalm-prayer

Almighty God, bring the kingdom of Christ, your anointed one, to its fullness. May the perfect offering of your Son, eternal priest of the new Jerusalem, be offered in every place to your name, and make all nations a holy people for you.

Ant. 2  God dwells in highest heaven; he has power to do all he wills, alleluia.

Advent: The Lord will come; he is true to his word. If he seems to delay, keep watch for him, for he will surely come, alleluia.

Lent, 2nd Sunday: We worship the one true God who made heaven and earth.

Lent, Passion (Palm) Sunday: The blood of Christ
    washes away our sins and makes us worthy to serve
    the living God.

Easter, 6th Sunday: You have been turned from faith in
    idols to the living God, alleluia.

## Psalm 115

### Praise of the true God

*You have renounced idol worship to serve the
living and true God* (1 Thessalonians 1:9).

Not to us, Lord, not to us,
    but to your name give the glory
    for the sake of your love and your truth,
    lest the heathen say: "Where is their God?"

But our God is in the heavens;
    he does whatever he wills.
    Their idols are silver and gold,
    the work of human hands.

They have mouths but they cannot speak;
    they have eyes but they cannot see;
    they have ears but they cannot hear;
    they have nostrils but they cannot smell.

With their hands they cannot feel;
    with their feet they cannot walk.
    No sound comes from their throats.
    Their makers will come to be like them
    and so will all who trust in them.

Sons of Israel, trust in the Lord;
    he is their help and their shield.
    Sons of Aaron, trust in the Lord;
    he is their help and their shield.

You who fear him, trust in the Lord;
    he is their help and their shield.
    He remembers us, and he will bless us; —

he will bless the sons of Israel.
He will bless the sons of Aaron.

The Lord will bless those who fear him,
the little no less than the great:
to you may the Lord grant increase,
to you and all your children.

May you be blessed by the Lord,
the maker of heaven and earth.
The heavens belong to the Lord
but the earth he has given to men.

The dead shall not praise the Lord,
nor those who go down into the silence.
But we who live bless the Lord
now and for ever. Amen.

Psalm-prayer

Father, creator and ruler of heaven and earth,
you made man in your likeness to subdue the earth
and master it, and to recognize the work of your
hands in created beauty. Grant that your children,
thus surrounded on all sides by signs of your presence, may live continually in Christ, praising you
through him and with him.

Ant. 3 **Praise God, all you who serve him, both
great and small, alleluia.**

Advent: The Lord our king and lawgiver will come to save
us.

Easter, 6th Sunday: Alleluia, salvation, glory and power
to our God, alleluia.

The following canticle is said with the **Alleluia**
when Evening Prayer is sung; when the office is
recited, the **Alleluia** may be said at the beginning
and end of each strophe.

Canticle                    See Revelation 19:1-7

### The wedding of the Lamb

Alleluia.
Salvation, glory, and power to our God:
(℟. Alleluia.)
his judgments are honest and true.
℟. Alleluia (alleluia).

Alleluia.
Sing praise to our God, all you his servants,
(℟. Alleluia.)
all who worship him reverently, great and small.
℟. Alleluia (alleluia).

Alleluia.
The Lord our all-powerful God is King;
(℟. Alleluia.)
let us rejoice, sing praise, and give him glory.
℟. Alleluia (alleluia).

Alleluia.
The wedding feast of the Lamb has begun,
(℟. Alleluia.)
and his bride is prepared to welcome him.
℟. Alleluia (alleluia).

---

## Lent

Lent, 2nd Sunday: **God did not spare his own Son but gave him up for us all.**

Lent, Passion (Palm) Sunday: **Christ bore our sins in his own body on the cross so that we might die to sin and be alive to all that is good.**

Canticle                    1 Peter 2:21-24

### The willing acceptance of his passion by Christ, the servant of God

Christ suffered for you,
and left you an example
to have you follow in his footsteps.

He did no wrong;
no deceit was found in his mouth.
When he was insulted,
he returned no insult.

When he was made to suffer,
he did not counter with threats.
Instead he delivered himself up
to the One who judges justly.

In his own body
he brought your sins to the cross,
so that all of us, dead to sin,
could live in accord with God's will.

By his wounds you were healed.

READING                    2 Thessalonians 2:13-14

But we ought to give thanks to God for you always, brothers loved by the Lord, because God
chose you as the firstfruits for salvation through
sanctification by the Spirit and belief in truth. To
this end he has [also] called you through our
gospel to possess the glory of our Lord Jesus
Christ.

RESPONSORY

Our Lord is great, mighty is his power.
— Our Lord is great, mighty is his power.

His wisdom is beyond compare,
— mighty is his power.

Glory to the Father . . .
— Our Lord is . . .

CANTICLE OF MARY, antiphon as in the Proper of
Seasons.

INTERCESSIONS

All praise and honor to Christ! He lives for ever to intercede for us, and he is able to save those who approach the Father in his name. Sustained by our faith, let us call upon him:

*Remember your people, Lord.*

As the day draws to a close, Sun of Justice, we invoke your name upon the whole human race,

— so that all men may enjoy your never failing light.

Preserve the covenant which you have ratified in your blood,

— cleanse and sanctify your Church.

Remember your assembly, Lord,

— your dwelling place.

Guide travelers along the path of peace and prosperity,

— so that they may reach their destinations in safety and joy.

Receive the souls of the dead, Lord,

— grant them your favor and the gift of eternal glory.

Our Father . . .

Concluding prayer, as in the Proper of Seasons.

Conclusion, as in the Ordinary, 29.

# MONDAY, WEEK II
## Invitatory

Lord, open my lips.

Ant. Come, let us sing joyful songs to the Lord.

Invitatory psalm, 22.

## Morning Prayer

The following verse and response are omitted when the hour begins with the invitatory.

God, come to my assistance. Glory to the Father. As it was in the beginning. Alleluia.

HYMN, no. 10 or 11. Outside Ordinary Time, see Guide, 578.

PSALMODY

Ant. 1   When will I come to the end of my pilgrimage and enter the presence of God?

Holy Week: Jesus said: My heart is nearly broken with sorrow; stay here and keep watch with me.

Easter: As a deer longs for flowing streams, so my soul longs for you, my God, alleluia.

## Psalm 42

Longing for the Lord's presence in his Temple

*Let all who thirst come; let all who desire it drink from the life-giving water* (Revelation 22:17).

Like the deer that yearns
for running streams,
so my soul is yearning
for you, my God.

My soul is thirsting for God,
the God of my life;
when can I enter and see
the face of God?

My tears have become my bread,
by night, by day,
as I hear it said all the day long:
"Where is your God?"

These things will I remember
as I pour out my soul:
how I would lead the rejoicing crowd
into the house of God,
amid cries of gladness and thanksgiving,
the throng wild with joy.

Why are you cast down, my soul,
why groan within me?
Hope in God; I will praise him still,
my savior and my God.

My soul is cast down within me
as I think of you,
from the country of Jordan and Mount Hermon,
from the Hill of Mizar.

Deep is calling on deep,
in the roar of waters:
your torrents and all your waves
swept over me.

By day the Lord will send
his loving kindness;
by night I will sing to him,
praise the God of my life.

I will say to God, my rock:
"Why have you forgotten me?
Why do I go mourning,
oppressed by the foe?"

With cries that pierce me to the heart,
my enemies revile me,
saying to me all the day long:
"Where is your God?"

Why are you cast down, my soul,
why groan within me?
Hope in God; I will praise him still,
my savior and my God.

Psalm-prayer

Father in heaven, when your strength takes possession of us we no longer say: Why are you cast down, my soul? So now that the surging waves of your indignation have passed over us, let us feel the healing calm of your forgiveness. Inspire us to yearn for you always, like the deer for running streams, until you satisfy every longing in heaven.

Ant. 2 Lord, show us the radiance of your mercy.

Holy Week: Now the time has come for this world to receive its sentence; now the prince of this world will be driven out.

Easter: Fill Zion with your praises, Lord, and let your wonders be proclaimed, alleluia.

Canticle   Sirach 36:1-5, 10-13

Prayer of entreaty for the holy city, Jerusalem

*This is eternal life: to know you, the one true God, and Jesus Christ whom you have sent* (John 17:3).

Come to our aid, O God of the universe,
and put all the nations in dread of you!
Raise your hand against the heathen,
that they may realize your power.

As you have used us to show them your holiness,
so now use them to show us your glory.
Thus they will know, as you know,
that there is no God but you.

Give new signs and work new wonders;
show forth the splendor of your right hand and
    arm.

Gather all the tribes of Jacob,
that they may inherit the land as of old.
Show mercy to the people called by your name;
Israel, whom you named your first-born.

Take pity on your holy city,
Jerusalem, your dwelling place.
Fill Zion with your majesty,
your temple with your glory.

Ant. 3 The vaults of heaven ring with your praise,
    O Lord.

Holy Week: Jesus, the beginning and end of our faith, endured the cross, heedless of the shame, and is seated now at the right hand of the throne of God.

Easter: The glory of God illumines the city; the Lamb of God is its light, alleluia.

Psalm 19A

Praise of the Lord, Creator of all

*The dawn from on high shall break upon us . . . to guide our feet into the way of peace* (Luke 1:78, 79).

The heavens proclaim the glory of God
and the firmament shows forth the work of his
    hands.
Day unto day takes up the story
and night unto night makes known the message.

No speech, no word, no voice is heard
yet their span extends through all the earth,
their words to the utmost bounds of the world.

There he has placed a tent for the sun;
it comes forth like a bridegroom coming from his
    tent,
rejoices like a champion to run its course.

At the end of the sky is the rising of the sun;
to the furthest end of the sky is its course.
There is nothing concealed from its burning heat.

Psalm-prayer

To enlighten the world, Father, you sent to us
your Word as the sun of truth and justice shining
upon mankind. Illumine our eyes that we may discern your glory in the many works of your hand.

READING                              Jeremiah 15:15-16

Remember me, Lord, visit me,
    and avenge me on my persecutors.
Because of your long-suffering banish me not;
    know that for you I have borne insult.
When I found your words, I devoured them;
    they became my joy and the happiness of my heart,
Because I bore your name,
    O Lord, God of hosts.

RESPONSORY

Sing for joy, God's chosen ones, give him the praise
    that is due.
— Sing for joy, God's chosen ones, give him the
    praise that is due.

Sing a new song to the Lord;
— give him the praise that is due.

Glory to the Father . . .
— Sing for joy . . .

CANTICLE OF ZECHARIAH

Ant. Blessed be the Lord, for he has come to his
people and set them free.

INTERCESSIONS

Our Savior has made us a nation of priests to offer
acceptable sacrifice to the Father. Let us call
upon him in gratitude:
*Preserve us in your ministry, Lord.*
Christ, eternal priest, you conferred the holy priesthood on your people,
— grant that we may offer spiritual sacrifices acceptable to the Father.
In your goodness pour out on us the fruits of your
Spirit,
— patience, kindness and gentleness.
May we love you and possess you, for you are love,
— and may every action of our lives praise you.
May we seek those things which are beneficial to
our brothers, without counting the cost,
— to help them on the way to salvation.

Our Father . . .

CONCLUDING PRAYER

Almighty Father,
you have brought us to the light of a new day:
keep us safe the whole day through
from every sinful inclination.
May all our thoughts, words and actions
aim at doing what is pleasing in your sight.

We ask this through our Lord Jesus Christ, your Son,
who lives and reigns with you and the Holy Spirit,
one God, for ever and ever.

Conclusion, as in the Ordinary, 29.

## Evening Prayer

God, come to my assistance. Glory to the Father.
As it was in the beginning. Alleluia.

HYMN, no. **41** or **47**. Outside Ordinary Time, see
Guide, **578**.

PSALMODY

Ant. 1 **Yours is more than mortal beauty; every
word you speak is full of grace.**

Holy Week: He had neither beauty, nor majesty, nothing
to attract our eyes.

Easter: Blessed is he who comes in the name of the
Lord, alleluia.

Psalm 45

The marriage of the king

*The Bridegroom is here; go out and welcome him*
(Matthew 25:6).

I

My heart overflows with noble words.
To the king I must speak the song I have made;
my tongue as nimble as the pen of a scribe.

You are the fairest of the children of men
and graciousness is poured upon your lips:
because God has blessed you for evermore.

O mighty one, gird your sword upon your thigh;
in splendor and state, ride on in triumph
for the cause of truth and goodness and right.

Take aim with your bow in your dread right hand.
Your arrows are sharp: peoples fall beneath you.
The foes of the king fall down and lose heart.

Your throne, O God, shall endure for ever.
A scepter of justice is the scepter of your king-
    dom.
Your love is for justice; your hatred for evil.

Therefore God, your God, has anointed you
with the oil of gladness above other kings:
your robes are fragrant with aloes and myrrh.

From the ivory palace you are greeted with music.
The daughters of kings are among your loved
    ones.
On your right stands the queen in gold of Ophir.

Ant. 2 **The Bridegroom is here; go out and welcome him.**

Holy Week: I will entrust all people to his care, for he
has given himself up to death for all.

Easter: Blessed are those who are called to the wedding
feast of the Lamb, alleluia.

## II

Listen, O daughter, give ear to my words:
forget your own people and your father's house.
So will the king desire your beauty:
he is your lord, pay homage to him.

And the people of Tyre shall come with gifts,
the richest of the people shall seek your favor.
The daughter of the king is clothed with splendor,
her robes embroidered with pearls set in gold.

She is led to the king with her maiden compan-
    ions.
They are escorted amid gladness and joy;
they pass within the palace of the king.

Sons shall be yours in place of your fathers:
you will make them princes over all the earth.
May this song make your name for ever remem-
    bered.
May the peoples praise you from age to age.

Psalm-prayer

When you took on flesh, Lord Jesus, you made a
marriage of mankind with God. Help us to be faithful to your word and endure our exile bravely, until
we are called to the heavenly marriage feast, to
which the Virgin Mary, exemplar of your Church,
has preceded us.

Ant. 3 **God planned in the fullness of time to restore all things in Christ.**

Holy Week: God has blessed us in Christ. Through him, at the cost of his blood, we have been redeemed.

Easter: From his fullness we have all received, grace upon grace, alleluia.

Canticle　　　　　Ephesians 1:3-10

God our Savior

Praised be the God and Father
of our Lord Jesus Christ
who has bestowed on us in Christ
every spiritual blessing in the heavens.

God chose us in him
before the world began
to be holy
and blameless in his sight.

He predestined us
to be his adopted sons through Jesus Christ,
such was his will and pleasure,
that all might praise the glorious favor
he has bestowed on us in his beloved.

In him and through his blood, we have been re-
　　　deemed,
and our sins forgiven,
so immeasurably generous
is God's favor to us.

God has given us the wisdom
to understand fully the mystery,
the plan he was pleased
to decree in Christ.

A plan to be carried out
in Christ, in the fullness of time,
to bring all things into one in him,
in the heavens and on earth.

READING　　　　　　　　1 Thessalonians 2:11-14

As you know, we treated each one of you as a
father treats his children, exhorting and encourag-
ing you and insisting that you conduct yourselves
as worthy of the God who calls you into his king-

dom and glory. And for this reason we too give thanks to God unceasingly, that, in receiving the word of God from hearing us, you received not a human word but, as it truly is, the word of God, which is now at work in you who believe.

RESPONSORY

Accept my prayer, O Lord, which rises up to you.
— Accept my prayer, O Lord, which rises up to you.

Like burning incense in your sight,
— which rises up to you.

Glory to the Father . . .
— Accept my prayer . . .

CANTICLE OF MARY

Ant. For ever will my soul proclaim the greatness of the Lord.

INTERCESSIONS

Let us praise Christ, who loves, nourishes and supports his Church. With faith let us cry out to him:
*Answer the prayers of your people, Lord.*
Lord Jesus, grant that all men be saved,
— and come to the knowledge of truth.
Preserve our holy father, Pope N., and N., our bishop,
— come with your power to help them.
Remember those who long for honest work,
— so that they may lead a life of peaceful security.
Lord, be the refuge of the poor,
— their help in distress.
We commend to your care all bishops, priests and deacons who have died,
— may they sing your praises for ever around your heavenly throne.

Our Father . . .

CONCLUDING PRAYER

Almighty Father,
you have given us the strength

to work throughout this day.
Receive our evening sacrifice of praise
in thanksgiving for your countless gifts.

We ask this through our Lord Jesus Christ, your Son,
who lives and reigns with you and the Holy Spirit,
one God, for ever and ever.

Conclusion, as in the Ordinary, 29.

# TUESDAY, WEEK II
## Invitatory

Lord, open my lips.

Ant. Come, let us worship the Lord, our mighty God.

Invitatory psalm, 22.

## Morning Prayer

The following verse and response are omitted when
the hour begins with the invitatory.

God, come to my assistance. Glory to the Father. As
it was in the beginning. Alleluia.

HYMN, no. 12 or 13. Outside Ordinary Time, see
Guide, 578.

PSALMODY

Ant. 1 Lord, send forth your light and your truth.

> Holy Week: O Lord, defend my cause; rescue me from de-
> ceitful and impious men.

> Easter: You have come to Mount Zion and to the city of the
> living God, alleluia.

### Psalm 43

Longing for the Temple

*I have come into the world to be its light* (John
12:46).

Defend me, O God, and plead my cause
against a godless nation.
From deceitful and cunning men
rescue me, O God.

Since you, O God, are my stronghold,
why have you rejected me?
Why do I go mourning
oppressed by the foe?

O send forth your light and your truth;
let these be my guide.
Let them bring me to your holy mountain
to the place where you dwell.

And I will come to the altar of God,
the God of my joy.
My redeemer, I will thank you on the harp,
O God, my God.

Why are you cast down, my soul,
why groan within me?
Hope in God; I will praise him still,
my savior and my God.

Psalm-prayer

Almighty Father, source of everlasting light, send forth your truth into our hearts and pour over us the brightness of your light.

Ant. 2  Lord, keep us safe all the days of our life.

> Holy Week: Lord, my God, you defended my cause; you ransomed my life.

> Easter: Lord, you have preserved my life from destruction, alleluia.

Canticle                                    Isaiah 38:10-14, 17-20

Anguish of a dying man and joy in his restoration

*I am living, I was dead . . . and I hold the keys of death* (Revelation 1:17, 18).

> Once I said,
> "In the noontime of life I must depart!
> To the gates of the nether world I shall be consigned
> for the rest of my years."

I said, "I shall see the Lord no more
in the land of the living.
No longer shall I behold my fellow men
among those who dwell in the world."

My dwelling, like a shepherd's tent,
is struck down and borne away from me;
you have folded up my life, like a weaver
who severs the last thread.

Day and night you give me over to torment;
I cry out until the dawn.
Like a lion he breaks all my bones;
day and night you give me over to torment.

Like a swallow I utter shrill cries;
I moan like a dove.
My eyes grow weak, gazing heaven-ward:
O Lord, I am in straits; be my surety!

You have preserved my life
from the pit of destruction,
when you cast behind your back
all my sins.

For it is not the nether world that gives you
      thanks,
nor death that praises you;
neither do those who go down into the pit
await your kindness.

The living, the living give you thanks,
as I do today.
Fathers declare to their sons,
O God, your faithfulness.

The Lord is our savior;
we shall sing to stringed instruments
in the house of the Lord
all the days of our life.

Ant. 3  To you, O God, our praise is due in Zion.

**Holy Week:** My servant, the Just One, will justify many by taking their sins on himself.

**Easter:** You have visited the earth and brought life-giving rain to fill it with plenty, alleluia.

Psalm 65

Solemn thanksgiving

*Zion represents heaven* (Origen).

To you our praise is due
in Zion, O God.
To you we pay our vows,
you who hear our prayer.

To you all flesh will come
with its burden of sin.
Too heavy for us, our offenses,
but you wipe them away.

Blessed is he whom you choose and call
to dwell in your courts.
We are filled with the blessings of your house,
of your holy temple.

You keep your pledge with wonders,
O God our savior,
the hope of all the earth
and of far distant isles.

You uphold the mountains with your strength,
you are girded with power.
You still the roaring of the seas,
the roaring of their waves
and the tumult of the peoples.

The ends of the earth stand in awe
at the sight of your wonders.
The lands of sunrise and sunset
you fill with your joy.

You care for the earth, give it water,
you fill it with riches.
Your river in heaven brims over
to provide its grain.

And thus you provide for the earth;
you drench its furrows,
you level it, soften it with showers,
you bless its growth.

You crown the year with your goodness.
Abundance flows in your steps,
in the pastures of the wilderness it flows.

The hills are girded with joy,
the meadows covered with flocks,
the valleys are decked with wheat.
They shout for joy, yes, they sing.

## Psalm-prayer

Lord God, hope of all the earth, hear the humble prayer of your children as we sing your praises. Pour out your Spirit on us so that our lives may bear fruit abundantly.

### READING                                              1 Thessalonians 5:2-6

For you yourselves know very well that the day of the Lord will come like a thief at night. When people are saying, "Peace and security," then sudden disaster comes upon them, like labor pains upon a pregnant woman, and they will not escape. But you, brothers, are not in darkness, for that day to overtake you like a thief. For all of you are children of the light and children of the day. We are not of the night or of darkness. Therefore, let us not sleep as the rest do, but let us stay alert and sober.

### RESPONSORY

Lord, listen to my cry; all my trust is in your promise.
— Lord, listen to my cry; all my trust is in your promise.

Dawn finds me watching, crying out for you,
— all my trust is in your promise.

Glory to the Father . . .
— Lord, listen to . . .

CANTICLE OF ZECHARIAH

Ant. **Lord, save us from the hands of all who hate us.**

INTERCESSIONS

Let us bless our Savior who enlightens the world
    by his resurrection. Let us humbly beg him:
    *Keep us, Lord, on your path.*
Lord Jesus, we honor your resurrection in our
    morning prayer,
— the hope of your glory enlightens our day.
Accept, Lord, our prayers and petitions,
— as the firstfruits of our day.
Grant that we may progress today in your love,
— and that all things may work together for our
    good and the good of all.
Make our light shine so brightly before men,
— that seeing our good works they may give glory
    to the Father.

Our Father . . .

CONCLUDING PRAYER

Lord Jesus Christ,
true light of the world,
you guide all mankind to salvation.
Give us the courage, strength and grace
to build a world of justice and peace,
ready for the coming of that kingdom,
where you live and reign with the Father and the
    Holy Spirit,
one God, for ever and ever.

Conclusion, as in the Ordinary, 29.

## Evening Prayer

God, come to my assistance. Glory to the Father.
As it was in the beginning. Alleluia.

HYMN, no. **42** or **37**. Outside Ordinary Time, see
Guide, **578**.

PSALMODY

Ant. 1 **You cannot serve both God and mammon.**

Holy Week: They insulted me and filled me with dread, but the Lord was at my side, like a mighty warrior.

Easter: Seek the things of heaven, not those that are on the earth, alleluia.

## Psalm 49
### Emptiness of riches

*It is difficult for a rich man to enter the kingdom of heaven* (Matthew 19:23).

I

Hear this, all you peoples,
give heed, all who dwell in the world,
men both low and high,
rich and poor alike!

My lips will speak words of wisdom.
My heart is full of insight.
I will turn my mind to a parable,
with the harp I will solve my problem.

Why should I fear in evil days
the malice of the foes who surround me,
men who trust in their wealth,
and boast of the vastness of their riches?

For no man can buy his own ransom,
or pay a price to God for his life.
The ransom of his soul is beyond him.
He cannot buy life without end,
nor avoid coming to the grave.

He knows that wise men and fools must both
   perish
and leave their wealth to others.
Their graves are their homes for ever,
their dwelling place from age to age,
though their names spread wide through the
   land.

In his riches, man lacks wisdom:
he is like the beasts that are destroyed.

Ant. 2 **Store up for yourselves treasure in heaven, says the Lord.**

Holy Week: Deliver me, Lord, and place me at your side, then let whoever will, lift his hand to strike me.

Easter: The Lord has rescued my life from the power of hell, alleluia.

II

This is the lot of those who trust in themselves,
who have others at their beck and call.
Like sheep they are driven to the grave,
where death shall be their shepherd
and the just shall become their rulers.

With the morning their outward show vanishes
and the grave becomes their home.
But God will ransom me from death
and take my soul to himself.

Then do not fear when a man grows rich,
when the glory of his house increases.
He takes nothing with him when he dies,
his glory does not follow him below.

Though he flattered himself while he lived:
"Men will praise me for all my success,"
yet he will go to join his fathers,
who will never see the light any more.

In his riches, man lacks wisdom:
he is like the beasts that are destroyed.

Psalm-prayer

Make our mouths speak your wisdom, Lord
Jesus, and help us to remember that you became
man and redeemed us from death that we might
merit the beauty of your light.

Ant. 3 **Adoration and glory belong by right to the Lamb who was slain.**

Holy Week: You were slain, Lord, and by your blood you have ransomed us for God.

Easter: Yours, O Lord, is majesty and power, glory and triumph, alleluia.

Canticle                    Revelation 4:11; 5:9, 10, 12

### Redemption hymn

O Lord our God, you are worthy
to receive glory and honor and power.

For you have created all things;
by your will they came to be and were made.

Worthy are you, O Lord,
to receive the scroll and break open its seals.

For you were slain;
with your blood you purchased for God
men of every race and tongue,
of every people and nation.

You made of them a kingdom,
and priests to serve our God,
and they shall reign on the earth.

Worthy is the Lamb that was slain
to receive power and riches,
wisdom and strength,
honor and glory and praise.

READING                          Romans 3:21-26

But now the righteousness of God has been manifested apart from the law, though testified to by the
law and the prophets, the righteousness of God
through faith in Jesus Christ for all who believe. For
there is no distinction; all have sinned and are deprived of the glory of God. They are justified freely by
his grace through the redemption in Christ Jesus,
whom God set forth as an expiation, through faith, by
his blood, to prove his righteousness because of the
forgiveness of sins previously committed, through
the forbearance of God—to prove his righteousness
in the present time, that he might be righteous and
justify the one who has faith in Jesus.

RESPONSORY

I shall know the fullness of joy, when I see your
    face, O Lord.
— I shall know the fullness of joy, when I see your
    face, O Lord.
Fulfillment and endless peace in your presence,
— when I see your face, O Lord.
Glory to the Father . . .
— I shall know . . .

CANTICLE OF MARY

Ant. Do great things for us, O Lord, for you are
    mighty, and holy is your name.

INTERCESSIONS

Let us praise Christ, the shepherd and guardian of
    our souls, who loves and protects his people.
    Placing our hope in him, we cry out:
    *Protect your people, Lord.*
Eternal shepherd, protect our bishop N.,
— and all the shepherds of your Church.
Look kindly on those who suffer persecution,
— hasten to free them from all adversity.
Have mercy on the needy, Lord,
— provide food for the hungry.
Enlighten all legislators,
— to enact laws in the spirit of wisdom and justice.
Come to the aid of our departed brothers and sisters,
    whom you have redeemed with your blood,
— make them worthy to enter your wedding feast.

Our Father . . .

CONCLUDING PRAYER

Father,
yours is the morning
and yours is the evening.
Let the Sun of Justice, Jesus Christ,

shine for ever in our hearts
and draw us to that light
where you live in radiant glory.

We ask this through our Lord Jesus Christ, your Son,
who lives and reigns with you and the Holy Spirit,
one God, for ever and ever.

Conclusion, as in the Ordinary, 29.

# WEDNESDAY, WEEK II

## Invitatory

Lord, open my lips.

Ant. Cry out with joy to the Lord, all the earth;
serve the Lord with gladness.

Invitatory psalm, 22.

## Morning Prayer

The following verse and response are omitted
when the hour begins with the invitatory.

God, come to my assistance. Glory to the Father.
As it was in the beginning. Alleluia.

HYMN, no. 14 or 15. Outside Ordinary Time, see
Guide, 578.

PSALMODY

Ant. 1  O God, all your ways are holy; what god can
compare with our God?

   Holy Week: In the day of my distress, I reached out with
   my hands to seek the Lord's help.

   Easter: The waters saw you, O God; you led your people
   through the sea, alleluia.


Psalm 77

Recalling God's works

*We suffer all kinds of afflictions and yet are not
overcome* (2 Corinthians 4:8).

I cry aloud to God,
cry aloud to God that he may hear me.

In the day of my distress I sought the Lord.
My hands were raised at night without ceasing;
my soul refused to be consoled.
I remembered my God and I groaned.
I pondered and my spirit fainted.

You withheld sleep from my eyes.
I was troubled, I could not speak.
I thought of the days of long ago
and remembered the years long past.
At night I mused within my heart.
I pondered and my spirit questioned.

"Will the Lord reject us for ever?
Will he show us his favor no more?
Has his love vanished for ever?
Has his promise come to an end?
Does God forget his mercy
or in anger withhold his compassion?"

I said: "This is what causes my grief;
that the way of the Most High has changed."
I remember the deeds of the Lord,
I remember your wonders of old,
I muse on all your works
and ponder your mighty deeds.

Your ways, O God, are holy.
What god is great as our God?
You are the God who works wonders.
You showed your power among the peoples.
Your strong arm redeemed your people,
the sons of Jacob and Joseph.

The waters saw you, O God,
the waters saw you and trembled;
the depths were moved with terror.—

The clouds poured down rain,
the skies sent forth their voice;
your arrows flashed to and fro.

Your thunder rolled round the sky,
your flashes lighted up the world.
The earth was moved and trembled
when your way led through the sea,
your path through the mighty waters,
and no one saw your footprints.

You guided your people like a flock
by the hand of Moses and Aaron.

Psalm-prayer

Father, you established your ancient covenant by
signs and wonders, but more wondrously you confirmed the new one through the sacrifice of your
Son. Guide your Church through the pathways of
life, that we may be led to the land of promise and
celebrate your name with lasting praise.

Ant. 2  My heart leaps up with joy to the Lord, for
he humbles only to exalt us.

Holy Week: If we have died with Christ, we believe that
we shall also live with Christ.

Easter: The Lord puts to death and raises to life, alleluia.

Canticle                    1 Samuel 2:1-10

The humble find joy in God

*He has cast down the mighty from their thrones
and has lifted up the lowly. He has filled the hungry with good things* (Luke 1:52-53).

My heart exults in the Lord,
my horn is exalted in my God.

I have swallowed up my enemies;
I rejoice in my victory.
There is no Holy One like the Lord;
there is no Rock like our God.

Speak boastfully no longer,
nor let arrogance issue from your mouths.
For an all-knowing God is the Lord,
a God who judges deeds.

The bows of the mighty are broken,
while the tottering gird on strength.
The well-fed hire themselves out for bread,
while the hungry batten on spoil.
The barren wife bears seven sons,
while the mother of many languishes.

The Lord puts to death and gives life;
he casts down to the nether world;
he raises up again.
The Lord makes poor and makes rich,
he humbles, he also exalts.

He raises the needy from the dust;
from the ash heap he lifts up the poor,
to seat them with nobles
and make a glorious throne their heritage.

For the pillars of the earth are the Lord's,
and he has set the world upon them.
He will guard the footsteps of his faithful ones,
but the wicked shall perish in the darkness.
For not by strength does man prevail;
the Lord's foes shall be shattered.

The Most High in heaven thunders;
the Lord judges the ends of the earth.
Now may he give strength to his king
and exalt the horn of his anointed!

Ant. 3 The Lord is king, let the earth rejoice.

Holy Week: God has made Christ Jesus our wisdom and
our holiness. By him we have been sanctified and redeemed.

Easter: A light has dawned for the just; joy has come to
the upright of heart, alleluia.

## Psalm 97

The glory of the Lord in his decrees for the world

*This psalm foretells a world-wide salvation and that peoples of all nations will believe in Christ* (Saint Athanasius).

The Lord is king, let earth rejoice,
let all the coastlands be glad.
Cloud and darkness are his raiment;
his throne, justice and right.

A fire prepares his path;
it burns up his foes on every side.
His lightnings light up the world,
the earth trembles at the sight.

The mountains melt like wax
before the Lord of all the earth.
The skies proclaim his justice;
all peoples see his glory.

Let those who serve idols be ashamed,
those who boast of their worthless gods.
All you spirits, worship him.

Zion hears and is glad;
the people of Judah rejoice
because of your judgments, O Lord.

For you indeed are the Lord,
most high above all the earth,
exalted far above all spirits.

The Lord loves those who hate evil:
he guards the souls of his saints;
he sets them free from the wicked.

Light shines forth for the just
and joy for the upright of heart.
Rejoice, you just, in the Lord;
give glory to his holy name.

Psalm-prayer

Father, you clothe the sky with light and the depths of the ocean with darkness. Among the sons of men you work wonders, and rain terror upon the enemy. Look upon your servants. Do not try us by fire but bring us rejoicing to the shelter of your home.

READING                                        Romans 8:35-39

What will separate us from the love of Christ? Will anguish, or distress, or persecution, or famine, or nakedness, or peril, or the sword? As it is written:

"For your sake we are being slain all the day;
    we are looked upon as sheep to be slaughtered."

No, in all these things we conquer overwhelmingly through him who loved us. For I am convinced that neither death, nor life, nor angels, nor principalities, nor present things, nor future things, nor powers, nor height, nor depth, nor any other creature will be able to separate us from the love of God in Christ Jesus our Lord.

RESPONSORY

I will bless the Lord all my life long.
— I will bless the Lord all my life long.

With a song of praise ever on my lips,
— all my life long.

Glory to the Father . . .
— I will bless . . .

CANTICLE OF ZECHARIAH

Ant. Let us serve the Lord in holiness all the days
    of our life.

INTERCESSIONS

Blessed be God our Savior, who promised to remain with his Church all days, until the end of the world. Let us give him thanks and call out:
    *Remain with us, Lord.*

Remain with us the whole day, Lord,
— let your grace be a sun that never sets.
We dedicate this day to you as an offering,
— do not let us offer anything that is evil.
May your gift of light pervade this whole day,
— that we may be the salt of the earth and the light of the world.
May the love of your Holy Spirit direct our hearts and our lips,
— and may we always act in accordance with your will.

Our Father . . .

CONCLUDING PRAYER

Lord,
as a new day dawns
send the radiance of your light
to shine in our hearts.
Make us true to your teaching;
keep us free from error and sin.

We ask this through our Lord Jesus Christ, your Son, who lives and reigns with you and the Holy Spirit, one God, for ever and ever.

Conclusion, as in the Ordinary, 29.

# Evening Prayer

God, come to my assistance. Glory to the Father. As it was in the beginning. Alleluia.

HYMN, no. 43 or 44. Outside Ordinary Time, see Guide, 578.

PSALMODY

Ant. 1   Eagerly we await the fulfillment of our hope, the glorious coming of our Savior.

    Holy Week: Evil men said: Let us make the just man suffer; he sets himself against our way of life.

    Easter: Do not let your hearts be troubled; have faith in me, alleluia.

## Psalm 62

### Peace in God

*May God, the source of our hope, fill your hearts with peace as you believe in him* (Romans 15:13).

In God alone is my soul at rest;
my help comes from him.
He alone is my rock, my stronghold,
my fortress: I stand firm.

How long will you all attack one man
to break him down,
as though he were a tottering wall,
or a tumbling fence?

Their plan is only to destroy:
they take pleasure in lies.
With their mouth they utter blessing
but in their heart they curse.

In God alone be at rest, my soul;
for my hope comes from him.
He alone is my rock, my stronghold,
my fortress: I stand firm.

In God is my safety and glory,
the rock of my strength.
Take refuge in God, all you people.
Trust him at all times.
Pour out your hearts before him
for God is our refuge.

Common folk are only a breath,
great men an illusion.
Placed in the scales, they rise;
they weigh less than a breath.

Do not put your trust in oppression
nor vain hopes on plunder.—

Do not set your heart on riches
even when they increase.

For God has said only one thing:
only two do I know:
that to God alone belongs power
and to you, Lord, love;
and that you repay each man
according to his deeds.

Psalm-prayer

Lord God, you reward each one according to his works. Hear us as we pour out our hearts to you, seeking your grace and secure protection. We look to you for our stable hope in a constantly changing world.

Ant. 2 May God turn his radiant face toward us and fill us with his blessings.

Holy Week: He took all our sins upon himself and asked forgiveness for our offenses.

Easter: Let the peoples praise you, Lord God; let them rejoice in your salvation, alleluia.

When psalm 67 is the invitatory psalm, psalm 95, 22, is used as the second psalm of Evening Prayer.

Psalm 67

People of all nations will worship the Lord

*You must know that God is offering his salvation to all the world* (Acts 28:28).

O God, be gracious and bless us
and let your face shed its light upon us.
So will your ways be known upon earth
and all nations learn your saving help.

Let the peoples praise you, O God;
let all the peoples praise you.

Let the nations be glad and exult
for you rule the world with justice.
With fairness you rule the peoples,
you guide the nations on earth.

Let the peoples praise you, O God;
let all the peoples praise you.

The earth has yielded its fruit
for God, our God, has blessed us.
May God still give us his blessing
till the ends of the earth revere him.

Psalm-prayer

Be gracious and bless us, Lord, and let your face
shed its light on us, so that we can make you known
with reverence and bring forth a harvest of justice.

Ant. 3 Through him all things were made; he
holds all creation together in himself.

Holy Week: In Christ we have found deliverance; through
his blood, the forgiveness of our sins.

Easter: His glory covers the heavens and his praise fills
the earth, alleluia.

Canticle     Colossians 1:12-20

Christ the first-born of all creation
and the first-born from the dead

Let us give thanks to the Father
for having made you worthy
to share the lot of the saints
in light.

He rescued us
from the power of darkness
and brought us
into the kingdom of his beloved Son.
Through him we have redemption,
the forgiveness of our sins.

He is the image of the invisible God,
the first-born of all creatures.
In him everything in heaven and on earth was
created,
things visible and invisible.

All were created through him;
all were created for him.
He is before all else that is.
In him everything continues in being.

It is he who is head of the body, the church!
he who is the beginning,
the first-born of the dead,
so that primacy may be his in everything.

It pleased God to make absolute fullness reside
in him
and, by means of him, to reconcile everything
in his person,
both on earth and in the heavens,
making peace through the blood of his cross.

READING                                    1 Peter 5:5b-11

And all of you, clothe yourselves with humility in
your dealings with one another, for:

"God opposes the proud
but bestows favor on the humble."

So humble yourselves under the mighty hand of God,
that he may exalt you in due time. Cast all your
worries upon him because he cares for you.

Be sober and vigilant. Your opponent the devil is
prowling around like a roaring lion looking for
[someone] to devour. Resist him, steadfast in faith,
knowing that your fellow believers throughout the
world undergo the same sufferings. The God of all
grace who called you to his eternal glory through
Christ [Jesus] will himself restore, confirm,
strengthen, and establish you after you have suffered a little. To him be dominion forever. Amen.

RESPONSORY

Keep us, O Lord, as the apple of your eye.
— Keep us, O Lord, as the apple of your eye.

Gather us under the shadow of your wings, and keep
us,
— as the apple of your eye.

Glory to the Father . . .
— Keep us, O Lord . . .

CANTICLE OF MARY

Ant. Lord, with the strength of your arm scatter the
proud, and lift up the lowly.

INTERCESSIONS

Beloved brothers and sisters, let us rejoice in our
God, for he takes great delight in bestowing benefits on his people. Let us fervently pray:
*Increase your grace and your peace, Lord.*
Eternal God, for whom a thousand years are like
the passing day,
— help us to remember that life is like a flower which
blossoms in the morning, but withers in the
evening.
Give your people manna to satisfy their hunger,
— and living water to quench their thirst for all
eternity.
Let your faithful ones seek and taste the things
that are above,
— and let them direct their work and their leisure
to your glory.
Grant us good weather, Lord,
— that we may reap the copious fruits of the earth.
(or:
Deliver us from all harm, Lord,
—and pour out your abundant blessings on our
homes.)
Show the faithful departed the vision of your face,
— let them rejoice in the contemplation of your
presence.
Our Father . . .

CONCLUDING PRAYER

Lord God,
holy is your name,

and renowned your compassion,
cherished by every generation.
Hear our evening prayer
and let us sing your praise,
and proclaim your greatness for ever.

We ask this through our Lord Jesus Christ, your Son,
who lives and reigns with you and the Holy Spirit,
one God, for ever and ever.

Conclusion, as in the Ordinary, 29.

# THURSDAY, WEEK II

## Invitatory

Lord, open my lips.

Ant. Come into the Lord's presence singing for joy.

Invitatory psalm, 22.

## Morning Prayer

The following verse and response are omitted
when the hour begins with the invitatory.

God, come to my assistance. Glory to the Father.
As it was in the beginning. Alleluia.

HYMN, no. 15 or 7. Outside Ordinary Time, see
Guide, 578.

PSALMODY

Ant. 1 Stir up your mighty power, Lord; come to
our aid.

Holy Week: Look, O Lord, and see my suffering. Come
quickly to my aid.

Easter: I am the vine; you are the branches, alleluia.


Psalm 80

Lord, come, take care of your vineyard

*Come, Lord Jesus* (Revelation 22:20).

O shepherd of Israel, hear us,
you who lead Joseph's flock,
shine forth from your cherubim throne
upon Ephraim, Benjamin, Manasseh.
O Lord, rouse up your might,
O Lord, come to our help.

God of hosts, bring us back;
let your face shine on us and we shall be saved.

Lord God of hosts, how long
will you frown on your people's plea?
You have fed them with tears for their bread,
an abundance of tears for their drink.
You have made us the taunt of our neighbors,
our enemies laugh us to scorn.

God of hosts, bring us back;
let your face shine on us and we shall be saved.

You brought a vine out of Egypt;
to plant it you drove out the nations.
Before it you cleared the ground;
it took root and spread through the land.

The mountains were covered with its shadow,
the cedars of God with its boughs.
It stretched out its branches to the sea,
to the Great River it stretched out its shoots.

Then why have you broken down its walls?
It is plucked by all who pass by.
It is ravaged by the boar of the forest,
devoured by the beasts of the field.

God of hosts, turn again, we implore,
look down from heaven and see.

Visit this vine and protect it,
the vine your right hand has planted.—

Men have burnt it with fire and destroyed it.
May they perish at the frown of your face.

May your hand be on the man you have chosen,
the man you have given your strength.
And we shall never forsake you again:
give us life that we may call upon your name.

God of hosts, bring us back;
let your face shine on us and we shall be saved.

Psalm-prayer

Lord God, eternal shepherd, you so tend the vineyard you planted that now it extends its branches even to the farthest coast. Look down on your Church and come to us. Help us remain in your Son as branches on the vine, that, planted firmly in your love, we may testify before the whole world to your great power working everywhere.

Ant. 2  The Lord has worked marvels for us; make
         it known to the ends of the world.

Holy Week: God is my savior; I trust in him and shall not
fear.

Easter: Rejoicing, you will draw water from the well-
springs of the Savior, alleluia.

                    Canticle            Isaiah 12:1-6
          Joy of God's ransomed people

*If anyone thirsts, let him come to me and drink*
(John 7:37).

I give you thanks, O Lord;
though you have been angry with me,
your anger has abated, and you have consoled
    me.

God indeed is my savior;
I am confident and unafraid.
My strength and my courage is the Lord,
and he has been my savior.

With joy you will draw water
at the fountain of salvation, and say on that day:
Give thanks to the Lord, acclaim his name;
among the nations make known his deeds,
proclaim how exalted is his name.

Sing praise to the Lord for his glorious achieve-
    ment;
let this be known throughout all the earth.

Shout with exultation, O city of Zion,
for great in your midst
is the Holy One of Israel!

Ant. 3  Ring out your joy to God our strength.

Holy Week: The Lord has fed us with the finest wheat; he
has filled us with honey from the rock.

Easter: The Lord has fed us with the finest wheat, alleluia.

### Psalm 81

Solemn renewal of the Covenant

*See that no one among you has a faithless heart*
(Hebrews 3:12).

Ring out your joy to God our strength,
shout in triumph to the God of Jacob.

Raise a song and sound the timbrel,
the sweet-sounding harp and the lute,
blow the trumpet at the new moon,
when the moon is full, on our feast.

For this is Israel's law,
a command of the God of Jacob.
He imposed it as a rule on Joseph,
when he went out against the land of Egypt.

A voice I did not know said to me:
"I freed your shoulder from the burden;
your hands were freed from the load.
You called in distress and I saved you.

I answered, concealed in the storm cloud,
at the waters of Meribah I tested you.
Listen, my people, to my warning,
O Israel, if only you would heed!

Let there be no foreign god among you,
no worship of an alien god.
I am the Lord your God,
who brought you from the land of Egypt.
Open wide your mouth and I will fill it.

But my people did not heed my voice
and Israel would not obey,
so I left them in their stubbornness of heart
to follow their own designs.

O that my people would heed me,
that Israel would walk in my ways!
At once I would subdue their foes,
turn my hand against their enemies.

The Lord's enemies would cringe at their feet
and their subjection would last for ever.
But Israel I would feed with finest wheat
and fill them with honey from the rock."

Psalm-prayer

Lord God, open our mouths to proclaim your
glory. Help us to leave sin behind and to rejoice in
professing your name.

READING                           Romans 14:12-13, 17-19

So [then] each of us shall give an account of himself [to God]. Then let us no longer judge one another, but rather resolve never to put a stumbling
block or hindrance in the way of a brother. So do
not let your good be reviled. For the kingdom of
God is not a matter of food and drink, but of righteousness, peace, and joy in the holy Spirit; who-

ever serves Christ in this way is pleasing to God
and approved by others. Let us then pursue what
leads to peace and to building up one another.

RESPONSORY

In the early hours of the morning, I think of you, O
   Lord.
— In the early hours of the morning, I think of you,
   O Lord.
Always you are there to help me.
— I think of you, O Lord.
Glory to the Father . . .
— In the early . . .

CANTICLE OF ZECHARIAH

Ant. Give your people knowledge of salvation, Lord,
      and forgive us our sins.

INTERCESSIONS

Blessed be God, our Father, who protects his children and never spurns their prayers. Let us
   humbly implore him:
   *Enlighten us, Lord.*
We thank you, Lord, for enlightening us through
   your Son,
— fill us with his light throughout the day.
Let your wisdom lead us today, Lord,
— that we may walk in the newness of life.
May we bear hardships with courage for your
   name's sake,
— and be generous in serving you.
Direct our thoughts, feelings and actions this day,
— help us to follow your providential guidance.

Our Father . . .

CONCLUDING PRAYER

Lord,
true light and source of all light,

listen to our morning prayer.
Turn our thoughts to what is holy
and may we ever live in the light of your love.

We ask this through our Lord Jesus Christ, your Son,
who lives and reigns with you and the Holy Spirit,
one God, for ever and ever.

Conclusion, as in the Ordinary, 29.

## Evening Prayer

God, come to my assistance. Glory to the Father.
As it was in the beginning. Alleluia.

HYMN, no. 45 or 38. Outside Ordinary Time, see
Guide, 578.

PSALMODY

Ant. 1  I have made you the light of all nations to
carry my salvation to the ends of the earth.

> Holy Week: Jesus Christ, the first-born from the dead
> and ruler of the kings of the earth, has made us a
> royal people to serve his God and Father.

> Easter: God has appointed him to judge the living and
> the dead, alleluia.

### Psalm 72

The Messiah's royal power

*Opening their treasures, they offered him gifts:*
*gold, frankincense and myrrh (Matthew 2:11).*

I

O God, give your judgment to the king,
to a king's son your justice,
that he may judge your people in justice
and your poor in right judgment.

May the mountains bring forth peace for the people
and the hills, justice.
May he defend the poor of the people
and save the children of the needy
and crush the oppressor.

He shall endure like the sun and the moon
from age to age.
He shall descend like rain on the meadow,
like raindrops on the earth.

In his days justice shall flourish
and peace till the moon fails.
He shall rule from sea to sea,
from the Great River to earth's bounds.

Before him his enemies shall fall,
his foes lick the dust.
The kings of Tarshish and the sea coasts
shall pay him tribute.

The kings of Sheba and Seba
shall bring him gifts.
Before him all kings shall fall prostrate,
all nations shall serve him.

Ant. 2  The Lord will save the children of the poor
and rescue them from slavery.

Holy Week: The Lord will be the champion of the helpless;
he will free the poor from the grip of the powerful.

Easter: All the peoples of the earth will be blessed in
him, alleluia.

II

For he shall save the poor when they cry
and the needy who are helpless.
He will have pity on the weak
and save the lives of the poor.

From oppression he will rescue their lives,
to him their blood is dear.
Long may he live,
may the gold of Sheba be given him.
They shall pray for him without ceasing
and bless him all the day.

May corn be abundant in the land
to the peaks of the mountains.
May its fruit rustle like Lebanon; —

may men flourish in the cities
like grass on the earth.

May his name be blessed for ever
and endure like the sun.
Every tribe shall be blessed in him,
all nations bless his name.

Blessed be the Lord, God of Israel,
who alone works wonders,
ever blessed his glorious name.
Let his glory fill the earth.

Amen! Amen!

Psalm-prayer

We call upon your name, Father, and pronounce
it blessed above the earth. Give your people the
fullness of peace and justice in your kingdom.

Ant. 3 Now the victorious reign of our God has
begun.

Holy Week: The saints won their victory over death
through the blood of the Lamb and the truth to which
they bore witness.

Easter: Christ yesterday and today: he is the same for
ever, alleluia.

Canticle                    Revelation 11:17-18; 12:10b-12a

The judgment of God

We praise you, the Lord God Almighty,
who is and who was.
You have assumed your great power,
you have begun your reign.

The nations have raged in anger,
but then came your day of wrath
and the moment to judge the dead:
the time to reward your servants the prophets
and the holy ones who revere you,
the great and the small alike.

Now have salvation and power come,
the reign of our God and the authority
of his Anointed One.
For the accuser of our brothers is cast out,
who night and day accused them before God.

They defeated him by the blood of the Lamb
and by the word of their testimony;
love for life did not deter them from death.
So rejoice, you heavens,
and you that dwell therein!

READING                                    1 Peter 1:18-23

Realize that you were ransomed from your futile
conduct, handed on by your ancestors, not with perishable things like silver or gold but with the precious
blood of Christ as of a spotless unblemished lamb. He
was known before the foundation of the world but revealed in the final time for you, who through him believe in God who raised him from the dead and gave
him glory, so that your faith and hope are in God.

Since you have purified yourselves by obedience to
the truth for sincere mutual love, love one another in-
tensely from a [pure] heart. You have been born
anew, not from perishable but from imperishable
seed, through the living and abiding word of God.

RESPONSORY

The Lord is my shepherd, I shall want for nothing.
— The Lord is my shepherd, I shall want for nothing.

He has brought me to green pastures.
— I shall want for nothing.

Glory to the Father . . .
— The Lord is . . .

CANTICLE OF MARY

Ant. If you hunger for holiness, God will satisfy your
       longing, good measure, and flowing over.

INTERCESSIONS

Lift up your hearts to our Lord and Savior who gives his people every spiritual blessing. In the spirit of devotion, let us ask him:

*Bless your people, Lord.*

Merciful God, strengthen N., our Pope, and N., our bishop,
— keep them free from harm.

Look favorably on our country, Lord,
— free us from all evil.

Call men to serve at your altar,
— and to follow you more closely in chastity, poverty and obedience.

Take care of your handmaidens vowed to virginity,
— that they may follow you, the divine Lamb, wherever you go.

May the dead rest in eternal peace,
— may their union with us be strengthened through the sharing of spiritual goods.

Our Father . . .

CONCLUDING PRAYER

Father of mercy,
hear our evening prayer of praise,
and let our hearts never waver
from the love of your law.
Lead us on through night's darkness
to the dawning of eternal life.

We ask this through our Lord Jesus Christ, your Son, who lives and reigns with you and the Holy Spirit, one God, for ever and ever.

Conclusion, as in the Ordinary, 29.

# FRIDAY, WEEK II

## Invitatory

Lord, open my lips.

Ant. Come, let us praise the Lord; in him is all our delight.

Invitatory psalm, 22.

## Morning Prayer

The following verse and response are omitted when the hour begins with the invitatory.

God, come to my assistance. Glory to the Father. As it was in the beginning. Alleluia.

HYMN, no. 16 or 91. Outside Ordinary Time, see Guide, 578.

PSALMODY

Ant. 1 A humble, contrite heart, O God, you will not spurn.

Easter: Have courage, my son; your sins are forgiven, alleluia.

### Psalm 51

O God, have mercy on me

*Your inmost being must be renewed, and you must put on the new man* (Ephesians 4:23-24).

Have mercy on me, God, in your kindness.
In your compassion blot out my offense.
O wash me more and more from my guilt
and cleanse me from my sin.

My offenses truly I know them;
my sin is always before me.
Against you, you alone, have I sinned;
what is evil in your sight I have done.

That you may be justified when you give sentence
and be without reproach when you judge.—

O see, in guilt I was born,
a sinner was I conceived.

Indeed you love truth in the heart;
then in the secret of my heart teach me wisdom.
O purify me, then I shall be clean;
O wash me, I shall be whiter than snow.

Make me hear rejoicing and gladness,
that the bones you have crushed may revive.
From my sins turn away your face
and blot out all my guilt.

A pure heart create for me, O God,
put a steadfast spirit within me.
Do not cast me away from your presence,
nor deprive me of your holy spirit.

Give me again the joy of your help;
with a spirit of fervor sustain me,
that I may teach transgressors your ways
and sinners may return to you.

O rescue me, God, my helper,
and my tongue shall ring out your goodness.
O Lord, open my lips
and my mouth shall declare your praise.

For in sacrifice you take no delight,
burnt offering from me you would refuse,
my sacrifice, a contrite spirit.
A humbled, contrite heart you will not spurn.

In your goodness, show favor to Zion:
rebuild the walls of Jerusalem.
Then you will be pleased with lawful sacrifice,
holocausts offered on your altar.

Psalm-prayer

Father, he who knew no sin was made sin for us, to save us and restore us to your friendship. Look upon our contrite heart and afflicted spirit and heal our

troubled conscience, so that in the joy and
strength of the Holy Spirit we may proclaim your
praise and glory before all the nations.

Ant. 2  Even in your anger, Lord, you will remem-
        ber compassion.

Easter: You go forth to save your people, to save your
        anointed one, alleluia.

Canticle                    Habakkuk 3:2-4, 13a, 15-19

God comes to judge

*Lift up your heads for your redemption is at hand*
(Luke 21:28).

O Lord, I have heard your renown,
and feared, O Lord, your work.
In the course of the years revive it,
in the course of the years make it known;
in your wrath remember compassion!

God comes from Teman,
the Holy One from Mount Paran.
Covered are the heavens with his glory,
and with his praise the earth is filled.

His splendor spreads like the light;
rays shine forth from beside him,
where his power is concealed.
You come forth to save your people,
to save your anointed one.

You tread the sea with your steeds
amid the churning of the deep waters.
I hear, and my body trembles;
at the sound, my lips quiver.

Decay invades my bones,
my legs tremble beneath me.
I await the day of distress
that will come upon the people who attack us.

For though the fig tree blossom not
nor fruit be on the vines,
though the yield of the olive fail
and the terraces produce no nourishment,

Though the flocks disappear from the fold
and there be no herd in the stalls,
yet will I rejoice in the Lord
and exult in my saving God.

God, my Lord, is my strength;
he makes my feet swift as those of hinds
and enables me to go upon the heights.

Ant. 3  O praise the Lord, Jerusalem!

Easter: Zion, give praise to your God; he has brought
peace to your borders, alleluia.

Psalm 147:12-20

The restoration of Jerusalem

*Come, I will show you the bride of the Lamb* (Revelation 21:9).

O praise the Lord, Jerusalem!
Zion, praise your God!

He has strengthened the bars of your gates,
he has blessed the children within you.
He established peace on your borders,
he feeds you with finest wheat.

He sends out his word to the earth
and swiftly runs his command.
He showers down snow white as wool,
he scatters hoar-frost like ashes.

He hurls down hailstones like crumbs.
The waters are frozen at his touch;
he sends forth his word and it melts them:
at the breath of his mouth the waters flow.

He makes his word known to Jacob,
to Israel his laws and decrees.—

He has not dealt thus with other nations;
he has not taught them his decrees.

## Psalm-prayer

Lord, you established peace within the borders of Jerusalem. Give the fullness of peace now to your faithful people. May peace rule us in this life and possess us in eternal life. You are about to fill us with the best of wheat; grant that what we see dimly now as in a mirror, we may come to perceive clearly in the brightness of your truth.

READING                    Ephesians 2:13-16

But now in Christ Jesus you who once were far off have become near by the blood of Christ. For he is our peace, he who made both one and broke down the dividing wall of enmity, through his flesh, abolishing the law with its commandments and legal claims, that he might create in himself one new person in place of the two, thus establishing peace, and might reconcile both with God, in one body, through the cross, putting that enmity to death by it.

RESPONSORY

The Lord, the Most High, has done good things for
   me.
In need I shall cry out to him.
— The Lord, the Most High, has done good things
   for me.
In need I shall cry out to him.

May he send his strength to rescue me.
— In need I shall cry out to him.

Glory to the Father . . .
— The Lord, the . . .

CANTICLE OF ZECHARIAH

Ant. Through the tender compassion of our God
   the dawn from on high shall break upon us.

INTERCESSIONS

Let us adore Christ who offered himself to the Father
through the Holy Spirit to cleanse us from the
works of death. Let us adore him and call upon
him with sincere hearts:

*In your will is our peace, Lord.*

From your generosity we have received the beginning
of this day,
— grant us also the beginning of new life.

You created all things, and now you provide for their
growth,
— may we always perceive your handiwork in creation.

With your own blood, you ratified the new and eternal covenant,
— may we remain faithful to that covenant by following your precepts.

On the cross, blood and water flowed from your side,
— may this saving stream wash away our sins and
gladden the City of God.

Our Father . . .

CONCLUDING PRAYER

All-powerful Father,
as now we bring you our songs of praise,
so may we sing your goodness
in the company of your saints for ever.

We ask this through our Lord Jesus Christ, your Son,
who lives and reigns with you and the Holy Spirit,
one God, for ever and ever.

Conclusion, as in the Ordinary, 29.

## Evening Prayer

God, come to my assistance. Glory to the Father.
As it was in the beginning. Alleluia.

HYMN, no. 46 or 39. Outside Ordinary Time, see
Guide, 578.

PSALMODY

Ant. 1  Lord, keep my soul from death, never let
         me stumble.

   Easter: The Lord has rescued my life from the grasp of
   hell, alleluia.

## Psalm 116:1-9

### Thanksgiving

*We must endure many trials before entering God's
kingdom* (Acts 14:21).

   I love the Lord for he has heard
   the cry of my appeal;
   for he turned his ear to me
   in the day when I called him.

   They surrounded me, the snares of death,
   with the anguish of the tomb;
   they caught me, sorrow and distress.
   I called on the Lord's name.

   O Lord my God, deliver me!

   How gracious is the Lord, and just;
   our God has compassion.
   The Lord protects the simple hearts;
   I was helpless so he saved me.

   Turn back, my soul, to your rest
   for the Lord has been good;
   he has kept my soul from death,
   my eyes from tears
   and my feet from stumbling.

   I will walk in the presence of the Lord
   in the land of the living.

Psalm-prayer

   God of power and mercy, through your Son's passion and resurrection you have freed us from the

bonds of death and the anguish of separation from you. Be ever with us on our pilgrimage; then we shall sing rather than weep. Keep our feet from stumbling, so that we may be able to follow you until we come to eternal rest.

Ant. 2 My help comes from the Lord, who made heaven and earth.

Easter: The Lord watches over his people, and protects them as the apple of his eye, alleluia.

## Psalm 121

### Guardian of his people

*Never again will they hunger and thirst, never again know scorching heat* (Revelation 7:16).

I lift up my eyes to the mountains:
from where shall come my help?
My help shall come from the Lord
who made heaven and earth.

May he never allow you to stumble!
Let him sleep not, your guard.
No, he sleeps not nor slumbers,
Israel's guard.

The Lord is your guard and your shade;
at your right side he stands.
By day the sun shall not smite you
nor the moon in the night.

The Lord will guard you from evil,
he will guard your soul.
The Lord will guard your going and coming
both now and for ever.

Psalm-prayer

Lord Jesus Christ, you have prepared a quiet place for us in your Father's eternal home. Watch over our welfare on this perilous journey, shade us from the burning heat of day, and keep our lives free of evil until the end.

Ant. 3  King of all the ages, your ways are perfect and true.

Easter: The Lord is my strength, I shall always praise him, for he has become my Savior, alleluia.

                    Canticle        Revelation 15:3-4
                 Hymn of adoration

Mighty and wonderful are your works,
Lord God Almighty!
Righteous and true are your ways,
O King of the nations!

Who would dare refuse you honor,
or the glory due your name, O Lord?

Since you alone are holy,
all nations shall come
and worship in your presence.
Your mighty deeds are clearly seen.

READING                          1 Corinthians 2:6-10a

Yet we do speak a wisdom to those who are mature, but not a wisdom of this age, nor of the rulers of this age who are passing away. Rather, we speak God's wisdom, mysterious, hidden, which God predetermined before the ages for our glory, and which none of the rulers of this age knew for, if they had known it, they would not have crucified the Lord of glory. But as it is written:

"What eye has not seen, and ear has not heard,
    and what has not entered the human heart,
    what God has prepared for those who love him,"

this God has revealed to us through the Spirit.

RESPONSORY

Christ died for our sins to make of us an offering to
    God.
— Christ died for our sins to make of us an offering
    to God.

He died to this world of sin, and rose in the power
   of the Spirit.
— To make of us an offering to God.

Glory to the Father . . .
— Christ died for our sins to make of us an offering
   to God.

Ant. Remember your mercy, Lord, the promise of
    mercy you made to our fathers.

INTERCESSIONS

Let us bless Christ, the compassionate and merciful Lord, who wipes away the tears of those who
   weep. Let us cry out to him in love and ask:
   *Have mercy on your people, Lord.*
Lord Jesus, you console the humble,
— be attentive to the tears of the poor.
Merciful God, hear the cries of the dying,
— comfort them with your presence.
Make exiles aware of your providential care,
— may they return to their home on earth and fi-
   nally enter their home in heaven.
Be merciful to sinners who have fallen away from
   your love,
— reconcile them to yourself and to your Church.
Save our brothers who have died,
— let them share in the fullness of redemption.

Our Father . . .

CONCLUDING PRAYER

God our Father,
the contradiction of the cross
proclaims your infinite wisdom.
Help us to see that the glory of your Son
is revealed in the suffering he freely accepted.
Give us faith to claim as our only glory

the cross of our Lord Jesus Christ,
who lives with you and the Holy Spirit,
one God, for ever and ever.

Conclusion, as in the Ordinary, 29.

# SATURDAY, WEEK II
## Invitatory

Lord, open my lips.

Ant. Let us listen to the voice of God; let us enter
into his rest.

Invitatory psalm, 22.

## Morning Prayer

The following verse and response are omitted
when the hour begins with the invitatory.

God, come to my assistance. Glory to the Father.
As it was in the beginning. Alleluia.

HYMN, no. 17 or 11. Outside Ordinary Time, see
Guide, 578.

PSALMODY

Ant. 1  As morning breaks we sing of your mercy,
Lord, and night will find us proclaiming
your fidelity.

Easter: You have filled me with gladness, Lord; I will
sing for joy at the works of your hands, alleluia.

Psalm 92
Praise of God the Creator

*Sing in praise of Christ's redeeming work* (Saint
Athanasius).

It is good to give thanks to the Lord,
to make music to your name, O Most High,
to proclaim your love in the morning
and your truth in the watches of the night, —

on the ten-stringed lyre and the lute,
with the murmuring sound of the harp.

Your deeds, O Lord, have made me glad;
for the work of your hands I shout with joy.
O Lord, how great are your works!
How deep are your designs!
The foolish man cannot know this
and the fool cannot understand.

Though the wicked spring up like grass
and all who do evil thrive:
they are doomed to be eternally destroyed.
But you, Lord, are eternally on high.
See how your enemies perish;
all doers of evil are scattered.

To me you give the wild-ox's strength;
you anoint me with the purest oil.
My eyes looked in triumph on my foes;
my ears heard gladly of their fall.
The just will flourish like the palm-tree
and grow like a Lebanon cedar.

Planted in the house of the Lord
they will flourish in the courts of our God,
still bearing fruit when they are old,
still full of sap, still green,
to proclaim that the Lord is just;
in him, my rock, there is no wrong.

Psalm-prayer

Take our shame away from us, Lord, and make
us rejoice in your saving works. May all who have
been chosen by your Son always abound in works
of faith, hope and love in your service.

Ant. 2  Extol the greatness of our God.

Easter: It is I who bring death and I who give life; I inflict
injury and I bring healing, alleluia.

Canticle                    Deuteronomy 32:1-12
              God's kindness to his people

*How often I have longed to gather your children as a*
*hen gathers her brood under her wing* (Matthew 23:
37).

Give ear, O heavens, while I speak;
let the earth hearken to the words of my mouth!
May my instruction soak in like the rain,
and my discourse permeate like the dew,
like a downpour upon the grass,
like a shower upon the crops:

For I will sing the Lord's renown.
Oh, proclaim the greatness of our God!
The Rock—how faultless are his deeds,
how right all his ways!
A faithful God, without deceit,
how just and upright he is!

Yet basely has he been treated by his degener-
ate children,
a perverse and crooked race!
Is the Lord to be thus repaid by you,
O stupid and foolish people?
Is he not your father who created you?
Has he not made you and established you?

Think back on the days of old,
reflect on the years of age upon age.
Ask your father and he will inform you,
ask your elders and they will tell you:

When the Most High assigned the nations their
heritage,
when he parceled out the descendants of Adam,
he set up the boundaries of the peoples
after the number of the sons of God;
while the Lord's own portion was Jacob,
his hereditary share was Israel.

He found them in a wilderness,
a wasteland of howling desert.
He shielded them and cared for them,
guarding them as the apple of his eye.

As an eagle incites its nestlings forth
by hovering over its brood,
so he spread his wings to receive them
and bore them up on his pinions.
The Lord alone was their leader,
no strange god was with him.

Ant. 3  How wonderful is your name, O Lord, in all
creation.

Easter: You have crowned your Anointed One with glory
and honor, alleluia.

Psalm 8

The majesty of the Lord and man's dignity

*The Father gave Christ lordship of creation and
made him head of the Church* (Ephesians 1:22).

How great is your name, O Lord our God,
through all the earth!

Your majesty is praised above the heavens;
on the lips of children and of babes
you have found praise to foil your enemy,
to silence the foe and the rebel.

When I see the heavens, the work of your hands,
the moon and the stars which you arranged,
what is man that you should keep him in mind,
mortal man that you care for him?

Yet you have made him little less than a god;
with glory and honor you crowned him,
gave him power over the works of your hands,
put all things under his feet.

All of them, sheep and cattle,
yes, even the savage beasts,

birds of the air, and fish
that make their way through the waters.

How great is your name, O Lord our God,
through all the earth!

Psalm-prayer

Almighty Lord, how wonderful is your name. You
have made every creature subject to you; make us
worthy to give you service.

READING                                    Romans 12:13-21

Contribute to the needs of the holy ones, exercise
hospitality. Bless those who persecute [you], bless
and do not curse them. Rejoice with those who rejoice, weep with those who weep. Have the same regard for one another; do not be haughty but associate
with the lowly; do not be wise in your own estimation. Do not repay anyone evil for evil; be concerned
for what is noble in the sight of all. If possible, on
your part, live at peace with all. Beloved, do not look
for revenge but leave room for the wrath; for it is written, "Vengeance is mine, I will repay, says the Lord."
Rather, "if your enemy is hungry, feed him; if he is
thirsty, give him something to drink; for by so doing
you will heap burning coals upon his head." Do not
be conquered by evil but conquer evil with good.

RESPONSORY

It is my joy, O God, to praise you with song.
— It is my joy, O God, to praise you with song.

To sing as I ponder your goodness,
— to praise you with song.

Glory to the Father . . .
— It is my . . .

CANTICLE OF ZECHARIAH

Ant. Lord, guide our feet into the way of peace.

INTERCESSIONS

Let us celebrate the kindness and wisdom of
    Christ. He offers his love and understanding to
    all men, especially to the suffering. Let us
    earnestly pray to him:
    *Perfect us in love, Lord.*

This morning we recall your resurrection,
— and we long for the benefits of your redemption.

Grant that we bear witness to you today, Lord,
— and offer an acceptable gift to the Father through
    you.

Enable us to see your image in all men,
— and to serve you in them.

Lord Jesus, you are the true vine and we are the
    branches,
— allow us to remain in you, to bear much fruit,
    and to give glory to the Father.

Our Father . . .

CONCLUDING PRAYER

Lord,
we praise you
with our lips,
and with our lives and hearts.
Our very existence is a gift from you;
to you we offer all that we have and are.

We ask this through our Lord Jesus Christ, your Son,
who lives and reigns with you and the Holy Spirit,
one God, for ever and ever.

Conclusion, as in the Ordinary, 29.

## WEEK III

## SUNDAY

### Evening Prayer I

God, come to my assistance. Glory to the Father. As it was in the beginning. Alleluia.

Hymn, no. 32 or 184. Outside Ordinary Time, see Guide, 578.

Psalmody

Ant. 1 **From the rising of the sun to its setting, may the name of the Lord be praised.**

Advent: Rejoice, Jerusalem, let your joy overflow; your Savior will come to you, alleluia.

Lent, 3rd Sunday: The Lord says: Turn away from sin and open your hearts to the Gospel.

Easter, 3rd and 7th Sunday: The Lord our God is high above the heavens; he raises up the lowly from the dust, alleluia.

Psalm 113

Praise the name of the Lord

*He has cast down the mighty and has lifted up the lowly* (Luke 1:52).

Praise, O servants of the Lord,
praise the name of the Lord!
May the name of the Lord be blessed
both now and for evermore!
From the rising of the sun to its setting
praised be the name of the Lord!

High above all nations is the Lord,
above the heavens his glory.—

Who is like the Lord, our God,
who has risen on high to his throne
yet stoops from the heights to look down,
to look down upon heaven and earth?

From the dust he lifts up the lowly,
from his misery he raises the poor
to set him in the company of princes,
yes, with the princes of his people.
To the childless wife he gives a home
and gladdens her heart with children.

Psalm-prayer

Lord Jesus, Word of God, surrendering the brightness of your glory you became man so that we may be raised from the dust to share your very being. May there be innumerable children of the Church to offer homage to your name from the rising of the sun to its setting.

Ant. 2  I shall take into my hand the saving chalice
and invoke the name of the Lord.

Advent: I, the Lord, am coming to save you; already I am near; soon I will free you from your sins.

Lent, 3rd Sunday: I will offer a sacrifice of praise and call upon the name of the Lord.

Easter, 3rd and 7th Sunday: Lord, you have broken the chains that held me bound; I will offer you a sacrifice of praise, alleluia.

Psalm 116:10-19

Thanksgiving in the Temple

*Through Christ let us offer God a continual sacrifice of praise* (Hebrews 13:15).

I trusted, even when I said:
"I am sorely afflicted,"
and when I said in my alarm:
"No man can be trusted."

How can I repay the Lord
for his goodness to me?
The cup of salvation I will raise;
I will call on the Lord's name.

My vows to the Lord I will fulfill
before all his people.
O precious in the eyes of the Lord
is the death of his faithful.

Your servant, Lord, your servant am I;
you have loosened my bonds.
A thanksgiving sacrifice I make:
I will call on the Lord's name.

My vows to the Lord I will fulfill
before all his people,
in the courts of the house of the Lord,
in your midst, O Jerusalem.

Psalm-prayer

Father, precious in your sight is the death of the saints, but precious above all is the love with which Christ suffered to redeem us. In this life we fill up in our own flesh what is still lacking in the sufferings of Christ; accept this as our sacrifice of praise, and we shall even now taste the joy of the new Jerusalem.

Ant. 3 The Lord Jesus humbled himself, and God exalted him for ever.

Advent: Lord, send the Lamb, the ruler of the earth, from the rock in the desert to the mountain of the daughter of Zion.

Lent, 3rd Sunday: No one takes my life away from me; I lay it down freely and I shall take it up again.

Easter, 3rd and 7th Sunday: Though he was the Son of God, Christ learned obedience through suffering; and for all who obey him, he has become the source of life, alleluia.

Canticle          Philippians 2:6-11

### Christ, God's holy servant

Though he was in the form of God,
Jesus did not deem equality with God
something to be grasped at.

Rather, he emptied himself
and took the form of a slave,
being born in the likeness of men.

He was known to be of human estate,
and it was thus that he humbled himself,
obediently accepting even death,
death on a cross!

Because of this,
God highly exalted him
and bestowed on him the name
above every other name,

So that at Jesus' name
every knee must bend
in the heavens, on the earth,
and under the earth,
and every tongue proclaim
to the glory of God the Father:
JESUS CHRIST IS LORD!

READING                            Hebrews 13:20-21

May the God of peace, who brought up from the
dead the great shepherd of the sheep by the blood
of the eternal covenant, Jesus our Lord, furnish
you with all that is good, that you may do his will.
May he carry out in you what is pleasing to him
through Jesus Christ, to whom be  glory forever
[and ever]. Amen.

RESPONSORY

Our hearts are filled with wonder as we contem-
    plate your works, O Lord.
— Our hearts are filled with wonder as we contem-
    plate your works, O Lord.

We praise the wisdom which wrought them all,
— as we contemplate your works, O Lord.

Glory to the Father . . .
— Our hearts are . . .

CANTICLE OF MARY, antiphon as in the Proper of Seasons.

INTERCESSIONS

Christ had compassion on the hungry and performed a miracle of love for them. Mindful of this, let us pray:
*Show us your love, Lord.*

Lord, we recognize that all the favors we have received today come through your generosity,
— do not let them return to you empty, but let them bear fruit.

Light and salvation of all nations, protect the missionaries you have sent into the world,
— enkindle in them the fire of your Spirit.

Grant that man may shape the world in keeping with human dignity,
— and respond generously to the needs of our time.

Healer of body and spirit, comfort the sick and be present to the dying,
— in your mercy visit and refresh us.

May the faithful departed be numbered among the saints,
— whose names are in the Book of Life.

Our Father . . .

Concluding prayer, as in the Proper of Seasons.

Conclusion, as in the Ordinary, 29.

## Invitatory

Lord, open my lips.

Ant. Come, let us sing to the Lord, and shout with joy to the Rock who saves us.

Invitatory psalm, 22.

## Morning Prayer

The following verse and response are omitted when the hour begins with the invitatory.

God, come to my assistance. Glory to the Father. As it was in the beginning. Alleluia.

HYMN, no. 1 or 151. Outside Ordinary Time, see Guide, 578.

PSALMODY

Ant. 1  Glorious is the Lord on high, alleluia.

> Advent: The Lord is coming without delay. He will reveal things kept hidden and show himself to all mankind, alleluia.

> Lent, 3rd Sunday: Your decrees, O Lord, are to be trusted; your truth is more powerful than the roaring of the seas.

> Easter, 3rd and 7th Sunday: The Lord is king, robed in splendor, alleluia.

Psalm 93

Splendor of God the Creator

*The Lord our mighty God now reigns supreme; let us rejoice and be glad and give him praise* (Revelation 19:6-7).

> The Lord is king, with majesty enrobed;
> the Lord has robed himself with might,
> he has girded himself with power.

> The world you made firm, not to be moved;
> your throne has stood firm from of old.
> From all eternity, O Lord, you are.

> The waters have lifted up, O Lord,
> the waters have lifted up their voice,
> the waters have lifted up their thunder.

> Greater than the roar of mighty waters,
> more glorious than the surgings of the sea,
> the Lord is glorious on high.

Truly your decrees are to be trusted.
Holiness is fitting to your house,
O Lord, until the end of time.

Psalm-prayer

All power and all authority in heaven and on earth
have been given to you, Lord Jesus; you rule with decrees that are firm and trustworthy. Be with us always so that we may make disciples whose holiness
will be worthy of your house.

Ant. 2 To you, Lord, be highest glory and praise
for ever, alleluia.

Advent: Mountains and hills shall be level, crooked
paths straight, rough ways smooth. Come, Lord, do
not delay, alleluia.

Lent, 3rd Sunday: Springs of water, bless the Lord;
praise and exalt him above all for ever.

Easter, 3rd and 7th Sunday: All creation will be freed; all
peoples will know the glory and freedom of God's children, alleluia.

Canticle      Daniel 3:57-88, 56

Let all creatures praise the Lord

*All you servants of the Lord, sing praise to him*
(Revelation 19:5).

Bless the Lord, all you works of the Lord.
Praise and exalt him above all forever.
Angels of the Lord, bless the Lord.
You heavens, bless the Lord.
All you waters above the heavens, bless the Lord.
All you hosts of the Lord, bless the Lord.
Sun and moon, bless the Lord.
Stars of heaven, bless the Lord.

Every shower and dew, bless the Lord.
All you winds, bless the Lord.
Fire and heat, bless the Lord.
Cold and chill, bless the Lord.

Dew and rain, bless the Lord.
Frost and chill, bless the Lord.
Ice and snow, bless the Lord.
Nights and days, bless the Lord.
Light and darkness, bless the Lord.
Lightnings and clouds, bless the Lord.

Let the earth bless the Lord.
Praise and exalt him above all forever.
Mountains and hills, bless the Lord.
Everything growing from the earth, bless the
Lord.
You springs, bless the Lord.
Seas and rivers, bless the Lord.
You dolphins and all water creatures, bless the
Lord.
All you birds of the air, bless the Lord.
All you beasts, wild and tame, bless the Lord.
You sons of men, bless the Lord.

O Israel, bless the Lord.
Praise and exalt him above all forever.
Priests of the Lord, bless the Lord.
Servants of the Lord, bless the Lord.
Spirits and souls of the just, bless the Lord.
Holy men of humble heart, bless the Lord.
Hananiah, Azariah, Mishael, bless the Lord.
Praise and exalt him above all forever.

Let us bless the Father, and the Son, and the
Holy Spirit.
Let us praise and exalt him above all forever.
Blessed are you, Lord, in the firmament of heaven.
Praiseworthy and glorious and exalted above
all forever.

At the end of the canticle the **Glory to the Father**
is not said.

Ant. 3 **Praise the Lord from the heavens, alleluia.**

Advent: I shall enfold Zion with my salvation and shed
my glory around Jerusalem, alleluia.

Lent, 3rd Sunday: All kings and peoples of the earth, give praise to God.

Easter, 3rd and 7th Sunday: The name of the Lord is praised in heaven and on earth, alleluia.

## Psalm 148

### Praise to the Lord, the Creator

*Praise and honor, glory and power for ever to him who sits upon the throne and to the Lamb* (Revelation 5:13).

Praise the Lord from the heavens,
praise him in the heights.
Praise him, all his angels,
praise him, all his host.

Praise him, sun and moon,
praise him, shining stars.
Praise him, highest heavens
and the waters above the heavens.

Let them praise the name of the Lord.
He commanded: they were made.
He fixed them for ever,
gave a law which shall not pass away.

Praise the Lord from the earth,
sea creatures and all oceans,
fire and hail, snow and mist,
stormy winds that obey his word;

all mountains and hills,
all fruit trees and cedars,
beasts, wild and tame,
reptiles and birds on the wing;

all earth's kings and peoples,
earth's princes and rulers;
young men and maidens,
old men together with children.

Let them praise the name of the Lord
for he alone is exalted.
The splendor of his name
reaches beyond heaven and earth.

He exalts the strength of his people.
He is the praise of all his saints,
of the sons of Israel,
of the people to whom he comes close.

Psalm-prayer

Lord, extolled in the heights by angelic powers,
you are also praised by all earth's creatures, each in
its own way. With all the splendor of heavenly worship, you still delight in such tokens of love as earth
can offer. May heaven and earth together acclaim you
as King; may the praise that is sung in heaven resound in the heart of every creature on earth.

READING                              Ezekiel 37:12b-14

Thus says the Lord God: O my people, I will open
your graves and have you rise from them, and bring
you back to the land of Israel. Then you shall know
that I am the Lord, when I open your graves and have
you rise from them, O my people! I will put my spirit
in you that you may live, and I will settle you upon
your land; thus you shall know that I am the Lord. I
have promised, and I will do it, says the Lord.

RESPONSORY

Christ, Son of the living God, have mercy on us.
— Christ, Son of the living God, have mercy on us.

You are seated at the right hand of the Father,
— have mercy on us.

Glory to the Father . . .
— Christ, Son of . . .

CANTICLE OF ZECHARIAH, antiphon as in the Proper
of Seasons.

INTERCESSIONS

Father, you sent the Holy Spirit to enlighten the hearts of men; hear us as we pray:
  *Enlighten your people, Lord.*
Blessed are you, O God, our light,
— you have given us a new day resplendent with your glory.
You enlightened the world through the resurrection of your Son,
— through your Church shed this light on all men.
You gave the disciples of your only-begotten Son the Spirit's gift of understanding,
— through the same Spirit keep the Church faithful to you.
Light of nations, remember those who remain in darkness,
— open their eyes and let them recognize you, the only true God.

Our Father . . .

Concluding prayer, as in the Proper of Seasons.

Conclusion, as in the Ordinary, 29.

## Evening Prayer II

God, come to my assistance. Glory to the Father. As it was in the beginning. Alleluia.

HYMN, no. 33 or 182. Outside Ordinary Time, see Guide, 578.

PSALMODY

Ant. 1  The Lord said to my Master: Sit at my right hand, alleluia.

   Advent: Our Lord will come to claim his glorious throne in the assembly of the princes.

   Lent, 3rd Sunday: Lord, all powerful King, free us for the sake of your name. Give us time to turn from our sins.

   Easter, 3rd and 7th Sunday: He purified us from our sins, and is seated on high at God's right hand, alleluia.

## Psalm 110:1-5, 7

### The Messiah, king and priest

*Christ's reign will last until all his enemies are made subject to him* (1 Corinthians 15:25).

The Lord's revelation to my Master:
"Sit on my right:
your foes I will put beneath your feet."

The Lord will wield from Zion
your scepter of power:
rule in the midst of all your foes.

A prince from the day of your birth
on the holy mountains;
from the womb before the dawn I begot you.

The Lord has sworn an oath he will not change.
"You are a priest for ever,
a priest like Melchizedek of old."

The Master standing at your right hand
will shatter kings in the day of his great wrath.

He shall drink from the stream by the wayside
and therefore he shall lift up his head.

Psalm-prayer

Father, we ask you to give us victory and peace. In Jesus Christ, our Lord and King, we are already seated at your right hand. We look forward to praising you in the fellowship of all your saints in our heavenly homeland.

Ant. 2  Our compassionate Lord has left us a memorial of his wonderful work, alleluia.

Advent: Let the mountains break out with joy and the hills with answering gladness, for the world's true light, the Lord, comes with power and might.

Lent, 3rd Sunday: We have been redeemed by the precious blood of Christ, the lamb without blemish.

Easter, 3rd and 7th Sunday: The Lord has redeemed his people, alleluia.

## Psalm 111

### God's marvelous works

*We are lost in wonder at all that you have done for us, our Lord and mighty God (Revelation 15:3).*

I will thank the Lord with all my heart
in the meeting of the just and their assembly.
Great are the works of the Lord;
to be pondered by all who love them.

Majestic and glorious his work,
his justice stands firm for ever.
He makes us remember his wonders.
The Lord is compassion and love.

He gives food to those who fear him;
keeps his covenant ever in mind.
He has shown his might to his people
by giving them the lands of the nations.

His works are justice and truth:
his precepts are all of them sure,
standing firm for ever and ever:
they are made in uprightness and truth.

He has sent deliverance to his people
and established his covenant for ever.
Holy his name, to be feared.

To fear the Lord is the first stage of wisdom;
all who do so prove themselves wise.
His praise shall last for ever!

Psalm-prayer

Merciful and gentle Lord, you are the crowning glory of all the saints. Give us, your children, the gift of obedience which is the beginning of wisdom, so that we may do what you command and be filled with your mercy.

Ant. 3  All power is yours, Lord God, our mighty King, alleluia.

Advent: Let us live in holiness and love as we patiently await our blessed hope, the coming of our Savior.

Easter, 3rd and 7th Sunday: Alleluia, our Lord is king; let us rejoice and give glory to him, alleluia.

The following canticle is said with the **Alleluia** when Evening Prayer is sung; when the office is recited, the **Alleluia** may be said at the beginning and end of each strophe.

Canticle                      See Revelation 19:1-7

The wedding of the Lamb

Alleluia.
Salvation, glory, and power to our God:
(℟. Alleluia.)
his judgments are honest and true.
℟. Alleluia (alleluia).

Alleluia.
Sing praise to our God, all you his servants,
(℟. Alleluia.)
all who worship him reverently, great and small.
℟. Alleluia (alleluia).

Alleluia.
The Lord our all-powerful God is King;
(℟. Alleluia.)
let us rejoice, sing praise, and give him glory.
℟. Alleluia (alleluia).

Alleluia.
The wedding feast of the Lamb has begun,
(℟. Alleluia.)
and his bride is prepared to welcome him.
℟. Alleluia (alleluia).

---

## Lent

Lent, 3rd Sunday: Ours were the sufferings he bore; ours the torments he endured.

Canticle        1 Peter 2:21-24

**The willing acceptance of his passion by Christ,
the servant of God**

Christ suffered for you,
and left you an example
to have you follow in his footsteps.

He did no wrong;
no deceit was found in his mouth.
When he was insulted,
he returned no insult.

When he was made to suffer,
he did not counter with threats.
Instead he delivered himself up
to the One who judges justly.

In his own body
he brought your sins to the cross,
so that all of us, dead to sin,
could live in accord with God's will.

By his wounds you were healed.

READING        1 Peter 1:3-7

Blessed be the God and Father of our Lord Jesus
Christ, who in his great mercy gave us a new birth to
a living hope through the resurrection of Jesus
Christ from the dead, to an inheritance that is imperishable, undefiled, and unfading, kept in heaven for
you who by the power of God are safeguarded
through faith, to a salvation that is ready to be revealed in the final time. In this you rejoice, although
now for a little while you may have to suffer through
various trials, so that the genuineness of your faith,
more precious than gold that is perishable even
though tested by fire, may prove to be for praise,
glory, and honor at the revelation of Jesus Christ.

RESPONSORY

The whole creation proclaims the greatness of your glory.
— The whole creation proclaims the greatness of your glory.

Eternal ages praise
— the greatness of your glory.

Glory to the Father . . .
— The whole creation . . .

CANTICLE OF MARY, antiphon as in the Proper of Seasons.

INTERCESSIONS

The world was created by the Word of God, re-created by his redemption, and it is continually renewed by his love. Rejoicing in him we call out:
*Renew the wonders of your love, Lord.*
We give thanks to God whose power is revealed in nature,
— and whose providence is revealed in history.
Through your Son, the herald of reconciliation, the victor of the cross,
— free us from empty fear and hopelessness.
May all those who love and pursue justice,
— work together without deceit to build a world of true peace.
Be with the oppressed, free the captives, console the sorrowing, feed the hungry, strengthen the weak,
— in all people reveal the victory of your cross.
After your Son's death and burial you raised him up again in glory,
— grant that the faithful departed may live with him.

Our Father . . .

Concluding prayer, as in the Proper of Seasons.

Conclusion, as in the Ordinary, 29.

## MONDAY, WEEK III
### Invitatory

Lord, open my lips.

Ant. Let us approach the Lord with praise and thanksgiving.

Invitatory psalm, 22.

### Morning Prayer

The following verse and response are omitted when the hour begins with the invitatory.

God, come to my assistance. Glory to the Father. As it was in the beginning. Alleluia.

HYMN, no. 2 or 132. Outside Ordinary Time, see Guide, 578.

PSALMODY

Ant. 1  Blessed are they who dwell in your house, O Lord.

December 17-23: The Lord, the ruler over the kings of the earth, will come; blessed are they who are ready to go and welcome him.

Easter: My heart and my flesh rejoice in the living God, alleluia.

### Psalm 84

Longing for God's Temple

*Here we do not have a lasting city; we seek a home that is yet to come* (Hebrews 13:14).

How lovely is your dwelling place,
Lord, God of hosts.

My soul is longing and yearning,
is yearning for the courts of the Lord.
My heart and my soul ring out their joy
to God, the living God.

The sparrow herself finds a home
and the swallow a nest for her brood;
she lays her young by your altars,
Lord of hosts, my king and my God.

They are happy, who dwell in your house,
for ever singing your praise.
They are happy, whose strength is in you,
in whose hearts are the roads to Zion.

As they go through the Bitter Valley
they make it a place of springs,
the autumn rain covers it with blessings.
They walk with ever growing strength,
they will see the God of gods in Zion.

O Lord God of hosts, hear my prayer,
give ear, O God of Jacob.
Turn your eyes, O God, our shield,
look on the face of your anointed.

One day within your courts
is better than a thousand elsewhere.
The threshold of the house of God
I prefer to the dwellings of the wicked.

For the Lord God is a rampart, a shield;
he will give us his favor and glory.
The Lord will not refuse any good
to those who walk without blame.

Lord, God of hosts,
happy the man who trusts in you!

Psalm-prayer

Bless your people, Lord. You have given us the law that we may walk from strength to strength and raise our minds to you from this valley of tears. May we receive the gifts you have gained for us.

Ant. 2  Come, let us climb the mountain of the Lord.

December 17-23: Sing a new song to the Lord; proclaim
his praises to the ends of the earth.

Easter: The house of the Lord has been raised on high,
and all the nations will go up to it, alleluia.

Canticle                Isaiah 2:2-5

The mountain of the Lord's dwelling towers above
every mountain

*All peoples shall come and worship in your presence* (Revelation 15:4).

> In days to come,
> the mountain of the Lord's house
> shall be established as the highest mountain
> and raised above the hills.
>
> All nations shall stream toward it;
> many peoples shall come and say:
> "Come, let us climb the Lord's mountain,
> to the house of the God of Jacob,
> that he may instruct us in his ways,
> and we may walk in his paths."
>
> For from Zion shall go forth instruction,
> and the word of the Lord from Jerusalem.
>
> He shall judge between the nations,
> and impose terms on many peoples.
> They shall beat their swords into plowshares
> and their spears into pruning hooks;
> one nation shall not raise the sword against
>     another,
> nor shall they train for war again.
>
> O house of Jacob, come,
> let us walk in the light of the Lord!

Ant. 3  Sing to the Lord and bless his name.

December 17-23: When the Son of Man comes to earth,
do you think he will find faith in men's hearts?

Easter: Proclaim this among the nations: the Lord is
king, alleluia.

## Psalm 96

### The Lord, king and judge of the world

*A new theme now inspires their praise of God; they belong to the Lamb (see Revelation 14:3).*

O sing a new song to the Lord,
sing to the Lord, all the earth.
O sing to the Lord, bless his name.

Proclaim his help day by day,
tell among the nations his glory
and his wonders among all the peoples.

The Lord is great and worthy of praise,
to be feared above all gods;
the gods of the heathens are naught.

It was the Lord who made the heavens,
his are majesty and state and power
and splendor in his holy place.

Give the Lord, you families of peoples,
give the Lord glory and power,
give the Lord the glory of his name.

Bring an offering and enter his courts,
worship the Lord in his temple.
O earth, tremble before him.

Proclaim to the nations: "God is king."
The world he made firm in its place;
he will judge the peoples in fairness.

Let the heavens rejoice and earth be glad,
let the sea and all within it thunder praise,
let the land and all it bears rejoice,
all the trees of the wood shout for joy

at the presence of the Lord for he comes,
he comes to rule the earth.
With justice he will rule the world,
he will judge the peoples with his truth.

Psalm-prayer

Lord, you have renewed the face of the earth. Your Church throughout the world sings you a new song, announcing your wonders to all. Through a virgin, you have brought forth a new birth in our world; through your miracles, a new power; through your suffering, a new patience; in your resurrection, a new hope, and in your ascension, new majesty.

READING                                     James 2:12-17

So speak and so act as people who will be judged by the law of freedom. For the judgment is merciless to one who has not shown mercy; mercy triumphs over judgment.

What good is it, my brothers, if someone says he has faith but does not have works? Can that faith save him? If a brother or sister has nothing to wear and has no food for the day, and one of you says to them, "Go in peace, keep warm, and eat well," but you do not give them the necessities of the body, what good is it? So also faith of itself, if it does not have works, is dead.

RESPONSORY

Blessed be the Lord our God, blessed from age to age.
— Blessed be the Lord our God, blessed from age to age.

His marvelous works are beyond compare,
— blessed from age to age.

Glory to the Father . . .
— Blessed be the . . .

CANTICLE OF ZECHARIAH

Ant. Blessed be the Lord our God.

INTERCESSIONS

Man was created to glorify God through his deeds. Let us earnestly pray:
*May we give glory to your name, Lord.*

We bless you, Creator of all things,
— for you have given us the goods of the earth and
   brought us to this day.
Look with favor on us as we begin our daily work,
— let us be fellow workers with you.
Make our work today benefit our brothers and sisters,
— that with them and for them we may build an
   earthly city, pleasing to you.
Grant joy and peace to us,
— and to all we meet this day.

Our Father . . .

CONCLUDING PRAYER

Lord God,
king of heaven and earth,
direct our minds and bodies throughout this day,
and make us holy.
Keep us faithful to your law in thought, word and deed.
Be our helper now and always,
free us from sin,
and bring us to salvation in that kingdom
where you live and reign with the Father and the
   Holy Spirit,
one God, for ever and ever.

Conclusion, as in the Ordinary, 29.

## Evening Prayer

God, come to my assistance. Glory to the Father.
As it was in the beginning. Alleluia.

HYMN, no. 34 or 41. Outside Ordinary Time, see
Guide, 578.

PSALMODY

Ant. 1  Our eyes are fixed intently on the Lord,
        waiting for his merciful help.

  December 17-23: The Lord, the ruler over the kings of
  the earth, will come; blessed are they who are ready to
  go and welcome him.

Easter: The Lord will be your light for ever; your God will be your glory, alleluia.

## Psalm 123

### The Lord, unfailing hope of his people

*Two blind men cried out: "Have pity on us, Lord, Son of David"* (Matthew 20:30).

> To you I have lifted up my eyes,
> you who dwell in the heavens:
> my eyes, like the eyes of slaves
> on the hand of their lords.

> Like the eyes of a servant
> on the hand of her mistress,
> so our eyes are on the Lord our God
> till he show us his mercy.

> Have mercy on us, Lord, have mercy.
> We are filled with contempt.
> Indeed all too full is our soul
> with the scorn of the rich,
> with the proud man's disdain.

Psalm-prayer

Father in heaven, we lift our eyes to you and pray: confound the scorn of the proud and graciously show us your mercy.

Ant. 2  Our help is in the name of the Lord who made heaven and earth.

December 17-23: Sing a new song to the Lord; proclaim his praises to the ends of the earth.

Easter: The snare was broken and we were set free, alleluia.

## Psalm 124

### Our help is in the name of the Lord

*The Lord said to Paul: "Fear not . . . I am with you"* (Acts 18:9-10).

> "If the Lord had not been on our side,"
> this is Israel's song.
> "If the Lord had not been on our side
> when men rose against us,—

then would they have swallowed us alive
when their anger was kindled.

Then would the waters have engulfed us,
the torrent gone over us;
over our head would have swept
the raging waters."

Blessed be the Lord who did not give us
a prey to their teeth!
Our life, like a bird, has escaped
from the snare of the fowler.

Indeed the snare has been broken
and we have escaped.
Our help is in the name of the Lord,
who made heaven and earth.

Psalm-prayer

Lord Jesus, you foretold that your disciples would
be despised on account of your name, but that not a
hair of their heads is ever forgotten. In times of persecution, defend and revive us by the power and comfort of the Holy Spirit, so that we can be freed from
our enemies and praise your saving help.

Ant. 3  God chose us in his Son to be his adopted
children.

December 17-23: When the Son of Man comes to earth,
do you think he will find faith in men's hearts?

Easter: When I am lifted up from the earth, I shall draw
all people to myself, alleluia.

Canticle          Ephesians 1:3-10

God our Savior

Praised be the God and Father
of our Lord Jesus Christ,
who has bestowed on us in Christ
every spiritual blessing in the heavens.

God chose us in him
before the world began
to be holy
and blameless in his sight.

He predestined us
to be his adopted sons through Jesus Christ,
such was his will and pleasure,
that all might praise the glorious favor
he has bestowed on us in his beloved.

In him and through his blood, we have been redeemed,
and our sins forgiven,
so immeasurably generous
is God's favor to us.

God has given us the wisdom
to understand fully the mystery,
the plan he was pleased
to decree in Christ.

A plan to be carried out
in Christ, in the fullness of time,
to bring all things into one in him,
in the heavens and on earth.

READING                                       James 4:11-12

Do not speak evil of one another, brothers. Whoever speaks evil of a brother or judges his brother
speaks evil of the law and judges the law. If you
judge the law, you are not a doer of the law but a
judge. There is one lawgiver and judge who is able
to save or to destroy. Who then are you to judge
your neighbor?

RESPONSORY

Lord, you alone can heal me, for I have grieved you
by my sins.
— Lord, you alone can heal me, for I have grieved
you by my sins.

Once more I say: O Lord, have mercy on me,
— for I have grieved you by my sins.

Glory to the Father . . .
— Lord, you alone can heal me, for I have grieved
you by my sins.

CANTICLE OF MARY

Ant. My soul proclaims the greatness of the Lord for
he has looked with favor on his lowly servant.

INTERCESSIONS

Christ desires to lead all men to salvation. Let us
implore him with all our heart:
*Draw all things to yourself, Lord.*
Through your precious blood, Lord, you redeemed
us from the slavery of sin,
— grant us the freedom of the sons of God.
Bestow your grace upon our bishop N., and upon
all bishops,
— may they administer your sacraments with fervent joy.
Grant that all who seek the truth may find it,
— and in finding it may they desire it all the more.
Be present to comfort widows, orphans and all the
abandoned, Lord,
— may they feel close to you and cling to you.
Receive our departed brethren into the heavenly
kingdom,
— where with the Father and the Holy Spirit you
will be all in all.

Our Father . . .

CONCLUDING PRAYER

God our Father,
at the close of day we come to you,
the light that never fades.
Shine in the darkness of our night
and forgive our sins and failings.

We ask this through our Lord Jesus Christ, your Son, who lives and reigns with you and the Holy Spirit, one God, for ever and ever.

Conclusion, as in the Ordinary, 29.

# TUESDAY, WEEK III

## Invitatory

Lord, open my lips.

Ant. Come, let us worship our mighty King and Lord.

Invitatory psalm, 22.

## Morning Prayer

The following verse and response are omitted when the hour begins with the invitatory.

God, come to my assistance. Glory to the Father. As it was in the beginning. Alleluia.

HYMN, no. 3 or 82. Outside Ordinary Time, see Guide, 578.

PSALMODY

Ant. 1 Lord, you have blessed your land; you have forgiven the sins of your people.

December 17-23: The Lord will come from his holy place to save his people.

Easter: You will turn back, O God, and bring us to life, and your people will rejoice in you, alleluia.

Psalm 85

Our salvation is near

God blessed the land when our Savior came to earth (Origen).

O Lord, you once favored your land
and revived the fortunes of Jacob,
you forgave the guilt of your people —

and covered all their sins.
You averted all your rage,
you calmed the heat of your anger.

Revive us now, God, our helper!
Put an end to your grievance against us.
Will you be angry with us for ever,
will your anger never cease?

Will you not restore again our life
that your people may rejoice in you?
Let us see, O Lord, your mercy
and give us your saving help.

I will hear what the Lord God has to say,
a voice that speaks of peace,
peace for his people and his friends
and those who turn to him in their hearts.
His help is near for those who fear him
and his glory will dwell in our land.

Mercy and faithfulness have met;
justice and peace have embraced.
Faithfulness shall spring from the earth
and justice look down from heaven.

The Lord will make us prosper
and our earth shall yield its fruit.
Justice shall march before him
and peace shall follow his steps.

Psalm-prayer

Show us your mercy, Lord; our misery is known
to us. May no evil desires prevail over us, for your
glory and love dwell in our hearts.

Ant. 2  My soul has yearned for you in the night, and
        as morning breaks I watch for your coming.

December 17-23: Zion is our mighty citadel, our saving
    Lord its wall and its defense; throw open the gates, for
    our God is here among us, alleluia.

Easter: We have placed all our hope in the Lord, and he has given us his peace, alleluia.

Canticle   Isaiah 26:1-4, 7-9, 12

Hymn after the defeat of the enemy

*The city wall had twelve foundation stones* (see Revelation 21:14).

A strong city have we;
he sets up walls and ramparts to protect us.
Open up the gates
to let in a nation that is just,
one that keeps faith.

A nation of firm purpose you keep in peace;
in peace, for its trust in you.
Trust in the Lord forever!
For the Lord is an eternal Rock.

The way of the just is smooth;
the path of the just you make level.
Yes, for your way and your judgments, O Lord,
we look to you;
your name and your title
are the desire of our souls.

My soul yearns for you in the night,
yes, my spirit within me keeps vigil for you;
when your judgment dawns upon the earth,
the world's inhabitants learn justice.

O Lord, you mete out peace to us,
for it is you who have accomplished all we have
done.

Ant. 3  Lord, let the light of your face shine upon
us.

December 17-23: Lord, make known your will throughout the earth; proclaim your salvation to every nation.

Easter: The earth has yielded its fruit; let the nations be
glad and sing for joy, alleluia.

## Psalm 67

People of all nations will worship the Lord

*You must know that God is offering his salvation to all the world* (Acts 28:28).

O God, be gracious and bless us
and let your face shed its light upon us.
So will your ways be known upon earth
and all nations learn your saving help.

Let the peoples praise you, O God;
let all the peoples praise you.

Let the nations be glad and exult
for you rule the world with justice.
With fairness you rule the peoples,
you guide the nations on earth.

Let the peoples praise you, O God;
let all the peoples praise you.

The earth has yielded its fruit
for God, our God, has blessed us.
May God still give us his blessing
till the ends of the earth revere him.

Let the peoples praise you, O God;
let all the peoples praise you.

Psalm-prayer

Be gracious and bless us, Lord, and let your face shed its light on us, so that we can make you known with reverence and bring forth a harvest of justice.

READING                                   1 John 4:12-15

No one has ever seen God. Yet, if we love one another, God remains in us, and his love is brought to perfection in us.

This is how we know that we remain in him and he in us, that he has given us of his Spirit. Moreover, we have seen and testify that the Father sent his Son as savior of the world. Whoever acknowledges that Jesus is the Son of God, God remains in him and he in God.

RESPONSORY

My God stands by me, all my trust is in him.
— My God stands by me, all my trust is in him.

I find refuge in him, and I am truly free;
— all my trust is in him.

Glory to the Father . . .
— My God stands . . .

CANTICLE OF ZECHARIAH

Ant. God has raised up for us a mighty Savior, as he promised of old through his holy prophets.

INTERCESSIONS

Lord Jesus, by your blood you have purchased for yourself a new people. We adore you and beseech you:
*Remember your people, Lord.*
Our King and our Redeemer, hear the praises of your Church at the beginning of this day,
— teach her to glorify your majesty without ceasing.
You are our hope and our strength, in you we trust,
— may we never despair.
Look kindly upon our weakness and hasten to our aid,
— for without you we can do nothing.
Remember the poor and the afflicted, do not let this day be a burden to them,
— but a consolation and a joy.

Our Father . . .

CONCLUDING PRAYER

God our Father,
yours is the beauty of creation
and the good things you have given us.
Help us to begin this day joyfully in your name
and to spend it in loving service
of you and our fellow man.

We ask this through our Lord Jesus Christ, your Son,
who lives and reigns with you and the Holy Spirit,
one God, for ever and ever.

Conclusion, as in the Ordinary, 29.

## Evening Prayer

God, come to my assistance. Glory to the Father.
As it was in the beginning. Alleluia.

HYMN, no. 35 or 42. Outside Ordinary Time, see
Guide, 578.

PSALMODY

Ant. 1 **The Lord surrounds his people with his
strength.**

December 17-23: The Lord will come from his holy place to
save his people.

Easter: Peace be with you; it is I, do not be afraid, alleluia.

### Psalm 125

The Lord, guardian of his people

*Peace to God's true Israel* (Galatians 6:16).

Those who put their trust in the Lord
are like Mount Zion, that cannot be shaken,
that stands for ever.

Jerusalem! The mountains surround her,
so the Lord surrounds his people
both now and for ever.

For the scepter of the wicked shall not rest
over the land of the just
for fear that the hands of the just
should turn to evil.

Do good, Lord, to those who are good,
to the upright of heart;
but the crooked and those who do evil,
drive them away!

On Israel, peace!

Psalm-prayer

Surround your people, Lord, within the safety of
your Church, which you preserve on its rock foundation. Do not let us stretch out our hands to evil
deeds, nor be destroyed by the insidious snares of
the enemy, but bring us to share the lot of the
saints in light.

Ant. 2    Unless you acquire the heart of a child, you
cannot enter the kingdom of God.

December 17-23: Zion is our mighty citadel, our saving
Lord its wall and its defense; throw open the gates, for
our God is here among us, alleluia.

Easter: Let Israel hope in the Lord, alleluia.

Psalm 131

Childlike trust in God

*Learn from me, for I am gentle and humble of
heart* (Matthew 11:29).

O Lord, my heart is not proud
nor haughty my eyes.
I have not gone after things too great
nor marvels beyond me.

Truly I have set my soul
in silence and peace.
As a child has rest in its mother's arms,
even so my soul.

O Israel, hope in the Lord
both now and for ever.

Psalm-prayer

Lord Jesus, gentle and humble of heart, you declared that whoever receives a little child in your name receives you, and you promised your kingdom to those who are like children. Never let pride reign in our hearts, but may the Father's compassion reward and embrace all who willingly bear your gentle yoke.

Ant. 3 Lord, you have made us a kingdom and priests for God our Father.

December 17-23: Lord, make known your will throughout the earth; proclaim your salvation to every nation.

Easter: Let all creation serve you, for all things came into being at your word, alleluia.

Canticle                          Revelation 4:11; 5:9, 10, 12
               Redemption hymn

O Lord our God, you are worthy
to receive glory and honor and power.

For you have created all things;
by your will they came to be and were made.

Worthy are you, O Lord,
to receive the scroll and break open its seals.

For you were slain;
with your blood you purchased for God
men of every race and tongue,
of every people and nation.

You made of them a kingdom,
and priests to serve our God,
and they shall reign on the earth.

Worthy is the Lamb that was slain
to receive power and riches, —

wisdom and strength,
   honor and glory and praise.

READING                                    Romans 12:9-12

Let love be sincere; hate what is evil, hold on to what is good; love one another with mutual affection; anticipate one another in showing honor. Do not grow slack in zeal, be fervent in spirit, serve the Lord. Rejoice in hope, endure in affliction, persevere in prayer.

RESPONSORY

Through all eternity, O Lord, your promise stands unshaken.
— Through all eternity, O Lord, your promise stands unshaken.

Your faithfulness will never fail;
— your promise stands unshaken.

Glory to the Father . . .
— Through all eternity . . .

CANTICLE OF MARY

Ant. My spirit rejoices in God my Savior.

INTERCESSIONS

God establishes his people in hope. Let us cry out to him with joy:
   *You are the hope of your people, Lord.*
We thank you, Lord,
— because in Christ you have given us all the treasures of wisdom and knowledge.
O God, in your hands are the hearts of the powerful; bestow your wisdom upon government leaders,
— may they draw from the fountain of your counsel and please you in thought and deed.
The talents of artists reflect your splendor,
— may their work give the world hope and joy.
You do not allow us to be tested beyond our ability,
— strengthen the weak and raise up the fallen.

Through your Son you promised to raise men up
    on the Last Day,
— do not forget those who have died.

Our Father . . .

CONCLUDING PRAYER

Lord,
may our evening prayer rise up to you,
and your blessing come down upon us.
May your help and salvation be ours
now and through all eternity.

We ask this through our Lord Jesus Christ, your Son,
who lives and reigns with you and the Holy Spirit,
one God, for ever and ever.

Conclusion, as in the Ordinary, 29.

# WEDNESDAY, WEEK III

## Invitatory

Lord, open my lips.

Ant. Come, let us worship before the Lord, our
    maker.

Invitatory psalm, 22.

## Morning Prayer

The following verse and response are omitted
when the hour begins with the invitatory.

God, come to my assistance. Glory to the Father.
As it was in the beginning. Alleluia.

HYMN, no. 4 or 5. Outside Ordinary Time, see
Guide, 578.

PSALMODY

Ant. 1  Give joy to your servant, Lord; to you I lift
    up my heart.

December 17-23: The Lord, the mighty God, will come
    forth from Zion to set his people free.

Easter: **People of every nation shall come and worship you, O Lord, alleluia.**

## Psalm 86

The prayer of the poor man in distress

*Blessed be God who comforts us in all our trials* (2 Corinthians 1:3, 4).

Turn your ear, O Lord, and give answer
for I am poor and needy.
Preserve my life, for I am faithful:
save the servant who trusts in you.

You are my God, have mercy on me, Lord,
for I cry to you all the day long.
Give joy to your servant, O Lord,
for to you I lift up my soul.

O Lord, you are good and forgiving,
full of love to all who call.
Give heed, O Lord, to my prayer
and attend to the sound of my voice.

In the day of distress I will call
and surely you will reply.
Among the gods there is none like you, O Lord;
nor work to compare with yours.

All the nations shall come to adore you
and glorify your name, O Lord:
for you are great and do marvellous deeds,
you who alone are God.

Show me, Lord, your way
so that I may walk in your truth.
Guide my heart to fear your name.

I will praise you, Lord my God, with all my heart
and glorify your name for ever;
for your love to me has been great:
you have saved me from the depths of the grave.

The proud have risen against me;
ruthless men seek my life:
to you they pay no heed.

But you, God of mercy and compassion,
slow to anger, O Lord,
abounding in love and truth,
turn and take pity on me.

O give your strength to your servant
and save your handmaid's son.
Show me a sign of your favor
that my foes may see to their shame
that you console me and give me your help.

Psalm-prayer

God of mercy and goodness, when Christ called
out to you in torment, you heard him and gave him
victory over death because of his love for you. We
already know the affection you have for us; fill us
with a greater love of your name, and we will proclaim you more boldly before men and happily lead
them to celebrate your glory.

Ant. 2  Blessed is the upright man, who speaks the
truth.

December 17-23: I shall not cease to plead with God for
Zion until he sends his Holy One in all his radiant
beauty.

Easter: Our eyes will see the King in all his radiant
beauty, alleluia.

Canticle        Isaiah 33:13-16

God's flawless judgment

*What God has promised is for you, for your chil-
dren, and for those still far away* (Acts 2:39).

Hear, you who are far off,
what I have done;
you who are near,
acknowledge my might.

On Zion sinners are in dread,
trembling grips the impious;
"Who of us can live with the consuming fire?
Who of us can live with the everlasting flames?"

He who practices virtue and speaks honestly,
who spurns what is gained by oppression,
brushing his hands
free of contact with a bribe,
stopping his ears lest he hear of bloodshed,
closing his eyes lest he look on evil.

He shall dwell on the heights,
his stronghold shall be the rocky fastness,
his food and drink
in steady supply.

Ant. 3   Let us celebrate with joy in the presence of
our Lord and King.

December 17-23: The Spirit of the Lord rests upon me; he
has sent me to preach his joyful message to the poor.

Easter: All peoples will see the saving power of our God,
alleluia.

Psalm 98

The Lord triumphs in his judgment

*This psalm tells of the Lord's first coming and that
people of all nations will believe in him* (Saint
Athanasius).

Sing a new song to the Lord
for he has worked wonders.
His right hand and his holy arm
have brought salvation.

The Lord has made known his salvation;
has shown his justice to the nations.
He has remembered his truth and love
for the house of Israel.

All the ends of the earth have seen
the salvation of our God.
Shout to the Lord, all the earth,
ring out your joy.

Sing psalms to the Lord with the harp
with the sound of music.
With trumpets and the sound of the horn
acclaim the King, the Lord.

Let the sea and all within it thunder;
the world, and all its peoples.
Let the rivers clap their hands
and the hills ring out their joy.

Rejoice at the presence of the Lord,
for he comes to rule the earth.
He will rule the world with justice
and the peoples with fairness.

Psalm-prayer

Lord Jesus, you have revealed your justice to all
nations. We stood condemned, and you came to be
judged in our place. Send your saving power on us
and, when you come in glory, bring your mercy to
those for whom you were condemned.

READING                                    Job 1:21; 2:10b

Naked I came forth from my mother's womb,
    and naked I shall go back again.
The Lord gave and the Lord has taken away;
    blessed be the name of the Lord!
We accept good things from God;
    and should we not accept evil?

RESPONSORY

Incline my heart according to your will, O God.
— Incline my heart according to your will, O God.

Speed my steps along your path,
— according to your will, O God.

Glory to the Father . . .
— Incline my heart . . .

CANTICLE OF ZECHARIAH

Ant. Show us your mercy, Lord; remember your
     holy covenant.

INTERCESSIONS

Christ nourishes and supports the Church for which
     he gave himself up to death. Let us ask him:
     *Remember your Church, Lord.*
You are the Good Shepherd who has given life and
     light today,
— make us grateful for these gifts.
Look with mercy on the flock you have gathered to-
     gether in your name,
— let no one whom the Father has given you perish.
Lead your Church in the way of your command-
     ments,
— may your Holy Spirit keep her faithful.
Nourish the Church at the banquet of your Word and
     Bread,
— strengthened by this food may she follow you in
     joy.

Our Father . . .

CONCLUDING PRAYER

Lord,
as daylight fills the sky,
fill us with your holy light.
May our lives mirror our love for you
whose wisdom has brought us into being,
and whose care guides us on our way.

We ask this through our Lord Jesus Christ, your Son,
who lives and reigns with you and the Holy Spirit,
one God, for ever and ever.

Conclusion, as in the Ordinary, 29.

## Evening Prayer

God, come to my assistance. Glory to the Father.
As it was in the beginning. Alleluia.

HYMN, no. 36 or 184. Outside Ordinary Time, see
Guide, 578.

PSALMODY

Ant. 1 Those who sow in tears will reap in joy.

December 17-23: The Lord, the mighty God, will come
forth from Zion to set his people free.

Easter: Your sorrow will be turned into joy, alleluia.

### Psalm 126

Joyful hope in God

*Just as you share in sufferings so you will share
in the divine glory* (2 Corinthians 1:7).

When the Lord delivered Zion from bondage,
it seemed like a dream.
Then was our mouth filled with laughter,
on our lips there were songs.

The heathens themselves said: "What marvels
the Lord worked for them!"
What marvels the Lord worked for us!
Indeed we were glad.

Deliver us, O Lord, from our bondage
as streams in dry land.
Those who are sowing in tears
will sing when they reap.

They go out, they go out, full of tears,
carrying seed for the sowing:
they come back, they come back, full of song,
carrying their sheaves.

Psalm-prayer

Lord, you have raised us from the earth; may you
let the seeds of justice, which we have sown in
tears, grow and increase in your sight. May we reap
in joy the harvest we hope for patiently.

Ant. 2 **May the Lord build our house and guard our city.**

December 17-23: I shall not cease to plead with God for Zion until he sends his Holy One in all his radiant beauty.

Easter: Whether we live or die, we are the Lord's, alleluia.

## Psalm 127

Apart from God our labors are worthless

*You are God's building* (1 Corinthians 3:9).

> If the Lord does not build the house,
> in vain do its builders labor;
> if the Lord does not watch over the city,
> in vain does the watchman keep vigil.
>
> In vain is your earlier rising,
> your going later to rest,
> you who toil for the bread you eat:
> when he pours gifts on his beloved while they
>     slumber.
>
> Truly sons are a gift from the Lord,
> a blessing, the fruit of the womb.
> Indeed the sons of youth
> are like arrows in the hand of a warrior.
>
> O the happiness of the man
> who has filled his quiver with these arrows!
> He will have no cause for shame
> when he disputes with his foes in the gateways.

Psalm-prayer

You command the seed to rise, Lord God, though the farmer is unaware. Grant that those who labor for you may trust not in their own work but in your help. Remembering that the land is brought to flower not with human tears but with those of your Son, may the Church rely only upon your gifts.

Ant. 3 He is the first-born of all creation; in every
way the primacy is his.

December 17-23: The Spirit of the Lord rests upon me;
he has sent me to preach his joyful message to the
poor.

Easter: From him, through him, and in him all things
exist; glory to him for ever, alleluia.

Canticle    Colossians 1:12-20

Christ the first-born of all creation and the first-born
from the dead

Let us give thanks to the Father
for having made you worthy
to share the lot of the saints
in light.

He rescued us
from the power of darkness
and brought us
into the kingdom of his beloved Son.
Through him we have redemption,
the forgiveness of our sins.

He is the image of the invisible God,
the first-born of all creatures.
In him everything in heaven and on earth was
created,
things visible and invisible.

All were created through him;
all were created for him.
He is before all else that is.
In him everything continues in being.

It is he who is head of the body, the church!
he who is the beginning,
the first-born of the dead,
so that primacy may be his in everything.

It pleased God to make absolute fullness reside
in him —

and, by means of him, to reconcile everything
in his person,
both on earth and in the heavens,
making peace through the blood of his cross.

READING                                    Ephesians 3:17-21

May Christ dwell in your hearts through faith; that
you, rooted and grounded in love, may have strength
to comprehend with all the holy ones what is the
breadth and length and height and depth, and to
know the love of Christ that surpasses knowledge, so
that you may be filled with all the fullness of God.

Now to him who is able to accomplish far more
than all we ask or imagine, by the power at work
within us, to him be glory in the church and in Christ
Jesus to all generations, forever and ever. Amen.

RESPONSORY

Claim me once more as your own, Lord, and have
mercy on me.
— Claim me once more as your own, Lord, and have
mercy on me.

Do not abandon me with the wicked;
— have mercy on me.

Glory to the Father . . .
— Claim me once . . .

CANTICLE OF MARY

Ant. The Almighty has done great things for me,
and holy is his Name.

INTERCESSIONS

Let us humbly pray to God who sent his Son as the
Savior and exemplar of his people:
*May your people praise you, Lord.*
Let us give thanks to God who chose us as the
firstfruits of salvation,

— and who called us to share in the glory of our
   Lord Jesus Christ.
May those who confess your holy name be united
   in your truth,
— and fervent in your love.
Creator of all things, your Son desired to work
   among men with his own hands,
— be mindful of all who earn their living by the
   sweat of their brow.
Be mindful of those who devote themselves to the
   service of their brothers,
— do not let them be deterred from their goals by
   discouraging results or lack of support.
Be merciful to the faithful departed,
— keep them from the power of the Evil One.

Our Father . . .

CONCLUDING PRAYER

Merciful Lord,
let the evening prayer of your Church
come before you.
May we do your work faithfully;
free us from sin
and make us secure in your love.

We ask this through our Lord Jesus Christ, your Son,
who lives and reigns with you and the Holy Spirit,
one God, for ever and ever.

Conclusion, as in the Ordinary, 29.

# THURSDAY, WEEK III

## Invitatory

Lord, open my lips.

Ant. Come, let us worship the Lord, for he is our
      God.

Invitatory psalm, 22.

## Morning Prayer

The following verse and response are omitted when the hour begins with the invitatory.

God, come to my assistance. Glory to the Father. As it was in the beginning. Alleluia.

HYMN, no. 6 or 14. Outside Ordinary Time, see Guide, 578.

PSALMODY

Ant. 1  Glorious things are said of you, O city of God.

> December 17-23: To you, O Lord, I lift up my soul; come and rescue me, for you are my refuge and my strength.

> Easter: City of God, you are the source of our life; with music and dance we shall rejoice in you, alleluia.

### Psalm 87
#### Jerusalem is mother of us all

*The heavenly Jerusalem is a free woman; she is our mother* (Galatians 4:26).

On the holy mountain is his city
cherished by the Lord.
The Lord prefers the gates of Zion
to all Jacob's dwellings.
Of you are told glorious things,
O city of God!

"Babylon and Egypt I will count
among those who know me;
Philistia, Tyre, Ethiopia,
these will be her children
and Zion shall be called 'Mother'
for all shall be her children."

It is he, the Lord Most High,
who gives each his place.
In his register of peoples he writes:
"These are her children,"
and while they dance they will sing:
"In you all find their home."

Psalm-prayer

Lord God, your only Son wept over ancient Jerusalem, soon to be destroyed for its lack of faith. He established the new Jerusalem firmly upon rock and made it the mother of the faithful. Make us rejoice in your Church, and grant that all people may be reborn into the freedom of your Spirit.

Ant. 2   The Lord, the mighty conqueror, will come; he will bring with him the prize of victory.

December 17-23: Bless those, O Lord, who have waited for your coming; let your prophets be proved true.

Easter: Like a shepherd he will gather the lambs in his arms and carry them close to his heart, alleluia.

Canticle         Isaiah 40:10-17

The Good Shepherd: God most high and most wise

*See, I come quickly; I have my reward in hand* (Revelation 22:12).

> Here comes with power
> the Lord God,
> who rules by his strong arm;
> here is his reward with him,
> his recompense before him.
>
> Like a shepherd he feeds his flock;
> in his arms he gathers the lambs,
> carrying them in his bosom,
> and leading the ewes with care.
>
> Who has cupped in his hand the waters of the sea,
> and marked off the heavens with a span?
> Who has held in a measure the dust of the earth,
> weighed the mountains in scales
> and the hills in a balance?
>
> Who has directed the spirit of the Lord,
> or has instructed him as his counselor?
> Whom did he consult to gain knowledge?—

Who taught him the path of judgment,
or showed him the way of understanding?

Behold, the nations count as a drop of the bucket,
as rust on the scales;
the coastlands weigh no more than powder.

Lebanon would not suffice for fuel,
nor its animals be enough for holocausts.
Before him all the nations are as nought,
as nothing and void he accounts them.

Ant. 3  Give praise to the Lord our God, bow down
before his holy mountain.

December 17-23: Turn to us, O Lord, make haste to help
your people.

Easter: Great is the Lord in Zion; he is exalted above all
the peoples, alleluia.

## Psalm 99

### Holy is the Lord our God

*Christ, higher than the Cherubim, when you took
our lowly nature you transformed our sinful world*
(Saint Athanasius).

The Lord is king; the peoples tremble.
He is throned on the cherubim; the earth quakes.
The Lord is great in Zion.

He is supreme over all the peoples.
Let them praise his name, so terrible and great.
He is holy, full of power.

You are a king who loves what is right;
you have established equity, justice and right;
you have established them in Jacob.

Exalt the Lord our God;
bow down before Zion, his footstool.
He the Lord is holy.

Among his priests were Aaron and Moses,
among those who invoked his name was Samuel.
They invoked the Lord and he answered.

To them he spoke in the pillar of cloud.
They did his will; they kept the law,
which he, the Lord, had given.

O Lord our God, you answered them.
For them you were a God who forgives;
yet you punished all their offenses.

Exalt the Lord our God;
bow down before his holy mountain
for the Lord our God is holy.

Psalm-prayer

God, you are the source of all holiness. Though
no one can see you and live, you give life most generously, and in an even greater way restore it. Sanctify your priests through your life-giving Word, and
consecrate your people in his blood until our eyes
see your face.

READING                                   1 Peter 4:8-11a

Let your love for one another be intense, because
love covers a multitude of sins. Be hospitable to one
another without complaining. As each one has received a gift, use it to serve one another as good stewards of God's varied grace. Whoever preaches, let it
be with the words of God; whoever serves, let it be
with the strength that God supplies, so that in all
things God may be glorified through Jesus Christ.

RESPONSORY

From the depths of my heart I cry to you; hear me,
   O Lord.
— From the depths of my heart I cry to you; hear
   me, O Lord.

I will do what you desire;
— hear me, O Lord.

Glory to the Father . . .
— From the depths . . .

CANTICLE OF ZECHARIAH

Ant. Let us serve the Lord in holiness, and he will
     save us from our enemies.

INTERCESSIONS

Let us joyfully cry out in thanks to God the Father
     whose love guides and nourishes his people:
     *May you be glorified, Lord, for all ages.*
Most merciful Father, we praise you for your love,
— for you wondrously created us and even more
     wondrously restored us to grace.
At the beginning of this day fill our hearts with zeal
     for serving you,
— so that our thoughts and actions may redound to
     your glory.
Purify our hearts of every evil desire,
— make us intent on doing your will.
Open our hearts to the needs of all men,
— fill us with brotherly love.

Our Father . . .

CONCLUDING PRAYER

All-powerful and ever-living God,
shine with the light of your radiance
on a people who live in the shadow of death.
Let the dawn from on high break upon us:
your Son our Lord Jesus Christ,
who lives and reigns with you and the Holy Spirit,
one God, for ever and ever.

Conclusion, as in the Ordinary, 29.

## Evening Prayer

God, come to my assistance. Glory to the Father.
As it was in the beginning. Alleluia.

HYMN, no. **37** or **45**. Outside Ordinary Time, see
Guide, **578**.

PSALMODY

Ant. 1 **Let your holy people rejoice, O Lord, as they enter your dwelling place.**

December 17-23: To you, O Lord, I lift up my soul; come and rescue me, for you are my refuge and my strength.

Easter: The Lord has given him the throne of David his father, alleluia.

## Psalm 132

### God's promises to the house of David

*The Lord God will give him the throne of his ancestor David* (Luke 1:32).

I

O Lord, remember David
and all the many hardships he endured,
the oath he swore to the Lord,
his vow to the Strong One of Jacob.

"I will not enter the house where I live
nor go to the bed where I rest.
I will give no sleep to my eyes,
to my eyelids I will give no slumber
till I find a place for the Lord,
a dwelling for the Strong One of Jacob."

At Ephrathah we heard of the ark;
we found it in the plains of Yearim.
"Let us go to the place of his dwelling;
let us go to kneel at his footstool."

Go up, Lord, to the place of your rest,
you and the ark of your strength.
Your priests shall be clothed with holiness:
your faithful shall ring out their joy.
For the sake of David your servant
do not reject your anointed.

Ant. 2 **The Lord has chosen Zion as his sanctuary.**

December 17-23: **Bless those, O Lord, who have waited for your coming; let your prophets be proved true.**

Easter: **Jesus Christ is supreme in his power. He is King of kings and Lord of lords, alleluia.**

## II

The Lord swore an oath to David;
he will not go back on his word:
"A son, the fruit of your body,
will I set upon your throne.

If they keep my covenant in truth
and my laws that I have taught them,
their sons also shall rule
on your throne from age to age."

For the Lord has chosen Zion;
he has desired it for his dwelling:
"This is my resting-place for ever,
here have I chosen to live.

I will greatly bless her produce,
I will fill her poor with bread.
I will clothe her priests with salvation
and her faithful shall ring out their joy.

There David's stock will flower:
I will prepare a lamp for my anointed.
I will cover his enemies with shame
but on him my crown shall shine."

### Psalm-prayer

You are our King, Lord God. Help us to find a place for you in our hearts. Clothe your priests with saving power, fill the needy with bread, and let your holiness shine on us all.

Ant. 3  The Father has given Christ all power, honor and kingship; all people will obey him.

December 17-23: Turn to us, O Lord, make haste to help your people.

Easter: Lord, who is your equal in power? Who is like you, majestic in holiness? alleluia.

Canticle                    Revelation 11:17-18; 12:10b-12a

The judgment of God

We praise you, the Lord God Almighty,
who is and who was.
You have assumed your great power,
you have begun your reign.

The nations have raged in anger,
but then came your day of wrath
and the moment to judge the dead:
the time to reward your servants the prophets
and the holy ones who revere you,
the great and the small alike.

Now have salvation and power come,
the reign of our God and the authority
of his Anointed One.
For the accuser of our brothers is cast out,
who night and day accused them before God.

They defeated him by the blood of the Lamb
and by the word of their testimony;
love for life did not deter them from death.
So rejoice, you heavens,
and you that dwell therein!

READING                              1 Peter 3:8-12

All of you, be of one mind, sympathetic, loving toward one another, compassionate, humble. Do not return evil for evil, or insult for insult; but, on the contrary, a blessing, because to this you were called, that you might inherit a blessing. For:

"Whoever would love life
    and see good days
must keep the tongue from evil
    and the lips from speaking deceit,

must turn from evil and do good,
    seek peace and follow after it.
For the eyes of the Lord are on the righteous
    and his ears turned to their prayer,
but the face of the Lord is against evildoers."

RESPONSORY

The Lord has given us food, bread of the finest wheat.
— The Lord has given us food, bread of the finest wheat.

Honey from the rock to our heart's content,
— bread of the finest wheat.

Glory to the Father . . .
— The Lord has . . .

CANTICLE OF MARY

Ant. God has cast down the mighty from their thrones, and has lifted up the lowly.

INTERCESSIONS

Let us call upon Christ, the Good Shepherd who comes to the aid of his people:
    *Hear us, O God, our refuge.*
Blessed are you, Lord, for you graciously called us into your holy Church,
— keep us within the Church until death.
You have given the care of all the churches to N., our Pope,
— give him unfailing faith, lively hope and loving concern.
Grant the grace of conversion to all sinners,
— and the grace of true repentance to all men.
You were willing to live as a stranger in our world,
— be mindful of those who are separated from family and homeland.
To all the departed who have hoped in you,
— grant eternal peace.

Our Father . . .

Concluding Prayer

Lord,
we thank you for guiding us
through the course of this day's work.
In your compassion forgive the sins
we have committed through human weakness.

We ask this through our Lord Jesus Christ, your Son,
who lives and reigns with you and the Holy Spirit,
one God, for ever and ever.

Conclusion, as in the Ordinary, 29.

# FRIDAY, WEEK III

## Invitatory

Lord, open my lips.

Ant. Come, let us give thanks to the Lord, for his
great love is without end.

Invitatory psalm, 22.

## Morning Prayer

The following verse and response are omitted
when the hour begins with the invitatory.

God, come to my assistance. Glory to the Father.
As it was in the beginning. Alleluia.

Hymn, no. 7 or 131. Outside Ordinary Time, see
Guide, 578.

Psalmody

Ant. 1  You alone I have grieved by my sin; have
pity on me, O Lord.

December 17-23: Our King will come from Zion; the
Lord, God-is-with-us, is his mighty name.

Easter: Lord, wash away my guilt, alleluia.

## Psalm 51

### O God, have mercy on me

*Your inmost being must be renewed, and you must put on the new man* (Ephesians 4:23-24).

Have mercy on me, God, in your kindness.
In your compassion blot out my offense.
O wash me more and more from my guilt
and cleanse me from my sin.

My offenses truly I know them;
my sin is always before me.
Against you, you alone, have I sinned;
what is evil in your sight I have done.

That you may be justified when you give sentence
and be without reproach when you judge.
O see, in guilt I was born,
a sinner was I conceived.

Indeed you love truth in the heart;
then in the secret of my heart teach me wisdom.
O purify me, then I shall be clean;
O wash me, I shall be whiter than snow.

Make me hear rejoicing and gladness,
that the bones you have crushed may revive.
From my sins turn away your face
and blot out all my guilt.

A pure heart create for me, O God,
put a steadfast spirit within me.
Do not cast me away from your presence,
nor deprive me of your holy spirit.

Give me again the joy of your help;
with a spirit of fervor sustain me,
that I may teach transgressors your ways
and sinners may return to you.

O rescue me, God, my helper,
and my tongue shall ring out your goodness.—

O Lord, open my lips
and my mouth shall declare your praise.

For in sacrifice you take no delight,
burnt offering from me you would refuse,
my sacrifice, a contrite spirit.
A humbled, contrite heart you will not spurn.

In your goodness, show favor to Zion:
rebuild the walls of Jerusalem.
Then you will be pleased with lawful sacrifice,
holocausts offered on your altar.

Psalm-prayer

Father, he who knew no sin was made sin for us,
to save us and restore us to your friendship. Look
upon our contrite heart and afflicted spirit and heal
our troubled conscience, so that in the joy and
strength of the Holy Spirit we may proclaim your
praise and glory before all the nations.

Ant. 2  Truly we know our offenses, Lord, for we
        have sinned against you.

December 17-23: Wait for the Lord and he will come to
you with his saving power.

Easter: Christ bore our sins in his own body as he hung
upon the cross, alleluia.

Canticle        Jeremiah 14:17-21

The lament of the people in war and famine

*The kingdom of God is at hand. Repent and believe
the Good News* (Mark 1:15).

Let my eyes stream with tears
day and night, without rest,
over the great destruction which overwhelms
the virgin daughter of my people,
over her incurable wound.

If I walk out into the field,
look! those slain by the sword; —

if I enter the city,
look! those consumed by hunger.
Even the prophet and the priest
forage in a land they know not.

Have you cast Judah off completely?
Is Zion loathsome to you?
Why have you struck us a blow
that cannot be healed?

We wait for peace, to no avail;
for a time of healing, but terror comes instead.
We recognize, O Lord, our wickedness,
the guilt of our fathers;
that we have sinned against you.

For your name's sake spurn us not,
disgrace not the throne of your glory;
remember your covenant with us, and break it
not.

Ant. 3 **The Lord is God; we are his people, the
flock he shepherds.**

December 17-23: Eagerly I watch for the Lord; I wait in
joyful hope for the coming of God my Savior.

Easter: Come into the Lord's presence singing for joy, alleluia.

When psalm 100 is the invitatory psalm, psalm 95,
22, is used as the third psalm at Morning Prayer.

## Psalm 100

The joyful song of those entering God's temple

*The Lord calls his ransomed people to sing songs
of victory* (Saint Athanasius).

Cry out with joy to the Lord, all the earth.
Serve the Lord with gladness.
Come before him, singing for joy.

Know that he, the Lord, is God.
He made us, we belong to him,
we are his people, the sheep of his flock.

Go within his gates, giving thanks.
Enter his courts with songs of praise.
Give thanks to him and bless his name.

Indeed, how good is the Lord,
eternal his merciful love.
He is faithful from age to age.

Psalm-prayer

God, devoted to us as a Father, you created us as
a sign of your power, and elected us your people to
show your goodness. Accept the thanks your children offer, that all men may enter your courts
praising you in song.

READING                                2 Corinthians 12:7-10

Because of the abundance of the revelations, that I
might not become too elated, a thorn in the flesh was
given to me, an angel of Satan, to beat me, to keep me
from being too elated. Three times I begged the Lord
about this, that it might leave me, but he said to me,
"My grace is sufficient for you, for power is made perfect in weakness." I will rather boast most gladly of
my weaknesses, in order that the power of Christ
may dwell with me. Therefore, I am content with
weaknesses, insults, hardships, persecutions, and
constraints, for the sake of Christ; for when I am
weak, then I am strong.

RESPONSORY

At daybreak, be merciful to me.
— At daybreak, be merciful to me.
Make known to me the path that I must walk.
— Be merciful to me.
Glory to the Father . . .
— At daybreak, be . . .

CANTICLE OF ZECHARIAH

Ant.  The Lord has come to his people and set them
      free.

INTERCESSIONS

Raising our eyes to Christ, who was born and died and rose again for his people, let us cry out:
*Save those you have redeemed by your blood, Lord.*

Blessed are you, Jesus, redeemer of mankind; you did not hesitate to undergo your passion and death,
— to redeem us by your precious blood.

You promised that you would provide living water, the fountain of eternal life,
— pour forth your Spirit upon all men.

You send disciples to preach the Gospel to all nations,
— help them to extend the victory of your cross.

You have given the sick and the suffering a share in your cross,
— give them patience and strength.

Our Father . . .

CONCLUDING PRAYER

Father all-powerful,
let your radiance dawn in our lives,
that we may walk in the light of your law
with you as our leader.

We ask this through our Lord Jesus Christ, your Son, who lives and reigns with you and the Holy Spirit, one God, for ever and ever.

Conclusion, as in the Ordinary, 29.

## Evening Prayer

God, come to my assistance. Glory to the Father. As it was in the beginning. Alleluia.

HYMN, no. 38 or 46. Outside Ordinary Time, see Guide, 578.

PSALMODY

Ant. 1  Great is the Lord, our God, transcending all other gods.

December 17-23: Our King will come from Zion; the
    Lord, God-is-with-us, is his mighty name.

Easter: I, the Lord, am your savior and redeemer, alleluia.

## Psalm 135

### Praise for the wonderful things God does for us

*He has won us for himself . . . and you must pro-
claim what he has done for you. He has called you
out of darkness into his own wonderful light* (see 1
Peter 2: 9).

### I

Praise the name of the Lord,
  praise him, servants of the Lord,
  who stand in the house of the Lord
  in the courts of the house of our God.

Praise the Lord for the Lord is good.
  Sing a psalm to his name for he is loving.
  For the Lord has chosen Jacob for himself
  and Israel for his own possession.

For I know the Lord is great,
  that our Lord is high above all gods.
  The Lord does whatever he wills,
  in heaven, on earth, in the seas.

He summons clouds from the ends of the earth;
  makes lightning produce the rain;
  from his treasuries he sends forth the wind.

The first-born of the Egyptians he smote,
  of man and beast alike.
  Signs and wonders he worked
  in the midst of your land, O Egypt,
  against Pharaoh and all his servants.

Nations in their greatness he struck
  and kings in their splendor he slew.
  Sihon, king of the Amorites,
  Og, the king of Bashan, —

and all the kingdoms of Canaan.
He let Israel inherit their land;
on his people their land he bestowed.

Ant. 2  House of Israel, bless the Lord! Sing psalms
to him, for he is merciful.

December 17-23: Wait for the Lord, and he will come to
you with his saving power.

Easter: Blessed is the kingdom of David our father which
has come among us, alleluia.

II

Lord, your name stands for ever,
unforgotten from age to age:
for the Lord does justice for his people;
the Lord takes pity on his servants.

Pagan idols are silver and gold,
the work of human hands.
They have mouths but they cannot speak;
they have eyes but they cannot see.

They have ears but they cannot hear;
there is never a breath on their lips.
Their makers will come to be like them
and so will all who trust in them!

Sons of Israel, bless the Lord!
Sons of Aaron, bless the Lord!
Sons of Levi, bless the Lord!
You who fear him, bless the Lord!

From Zion may the Lord be blessed,
he who dwells in Jerusalem!

Psalm-prayer

Father, your name and your memory last for ever.
We stand to pray in your house and praise you with
psalms of joy. We ask you in your kindness to have
mercy on us in our lowliness.

Ant. 3 **All nations will come and worship before you, O Lord.**

December 17-23: Eagerly I watch for the Lord; I wait in joyful hope for the coming of God my Savior.

Easter: Let us sing to the Lord, glorious in his triumph, alleluia.

Canticle             Revelation 15:3-4

### Hymn of adoration

Mighty and wonderful are your works,
Lord God Almighty!
Righteous and true are your ways,
O King of the nations!

Who would dare refuse you honor,
or the glory due your name, O Lord?

Since you alone are holy,
all nations shall come
and worship in your presence.
Your mighty deeds are clearly seen.

READING                        James 1:2-8

Consider it all joy, my brothers, when you encounter various trials, for you know that the testing of your faith produces perseverance. And let perseverance be perfect, so that you may be perfect and complete, lacking in nothing. But if any of you lacks wisdom, he should ask God who gives to all generously and ungrudgingly, and he will be given it. But he should ask in faith, not doubting, for the one who doubts is like a wave of the sea that is driven and tossed about by the wind. For that person must not suppose that he will receive anything from the Lord, since he is a man of two minds, unstable in all his ways.

RESPONSORY

Christ loved us and washed away our sins, in his own blood.
— Christ loved us and washed away our sins, in his own blood.

He made us a nation of kings and priests,
— in his own blood.

Glory to the Father . . .
— Christ loved us . . .

CANTICLE OF MARY

Ant. The Lord has come to the help of his servants, for he has remembered his promise of mercy.

INTERCESSIONS

Because of our sins the Father gave the Lord Jesus up to death, and for our justification he raised him up again. Let us pray:
*Have mercy on your people, Lord.*
Hear our prayers and spare us as we confess our sins,
— grant us forgiveness and peace.
Your Apostle said: "Where sin abounds, grace abounds all the more,"
— forgive us our transgressions.
Lord, we have sinned, yet we have also acknowledged your infinite mercy,
— bring us to conversion.
Save your people from their sins, Lord,
— make them pleasing to you.
You opened Paradise to the thief who believed in you,
— do not close the gates of heaven to the faithful departed.

Our Father . . .

CONCLUDING PRAYER

Father,
in your loving plan
Christ your Son became the price of our salvation.
May we be united with him in his suffering
so that we may experience
the power of his resurrection
in the kingdom
where he lives and reigns with you and the Holy Spirit,
one God, for ever and ever.

Conclusion, as in the Ordinary, 29.

## SATURDAY, WEEK III

### Invitatory

Lord, open my lips.

Ant. Come, let us worship God who holds the world
and its wonders in his creating hand.

Invitatory psalm, 22.

### Morning Prayer

The following verse and response are omitted
when the hour begins with the invitatory.

God, come to my assistance. Glory to the Father.
As it was in the beginning. Alleluia.

HYMN, no. 8 or 12. Outside Ordinary Time, see
Guide, 578.

PSALMODY

Ant. 1  Lord, you are near to us, and all your ways
are true.

December 17-23: Our God will come from Lebanon; he
shall be as brilliant as the sun.

Easter: The words I have spoken to you are spirit and
life, alleluia.

Psalm 119:145-152
XIX (Koph)

I call with all my heart; Lord, hear me,
I will keep your commands.
I call upon you, save me
and I will do your will.

I rise before dawn and cry for help,
I hope in your word.
My eyes watch through the night
to ponder your promise.

In your love hear my voice, O Lord;
give me life by your decrees.—

Those who harm me unjustly draw near:
they are far from your law.

But you, O Lord, are close:
your commands are truth.
Long have I known that your will
is established for ever.

Psalm-prayer

Save us by the power of your hand, Father, for
our enemies have ignored your words. May the fire
of your word consume our sins and its brightness
illumine our hearts.

Ant. 2  Wisdom of God, be with me, always at work
in me.

December 17-23: May the Holy One from heaven come
down like gentle rain; may the earth burst into blossom and bear the tender Savior.

Easter: Lord, you have built your temple and altar on
your holy mountain, alleluia.

Canticle          Wisdom 9:1-6, 9-11

Lord, give me wisdom

*I will inspire you with wisdom which your adver-
saries will be unable to resist* (Luke 21:15).

God of my fathers, Lord of mercy,
you who have made all things by your word
and in your wisdom have established man
to rule the creatures produced by you,
to govern the world in holiness and justice,
and to render judgment in integrity of heart:

Give me Wisdom, the attendant at your throne,
and reject me not from among your children;
for I am your servant, the son of your handmaid,
a man weak and short-lived
and lacking in comprehension of judgment and
of laws.

Indeed, though one be perfect among the sons of
    men,
if Wisdom, who comes from you, be not with him,
he shall be held in no esteem.

Now with you is Wisdom, who knows your works
and was present when you made the world;
who understands what is pleasing in your eyes
and what is conformable with your commands.

Send her forth from your holy heavens
and from your glorious throne dispatch her
that she may be with me and work with me,
that I may know what is your pleasure.

For she knows and understands all things,
and will guide me discreetly in my affairs
and safeguard me by her glory.

Ant. 3 The Lord remains faithful to his promise
    for ever.

December 17-23: Israel, prepare yourself to meet the
    Lord, for he is coming.

Easter: I am the way, the truth and the life, alleluia.


Psalm 117

Praise for God's loving compassion

*I affirm that . . . the Gentile peoples are to praise
God because of his mercy* (Romans 15:8-9).

O praise the Lord, all you nations,
acclaim him, all you peoples!

Strong is his love for us;
he is faithful for ever.

Psalm-prayer

God our Father, may all nations and peoples
praise you. May Jesus, who is called faithful and
true and who lives with you eternally, possess our
hearts for ever.

READING                              Philippians 2:2-4, 14-16

Complete my joy by being of the same mind, with the same love, united in heart, thinking one thing. Do nothing out of selfishness or out of vainglory; rather, humbly regard others as more important than yourselves, each looking out not for his own interests, but [also] everyone for those of others.

Do everything without grumbling or questioning, that you may be blameless and innocent, children of God without blemish in the midst of a crooked and perverse generation, among whom you shine like lights in the world, as you hold on to the word of life, so that my boast for the day of Christ may be that I did not run in vain or labor in vain.

RESPONSORY

I cry to you, O Lord, for you are my refuge.
— I cry to you, O Lord, for you are my refuge.

You are all I desire in the land of the living,
— for you are my refuge.

Glory to the Father . . .
— I cry to . . .

CANTICLE OF ZECHARIAH

Ant. Lord, shine on those who dwell in darkness and the shadow of death.

INTERCESSIONS

With confidence let us pray to the Father who willed that the Virgin Mary should surpass all creatures in heaven and earth:
*Look upon the Mother of your Son and hear our prayer.*
We are grateful to you, Father of mercy, for you gave us Mary to be our mother and our model,
— through her intercession cleanse our hearts.
You inspired Mary to be attentive to your word and faithful in your service,

— through her intercession give us the gifts of the
    Holy Spirit.
You strengthened Mary at the foot of the cross and
    filled her with joy at the resurrection of your Son,
— through her intercession relieve our distress and
    strengthen our hope.

Our Father . . .

CONCLUDING PRAYER

God our Father,
fountain and source of our salvation,
may we proclaim your glory every day of our lives,
that we may sing your praise for ever in heaven.

We ask this through our Lord Jesus Christ, your
Son,
who lives and reigns with you and the Holy Spirit,
one God, for ever and ever.

Conclusion, as in the Ordinary, 29.

# WEEK IV

## SUNDAY

### Evening Prayer I

God, come to my assistance. Glory to the Father.
As it was in the beginning. Alleluia.

HYMN, no. 39 or 182. Outside Ordinary Time, see
Guide, 578.

PSALMODY

Ant. 1 Pray for the peace of Jerusalem.

> Advent: He comes, the desire of all human hearts; his
> dwelling place shall be resplendent with glory, alleluia.

> Lent, 4th Sunday: Let us go to God's house with rejoicing.

> Easter, 4th Sunday: May the peace of Christ fill your
> hearts with joy, alleluia.

#### Psalm 122

#### Holy city Jerusalem

*You have come to Mount Zion, to the city of the
living God, heavenly Jerusalem* (Hebrews 12:22).

> I rejoiced when I heard them say:
> "Let us go to God's house."
> And now our feet are standing
> within your gates, O Jerusalem.

> Jerusalem is built as a city
> strongly compact.
> It is there that the tribes go up,
> the tribes of the Lord.

> For Israel's law it is,
> there to praise the Lord's name.—

There were set the thrones of judgment
of the house of David.

For the peace of Jerusalem pray:
"Peace be to your homes!
May peace reign in your walls,
in your palaces, peace!"

For love of my brethren and friends
I say: "Peace upon you!"
For love of the house of the Lord
I will ask for your good.

Psalm-prayer

When you rose from the dead, Lord Jesus, you
formed the Church into your new body and made of
it the new Jerusalem, united in your Spirit. Give us
peace in our day. Make all nations come to your
Church to share your gifts in fellowship, that they
may render you thanks without end and come to
your eternal city.

Ant. 2  **From the morning watch until night, I have
waited trustingly for the Lord.**

Advent: Come, Lord, do not delay; free your people from
their sinfulness.

Lent, 4th Sunday: Awake from your sleep, rise from the
dead, and Christ will give you light.

Easter, 4th Sunday: With your own blood, you have redeemed us for God, alleluia.

## Psalm 130

A cry from the depths

*He himself will save his people from their sins*
(Mat-thew 1:21).

Out of the depths I cry to you, O Lord,
Lord, hear my voice!
O let your ears be attentive
to the voice of my pleading.

If you, O Lord, should mark our guilt,
Lord, who would survive?
But with you is found forgiveness:
for this we revere you.

My soul is waiting for the Lord,
I count on his word.
My soul is longing for the Lord
more than watchman for daybreak.
Let the watchman count on daybreak
and Israel on the Lord.

Because with the Lord there is mercy
and fullness of redemption,
Israel indeed he will redeem
from all its iniquity.

Psalm-prayer

Listen with compassion to our prayers, Lord. The forgiveness of sins is yours. Do not look on the wrong we have done, but grant us your merciful kindness.

Ant. 3  Let everything in heaven and on earth bend the knee at the name of Jesus.

Advent: The fullness of time has come upon us at last: God sends his Son into the world.

Lent, 4th Sunday: So great was God's love for us that when we were dead because of our sins, he brought us to life in Christ Jesus.

Easter, 4th Sunday: Was it not necessary for Christ to suffer and so enter into his glory? alleluia.

Canticle     Philippians 2:6-11

Christ, God's holy servant

Though he was in the form of God,
Jesus did not deem equality with God
something to be grasped at.

Rather, he emptied himself
and took the form of a slave,
being born in the likeness of men.

He was known to be of human estate,
and it was thus that he humbled himself,
obediently accepting even death,
death on a cross!

Because of this,
God highly exalted him
and bestowed on him the name
above every other name,

So that at Jesus' name
every knee must bend
in the heavens, on the earth,
and under the earth,
and every tongue proclaim
to the glory of God the Father:
JESUS CHRIST IS LORD!

READING                                    2 Peter 1:19-21

We possess the prophetic message that is alto-
gether reliable. You will do well to be attentive to it,
as to a lamp shining in a dark place, until day
dawns and the morning star rises in your hearts.
Know this first of all, that there is no prophecy of
scripture that is a matter of personal interpreta-
tion, for no prophecy ever came through human
will; but rather human beings moved by the holy
Spirit spoke under the influence of God.

RESPONSORY

From the rising of the sun to its setting,
    may the name of the Lord be praised.
— From the rising of the sun to its setting,
    may the name of the Lord be praised.

His splendor reaches far beyond the heavens;
— may the name of the Lord be praised.

Glory to the Father . . .
— From the rising . . .

Canticle of Mary, antiphon as in the Proper of Seasons.

Intercessions

Everyone who waits for the Lord finds joy. Now we pray to him:
*Look on us with favor, Lord, and hear us.*
Faithful witness, firstborn of the dead, you washed away our sins in your blood,
— make us always remember your wonderful works.
You called men to be heralds of your good news,
— make them strong and faithful messengers of your kingdom.
King of peace, send your Spirit on the leaders of the world,
— turn their eyes toward the poor and suffering.
Protect and defend those who are discriminated against because of race, color, class, language or religion,
— that they may be accorded the rights and dignity which are theirs.
May all who died in your love share in your happiness,
— with Mary, our mother, and all your holy ones.

Our Father . . .

Concluding prayer, as in the Proper of Seasons.
Conclusion, as in the Ordinary, 29.

## Invitatory

Lord, open my lips.

Ant.  Come, worship the Lord, for we are his people, the flock he shepherds, alleluia.

Invitatory psalm, 22.

## Morning Prayer

The following verse and response are omitted when the hour begins with the invitatory.

God, come to my assistance. Glory to the Father. As it was in the beginning. Alleluia.

HYMN, no. 9 or 19. Outside Ordinary Time, see Guide, 578.

PSALMODY

Ant. 1  **Praise the Lord, for his loving kindness will never fail, alleluia.**

> Advent: Sound the trumpet in Zion; the day of the Lord is near; he comes to save us, alleluia.

If this Sunday occurs on December 24, the antiphons are said as below, 378.

> Lent, 4th Sunday: O God, my God, I give you thanks; you are my God, I shall proclaim your glory.

> Easter, 4th Sunday: I shall not die but live and proclaim the works of the Lord, alleluia.

Psalm 118

Song of joy for salvation

*This Jesus is the stone which, rejected by you builders, has become the chief stone supporting all the rest* (Acts 4:11).

Give thanks to the Lord for he is good,
for his love endures for ever.

Let the sons of Israel say:
"His love endures for ever."
Let the sons of Aaron say:
"His love endures for ever."
Let those who fear the Lord say:
"His love endures for ever."

I called to the Lord in my distress;
he answered and freed me.
The Lord is at my side; I do not fear.
What can man do against me?
The Lord is at my side as my helper:
I shall look down on my foes.

It is better to take refuge in the Lord
than to trust in men:—

it is better to take refuge in the Lord
than to trust in princes.

The nations all encompassed me;
in the Lord's name I crushed them.
They compassed me, compassed me about;
in the Lord's name I crushed them.
They compassed me about like bees;
they blazed like a fire among thorns.
In the Lord's name I crushed them.

I was hard-pressed and was falling
but the Lord came to help me.
The Lord is my strength and my song;
he is my savior.
There are shouts of joy and victory
in the tents of the just.

The Lord's right hand has triumphed;
his right hand raised me.
The Lord's right hand has triumphed;
I shall not die, I shall live
and recount his deeds.
I was punished, I was punished by the Lord,
but not doomed to die.

Open to me the gates of holiness:
I will enter and give thanks.
This is the Lord's own gate
where the just may enter.
I will thank you for you have answered
and you are my savior.

The stone which the builders rejected
has become the corner stone.
This is the work of the Lord,
a marvel in our eyes.
This day was made by the Lord;
we rejoice and are glad.

O Lord, grant us salvation;
O Lord, grant success.
Blessed in the name of the Lord
is he who comes.
We bless you from the house of the Lord;
the Lord God is our light.

Go forward in procession with branches
even to the altar.
You are my God, I thank you.
My God, I praise you.
Give thanks to the Lord for he is good;
for his love endures for ever.

Psalm-prayer

Lord God, you have given us the great day of
rejoicing: Jesus Christ, the stone rejected by the
builders, has become the cornerstone of the Church,
our spiritual home. Shed upon your Church the rays
of your glory, that it may be seen as the gate of salvation open to all nations. Let cries of joy and exultation ring out from its tents, to celebrate the wonder
of Christ's resurrection.

Ant. 2  Alleluia! Bless the Lord, all you works of
the Lord, alleluia!

Advent: The Lord is here; go out to meet him, saying:
Great his birth, eternal his kingdom: Strong God,
Ruler of all, Prince of Peace, alleluia.

Lent, 4th Sunday: God of might, deliver us; free us from
the power of the enemy.

Easter, 4th Sunday: Blessed be your holy and glorious
name, O Lord, alleluia.

Canticle            Daniel 3:52-57

Let all creatures praise the Lord

*The Creator . . . is blessed for ever* (Romans 1:25).

Blessed are you, O Lord, the God of our fathers,
praiseworthy and exalted above all forever.

And blessed is your holy and glorious name,
praiseworthy and exalted above all for all ages.

Blessed are you in the temple of your holy glory,
praiseworthy and glorious above all forever.

Blessed are you on the throne of your kingdom,
praiseworthy and exalted above all forever.

Blessed are you who look into the depths
from your throne upon the cherubim,
praiseworthy and glorious above all forever.

Blessed are you in the firmament of heaven,
praiseworthy and glorious forever.

Bless the Lord, all you works of the Lord,
praise and exalt him above all forever.

Ant. 3  Let everything that breathes give praise to
the Lord, alleluia.

Advent: Your all-powerful Word, O Lord, will come to
earth from his throne of glory, alleluia.

Lent, 4th Sunday: Praise God for his mighty deeds.

Easter, 4th Sunday: Give honor and praise to our God; all
that he does is perfect and all his ways are true, alleluia.

Psalm 150
Praise the Lord

*Let mind and heart be in your song: this is to glo-
rify God with your whole self* (Hesychius).

Praise God in his holy place,
praise him in his mighty heavens.
Praise him for his powerful deeds,
praise his surpassing greatness.

O praise him with sound of trumpet,
praise him with lute and harp.
Praise him with timbrel and dance,
praise him with strings and pipes.

O praise him with resounding cymbals,
praise him with clashing of cymbals.

Let everything that lives and that breathes
give praise to the Lord.

## Psalm-prayer

Lord God, maker of heaven and earth and of all
created things, you make your just ones holy and
you justify sinners who confess your name. Hear
us as we humbly pray to you: give us eternal joy
with your saints.

READING                                    2 Timothy 2:8, 11-13

Remember Jesus Christ, raised from the dead, a
descendant of David: such is my gospel. This saying is trustworthy:

If we have died with him
    we shall also live with him;
if we persevere
    we shall also reign with him.
But if we deny him
    he will deny us.
If we are unfaithful
    he remains faithful,
    for he cannot deny himself.

RESPONSORY

We give thanks to you, O God, as we call upon your
    name.
— We give thanks to you, O God, as we call upon
    your name.

We cry aloud how marvelous you are,
— as we call upon your name.

Glory to the Father . . .
— We give thanks . . .

CANTICLE OF ZECHARIAH, antiphon as in the Proper of
Seasons.

INTERCESSIONS

Open your hearts to praise the God of power and
    goodness, for he loves us and knows our needs:
    *We praise you, Lord, and trust in you.*

We bless you, almighty God, King of the universe,
    because you called us while we were yet sinners,
— to acknowledge your truth and to serve your
    majesty.
O God, you opened the gates of mercy for us,
— let us never turn aside from the path of life.
As we celebrate the resurrection of your beloved Son,
— help us to spend this day in the spirit of joy.
Give to your faithful, O Lord, a prayerful spirit of grat-
    itude,
— that we may thank you for all your gifts.

Our Father . . .

Concluding prayer, as in the Proper of Seasons.

Conclusion, as in the Ordinary, 29.

## Evening Prayer II

God, come to my assistance. Glory to the Father.
As it was in the beginning. Alleluia.

HYMN, no. **40** or **184**. Outside Ordinary Time, see
Guide, **578**.

PSALMODY

Ant. 1  In eternal splendor, before the dawn of light
          on earth, I have begotten you, alleluia.

    Advent: See how glorious he is, coming forth as Savior of
    all peoples!

    Lent, 4th Sunday: God has appointed Christ to be judge
    of the living and the dead.

    Easter, 4th Sunday: Seek the things that are above
    where Christ is seated at God's right hand, alleluia.

Psalm 110:1-5, 7

The Messiah, king and priest

*Christ's reign will last until all his enemies are
made subject to him* (1 Corinthians 15:25).

The Lord's revelation to my Master:
"Sit on my right:
your foes I will put beneath your feet."

The Lord will wield from Zion
your scepter of power:
rule in the midst of all your foes.

A prince from the day of your birth
on the holy mountains;
from the womb before the dawn I begot you.

The Lord has sworn an oath he will not change.
"You are a priest for ever,
a priest like Melchizedek of old."

The Master standing at your right hand
will shatter kings in the day of his great wrath.

He shall drink from the stream by the wayside
and therefore he shall lift up his head.

Psalm-prayer

Father, we ask you to give us victory and peace.
In Jesus Christ, our Lord and King, we are already
seated at your right hand. We look forward to praising you in the fellowship of all your saints in our
heavenly homeland.

Ant. 2  Blessed are they who hunger and thirst for
holiness; they will be satisfied.

Advent: Crooked paths will be straightened and rough
ways made smooth. Come, O Lord, do not delay, alleluia.

Lent, 4th Sunday: Happy the man who shows mercy for
the Lord's sake; he will stand firm for ever.

Easter, 4th Sunday: In the darkness he dawns: a light for
upright hearts, alleluia.

## Psalm 112

### The happiness of the just man

*Live as children born of the light. Light produces every kind of goodness and justice and truth* (Ephesians 5:8-9).

Happy the man who fears the Lord,
who takes delight in all his commands.
His sons will be powerful on earth;
the children of the upright are blessed.

Riches and wealth are in his house;
his justice stands firm for ever.
He is a light in the darkness for the upright:
he is generous, merciful and just.

The good man takes pity and lends,
he conducts his affairs with honor.
The just man will never waver:
he will be remembered for ever.

He has no fear of evil news;
with a firm heart he trusts in the Lord.
With a steadfast heart he will not fear;
he will see the downfall of his foes.

Open-handed, he gives to the poor;
his justice stands firm for ever.
His head will be raised in glory.

The wicked man sees and is angry,
grinds his teeth and fades away;
the desire of the wicked leads to doom.

## Psalm-prayer

Lord God, you are the eternal light which illumines the hearts of good people. Help us to love you, to rejoice in your glory, and so to live in this world as to avoid harsh judgment in the next. May we come to see the light of your countenance.

Ant. 3 **Praise God, all you who serve him, both great and small, alleluia.**

Advent: Ever wider will his kingdom spread, eternally at peace, alleluia.

Easter, 4th Sunday: Alleluia, salvation, glory and power to our God, alleluia.

The following canticle is said with the **Alleluia** when Evening Prayer is sung; when the office is recited, the **Alleluia** may be said at the beginning and end of each strophe.

Canticle                              See Revelation 19:1-7

### The wedding of the Lamb

Alleluia.
Salvation, glory, and power to our God:
(R̷. Alleluia.)
his judgments are honest and true.
R̷. Alleluia (alleluia).

Alleluia.
Sing praise to our God, all you his servants,
(R̷. Alleluia.)
all who worship him reverently, great and small.
R̷. Alleluia (alleluia).

Alleluia.
The Lord our all-powerful God is King;
(R̷. Alleluia.)
let us rejoice, sing praise, and give him glory.
R̷. Alleluia (alleluia).

Alleluia.
The wedding feast of the Lamb has begun,
(R̷. Alleluia.)
and his bride is prepared to welcome him.
R̷. Alleluia (alleluia).

## Lent

Lent, 4th Sunday: Those things, which God foretold through his prophets concerning the sufferings that Christ would endure, have been fulfilled.

### Canticle                    1 Peter 2:21-24

The willing acceptance of his passion by Christ, the servant of God

Christ suffered for you,
and left you an example
to have you follow in his footsteps.

He did no wrong;
no deceit was found in his mouth.
When he was insulted,
he returned no insult.

When he was made to suffer,
he did not counter with threats.
Instead he delivered himself up
to the One who judges justly.

In his own body
he brought your sins to the cross,
so that all of us, dead to sin,
could live in accord with God's will.

By his wounds you were healed.

---

READING                           Hebrews 12:22-24

You have approached Mount Zion and the city of the living God, the heavenly Jerusalem, and countless angels in festal gathering, and the assembly of the firstborn enrolled in heaven, and God the judge of all, and the spirits of the just made perfect, and Jesus, the mediator of a new covenant, and the sprinkled blood that speaks more eloquently than that of Abel.

RESPONSORY

Our Lord is great, mighty is his power.
— Our Lord is great, mighty is his power.

His wisdom is beyond compare,
— mighty is his power.

Glory to the Father . . .
— Our Lord is . . .

CANTICLE OF MARY, antiphon as in the Proper of Seasons.

INTERCESSIONS

Rejoicing in the Lord, from whom all good things come, let us pray:
*Lord, hear our prayer.*
Father and Lord of all, you sent your Son into the world, that your name might be glorified in every place,
— strengthen the witness of your Church among the nations.
Make us obedient to the teachings of your apostles,
— and bound to the truth of our faith.
As you love the innocent,
— render justice to those who are wronged.
Free those in bondage and give sight to the blind,
— raise up the fallen and protect the stranger.
Fulfill your promise to those who already sleep in your peace,
— through your Son grant them a blessed resurrection.

Our Father . . .

Concluding prayer, as in the Proper of Seasons.

Conclusion, as in the Ordinary, 29.

## MONDAY, WEEK IV

### Invitatory

Lord, open my lips.

Ant. Come, let us sing joyful songs to the Lord.

Invitatory psalm, 22.

### Morning Prayer

The following verse and response are omitted when the hour begins with the invitatory.

God, come to my assistance. Glory to the Father. As it was in the beginning. Alleluia.

HYMN, no. 11 or 10. Outside Ordinary Time, see Guide, 578.

PSALMODY

Ant. 1 Each morning, Lord, you fill us with your kindness.

December 17-23: The Lord, the ruler over the kings of the earth, will come; blessed are they who are ready to go and welcome him.

Easter: Let the splendor of the Lord our God be upon us, alleluia.

### Psalm 90

May we live in the radiance of God

*There is no time with God: a thousand years, a single day: it is all one* (2 Peter 3:8).

O Lord, you have been our refuge
from one generation to the next.
Before the mountains were born
or the earth or the world brought forth,
you are God, without beginning or end.

You turn men back to dust
and say: "Go back, sons of men."
To your eyes a thousand years
are like yesterday, come and gone,
no more than a watch in the night.

You sweep men away like a dream,
like grass which springs up in the morning.
In the morning it springs up and flowers:
by evening it withers and fades.

So we are destroyed in your anger,
struck with terror in your fury.
Our guilt lies open before you;
our secrets in the light of your face.

All our days pass away in your anger.
Our life is over like a sigh.
Our span is seventy years
or eighty for those who are strong.

And most of these are emptiness and pain.
They pass swiftly and we are gone.
Who understands the power of your anger
and fears the strength of your fury?

Make us know the shortness of our life
that we may gain wisdom of heart.
Lord, relent! Is your anger for ever?
Show pity to your servants.

In the morning, fill us with your love;
we shall exult and rejoice all our days.
Give us joy to balance our affliction
for the years when we knew misfortune.

Show forth your work to your servants;
let your glory shine on their children.
Let the favor of the Lord be upon us:
give success to the work of our hands,
give success to the work of our hands.

Psalm-prayer

Eternal Father, you give us life despite our guilt
and even add days and years to our lives in order to
bring us wisdom. Make us love and obey you, so
that the works of our hands may always display

what your hands have done, until the day we gaze
upon the beauty of your face.

Ant. 2  **From the farthest bounds of earth, may God
be praised!**

December 17-23: Sing a new song to the Lord, proclaim his
praises to the ends of the earth.

Easter: I will turn darkness into light before them, alleluia.

Canticle        Isaiah 42:10-16

God victor and savior

*They were singing a new hymn before the throne
of God* (Revelation 14:3).

Sing to the Lord a new song,
his praise from the end of the earth:

Let the sea and what fills it resound,
the coastlands, and those who dwell in them.
Let the steppe and its cities cry out,
the villages where Kedar dwells;

let the inhabitants of Sela exult,
and shout from the top of the mountains.
Let them give glory to the Lord,
and utter his praise in the coastlands.

The Lord goes forth like a hero,
like a warrior he stirs up his ardor;
he shouts out his battle cry,
against his enemies he shows his might:

I have looked away, and kept silence,
I have said nothing, holding myself in;
but now, I cry out as a woman in labor,
gasping and panting.

I will lay waste mountains and hills,
all their herbage I will dry up;
I will turn the rivers into marshes,
and the marshes I will dry up.

I will lead the blind on their journey;
   by paths unknown I will guide them.
I will turn darkness into light before them,
   and make crooked ways straight.

Ant. 3  You who stand in his sanctuary, praise the
          name of the Lord.

December 17-23: When the Son of Man comes to earth,
   do you think he will find faith in men's hearts?

Easter: The Lord does whatever he wills, alleluia.

Psalm 135:1-12

Praise for the wonderful things God does for us

*He has won you for himself . . . and you must pro-*
*claim what he has done for you: he has called you*
*out of darkness into his own wonderful light* (1
Peter 2:9).

Praise the name of the Lord,
   praise him, servants of the Lord,
who stand in the house of the Lord,
   in the courts of the house of our God.

Praise the Lord for the Lord is good.
   Sing a psalm to his name for he is loving.
For the Lord has chosen Jacob for himself
   and Israel for his own possession.

For I know the Lord is great,
   that our Lord is high above all gods.
The Lord does whatever he wills,
   in heaven, on earth, in the seas.

He summons clouds from the ends of the earth;
   makes lightning produce the rain;
from his treasuries he sends forth the wind.

The first-born of the Egyptians he smote,
   of man and beast alike.
Signs and wonders he worked
   in the midst of your land, O Egypt,
against Pharaoh and all his servants.

Nations in their greatness he struck
and kings in their splendor he slew.
Sihon, king of the Amorites,
Og, the king of Bashan,
and all the kingdoms of Canaan.
He let Israel inherit their land;
on his people their land he bestowed.

Psalm-prayer

Father, your name and your memory last for ever.
We stand to pray in your house and praise you with
psalms of joy. We ask you in your kindness to have
mercy on us in our lowliness.

READING                                   Judith 8:25-27

We should be grateful to the Lord our God, for
putting us to the test, as he did our forefathers. Recall how he dealt with Abraham, and how he tried
Isaac, and all that happened to Jacob in Syrian Meso-
potamia while he was tending the flocks of Laban, his
mother's brother. Not for vengeance did the Lord put
them in the crucible to try their hearts, nor has he
done so with us. It is by way of admonition that he
chastises those who are close to him.

RESPONSORY

Sing for joy, God's chosen ones, give him the praise
    that is due.
— Sing for joy, God's chosen ones, give him the
    praise that is due.

Sing a new song to the Lord;
— give him the praise that is due.

Glory to the Father . . .
— Sing for joy . . .

CANTICLE OF ZECHARIAH

Ant. Blessed be the Lord, for he has come to his
    people and set them free.

INTERCESSIONS

Because Christ hears and saves those who hope in
   him, let us pray:
   *We praise you, Lord, we hope in you.*
We thank you because you are rich in mercy,
— and for the abundant love with which you have
   loved us.
With the Father you are always at work in the world,
— make all things new through the power of your
   Holy Spirit.
Open our eyes and the eyes of our brothers,
— to see your wonders this day.
You call us today to your service,
— make us stewards of your many gifts.

Our Father . . .

CONCLUDING PRAYER

God our creator,
you gave us the earth to cultivate
and the sun to serve our needs.
Help us to spend this day
for your glory and our neighbor's good.

We ask this through our Lord Jesus Christ, your Son,
who lives and reigns with you and the Holy Spirit,
one God, for ever and ever.

Conclusion, as in the Ordinary, 29.

### Evening Prayer

God, come to my assistance. Glory to the Father.
As it was in the beginning. Alleluia.

HYMN, no. 41 or 35. Outside Ordinary Time, see
Guide, 578.

PSALMODY

Ant. 1  Give thanks to the Lord, for his great love is
            without end.

December 17-23: The Lord, the ruler over the kings of the earth, will come; blessed are they who are ready to go and welcome him.

Easter: Whoever is in Christ is a new creature, alleluia.

## Psalm 136

### Easter hymn

*We praise God by recalling his marvelous deeds* (Cas-siodorus).

### I

O give thanks to the Lord for he is good,
for his love endures for ever.
Give thanks to the God of gods,
for his love endures for ever.
Give thanks to the Lord of lords,
for his love endures for ever;

who alone has wrought marvellous works,
for his love endures for ever;
whose wisdom it was made the skies,
for his love endures for ever;
who fixed the earth firmly on the seas,
for his love endures for ever.

It was he who made the great lights,
for his love endures for ever,
the sun to rule in the day,
for his love endures for ever,
the moon and stars in the night,
for his love endures for ever.

Ant. 2 **Great and wonderful are your deeds, Lord God the Almighty.**

December 17-23: Sing a new song to the Lord, proclaim his praises to the ends of the earth.

Easter: Let us love God, for he has first loved us, alleluia.

## II

The first-born of the Egyptians he smote,
for his love endures for ever.
He brought Israel out from their midst,
for his love endures for ever;
arm outstretched, with power in his hand,
for his love endures for ever.

He divided the Red Sea in two,
for his love endures for ever;
he made Israel pass through the midst,
for his love endures for ever;
he flung Pharaoh and his force in the sea,
for his love endures for ever.

Through the desert his people he led,
for his love endures for ever.
Nations in their greatness he struck,
for his love endures for ever.
Kings in their splendor he slew,
for his love endures for ever.

Sihon, king of the Amorites,
for his love endures for ever;
and Og, the king of Bashan,
for his love endures for ever.

He let Israel inherit their land,
for his love endures for ever.
On his servant their land he bestowed,
for his love endures for ever.
He remembered us in our distress,
for his love endures for ever.

And he snatched us away from our foes,
for his love endures for ever.
He gives food to all living things,
for his love endures for ever.
To the God of heaven give thanks,
for his love endures for ever.

**Psalm-prayer**

Almighty God, remember our lowliness and have mercy. Once you gave our fathers a foreign land to inherit. Free us today from sin and give us a share in your inheritance.

Ant. 3 God planned in the fullness of time to restore all things in Christ.

December 17-23: When the Son of Man comes to earth, do you think he will find faith in men's hearts?

Easter: From his fullness we have all received, grace upon grace, alleluia.

Canticle        Ephesians 1:3-10

God our Savior

Praised be the God and Father
of our Lord Jesus Christ,
who has bestowed on us in Christ
every spiritual blessing in the heavens.

God chose us in him
before the world began
to be holy
and blameless in his sight.

He predestined us
to be his adopted sons through Jesus Christ,
such was his will and pleasure,
that all might praise the glorious favor
he has bestowed on us in his beloved.

In him and through his blood, we have been redeemed,
and our sins forgiven,
so immeasurably generous
is God's favor to us.

God has given us the wisdom
to understand fully the mystery,
the plan he was pleased
to decree in Christ.

A plan to be carried out
in Christ, in the fullness of time,
to bring all things into one in him,
in the heavens and on earth.

READING                    1 Thessalonians 3:12-13

And may the Lord make you increase and abound
in love for one another and for all, just as we have for
you, so as to strengthen your hearts, to be blameless
in holiness before our God and Father at the coming
of our Lord Jesus with all his holy ones.

RESPONSORY

Accept my prayer, O Lord, which rises up to you.
— Accept my prayer, O Lord, which rises up to you.

Like burning incense in your sight,
— which rises up to you.

Glory to the Father . . .
— Accept my prayer . . .

CANTICLE OF MARY

Ant. For ever will my soul proclaim the greatness
of the Lord.

INTERCESSIONS

Jesus does not abandon those who hope in him;
therefore, let us humbly ask him:
*Our Lord and our God, hear us.*
Christ our light, brighten your Church with your
splendor,
— so that it may be for the nations the great sacrament of your love.
Watch over the priests and ministers of your Church,
— so that after they have preached to others, they
themselves may remain faithful in your service.
Through your blood you gave peace to the world,
— turn away the sin of strife, the scourge of war.

O Lord, help married couples with an abundance of
  your grace,
— so that they may better symbolize the mystery of
  your Church.
In your mercy forgive the sins of all the dead,
— that they may live with your saints.

Our Father . . .

CONCLUDING PRAYER

Stay with us, Lord Jesus,
for evening draws near,
and be our companion on our way
to set our hearts on fire with new hope.
Help us to recognize your presence among us
in the Scriptures we read,
and in the breaking of bread.

You live and reign with the Father and the Holy Spirit,
one God, for ever and ever.

Conclusion, as in the Ordinary, 29.

# TUESDAY, WEEK IV

## Invitatory

Lord, open my lips.

Ant. Come, let us worship the Lord, our mighty God.

Invitatory psalm, 22.

## Morning Prayer

The following verse and response are omitted when
the hour begins with the invitatory.

God, come to my assistance. Glory to the Father. As it
was in the beginning. Alleluia.

HYMN, no. 13 or 20. Outside Ordinary Time, see
Guide, 578.

PSALMODY

Ant. 1 I will sing to you, O Lord; I will learn from
        you the way of perfection.

December 17-23: The Lord will come from his holy place to save his people.

Easter: Whoever does the will of my Father will enter the kingdom of heaven, alleluia.

## Psalm 101

### Avowal of a good ruler

*If you love me, keep my commandments* (John 14:15).

My song is of mercy and justice;
I sing to you, O Lord.
I will walk in the way of perfection.
O when, Lord, will you come?

I will walk with blameless heart
within my house;
I will not set before my eyes
whatever is base.

I will hate the ways of the crooked;
they shall not be my friends.
The false-hearted must keep far away;
the wicked I disown.

The man who slanders his neighbor in secret
I will bring to silence.
The man of proud looks and haughty heart
I will never endure.

I look to the faithful in the land
that they may dwell with me.
He who walks in the way of perfection
shall be my friend.

No man who practices deceit
shall live within my house.
No man who utters lies shall stand
before my eyes.

Morning by morning I will silence
all the wicked in the land, —

uprooting from the city of the Lord
all who do evil.

## Psalm-prayer

So that your people may walk in innocence, you
came to us, Lord Jesus, and told us to be holy as
your Father is holy. Help your children to love what
is truly perfect, so that we may neither speak what is
evil nor do what is wrong. Let us stand in your sight
and celebrate with you the Father's love and justice.

Ant. 2 Lord, do not withhold your compassion
from us.

December 17-23: Zion is our mighty citadel, our saving
Lord its wall and its defense; throw open the gates, for
our God is here among us, alleluia.

Easter: Let all the nations, O Lord, know the depths of
your loving mercy for us, alleluia.

Canticle                          Daniel 3:26, 27, 29, 34-41

Azariah's prayer in the furnace

*With your whole hearts turn to God and he will
blot out all your sins* (Acts 3:19).

Blessed are you, and praiseworthy,
O Lord, the God of our fathers,
and glorious forever is your name.

For you are just in all you have done;
all your deeds are faultless, all your ways right,
and all your judgments proper.

For we have sinned and transgressed
by departing from you,
and we have done every kind of evil.

For your name's sake, do not deliver us up forever,
or make void your covenant.

Do not take away your mercy from us,
for the sake of Abraham, your beloved,
Isaac your servant, and Israel your holy one,

to whom you promised to multiply their offspring
like the stars of heaven,
or the sand on the shore of the sea.

For we are reduced, O Lord, beyond any other
    nation,
brought low everywhere in the world this day
because of our sins.

We have in our day no prince, prophet, or leader,
no holocaust, sacrifice, oblation, or incense,
no place to offer first fruits, to find favor with
    you.

But with contrite heart and humble spirit
let us be received;
as though it were holocausts of rams and bul-
    locks,
or thousands of fat lambs,
so let our sacrifice be in your presence today
as we follow you unreservedly;
for those who trust in you cannot be put to
    shame.

And now we follow you with our whole heart,
we fear you and we pray to you.

Ant. 3  O God, I will sing to you a new song.

December 17-23: Lord, make known your will throughout the earth; proclaim your salvation to every nation.

Easter: The Lord is my refuge and my savior, alleluia.

Psalm 144: 1-10
Prayer for victory and peace

*I can do all things in him who strengthens me*
(Philippians 4:13).

Blessed be the Lord, my rock,
who trains my arms for battle,
who prepares my hands for war.

He is my love, my fortress;
he is my stronghold, my savior,
my shield, my place of refuge.
He brings peoples under my rule.

Lord, what is man that you care for him,
mortal man, that you keep him in mind;
man, who is merely a breath,
whose life fades like a passing shadow?

Lower your heavens and come down;
touch the mountains; wreathe them in smoke.
Flash your lightnings; rout the foe,
shoot your arrows and put them to flight.

Reach down from heaven and save me;
draw me out from the mighty waters,
from the hands of alien foes
whose mouths are filled with lies,
whose hands are raised in perjury.

To you, O God, will I sing a new song;
I will play on the ten-stringed harp
to you who give kings their victory,
who set David your servant free.

## Psalm-prayer

Lord, God of strength, you gave your Son victory
over death. Direct your Church's fight against evil
in the world. Clothe us with the weapons of light
and unite us under the one banner of love, that we
may receive our eternal reward after the battle of
earthly life.

READING                                    Isaiah 55:1-3

All you who are thirsty,
    come to the water!
You who have no money,
    come, receive grain and eat;

Come, without paying and without cost,
  drink wine and milk!
Why spend your money for what is not bread;
  your wages for what fails to satisfy?
Heed me, and you shall eat well,
  you shall delight in rich fare.
Come to me heedfully,
  listen, that you may have life.
I will renew with you the everlasting covenant,
  the benefits assured to David.

RESPONSORY

Lord, listen to my cry; all my trust is in your promise.
— Lord, listen to my cry; all my trust is in your promise.

Dawn finds me watching, crying out for you.
— All my trust is in your promise.

Glory to the Father . . .
— Lord, listen to . . .

CANTICLE OF ZECHARIAH

Ant. Lord, save us from the hands of all who hate us.

INTERCESSIONS

To the God who gives us the joy of praising him this morning, and who strengthens our hope, let us pray:
  *Hear us, O Lord, for the glory of your name.*
We thank you, God and Father of Jesus our Savior,
— for the knowledge and immortality you have given us through him.
Make us humble of heart,
— help us to serve one another out of reverence for Christ.
Pour out your Spirit on us, your servants,
— make us sincere in our love for each other.
You instructed man to labor and to exercise dominion over the earth,

— may our work honor you and sanctify our brothers and sisters.

Our Father . . .

CONCLUDING PRAYER

Increase in us, Lord, the faith you have given us,
and bring to a harvest worthy of heaven
the praise we offer you at the beginning of this new
    day.

We ask this through our Lord Jesus Christ, your Son,
who lives and reigns with you and the Holy Spirit,
one God, for ever and ever.

Conclusion, as in the Ordinary, 29.

## Evening Prayer

God, come to my assistance. Glory to the Father.
As it was in the beginning. Alleluia.

HYMN, no. **42** or **47**. Outside Ordinary Time, see
Guide, 578.

PSALMODY

Ant. 1  **If I forget you, Jerusalem, let my right hand
          wither.**

  December 17-23: The Lord will come from his holy place
    to save his people.

  Easter: Sing for us one of Zion's songs, alleluia.

Psalm 137:1-6

By the rivers of Babylon

*The Babylonian captivity is a type of our spiritual
captivity* (Saint Hilary).

  By the rivers of Babylon
    there we sat and wept,
    remembering Zion;
  on the poplars that grew there
    we hung up our harps.

For it was there that they asked us,
our captors, for songs,
our oppressors, for joy.
"Sing to us," they said,
"one of Zion's songs."

O how could we sing
the song of the Lord
on alien soil?
If I forget you, Jerusalem,
let my right hand wither!

O let my tongue
cleave to my mouth
if I remember you not,
if I prize not Jerusalem
above all my joys!

Psalm-prayer

Lord, remember your pilgrim Church. We sit
weeping at the streams of Babylon. Do not let us be
drawn into the current of the passing world, but
free us from every evil and raise our thoughts to
the heavenly Jerusalem.

Ant. 2  In the presence of the angels I will sing to
you, my God.

December 17-23: Zion is our mighty citadel, our saving
Lord its wall and its defense; throw open the gates, for
our God is here among us, alleluia.

Easter: Though I am surrounded by affliction, you preserve my life, alleluia.

Psalm 138

Thanksgiving

*The kings of the earth will bring his glory and
honor into the holy city* (see Revelation 21:24).

I thank you, Lord, with all my heart,
you have heard the words of my mouth.—

In the presence of the angels I will bless you.
I will adore before your holy temple.

I thank you for your faithfulness and love
which excel all we ever knew of you.
On the day I called, you answered;
you increased the strength of my soul.

All earth's kings shall thank you
when they hear the words of your mouth.
They shall sing of the Lord's ways:
"How great is the glory of the Lord!"

The Lord is high yet he looks on the lowly
and the haughty he knows from afar.
Though I walk in the midst of affliction
you give me life and frustrate my foes.

You stretch out your hand and save me,
your hand will do all things for me.
Your love, O Lord, is eternal,
discard not the work of your hands.

Psalm-prayer

Listen to the prayers of your Church, Lord God;
in the presence of the angels we praise your name.
You keep the proud at a distance and look upon the
lowly with favor. Stretch out your hand to us in our
suffering, perfect in us the work of your love and
bring us to life.

Ant. 3 Adoration and glory belong by right to the
Lamb who was slain.

December 17-23: Lord, make known your will throughout the earth; proclaim your salvation to every nation.

Easter: Yours, O Lord, is majesty and power, glory and
triumph, alleluia.

Canticle                    Revelation 4:11; 5:9, 10, 12

### Redemption hymn

O Lord our God, you are worthy
to receive glory and honor and power.

For you have created all things;
by your will they came to be and were made.

Worthy are you, O Lord,
to receive the scroll and break open its seals.

For you were slain;
with your blood you purchased for God
men of every race and tongue,
of every people and nation.

You made of them a kingdom,
and priests to serve our God,
and they shall reign on the earth.

Worthy is the Lamb that was slain
to receive power and riches,
wisdom and strength,
honor and glory and praise.

READING                                Colossians 3:15-17

Let the peace of Christ control your hearts, the peace into which you were also called in one body. And be thankful. Let the word of Christ dwell in you richly, as in all wisdom you teach and admonish one another, singing psalms, hymns, and spiritual songs with gratitude in your hearts to God. And whatever you do, in word or in deed, do everything in the name of the Lord Jesus, giving thanks to God the Father through him.

RESPONSORY

I shall know the fullness of joy,
    when I see your face, O Lord.
— I shall know the fullness of joy,
    when I see your face, O Lord.

Fulfillment and endless peace in your presence,
— when I see your face, O Lord.

Glory to the Father . . .
— I shall know . . .

CANTICLE OF MARY

Ant. Do great things for us, O Lord, for you are
mighty, and holy is your name.

INTERCESSIONS

Let us praise Christ who gives power and strength to
his people, and let us entreat him with sincere
hearts:
*Hear us, O Lord, and we shall praise you for ever.*
Christ, our strength, you called your faithful ones to
your truth,
— mercifully grant them faith and perseverance.
Direct our leaders according to your will,
— and help them to keep us in peace.
You provided bread for the hungry crowd,
— teach us to share our resources with the needy.
Do not direct world leaders to give attention only to
the needs of their own nations,
— but give them, above all, a respect and a deep concern for all peoples.
Grant blessed life and resurrection to our brothers
and sisters who have fallen asleep,
— and may all those who have believed in you share
in your glory.

Our Father . . .

CONCLUDING PRAYER

Lord,
may our evening prayer come before you
and let the faith our lips profess
live in the prayerful thoughts of our hearts.

We ask this through our Lord Jesus Christ, your Son,
who lives and reigns with you and the Holy Spirit,
one God, for ever and ever.

Conclusion, as in the Ordinary, 29.

# WEDNESDAY, WEEK IV

## Invitatory

Lord, open my lips.

Ant. Cry out with joy to the Lord, all the earth,
serve the Lord with gladness.

Invitatory psalm, 22.

## Morning Prayer

The following verse and response are omitted
when the hour begins with the invitatory.

God, come to my assistance. Glory to the Father.
As it was in the beginning. Alleluia.

HYMN, no. 14 or 20. Outside Ordinary Time, see
Guide, 578.

PSALMODY

Ant. 1  My heart is ready, O God, my heart is ready.

December 17-23: The Lord, the mighty God, will come
forth from Zion to set his people free.

Easter: O God, arise above the heavens, alleluia.

### Psalm 108

Praise of God and a plea for help

*Since the Son of God has been exalted above the*
*heavens, his glory is proclaimed through all the*
*earth* (Arnobius).

My heart is ready, O God;
I will sing, sing your praise.
Awake, my soul;
awake, lyre and harp.
I will awake the dawn.

I will thank you, Lord, among the peoples,
among the nations I will praise you,
for your love reaches to the heavens
and your truth to the skies. —

O God, arise above the heavens;
may your glory shine on earth!

O come and deliver your friends;
help with your right hand and reply.
From his holy place God has made this promise:
"I will triumph and divide the land of Shechem;
I will measure out the valley of Succoth.

Gilead is mine and Manasseh.
Ephraim I take for my helmet,
Judah for my commander's staff.
Moab I will use for my washbowl,
on Edom I will plant my shoe.
Over the Philistines I will shout in triumph."

But who will lead me to conquer the fortress?
Who will bring me face to face with Edom?
Will you utterly reject us, O God,
and no longer march with our armies?

Give us help against the foe:
for the help of man is vain.
With God we shall do bravely
and he will trample down our foes.

Psalm-prayer

Accept the prayers of your servants, Lord, and
prepare our hearts to praise your holy name. Come
to our aid in times of trouble, and make us worthy
to sing you songs of thanksgiving.

Ant. 2  The Lord has robed me with grace and salvation.

December 17-23: I shall not cease to plead with God for
Zion until he sends his Holy One in all his radiant
beauty.

Easter: The Lord will make praise and justice blossom
before all the nations, alleluia.

Canticle     Isaiah 61:10—62:5

The prophet's joy in the vision of a new Jerusalem

*I saw the holy city, new Jerusalem, with the beauty
of a bride adorned for her husband* (Revelation 21:2).

I rejoice heartily in the Lord,
in my God is the joy of my soul;
for he has clothed me with a robe of salvation,
and wrapped me in a mantle of justice,
like a bridegroom adorned with a diadem,
like a bride bedecked with her jewels.

As the earth brings forth its plants,
and a garden makes its growth spring up,
so will the Lord God make justice and praise
spring up before all the nations.

For Zion's sake I will not be silent,
for Jerusalem's sake I will not be quiet,
until her vindication shines forth like the dawn
and her victory like a burning torch.

Nations shall behold your vindication,
and all kings your glory;
you shall be called by a new name
pronounced by the mouth of the Lord.
You shall be a glorious crown in the hand of
    the Lord,
a royal diadem held by your God.

No more shall men call you "Forsaken,"
or your land "Desolate,"
but you shall be called "My delight,"
and your land "Espoused."
For the Lord delights in you,
and makes your land his spouse.

As a young man marries a virgin,
your Builder shall marry you;
and as a bridegroom rejoices in his bride
so shall your God rejoice in you.

Ant. 3  I will praise my God all the days of my life.

December 17-23: The Spirit of the Lord rests upon me;
he has sent me to preach his joyful message to the
poor.

Easter: Zion, the Lord, your God, will reign for ever, alleluia.

## Psalm 146

Those who trust in God know what it is to be happy

*To praise God in our lives means all we do must be
for his glory* (Arnobius).

My soul, give praise to the Lord;
I will praise the Lord all my days,
make music to my God while I live.

Put no trust in princes,
in mortal men in whom there is no help.
Take their breath, they return to clay
and their plans that day come to nothing.

He is happy who is helped by Jacob's God,
whose hope is in the Lord his God,
who alone made heaven and earth,
the seas and all they contain.

It is he who keeps faith for ever,
who is just to those who are oppressed.
It is he who gives bread to the hungry,
the Lord, who sets prisoners free,

the Lord who gives sight to the blind,
who raises up those who are bowed down,
the Lord, who protects the stranger
and upholds the widow and orphan.

It is the Lord who loves the just
but thwarts the path of the wicked.
The Lord will reign for ever,
Zion's God, from age to age.

Psalm-prayer

God of glory and power, those who have put all
their trust in you are happy indeed. Shine the
brightness of your light on us, that we may love
you always with a pure heart.

READING                          Deuteronomy 4:39-40a

Know, and fix in your heart, that the Lord is God
in the heavens above and on earth below, and that
there is no other. You must keep his statutes and
commandments which I enjoin on you today.

RESPONSORY

I will bless the Lord all my life long.
— I will bless the Lord all my life long.

With a song of praise ever on my lips,
— all my life long.

Glory to the Father . . .
— I will bless . . .

CANTICLE OF ZECHARIAH

Ant. Let us serve the Lord in holiness all the days
of our life.

INTERCESSIONS

Christ, the splendor of the Father's glory, enlightens
us with his word. With deep love we call upon him:
*Hear us, King of eternal glory.*
Blessed are you, the alpha and the omega of our faith,
— for you called us out of darkness into your marvelous light.
You enabled the blind to see, the deaf to hear,
— help our unbelief.
Lord, keep us in your love, preserve our community,
— do not let us become separated from one another.
Give us strength in temptation, endurance in trial,
— and gratitude in prosperity.

Our Father . . .

CONCLUDING PRAYER

Father,
keep in mind your holy covenant,
sealed with the blood of the Lamb.
Forgive the sins of your people
and let this new day bring us closer to salvation.

We ask this through our Lord Jesus Christ, your Son,
who lives and reigns with you and the Holy Spirit,
one God, for ever and ever.

Conclusion, as in the Ordinary, 29.

## Evening Prayer

God, come to my assistance. Glory to the Father.
As it was in the beginning. Alleluia.

HYMN, no. 43 or 44. Outside Ordinary Time, see
Guide, 578.

PSALMODY

Ant. 1  Lord, how wonderful is your wisdom, so far
beyond my understanding.

December 17-23: The Lord, the mighty God, will come
forth from Zion to set his people free.

Easter: The night will be as clear as day, alleluia.

Psalm 139:1-18, 23-24
God sees all that is

*Who has known the mind of God, who has been his
counselor?* (Romans 11:34).

I

O Lord, you search me and you know me,
you know my resting and my rising,
you discern my purpose from afar.
You mark when I walk or lie down,
all my ways lie open to you.

Before ever a word is on my tongue
you know it, O Lord, through and through.
Behind and before you besiege me,
your hand ever laid upon me.
Too wonderful for me, this knowledge,
too high, beyond my reach.

O where can I go from your spirit,
or where can I flee from your face?
If I climb the heavens, you are there.
If I lie in the grave, you are there.

If I take the wings of the dawn
and dwell at the sea's furthest end,
even there your hand would lead me,
your right hand would hold me fast.

If I say: "Let the darkness hide me
and the light around me be night,"
even darkness is not dark for you
and the night is as clear as the day.

Ant. 2  I am the Lord: I search the mind and probe
the heart; I give to each one as his deeds deserve.

December 17-23: I shall not cease to plead with God for
Zion until he sends his Holy One in all his radiant
beauty.

Easter: I know my sheep and mine know me, alleluia.

II

For it was you who created my being,
knit me together in my mother's womb.
I thank you for the wonder of my being,
for the wonders of all your creation.

Already you knew my soul,
my body held no secret from you
when I was being fashioned in secret
and molded in the depths of the earth.

Your eyes saw all my actions,
they were all of them written in your book;
every one of my days was decreed
before one of them came into being.

To me, how mysterious your thoughts,
the sum of them not to be numbered!
If I count them, they are more than the sand;
to finish, I must be eternal, like you.

O search me, God, and know my heart.
O test me and know my thoughts.
See that I follow not the wrong path
and lead me in the path of life eternal.

Psalm-prayer

You watch over heaven and earth, Lord Jesus.
Your death brought light to the dead; your resurrection gave joy to the saints; your ascension made the angels rejoice. Your power exceeds all power. Lead us to life eternal, and watch over us with your love. May your friends be filled with honor and join you in heaven.

Ant. 3 Through him all things were made; he holds all creation together in himself.

December 17-23: The Spirit of the Lord rests upon me; he has sent me to preach his joyful message to the poor.

Easter: His glory covers the heavens and his praise fills the earth, alleluia.

Canticle    Colossians 1:12-20

Christ the first-born of all creation
and the first-born from the dead

Let us give thanks to the Father
for having made you worthy
to share the lot of the saints
in light.

He rescued us
from the power of darkness
and brought us
into the kingdom of his beloved Son.
Through him we have redemption,
the forgiveness of our sins.

He is the image of the invisible God,
the first-born of all creatures.
In him everything in heaven and on earth was
    created,
things visible and invisible.

All were created through him;
all were created for him.
He is before all else that is.
In him everything continues in being.

It is he who is head of the body, the church!
he who is the beginning,
the first-born of the dead,
so that primacy may be his in everything.

It pleased God to make absolute fullness reside
    in him
and, by means of him, to reconcile everything
    in his person,
both on earth and in the heavens,
making peace through the blood of his cross.

READING                                      1 John 2:3-6

The way we may be sure that we know him is to
keep his commandments. Whoever says, "I know
him," but does not keep his commandments is a
liar, and the truth is not in him. But whoever keeps
his word, the love of God is truly perfected in him.
This is the way we may know that we are in union
with him: whoever claims to abide in him ought to
live [just] as he lived.

RESPONSORY

Keep us, O Lord, as the apple of your eye.
— Keep us, O Lord, as the apple of your eye.

Gather us under the shadow of your wings, and keep us,
— as the apple of your eye.

Glory to the Father . . .
— Keep us, O Lord . . .

CANTICLE OF MARY

Ant. Lord, with the strength of your arm scatter the proud and lift up the lowly.

INTERCESSIONS

With joyful hearts, let us praise the Eternal Father whose mercy toward his people is exalted to the heavens:
*Let all who hope in you rejoice, Lord.*
Remember, Lord, that you sent your Son into the world to be its savior, not its judge,
— let his glorious death bring us salvation.
You ordained your priests to be ministers of Christ and stewards of your marvelous gifts,
— fill them with fidelity, wisdom and love.
You have called men and women to chastity for the sake of the kingdom,
— let them faithfully follow your Son.
From the beginning you intended husband and wife to be one,
— keep all families united in sincere love.
You sent Christ Jesus into the world to absolve the sins of men,
— free all the dead from their sins.

Our Father . . .

CONCLUDING PRAYER

God our Father,
you have filled the hungry with the good things of
 heaven.
Keep in mind your infinite compassion.
Look upon our poverty:
and let us share the riches of your life and love.

We ask this through our Lord Jesus Christ, your Son,
who lives and reigns with you and the Holy Spirit,
one God, for ever and ever.

Conclusion, as in the Ordinary, 29.

# THURSDAY, WEEK IV

## Invitatory

Lord, open my lips.

Ant. Come into the Lord's presence singing for joy.

Invitatory psalm, 22.

## Morning Prayer

The following verse and response are omitted
when the hour begins with the invitatory.

God, come to my assistance. Glory to the Father.
As it was in the beginning. Alleluia.

HYMN, no. 15 or 10. Outside Ordinary Time, see
Guide, 578.

PSALMODY

Ant. 1 At daybreak, be merciful to me, O Lord.

December 17-23: To you, O Lord, I lift up my soul; come
 and rescue me, for you are my refuge and my
 strength.

Easter: Be true to your name, O Lord, and preserve my
 life, alleluia.

## Psalm 143:1-11

### Prayer in distress

*A man is not justified by observance of the law but only through faith in Jesus Christ* (Galatians 2:16).

Lord, listen to my prayer:
turn your ear to my appeal.
You are faithful, you are just; give answer.
Do not call your servant to judgment
for no one is just in your sight.

The enemy pursues my soul;
he has crushed my life to the ground;
he has made me dwell in darkness
like the dead, long forgotten.
Therefore my spirit fails;
my heart is numb within me.

I remember the days that are past:
I ponder all your works.
I muse on what your hand has wrought
and to you I stretch out my hands.
Like a parched land my soul thirsts for you.

Lord, make haste and answer;
for my spirit fails within me.
Do not hide your face
lest I become like those in the grave.

In the morning let me know your love
for I put my trust in you.
Make me know the way I should walk:
to you I lift up my soul.

Rescue me, Lord, from my enemies;
I have fled to you for refuge.
Teach me to do your will
for you, O Lord, are my God.
Let your good spirit guide me
in ways that are level and smooth.

For your name's sake, Lord, save my life;
in your justice save my soul from distress.

Psalm-prayer

Lord Jesus, early in the morning of your resurrection, you made your love known and brought the
first light of dawn to those who dwell in darkness.
Your death has opened a path for us. Do not enter
into judgment with your servants; let your Holy
Spirit guide us together into the land of justice.

Ant. 2  The Lord will make a river of peace flow
through Jerusalem.

December 17-23: Bless those, O Lord, who have waited
for your coming; let your prophets be proved true.

Easter: I will see you again and your hearts will rejoice,
alleluia.

Canticle        Isaiah 66:10-14a
Joys of heaven

*The heavenly Jerusalem is a free woman and our*
*mother* (Galatians 4:26).

Rejoice with Jerusalem and be glad because of
her,
all you who love her;
exult, exult with her,
all you who were mourning over her!

Oh, that you may suck fully
of the milk of her comfort,
that you may nurse with delight
at her abundant breasts!

For thus says the Lord:
Lo, I will spread prosperity over her like a river,
and the wealth of the nations like an overflowing torrent.

As nurslings, you shall be carried in her arms,
and fondled in her lap;
as a mother comforts her son,
so will I comfort you;
in Jerusalem you shall find your comfort.

When you see this, your heart shall rejoice,
and your bodies flourish like the grass.

Ant. 3  Let us joyfully praise the Lord our God.

December 17-23: Turn to us, O Lord, make haste to help
your people.

Easter: The Lord rebuilds Jerusalem and heals the bro-
kenhearted, alleluia.

### Psalm 147:1-11

The loving kindness of God who can do all he wills

*You are God: we praise you; you are the Lord: we
acclaim you.*

Praise the Lord for he is good;
sing to our God for he is loving:
to him our praise is due.

The Lord builds up Jerusalem
and brings back Israel's exiles,
he heals the broken-hearted,
he binds up all their wounds.
He fixes the number of the stars;
he calls each one by its name.

Our Lord is great and almighty;
his wisdom can never be measured.
The Lord raises the lowly;
he humbles the wicked to the dust.
O sing to the Lord, giving thanks;
sing psalms to our God with the harp.

He covers the heavens with clouds;
he prepares the rain for the earth,
making mountains sprout with grass —

and with plants to serve man's needs.
He provides the beasts with their food
and young ravens that call upon him.

His delight is not in horses
nor his pleasure in warriors' strength.
The Lord delights in those who revere him,
in those who wait for his love.

Psalm-prayer

God our Father, great builder of the heavenly Jerusalem, you know the number of the stars and call
each of them by name. Heal hearts that are broken,
gather together those who have been scattered, and
enrich us all from the plenitude of your eternal wisdom.

READING                                    Romans 8:18-21

The sufferings of this present time are as nothing
compared with the glory to be revealed for us. For
creation awaits with eager expectation the revelation
of the children of God; for creation was made subject
to futility, not of its own accord but because of the
one who subjected it, in hope that creation itself
would be set free from slavery to corruption and
share in the glorious freedom of the children of God.

RESPONSORY

In the early hours of the morning, I think of you, O
    Lord.
— In the early hours of the morning, I think of you,
    O Lord.
Always you are there to help me,
— I think of you, O Lord.
Glory to the Father . . .
— In the early . . .

CANTICLE OF ZECHARIAH

Ant.  Give your people knowledge of salvation, Lord,
      and forgive us our sins.

INTERCESSIONS

Let us pray to God, who gives salvation to his people:
*You are our life, O Lord.*

Blessed are you, Father of our Lord Jesus Christ, for
by your mercy we have been reborn to a living hope,
— through the resurrection of Jesus Christ from the
dead.

You made man in your image and renewed him in
Christ,
— mold us into the likeness of your Son.

Pour out your love through the Holy Spirit,
— heal our hearts, wounded by hatred and jealousy.

Today grant work to laborers, bread to the hungry, joy
to the sorrowful,
— grace and redemption to all men.

Our Father . . .

CONCLUDING PRAYER

Lord,
let the knowledge of salvation
enlighten our hearts,
so that, freed from fear and from the power of our enemies,
we may serve you faithfully all the days of our life.

We ask this through our Lord Jesus Christ, your Son,
who lives and reigns with you and the Holy Spirit,
one God, for ever and ever.

Conclusion, as in the Ordinary, 29.

## Evening Prayer

God, come to my assistance. Glory to the Father.
As it was in the beginning. Alleluia.

HYMN, no. **45** or 33. Outside Ordinary Time, see
Guide, 578.

PSALMODY

Ant. 1 He is my comfort and my refuge. In him I
put my trust.

December 17-23: To you, O Lord, I lift up my soul; come
and rescue me, for you are my refuge and my strength.

Easter: The Lord is my stronghold and my savior, alleluia.

## Psalm 144

### Prayer for victory and peace

*Christ learned the art of warfare when he over-*
*came the world, as he said: "I have overcome the*
*world"* (Saint Hilary).

### I

Blessed be the Lord, my rock
who trains my arms for battle,
who prepares my hands for war.

He is my love, my fortress;
he is my stronghold, my savior,
my shield, my place of refuge.
He brings peoples under my rule.

Lord, what is man that you care for him,
mortal man, that you keep him in mind;
man, who is merely a breath,
whose life fades like a shadow?

Lower your heavens and come down;
touch the mountains; wreathe them in smoke.
Flash your lightnings; rout the foe,
shoot your arrows and put them to flight.

Reach down from heaven and save me;
draw me out from the mighty waters,
from the hands of alien foes
whose mouths are filled with lies,
whose hands are raised in perjury.

Ant. 2 Blessed are the people whose God is the
Lord.

December 17-23: Bless those, O Lord, who have waited
for your coming; let your prophets be proved true.

Easter: Thanks be to God who has given us the victory
through our Lord Jesus Christ, alleluia.

## II

To you, O God, will I sing a new song;
I will play on the ten-stringed harp
to you who give kings their victory,
who set David your servant free.

You set him free from the evil sword;
you rescued him from alien foes
whose mouths were filled with lies,
whose hands were raised in perjury.

Let our sons then flourish like saplings
grown tall and strong from their youth:
our daughters graceful as columns,
adorned as though for a palace.

Let our barns be filled to overflowing
with crops of every kind;
our sheep increasing by thousands,
myriads of sheep in our fields,
our cattle heavy with young,

no ruined wall, no exile,
no sound of weeping in our streets.
Happy the people with such blessings;
happy the people whose God is the Lord.

Psalm-prayer

Lord, God of strength, you gave your Son victory
over death. Direct your Church's fight against evil in
the world. Clothe us with the weapons of light and
unite us under the one banner of love, that we may receive our eternal reward after the battle of earthly life.

Ant. 3 Now the victorious reign of our God has
       begun.

December 17-23: Turn to us, O Lord, make haste to help
    your people.

Easter: Christ yesterday and today: he is the same for
    ever, alleluia.

Canticle                    Revelation 11:17-18; 12:10b-12a

### The judgment of God

We praise you, the Lord God Almighty,
who is and who was.
You have assumed your great power,
you have begun your reign.

The nations have raged in anger,
but then came your day of wrath
and the moment to judge the dead:
the time to reward your servants the prophets
and the holy ones who revere you,
the great and the small alike.

Now have salvation and power come,
the reign of our God and the authority
of his Anointed One.
For the accuser of our brothers is cast out,
who night and day accused them before God.

They defeated him by the blood of the Lamb
and by the word of their testimony;
love for life did not deter them from death.
So rejoice, you heavens,
and you that dwell therein!

READING                     See Colossians 1:21-23

You who once were alienated and hostile in mind
because of evil deeds he has now reconciled in his
fleshly body through his death, to present you holy,
without blemish, and irreproachable before him,
provided that you persevere in the faith, firmly
grounded, stable, and not shifting from the hope of
the gospel that you heard, which has been preached
to every creature under heaven.

RESPONSORY

The Lord is my shepherd, I shall want for nothing.
— The Lord is my shepherd, I shall want for nothing.

He has brought me to green pastures.
— I shall want for nothing.

Glory to the Father . . .
— The Lord is . . .

CANTICLE OF MARY

Ant. If you hunger for holiness, God will satisfy
your longing, good measure, and flowing over.

INTERCESSIONS

Let us pray to Christ, the light of the nations and
the joy of every living creature:
*Give us light, peace and security, Lord.*
Brilliant Light, Word of the Father, you came to
save all men,
— lead the catechumens of your Church into your
marvelous light.
Overlook our sins, Lord,
— for you are the source of forgiveness.
Lord, it is your will that men use their minds to un-
lock nature's secrets and master the world,
— may the arts and sciences advance your glory
and the happiness of all peoples.
Look kindly on those who have dedicated themselves to the service of their fellow men,
— may they fulfill their work freely and completely.
Lord, you open the way and no one can close it,
— lead into your light those who have fallen asleep
in the hope of resurrection.

Our Father . . .

CONCLUDING PRAYER

Lord,
hear the evening prayers we bring before you:
help us to follow in the footsteps of your Son
so that we may produce an abundant harvest of
goodness
in patience and in faith.

We ask this through our Lord Jesus Christ, your Son, who lives and reigns with you and the Holy Spirit, one God, for ever and ever.

Conclusion, as in the Ordinary, 29.

## FRIDAY, WEEK IV
### Invitatory

Lord, open my lips.

Ant. Come, let us praise the Lord; in him is all our delight.

Invitatory psalm, 22.

### Morning Prayer

The following verse and response are omitted when the hour begins with the invitatory.

God, come to my assistance. Glory to the Father. As it was in the beginning. Alleluia.

HYMN, no. 16 or 151. Outside Ordinary Time, see Guide, 578.

PSALMODY

Ant. 1 Create a clean heart in me, O God; renew in me a steadfast spirit.

December 17-23: Our King will come from Zion; the Lord, God-is-with-us, is his mighty name.

Easter: Christ gave himself up for us as a sacrificial offering to God, alleluia.

### Psalm 51

O God, have mercy on me

*Your inmost being must be renewed, and you must put on the new man* (Ephesians 4:23-24).

Have mercy on me, God, in your kindness.
In your compassion blot out my offense. —

O wash me more and more from my guilt
and cleanse me from my sin.

My offenses truly I know them;
my sin is always before me.
Against you, you alone, have I sinned;
what is evil in your sight I have done.

That you may be justified when you give sentence
and be without reproach when you judge.
O see, in guilt I was born,
a sinner was I conceived.

Indeed you love truth in the heart;
then in the secret of my heart teach me wisdom.
O purify me, then I shall be clean;
O wash me, I shall be whiter than snow.

Make me hear rejoicing and gladness,
that the bones you have crushed may revive.
From my sins turn away your face
and blot out all my guilt.

A pure heart create for me, O God,
put a steadfast spirit within me.
Do not cast me away from your presence,
nor deprive me of your holy spirit.

Give me again the joy of your help;
with a spirit of fervor sustain me,
that I may teach transgressors your ways
and sinners may return to you.

O rescue me, God, my helper,
and my tongue shall ring out your goodness.
O Lord, open my lips
and my mouth shall declare your praise.

For in sacrifice you take no delight,
burnt offering from me you would refuse,
my sacrifice, a contrite spirit.
A humbled, contrite heart you will not spurn.

In your goodness, show favor to Zion:
rebuild the walls of Jerusalem.
Then you will be pleased with lawful sacrifice,
holocausts offered on your altar.

## Psalm-prayer

Father, he who knew no sin was made sin for us,
to save us and restore us to your friendship. Look
upon our contrite heart and afflicted spirit and heal
our troubled conscience, so that in the joy and
strength of the Holy Spirit we may proclaim your
praise and glory before all the nations.

Ant. 2  Rejoice, Jerusalem, for through you all men
will be gathered to the Lord.

December 17-23: Wait for the Lord and he will come to
you with his saving power.

Easter: Jerusalem, city of God, you will shine with a radiant light, alleluia.

## Canticle                                Tobit 13:8-11, 13-15

Thanksgiving for the people's deliverance

*He showed me the holy city Jerusalem which
shone with the glory of God* (Revelation 21:10-11).

Let all men speak of the Lord's majesty,
and sing his praises in Jerusalem.

O Jerusalem, holy city,
he scourged you for the works of your hands,
but will again pity the children of the righteous.

Praise the Lord for his goodness,
and bless the King of the ages,
so that his tent may be rebuilt in you with joy.

May he gladden within you all who were captives;
all who were ravaged may he cherish within you
for all generations to come.

A bright light will shine to all parts of the earth;
many nations shall come to you from afar,
and the inhabitants of all the limits of the earth,
drawn to you by the name of the Lord God,
bearing in their hands their gifts for the King of
    heaven.

Every generation shall give joyful praise in you,
and shall call you the chosen one,
through all ages forever.

Go, then, rejoice over the children of the righ-
    teous,
who shall be gathered together
and shall bless the Lord of the ages.

Happy are those who love you,
and happy those who rejoice in your prosperity.

Happy are all the men who shall grieve over you,
over all your chastisements,

for they shall rejoice in you
as they behold all your joy forever.

My spirit blesses the Lord, the great King.

Ant. 3  Zion, praise your God, who sent his Word
        to renew the earth.

December 17-23: Eagerly I watch for the Lord; I wait in
joyful hope for the coming of God my Savior.

Easter: I saw the new Jerusalem, coming down from
heaven, alleluia.

Psalm 147:12-20

The restoration of Jerusalem

*Come, I will show you the bride of the Lamb* (Revelation 21:9).

O praise the Lord, Jerusalem!
Zion, praise your God!

He has strengthened the bars of your gates,
he has blessed the children within you.
He established peace on your borders,
he feeds you with finest wheat.

He sends out his word to the earth
and swiftly runs his command.
He showers down snow white as wool,
he scatters hoar-frost like ashes.

He hurls down hailstones like crumbs.
The waters are frozen at his touch;
he sends forth his word and it melts them:
at the breath of his mouth the waters flow.

He makes his word known to Jacob,
to Israel his laws and decrees.
He has not dealt thus with other nations;
he has not taught them his decrees.

Psalm-prayer

All-powerful God, it is through your Church, generously endowed with gifts of grace and fortified by the Holy Spirit, that you send out your word to all nations. Strengthen your Church with the best of all food and make it dauntless in faith. Multiply its children to celebrate with one accord the mysteries of your love at the altar on high.

READING                                    Galatians 2:16, 19-20

Knowing that a person is not justified by works of the law but through faith in Jesus Christ, even we have believed in Christ Jesus that we may be justified by faith in Christ and not by works of the law, because by works of the law no one will be justified. For through the law I died to the law, that I might live for God. I have been crucified with Christ; yet I live, no longer I, but Christ lives in me; insofar as I now live in the flesh, I live by faith in the Son of God who has loved me and given himself up for me.

## RESPONSORY

The Lord, the Most High, has done good things for me.
In need I shall cry out to him.
— The Lord, the Most High, has done good things for me.
In need I shall cry out to him.

May he send his strength to rescue me.
— In need I shall cry out to him.

Glory to the Father . . .
— The Lord, the . . .

## CANTICLE OF ZECHARIAH

Ant. Through the tender compassion of our God the dawn from on high shall break upon us.

## INTERCESSIONS

We trust in God's concern for every person he has created and redeemed through his Son. Let us, therefore, renew our prayer to him:
*Fulfill the good work you have begun in us, Lord.*
O God of mercy, guide us toward spiritual growth,
— fill our minds with the thoughts of truth, justice and love.
For your name's sake, do not abandon us for ever,
— and do not annul your covenant.
Accept us, for our hearts are humble and our spirits contrite,
— and those who trust in you shall not be put to shame.
You have called us to a prophetic vocation in Christ,
— help us proclaim your mighty deeds.

Our Father . . .

## CONCLUDING PRAYER

Lord,
fill our hearts with your love
as morning fills the sky.

By living your law may we have
your peace in this life
and endless joy in the life to come.

We ask this through our Lord Jesus Christ, your Son,
who lives and reigns with you and the Holy Spirit,
one God, for ever and ever.

Conclusion, as in the Ordinary, 29.

## Evening Prayer

God, come to my assistance. Glory to the Father.
As it was in the beginning. Alleluia.

HYMN, no. 46 or 38. Outside Ordinary Time, see
Guide, 578.

PSALMODY

Ant. 1 Day after day I will bless you, Lord; I will
tell of your marvelous deeds.

December 17-23: Our King will come from Zion; the
Lord, God-is-with-us, is his mighty name.

Easter: God so loved the world that he gave us his only
Son, alleluia.

### Psalm 145

Praise of God's majesty

*Lord, you are the Just One, who was and who is*
(Revelation 16:5).

I

I will give you glory, O God my King,
I will bless your name for ever.

I will bless you day after day
and praise your name for ever.
The Lord is great, highly to be praised,
his greatness cannot be measured.

Age to age shall proclaim your works,
shall declare your mighty deeds,
shall speak of your splendor and glory,
tell the tale of your wonderful works.

They will speak of your terrible deeds,
recount your greatness and might.
They will recall your abundant goodness;
age to age shall ring out your justice.

The Lord is kind and full of compassion,
slow to anger, abounding in love.
How good is the Lord to all,
compassionate to all his creatures.

All your creatures shall thank you, O Lord,
and your friends shall repeat their blessing.
They shall speak of the glory of your reign
and declare your might, O God,

to make known to men your mighty deeds
and the glorious splendor of your reign.
Yours is an everlasting kingdom;
your rule lasts from age to age.

Ant. 2  To you alone, Lord, we look with confidence;
you are ever close to those who call upon you.

December 17-23: Wait for the Lord and he will come to
you with his saving power.

Easter: To the King of ages, immortal and invisible, be
all honor and glory, alleluia.

II

The Lord is faithful in all his words
and loving in all his deeds.
The Lord supports all who fall
and raises all who are bowed down.

The eyes of all creatures look to you
and you give them their food in due time.
You open wide your hand,
grant the desires of all who live.

The Lord is just in all his ways
and loving in all his deeds.—

He is close to all who call him,
who call on him from their hearts.

He grants the desires of those who fear him,
he hears their cry and he saves them.
The Lord protects all who love him;
but the wicked he will utterly destroy.

Let me speak the praise of the Lord,
let all mankind bless his holy name
for ever, for ages unending.

Psalm-prayer

Lord, be near to all who call upon you in truth,
and increase the dedication of those who revere
you. Hear their prayers and save them, that they
may always love you and praise your holy name.

Ant. 3  King of all the ages, your ways are perfect
and true.

December 17-23: Eagerly I watch for the Lord; I wait in
joyful hope for the coming of God my Savior.

Easter: The Lord is my strength, I shall always praise
him, for he has become my savior, alleluia.

Canticle          Revelation 15:3-4

Hymn of adoration

Mighty and wonderful are your works,
Lord God Almighty!
Righteous and true are your ways,
O King of the nations!

Who would dare refuse you honor,
or the glory due your name, O Lord?

Since you alone are holy,
all nations shall come
and worship in your presence.
Your mighty deeds are clearly seen.

READING                    Romans 8:1-2, 10-11

Now there is no condemnation for those who are in Christ Jesus. For the law of the spirit of life in Christ Jesus has freed you from the law of sin and death. If Christ is in you, although the body is dead because of sin, the spirit is alive because of righteousness. If the Spirit of the one who raised Jesus from the dead dwells in you, the one who raised Christ from the dead will give life to your mortal bodies also, through his Spirit that dwells in you.

RESPONSORY

Christ died for our sins to make of us an offering to God.
— Christ died for our sins to make of us an offering to God.

He died to this world of sin, and rose in the power of the Spirit,
— to make of us an offering to God.

Glory to the Father . . .
— Christ died for . . .

CANTICLE OF MARY

Ant. Remember your mercy, Lord, the promise of mercy you made to our fathers.

INTERCESSIONS

Let us pray to Christ, the source of hope for all who know his name:
  Lord, have mercy.
Christ, our frail humanity is prone to fall,
— strengthen us through your help.
Left to itself, our nature is inclined to sin,
— let your love always restore it to grace.
Lord, sin offends you, repentance pleases you,
— do not punish us in your wrath even when we have sinned.

You forgave the penitent woman, and placed the wandering sheep on your shoulders,
— do not deprive us of your mercy.

By your death on the cross you opened the gates of heaven,
— admit into your kingdom all who hoped in you.

Our Father . . .

CONCLUDING PRAYER

God our Father,
you brought salvation to all mankind
through the suffering of Christ your Son.
May your people strive to offer themselves to you
as a living sacrifice
and be filled with the abundance of your love.

We ask this through our Lord Jesus Christ, your Son,
who lives and reigns with you and the Holy Spirit,
one God, for ever and ever.

Conclusion, as in the Ordinary, 29.

# SATURDAY, WEEK IV

## Invitatory

Lord, open my lips.

Ant. Let us listen to the voice of God; let us enter into his rest.

Invitatory psalm, 22.

## Morning Prayer

The following verse and response are omitted when the hour begins with the invitatory.

God, come to my assistance. Glory to the Father.
As it was in the beginning. Alleluia.

HYMN, no. 17 or 132. Outside Ordinary Time, see Guide, 578.

PSALMODY

Ant. 1  We do well to sing to your name, Most High,
and proclaim your mercy at daybreak.

December 24: Bethlehem in Judah's land, how glorious
your future! The king who will rule my people comes
from you.

Easter: How wonderful are your works, O Lord, alleluia.

### Psalm 92
#### Praise of God the creator

*Sing in praise of Christ's redeeming work* (Saint
Athanasius).

It is good to give thanks to the Lord,
to make music to your name, O Most High,
to proclaim your love in the morning
and your truth in the watches of the night,
on the ten-stringed lyre and the lute,
with the murmuring sound of the harp.

Your deeds, O Lord, have made me glad;
for the work of your hands I shout with joy.
O Lord, how great are your works!
How deep are your designs!
The foolish man cannot know this
and the fool cannot understand.

Though the wicked spring up like grass
and all who do evil thrive:
they are doomed to be eternally destroyed.
But you, Lord, are eternally on high.
See how your enemies perish;
all doers of evil are scattered.

To me you give the wild-ox's strength;
you anoint me with the purest oil.
My eyes looked in triumph on my foes;
my ears heard gladly of their fall.
The just will flourish like the palm-tree
and grow like a Lebanon cedar.

Planted in the house of the Lord,
they will flourish in the courts of our God,
still bearing fruit when they are old,
still full of sap, still green,
to proclaim that the Lord is just.
In him, my rock, there is no wrong.

Psalm-prayer

Take our shame away from us, Lord, and make
us rejoice in your saving works. May all who have
been chosen by your Son always abound in works
of faith, hope and love in your service.

Ant. 2  I will create a new heart in you, and breathe
into you a new spirit.

December 24: Lift up your heads and see; your redemption is now at hand.

Easter: I will pour cleansing water upon you, alleluia.

Canticle        Ezekiel 36:24-28

The Lord will renew his people

*They will be his own people, and God himself will
be with them, their own God* (Revelation 21:3).

I will take you away from among the nations,
gather you from all the foreign lands,
and bring you back to your own land.

I will sprinkle clean water upon you
to cleanse you from all your impurities,
and from all your idols I will cleanse you.

I will give you a new heart
and place a new spirit within you,
taking from your bodies your stony hearts
and giving you natural hearts.

I will put my spirit within you
and make you live by my statutes,
careful to observe my decrees.

You shall live in the land I gave your fathers;
you shall be my people,
and I will be your God.

Ant. 3  On the lips of children and infants you have
found perfect praise.

December 24: The day has come at last when Mary will
bring forth her firstborn Son.

Easter: All things are yours, and you are Christ's, and
Christ is God's, alleluia.

## Psalm 8

The majesty of the Lord and man's dignity

*The Father gave Christ lordship of creation and
made him head of the Church* (Ephesians 1:22).

How great is your name, O Lord our God,
through all the earth!

Your majesty is praised above the heavens;
on the lips of children and of babes
you have found praise to foil your enemy,
to silence the foe and the rebel.

When I see the heavens, the work of your hands,
the moon and the stars which you arranged,
what is man that you should keep him in mind,
mortal man that you care for him?

Yet you have made him little less than a god;
with glory and honor you crowned him,
gave him power over the works of your hand,
put all things under his feet.

All of them, sheep and cattle,
yes, even the savage beasts,
birds of the air, and fish
that make their way through the waters.

How great is your name, O Lord our God,
through all the earth!

Psalm-prayer

Almighty Lord, how wonderful is your name. You have made every creature subject to you; make us worthy to give you service.

READING                                    2 Peter 3:13-15a

According to his promise we await new heavens and a new earth in which righteousness dwells. Therefore, beloved, since you await these things, be eager to be found without spot or blemish before him, at peace. And consider the patience of our Lord as salvation.

RESPONSORY

It is my joy, O God, to praise you with song.
— It is my joy, O God, to praise you with song.

To sing as I ponder your goodness,
— to praise you with song.

Glory to the Father . . .
— It is my . . .

CANTICLE OF ZECHARIAH

Ant. Lord, guide our feet into the way of peace.

INTERCESSIONS

Let us adore God, who has given hope and life to the world, through his Son, and let us humbly ask him:
    Lord, hear us.
Lord, Father of all, you have brought us to the dawn of this day,
— make us live with Christ and praise your glory.
You have poured out faith, hope and love upon us,
— keep them firmly rooted in our hearts.
Lord, let our eyes be always raised up to you,
— so that we may swiftly answer your call.
Protect us from the snares and enticements of evil,
— keep our feet from stumbling.

Our Father . . .

CONCLUDING PRAYER

All-powerful and ever-living God,
splendor of true light, and never-ending day:
let the radiance of your coming
banish from our minds
the darkness of sin.

We ask this through our Lord Jesus Christ, your Son,
who lives and reigns with you and the Holy Spirit,
one God, for ever and ever.

Conclusion, as in the Ordinary, 29.

# NIGHT PRAYER

INTRODUCTION

God, come to my assistance.
— Lord, make haste to help me.

Glory to the Father, and to the Son, and to the Holy
    Spirit:
as it was in the beginning, is now, and will be for
    ever. Amen (alleluia).

A brief examination of conscience may be made.
In the communal celebration of the office, a peni-
tential rite using the formulas of the Mass may be
inserted here.

HYMN, no. 33 or 34, 42, 48-53, 99, 184.

## AFTER EVENING PRAYER I
## ON SUNDAYS AND SOLEMNITIES

PSALMODY

Ant. 1  Have mercy, Lord, and hear my prayer.
    Easter: Alleluia, alleluia, alleluia.

Psalm 4

Thanksgiving

*The resurrection of Christ was God's supreme and
wholly marvelous work* (Saint Augustine).

    When I call, answer me, O God of justice;
    from anguish you released me; have mercy and
        hear me!

    O men, how long will your hearts be closed,
    will you love what is futile and seek what is false?

    It is the Lord who grants favors to those whom
        he loves;
    the Lord hears me whenever I call him.

Fear him; do not sin: ponder on your bed and
    be still.
Make justice your sacrifice and trust in the Lord.

"What can bring us happiness?" many say.
Let the light of your face shine on us, O Lord.

You have put into my heart a greater joy
than they have from abundance of corn and new
    wine.

I will lie down in peace and sleep comes at once
for you alone, Lord, make me dwell in safety.

Ant. 2  In the silent hours of night, bless the Lord.


Psalm 134

Evening prayer in the Temple

*Praise our God, all you his servants, you who fear
him, small and great* (Revelation 19:5).

O come, bless the Lord,
all you who serve the Lord,
who stand in the house of the Lord,
in the courts of the house of our God.

Lift up your hands to the holy place
and bless the Lord through the night.

May the Lord bless you from Zion,
he who made both heaven and earth.


READING                                Deuteronomy 6:4-7

Hear, O Israel! The Lord is our God, the Lord
alone! Therefore, you shall love the Lord, your God,
with all your heart, and with all your soul, and with
all your strength. Take to heart these words which I
enjoin on you today. Drill them into your children.
Speak of them at home and abroad, whether you
are busy or at rest.

RESPONSORY

Into your hands, Lord, I commend my spirit.
— Into your hands, Lord, I commend my spirit.

You have redeemed us, Lord God of truth.
— I commend my spirit.

Glory to the Father . . .
— Into your hands . . .

Octave of Easter:

This is the day the Lord has made; let us rejoice and be glad, alleluia.

Easter:

Into your hands, Lord, I commend my spirit, alleluia, alleluia.
— Into your hands, Lord, I commend my spirit, alleluia, alleluia.

You have redeemed us, Lord God of truth,
— alleluia, alleluia.

Glory to the Father . . .
— Into your hands . . .

Ant. 3  Protect us, Lord, as we stay awake; watch over us as we sleep, that awake, we may keep watch with Christ, and asleep, rest in his peace (alleluia).

GOSPEL CANTICLE                              Luke 2:29-32

Christ is the light of the nations
and the glory of Israel

Lord, now you let your servant go in peace;
your word has been fulfilled:

my own eyes have seen the salvation
which you have prepared in the sight of every people:

a light to reveal you to the nations
and the glory of your people Israel.

CONCLUDING PRAYER

On Sundays and during the octave of Easter:

Lord,
be with us throughout this night.
When day comes may we rise from sleep
to rejoice in the resurrection of your Christ,
who lives and reigns for ever and ever.

Or: on solemnities that do not occur on Sunday:

Lord,
we beg you to visit this house
and banish from it
all the deadly power of the enemy.
May your holy angels dwell here
to keep us in peace,
and may your blessing be upon us always.

We ask this through Christ our Lord.

CONCLUSION

The blessing is said, even in individual recitation:

May the all-powerful Lord grant us a restful night
and a peaceful death.
— Amen.

Antiphon of the Blessed Virgin Mary, as on 352.

# AFTER EVENING PRAYER II
# ON SUNDAYS AND SOLEMNITIES

PSALMODY

Ant. **Night holds no terrors for me sleeping under
God's wings.**

Easter: Alleluia, alleluia, alleluia.

### Psalm 91
Safe in God's sheltering care

*I have given you the power to tread upon serpents
and scorpions* (Luke 10:19).

He who dwells in the shelter of the Most High
and abides in the shade of the Almighty
says to the Lord: "My refuge,
my stronghold, my God in whom I trust!"

It is he who will free you from the snare
of the fowler who seeks to destroy you;
he will conceal you with his pinions
and under his wings you will find refuge.

You will not fear the terror of the night
nor the arrow that flies by day,
nor the plague that prowls in the darkness
nor the scourge that lays waste at noon.

A thousand may fall at your side,
ten thousand fall at your right,
you, it will never approach;
his faithfulness is buckler and shield.

Your eyes have only to look
to see how the wicked are repaid,
you who have said: "Lord, my refuge!"
and have made the Most High your dwelling.

Upon you no evil shall fall,
no plague approach where you dwell.
For you has he commanded his angels,
to keep you in all your ways.

They shall bear you upon their hands
lest you strike your foot against a stone.
On the lion and the viper you will tread
and trample the young lion and the dragon.

Since he clings to me in love, I will free him;
protect him for he knows my name.
When he calls I shall answer: "I am with you."
I will save him in distress and give him glory.

With length of life I will content him;
I shall let him see my saving power.

READING                          Revelation 22:4-5

They will look upon his face, and his name will be on their foreheads. Night will be no more, nor will they need light from lamp or sun, for the Lord God shall give them light, and they shall reign forever and ever.

RESPONSORY

Into your hands, Lord, I commend my spirit.
— Into your hands, Lord, I commend my spirit.

You have redeemed us, Lord God of truth.
— I commend my spirit.

Glory to the Father . . .
— Into your hands . . .

Easter Triduum:

For our sake Christ was obedient, accepting even death, *(Good Friday, add:)* death on a cross. *(Holy Saturday, add further:)* Therefore God raised him on high and gave him the name above all other names.

Octave of Easter:

This is the day the Lord has made; let us rejoice and be glad, alleluia.

Easter:

Into your hands, Lord, I commend my spirit, alleluia, alleluia.
— Into your hands, Lord, I commend my spirit, alleluia, alleluia.

You have redeemed us, Lord God of truth,
— alleluia, alleluia.

Glory to the Father . . .
— Into your hands . . .

Ant. Protect us, Lord, as we stay awake; watch over us as we sleep, that awake, we may keep watch with Christ, and asleep, rest in his peace (alleluia).

### Christ is the light of the nations and the glory of Israel

Lord, now you let your servant go in peace;
your word has been fulfilled:

my own eyes have seen the salvation
which you have prepared in the sight of every people:

a light to reveal you to the nations
and the glory of your people Israel.

Concluding Prayer

On Sundays and during the octave of Easter:
Lord,
we have celebrated today
the mystery of the rising of Christ to new life.
May we now rest in your peace,
safe from all that could harm us,
and rise again refreshed and joyful,
to praise you throughout another day.
We ask this through Christ our Lord.

Or: on solemnities that do not occur on Sunday:
Lord,
we beg you to visit this house
and banish from it
all the deadly power of the enemy.
May your holy angels dwell here
to keep us in peace,
and may your blessing be upon us always.
We ask this through Christ our Lord.

Conclusion

The blessing is said, even in individual recitation:

May the all-powerful Lord grant us a restful night
and a peaceful death.
— Amen.

Antiphon of the Blessed Virgin Mary, as on 352.

# MONDAY

PSALMODY

**Ant.** O Lord, our God, unwearied is your love for us.

Easter: Alleluia, alleluia, alleluia.

## Psalm 86

### Poor man's prayer in trouble

*Blessed be God who comforts us in all our trials* (2 Corinthians 1:3, 4).

Turn your ear, O Lord, and give answer
for I am poor and needy.
Preserve my life, for I am faithful:
save the servant who trusts in you.

You are my God; have mercy on me, Lord,
for I cry to you all day long.
Give joy to your servant, O Lord,
for to you I lift up my soul.

O Lord, you are good and forgiving,
full of love to all who call.
Give heed, O Lord, to my prayer
and attend to the sound of my voice.

In the day of distress I will call
and surely you will reply.
Among the gods there is none like you, O Lord;
nor work to compare with yours.

All the nations shall come to adore you
and glorify your name, O Lord:
for you are great and do marvellous deeds,
you who alone are God.

Show me, Lord, your way
so that I may walk in your truth.
Guide my heart to fear your name.

I will praise you, Lord my God, with all my heart
and glorify your name for ever;
for your love to me has been great:
you have saved me from the depths of the grave.

The proud have risen against me;
ruthless men seek my life:
to you they pay no heed.

But you, God of mercy and compassion,
slow to anger, O Lord,
abounding in love and truth,
turn and take pity on me.

O give your strength to your servant
and save your handmaid's son.
Show me a sign of your favor
that my foes may see to their shame
that you console me and give me your help.

READING                              1 Thessalonians 5:9-10

God did not destine us for wrath, but to gain salvation through our Lord Jesus Christ, who died for
us, so that whether we are awake or asleep we may
live together with him.

RESPONSORY

Into your hands, Lord, I commend my spirit.
— Into your hands, Lord, I commend my spirit.
You have redeemed us, Lord God of truth.
— I commend my spirit.
Glory to the Father . . .
— Into your hands . . .

During the octave of Easter, in place of the responsory, the antiphon This is the day the Lord has
made; let us rejoice and be glad, alleluia, is said.

Easter:

Into your hands, Lord, I commend my spirit, alleluia, alleluia.

— Into your hands, Lord, I commend my spirit, alleluia, alleluia.

You have redeemed us, Lord God of truth,
— alleluia, alleluia.

Glory to the Father . . .
— Into your hands . . .

Ant. Protect us, Lord, as we stay awake; watch over us as we sleep, that awake, we may keep watch with Christ, and asleep, rest in his peace (alleluia).

GOSPEL CANTICLE                                    Luke 2:29-32

Christ is the light of the nations and
the glory of Israel

Lord, now you let your servant go in peace;
your word has been fulfilled:

my own eyes have seen the salvation
which you have prepared in the sight of every
people:

a light to reveal you to the nations
and the glory of your people Israel.

CONCLUDING PRAYER

Lord,
give our bodies restful sleep
and let the work we have done today
bear fruit in eternal life.

We ask this through Christ our Lord.

CONCLUSION

The blessing is said, even in individual recitation:

May the all-powerful Lord grant us a restful night
and a peaceful death.
— Amen.

Antiphon of the Blessed Virgin Mary, as on 352.

# TUESDAY

PSALMODY

Ant. Do not hide your face from me; in you I put
my trust.

Easter: Alleluia, alleluia, alleluia.

### Psalm 143:1-11

#### Prayer in distress

*Only by faith in Jesus Christ is a man made holy
in God's sight. No observance of the law can
achieve this* (Galatians 2:16).

Lord, listen to my prayer:
turn your ear to my appeal.
You are faithful, you are just; give answer.
Do not call your servant to judgment
for no one is just in your sight.

The enemy pursues my soul;
he has crushed my life to the ground;
he has made me dwell in darkness
like the dead, long forgotten.
Therefore my spirit fails;
my heart is numb within me.

I remember the days that are past:
I ponder all your works.
I muse on what your hand has wrought
and to you I stretch out my hands.
Like a parched land my soul thirsts for you.

Lord, make haste and answer;
for my spirit fails within me.
Do not hide your face
lest I become like those in the grave.

In the morning let me know your love
for I put my trust in you.—

Make me know the way I should walk:
to you I lift up my soul.

Rescue me, Lord, from my enemies;
I have fled to you for refuge.
Teach me to do your will
for you, O Lord, are my God.
Let your good spirit guide me
in ways that are level and smooth.

For your name's sake, Lord, save my life;
in your justice save my soul from distress.

READING                                    1 Peter 5:8-9a

Be sober and vigilant. Your opponent the devil is
prowling around like a roaring lion looking for
[someone] to devour. Resist him, steadfast in faith.

RESPONSORY

Into your hands, Lord, I commend my spirit.
— Into your hands, Lord, I commend my spirit.

You have redeemed us, Lord God of truth.
— I commend my spirit.

Glory to the Father . . .
— Into your hands . . .

During the octave of Easter, in place of the responsory, the antiphon This is the day the Lord has
made; let us rejoice and be glad, alleluia, is said.

Easter:

Into your hands, Lord, I commend my spirit, alleluia, alleluia.
— Into your hands, Lord, I commend my spirit, alleluia, alleluia.

You have redeemed us, Lord God of truth,
— alleluia, alleluia.

Glory to the Father . . .
— Into your hands . . .

Ant.  **Protect us, Lord, as we stay awake; watch over us as we sleep, that awake, we may keep watch with Christ, and asleep, rest in his peace (alleluia).**

GOSPEL CANTICLE                          Luke 2:29-32

Christ is the light of the nations and
the glory of Israel

Lord, now you let your servant go in peace;
your word has been fulfilled:

my own eyes have seen the salvation
which you have prepared in the sight of every
people:

a light to reveal you to the nations
and the glory of your people Israel.

CONCLUDING PRAYER

Lord,
fill this night with your radiance.
May we sleep in peace and rise with joy
to welcome the light of a new day in your name.

We ask this through Christ our Lord.

CONCLUSION

The blessing is said, even in individual recitation:

May the all-powerful Lord grant us a restful night
and a peaceful death.
— Amen.

Antiphon of the Blessed Virgin Mary, as on 352.

# WEDNESDAY

PSALMODY

Ant. 1  **Lord God, be my refuge and my strength.**

Easter: **Alleluia, alleluia, alleluia.**

## Psalm 31:1-6

### Trustful prayer in adversity

*Father, into your hands I commend my spirit*
(Luke 23:46).

In you, O Lord, I take refuge.
Let me never be put to shame.
In your justice, set me free,
hear me and speedily rescue me.

Be a rock of refuge for me,
a mighty stronghold to save me,
for you are my rock, my stronghold.
For your name's sake, lead me and guide me.

Release me from the snares they have hidden
for you are my refuge, Lord.
Into your hands I commend my spirit.
It is you who will redeem me, Lord.

Ant. 2   Out of the depths I cry to you, Lord.

## Psalm 130

### A cry from the depths

*He will save his people from their sins* (Matthew
1:21).

Out of the depths I cry to you, O Lord,
Lord, hear my voice!
O let your ears be attentive
to the voice of my pleading.

If you, O Lord, should mark our guilt,
Lord, who would survive?
But with you is found forgiveness:
for this we revere you.

My soul is waiting for the Lord,
I count on his word.
My soul is longing for the Lord
more than watchman for daybreak.—

Let the watchman count on daybreak
and Israel on the Lord.

Because with the Lord there is mercy
and fullness of redemption,
Israel indeed he will redeem
from all its iniquity.

READING                              Ephesians 4:26-27

Be angry but do not sin; do not let the sun set on
your anger, and do not leave room for the devil.

RESPONSORY

Into your hands, Lord, I commend my spirit.
— Into your hands, Lord, I commend my spirit.

You have redeemed us, Lord God of truth.
— I commend my spirit.

Glory to the Father . . .
— Into your hands . . .

During the octave of Easter, in place of the responsory, the antiphon This is the day the Lord has
made; let us rejoice and be glad, alleluia, is said.

Easter:

Into your hands, Lord, I commend my spirit, al-
    leluia, alleluia.
— Into your hands, Lord, I commend my spirit, al-
    leluia, alleluia.

You have redeemed us, Lord God of truth,
— alleluia, alleluia.

Glory to the Father . . .
— Into your hands . . .

Ant.  Protect us, Lord, as we stay awake; watch over
      us as we sleep, that awake, we may keep
      watch with Christ, and asleep, rest in his
      peace (alleluia).

GOSPEL CANTICLE                    Luke 2:29-32

> Christ is the light of the nations and
> the glory of Israel

Lord, now you let your servant go in peace;
your word has been fulfilled:

my own eyes have seen the salvation
which you have prepared in the sight of every
   people:

a light to reveal you to the nations
and the glory of your people Israel.

CONCLUDING PRAYER

Lord Jesus Christ,
you have given your followers
an example of gentleness and humility,
a task that is easy, a burden that is light.
Accept the prayers and work of this day,
and give us the rest that will strengthen us
to render more faithful service to you
who live and reign for ever and ever.

CONCLUSION

The blessing is said, even in individual recitation:
May the all-powerful Lord grant us a restful night
and a peaceful death.
— Amen.

Antiphon of the Blessed Virgin Mary, as on 352.

# THURSDAY

PSALMODY

Ant. In you, my God, my body will rest in hope.

Easter: Alleluia, alleluia, alleluia.

## Psalm 16

### God is my portion, my inheritance

*The Father raised up Jesus from the dead and broke the bonds of death* (Acts 2:24).

Preserve me, God, I take refuge in you.
I say to the Lord: "You are my God.
My happiness lies in you alone."

He has put into my heart a marvellous love
for the faithful ones who dwell in his land.
Those who choose other gods increase their
    sorrows.
Never will I offer their offerings of blood.
Never will I take their name upon my lips.

O Lord, it is you who are my portion and cup;
it is you yourself who are my prize.
The lot marked out for me is my delight:
welcome indeed the heritage that falls to me!

I will bless the Lord who gives me counsel,
who even at night directs my heart.
I keep the Lord ever in my sight:
since he is at my right hand, I shall stand firm.

And so my heart rejoices, my soul is glad;
even my body shall rest in safety.
For you will not leave my soul among the dead,
nor let your beloved know decay.

You will show me the path of life,
the fullness of joy in your presence,
at your right hand happiness for ever.

READING                          1 Thessalonians 5:23

May the God of peace himself make you perfectly holy and may you entirely, spirit, soul, and body, be preserved blameless for the coming of our Lord Jesus Christ.

RESPONSORY

Into your hands, Lord, I commend my spirit.
— Into your hands, Lord, I commend my spirit.

You have redeemed us, Lord God of truth.
— I commend my spirit.

Glory to the Father . . .
— Into your hands . . .

During the octave of Easter, in place of the responsory, the antiphon This is the day the Lord has made; let us rejoice and be glad, alleluia, is said.

Easter:

Into your hands, Lord, I commend my spirit, alleluia, alleluia.
— Into your hands, Lord, I commend my spirit, alleluia, alleluia.

You have redeemed us, Lord God of truth,
— alleluia, alleluia.

Glory to the Father . . .
— Into your hands . . .

Ant. Protect us, Lord, as we stay awake; watch over us as we sleep, that awake, we may keep watch with Christ, and asleep, rest in his peace (alleluia).

GOSPEL CANTICLE                          Luke 2:29-32

Christ is the light of the nations and
the glory of Israel

Lord, now you let your servant go in peace;
your word has been fulfilled:

my own eyes have seen the salvation
which you have prepared in the sight of every
people:

a light to reveal you to the nations
and the glory of your people Israel.

CONCLUDING PRAYER

Lord God,
send peaceful sleep
to refresh our tired bodies.
May your help always renew us
and keep us strong in your service.

We ask this through Christ our Lord.

CONCLUSION

The blessing is said, even in individual recitation:

May the all-powerful Lord grant us a restful night
and a peaceful death.
— Amen.

Antiphon of the Blessed Virgin Mary, as on 352.

# FRIDAY

PSALMODY

Ant.  Day and night I cry to you, my God.

Easter: Alleluia, alleluia, alleluia.

## Psalm 88

### Prayer of a sick person

*This is your hour when darkness reigns* (Luke 22:53).

Lord my God, I call for help by day;
I cry at night before you.
Let my prayer come into your presence.
O turn your ear to my cry.

For my soul is filled with evils;
my life is on the brink of the grave.
I am reckoned as one in the tomb:
I have reached the end of my strength,

like one alone among the dead;
like the slain lying in their graves;
like those you remember no more,
cut off, as they are, from your hand.

You have laid me in the depths of the tomb,
in places that are dark, in the depths.
Your anger weighs down upon me:
I am drowned beneath your waves.

You have taken away my friends
and made me hateful in their sight.
Imprisoned, I cannot escape;
my eyes are sunken with grief.

I call to you, Lord, all the day long;
to you I stretch out my hands.
Will you work your wonders for the dead?
Will the shades stand and praise you?

Will your love be told in the grave
or your faithfulness among the dead?
Will your wonders be known in the dark
or your justice in the land of oblivion?

As for me, Lord, I call to you for help:
in the morning my prayer comes before you.
Lord, why do you reject me?
Why do you hide your face?

Wretched, close to death from my youth,
I have borne your trials; I am numb.
Your fury has swept down upon me;
your terrors have utterly destroyed me.

They surround me all the day like a flood,
they assail me all together.
Friend and neighbor you have taken away:
my one companion is darkness.

READING                                      Jeremiah 14:9a

You are in our midst, O Lord,
  your name we bear:
  do not forsake us, O Lord, our God!

RESPONSORY

Into your hands, Lord, I commend my spirit.
— Into your hands, Lord, I commend my spirit.

You have redeemed us, Lord God of truth.
— I commend my spirit.

Glory to the Father . . .
— Into your hands . . .

During the octave of Easter, in place of the responsory, the antiphon **This is the day the Lord has
made; let us rejoice and be glad, alleluia,** is said.

Easter:

Into your hands, Lord, I commend my spirit, alleluia, alleluia.
— Into your hands, Lord, I commend my spirit, alleluia, alleluia.

You have redeemed us, Lord God of truth,
— alleluia, alleluia.

Glory to the Father . . .
— Into your hands . . .

Ant.  **Protect us, Lord, as we stay awake; watch over
      us as we sleep, that awake, we may keep
      watch with Christ, and asleep, rest in his
      peace (alleluia).**

GOSPEL CANTICLE                                Luke 2:29-32

Christ is the light of the nations and
        the glory of Israel

Lord, now you let your servant go in peace;
your word has been fulfilled:

my own eyes have seen the salvation
which you have prepared in the sight of every
  people:

a light to reveal you to the nations
and the glory of your people Israel.

CONCLUDING PRAYER

All-powerful God,
keep us united with your Son
in his death and burial
so that we may rise to new life with him,
who lives and reigns for ever and ever.

CONCLUSION

The blessing is said, even in individual recitation:

May the all-powerful Lord grant us a restful night
and a peaceful death.
— Amen.

Antiphon of the Blessed Virgin Mary, as on 352.

## Antiphons in Honor of the Blessed Virgin

Then one of the antiphons in honor of Mary is
said. Other hymns approved by the conference of
bishops may be used.

Hail, holy Queen, mother of mercy,
our life, our sweetness, and our hope.
To you do we cry,
poor banished children of Eve.
To you do we send up our sighs
mourning and weeping in this vale of tears.
Turn then, most gracious advocate,
your eyes of mercy toward us,
and after this exile
show us the blessed fruit of your womb, Jesus.
O clement, O loving,
O sweet Virgin Mary.

Or:

Loving mother of the Redeemer,
gate of heaven, star of the sea,
assist your people who have fallen yet strive to
    rise again.
To the wonderment of nature you bore your
    Creator,
yet remained a virgin after as before.
You who received Gabriel's joyful greeting,
have pity on us poor sinners.

Or:

Hail Mary, full of grace,
the Lord is with you!
Blessed are you among women,
and blessed is the fruit of your womb, Jesus.
Holy Mary, Mother of God,
pray for us sinners,
now and at the hour of our death.

Or:

Queen of heaven, rejoice, alleluia.
The Son whom you merited to bear, alleluia,
has risen as he said, alleluia.

Rejoice and be glad, O Virgin Mary, alleluia!
For the Lord has truly risen, alleluia.

Or:

Alma Redemptoris Mater, quae pervia caeli
   porta manes, et stella maris, succurre cadenti,
surgere qui curat, populo: tu quae genuisti,
   natura mirante, tuum sanctum Genitorem,
Virgo prius ac posterius, Gabrielis ab ore
   sumens illud Ave, peccatorum miserere.

Or:

Ave, Regina caelorum,
ave, Domina angelorum,
salve, radix, salve, porta,
ex qua mundo lux est orta.

Gaude, Virgo gloriosa,
super omnes speciosa;
vale, o valde decora,
et pro nobis Christum exora.

Or:

Salve, Regina, mater misericordiae;
   vita, dulcedo et spes nostra, salve,
Ad te clamamus, exsules filii Evae.
Ad te suspiramus, gementes et flentes
   in hac lacrimarum valle.

Eia ergo, advocata nostra,
   illos tuos misericordes oculos
   ad nos converte.
Et Iesum, benedictum fructum ventris tui,
   nobis post hoc exsilium ostende.
O clemens, o pia, o dulcis Virgo Maria.

Or:

Regina caeli, laetare, alleluia,
   quia quem meruisti portare, alleluia,
resurrexit sicut dixit, alleluia;
   ora pro nobis Deum, alleluia.

Gaude et laetare, Virgo Maria, alleluia.
Quia surrexit Dominus vere, alleluia.

# PROPER OF SEASONS

This section contains a selection of texts so that the season of the year may be taken into account when any office is celebrated. The full variety of seasonal texts will be found in *The Liturgy of the Hours* and *Christian Prayer*.

Unless otherwise indicated, the Psalmody is as given in the Four-Week Psalter. The hymn, unless it is indicated, is to be chosen from the Liturgical Guide for Hymns, 578-582.

# ADVENT SEASON

One week of texts is provided for the Advent Season. These texts may be repeated throughout the season. The hymns for Advent are indicated in the Liturgical Guide, 578.

INVITATORY

The antiphons for the invitatory psalm of Morning Prayer are:

To Dec. 16: Come, let us worship the Lord, the King who is to come.

Dec. 17-23: The Lord is close at hand; come, let us worship him.

Dec 24: Today you will know the Lord is coming, and in the morning you will see his glory.

The psalms and canticle with their antiphons are from the current day in the Psalter.

# SUNDAY

## Evening Prayer I

READING                                    1 Thessalonians 5:19-24

Do not quench the Spirit. Do not despise prophetic utterances. Test everything; retain what is good. Refrain from every kind of evil.

May the God of peace himself make you perfectly holy and may you entirely, spirit, soul, and body, be preserved blameless for the coming of our Lord Jesus Christ. The one who calls you is faithful, and he will also accomplish it.

RESPONSORY

Lord, show us your mercy and love.
— Lord, show us your mercy and love.

And grant us your salvation,
— your mercy and love.

Glory to the Father . . .
— Lord, show us . . .

CANTICLE OF MARY

Ant. See the Lord coming from afar; his splendor fills the earth.

INTERCESSIONS

Jesus Christ is the joy and happiness of all who look forward to his coming. Let us call upon him and say:

*Come, Lord, and do not delay!*

In joy, we wait for your coming,
— come, Lord Jesus.

Before time began, you shared life with the Father,
— come now and save us.

You created the world and all who live in it,
— come to redeem the work of your hands.

You did not hesitate to become man, subject to death,
— come to free us from the power of death.

You came to give us life to the full,
— come and give us your unending life.

You desire all people to live in love in your kingdom,
— come and bring together those who long to see you face to face.

Our Father . . .

CONCLUDING PRAYER

All-powerful God,
increase our strength of will for doing good
that Christ may find an eager welcome at his coming
and call us to his side in the kingdom of heaven,
where he lives and reigns with you and the Holy Spirit,
one God, for ever and ever.

## Alternative Prayer

Father in heaven,
our hearts desire the warmth of your love
and our minds are searching for the light of your Word.

Increase our longing for Christ our Savior
and give us the strength to grow in love,
that the dawn of his coming
may find us rejoicing in his presence
and welcoming the light of his truth.

We ask this in the name of Jesus the Lord.

## Invitatory

Ant.  Come, let us worship the Lord, the King who
      is to come.

Invitatory psalm, as in the Ordinary, 22.

## Morning Prayer

READING                            Romans 13:11-14

It is the hour now for you to awake from sleep. For
our salvation is nearer now than when we first believed; the night is advanced, the day is at hand. Let
us then throw off the works of darkness [and] put on
the armor of light; let us conduct ourselves properly
as in the day, not in orgies and drunkenness, not in
promiscuity and licentiousness, not in rivalry and
jealousy. But put on the Lord Jesus Christ, and make
no provision for the desires of the flesh.

RESPONSORY

Christ, Son of the living God, have mercy on us.
— Christ, Son of the living God, have mercy on us.

You are the one who is to come,
— have mercy on us.

Glory to the Father . . .
— Christ, Son of the living God, have mercy on us.

CANTICLE OF ZECHARIAH

Ant. The Holy Spirit will come upon you, Mary; you have no need to be afraid. You will carry in your womb the Son of God, alleluia.

INTERCESSIONS

To God our Father, who has given us the grace to wait in joyful hope for the revelation of our Lord Jesus Christ, let us make our prayer:
   *Show us your mercy, Lord.*
Sanctify us in mind and body,
— keep us without sin until the coming of your Son.
Make us walk this day in holiness,
— and live upright and devout lives in this world.
May we be clothed in our Lord Jesus Christ,
— and filled with the Holy Spirit.
Lord, help us to stand watchful and ready,
— until your Son is revealed in all his glory.

Our Father . . .

CONCLUDING PRAYER

All-powerful God,
increase our strength of will for doing good
that Christ may find an eager welcome at his coming
and call us to his side in the kingdom of heaven,
where he lives and reigns with you and the Holy Spirit,
one God, for ever and ever.

Alternative Prayer

Father in heaven,
our hearts desire the warmth of your love
and our minds are searching for the light of your Word.
Increase our longing for Christ our Savior
and give us the strength to grow in love,
that the dawn of his coming

may find us rejoicing in his presence
and welcoming the light of his truth.

We ask this in the name of Jesus the Lord.

## Evening Prayer II

READING                              Philippians 4:4-7

Rejoice in the Lord always. I shall say it again: rejoice! Your kindness should be known to all. The
Lord is near. Have no anxiety at all, but in everything, by prayer and petition, with thanksgiving,
make your requests known to God. Then the peace
of God that surpasses all understanding will guard
your hearts and minds in Christ Jesus.

RESPONSORY

Lord, show us your mercy and love.
— Lord, show us your mercy and love.

And grant us your salvation,
— your mercy and love.

Glory to the Father . . .
— Lord, show us . . .

CANTICLE OF MARY

Ant. Do not be afraid, Mary, you have found favor
      with God; you will conceive and give birth to a
      Son, alleluia.

INTERCESSIONS

To Jesus Christ, our Redeemer, the way, the truth,
    and the life, let us make our humble prayer:
    *Come and stay with us, Lord.*
Son of the Most High, your coming was announced
    to the Virgin Mary by Gabriel,
— come and rule over your people for ever.

Holy One of God, in your presence John the Baptist
  leapt in Elizabeth's womb,
— bring the joy of salvation to all the earth.
Jesus the Savior, the angel revealed your name to
  Joseph the just man,
— come and save your people from their sins.
Light of the world, for whom Simeon and all the
  just waited,
— come and comfort us.
O Rising Sun that never sets, Zechariah foretold
  that you would visit us from above,
— come and shine on those who dwell in darkness
  and the shadow of death.

Our Father . . .

CONCLUDING PRAYER

All-powerful God,
increase our strength of will for doing good
that Christ may find an eager welcome at his coming
and call us to his side in the kingdom of heaven,
where he lives and reigns with you and the Holy
  Spirit,
one God, for ever and ever.

## Alternative Prayer

Father in heaven,
our hearts desire the warmth of your love
and our minds are searching for the light of your
  Word.
Increase our longing for Christ our Savior
and give us the strength to grow in love,
that the dawn of his coming
may find us rejoicing in his presence
and welcoming the light of his truth.

We ask this in the name of Jesus the Lord.

# MONDAY

## Morning Prayer

Isaiah 2:3-4

Come, let us climb the Lord's mountain,
  to the house of the God of Jacob,
That he may instruct us in his ways,
  and we may walk in his paths.
For from Zion shall go forth instruction,
  and the word of the Lord from Jerusalem.

He shall judge between the nations,
  and impose terms on many peoples.
They shall beat their swords into plowshares
  and their spears into pruning hooks;
One nation shall not raise the sword against another,
  nor shall they train for war again.

RESPONSORY

Your light will come, Jerusalem;
the Lord will dawn on you in radiant beauty.
— Your light will come, Jerusalem;
the Lord will dawn on you in radiant beauty.

You will see his glory within you;
— the Lord will dawn on you in radiant beauty.

Glory to the Father . . .
— Your light will . . .

CANTICLE OF ZECHARIAH

Ant.  Lift up your eyes, Jerusalem, and see the
      great power of your King; your Savior comes
      to set you free.

INTERCESSIONS

Christ the Lord, Son of the living God, light from
  light, leads us into the light and reveals his holiness. With confidence let us make our prayer:

*Come, Lord Jesus!*
Light that never fades, dispel the mists about us,
— awaken our faith from sleep.
Guard us from all harm today,
— may your glory fill us with joy.
Give us unfailing gentleness at all times,
— toward everyone we meet.
Come to create a new earth for us,
— where there will be justice and peace.

Our Father . . .

CONCLUDING PRAYER

Lord our God,
help us to prepare
for the coming of Christ your Son.
May he find us waiting,
eager in joyful prayer.

We ask this through our Lord Jesus Christ, your Son,
who lives and reigns with you and the Holy Spirit,
one God, for ever and ever.

## Evening Prayer

READING                                    Philippians 3:20b-21

We also await a savior, the Lord Jesus Christ. He
will change our lowly body to conform with his glorified body by the power that enables him also to
bring all things into subjection to himself.

RESPONSORY

Come and set us free, Lord God of power and
might.
— Come and set us free, Lord God of power and
   might.

Let your face shine upon us and we shall be saved,
— Lord God of power and might.

Glory to the Father . . .
— Come and set . . .

CANTICLE OF MARY

Ant. The angel of the Lord brought God's message
to Mary, and she conceived by the power of
the Holy Spirit, alleluia.

INTERCESSIONS

We cry to the Lord, who will come to bring us salvation:
*Come, Lord, and save us!*
Lord Jesus Christ, our God, Savior of all,
— come swiftly and save us.
Lord, by your coming into this world,
— free us from the sin of the world.
You came from the Father,
— show us the path that leads to him.
You were conceived by the Holy Spirit,
— by your word renew the same Spirit in our
hearts.
You became incarnate from the Virgin Mary,
— free our bodies from corruption.
Lord, be mindful of all men,
— who from the beginning of time have placed their
trust in you.

Our Father . . .

CONCLUDING PRAYER

Lord our God,
help us to prepare
for the coming of Christ your Son.
May he find us waiting,
eager in joyful prayer.

We ask this through our Lord Jesus Christ, your Son,
who lives and reigns with you and the Holy Spirit,
one God, for ever and ever.

# TUESDAY

## Morning Prayer

READING                                      Genesis 49:8-10

You, Judah, shall your brothers praise
  —your hand on the neck of your enemies;
  the sons of your father shall bow down to you.
Judah, like a lion's whelp,
  you have grown up on prey, my son.
He crouches like a lion recumbent,
  the king of beasts—who would dare rouse him?
The scepter shall never depart from Judah,
  or the mace from between his legs,
While tribute is brought to him,
  and he receives the people's homage.

RESPONSORY

Your light will come, Jerusalem;
the Lord will dawn on you in radiant beauty.
— Your light will come, Jerusalem;
the Lord will dawn on you in radiant beauty.

You will see his glory within you;
— the Lord will dawn on you in radiant beauty.

Glory to the Father . . .
— Your light will . . .

CANTICLE OF ZECHARIAH

Ant. From the root of Jesse a flower will blossom,
      the glory of the Lord will fill the earth, and all
      creation shall see the saving power of God.

INTERCESSIONS

God the almighty Father stretches forth his hand
  again to take possession of the remnant of his
  people. Let us make our prayer to him:
  *Lord, may your kingdom come.*

Lord, grant that our works of penance may please
    you,
— and that we may be ready for your kingdom
    which is so near.
Prepare a path in our hearts for the coming of your
    Word,
— and let his glory be revealed among us.
Bring low the mountains of our pride,
— and fill up the valleys of our weakness.
Break down the wall of hatred that divides the na-
    tions,
— and make level for mankind the paths to peace.
Our Father . . .

CONCLUDING PRAYER

God of mercy and consolation,
help us in our weakness and free us from sin.
Hear our prayers
that we may rejoice at the coming of your Son,
who lives and reigns with you and the Holy Spirit,
one God, for ever and ever.

## Evening Prayer

READING                                    I Corinthians 1:4-9

I give thanks to my God always on your account
for the grace of God bestowed on you in Christ
Jesus, that in him you were enriched in every way,
with all discourse and all knowledge, as the testimony to Christ was confirmed among you, so that
you are not lacking in any spiritual gift as you wait
for the revelation of our Lord Jesus Christ. He will
keep you firm to the end, irreproachable on the day
of our Lord Jesus [Christ]. God is faithful, and by
him you were called to fellowship with his Son,
Jesus Christ our Lord.

RESPONSORY

Come and set us free, Lord God of power and might.
— Come and set us free, Lord God of power and might.

Let your face shine upon us and we shall be saved,
— Lord God of power and might.

Glory to the Father . . .
— Come and set . . .

CANTICLE OF MARY

Ant. Seek the Lord while he may be found; call on him while he is near, alleluia.

INTERCESSIONS

To the eternal Word who became man to reveal to us the new and living way, let us make our humble prayer:
Come, Lord, and save us.
God, in whom we live and move and have our being,
— come and teach us that you have made us your own.
You are not far from each of us,
— show yourself to all who search for you.
Father of the poor and consoler of the afflicted,
— set captives free, give joy to those who mourn.
You hate death and love life,
— free all mankind from eternal death.

Our Father . . .

CONCLUDING PRAYER

God of mercy and consolation,
help us in our weakness and free us from sin.
Hear our prayers
that we may rejoice at the coming of your Son,
who lives and reigns with you and the Holy Spirit,
one God, for ever and ever.

# WEDNESDAY

## Morning Prayer

READING                                        Isaiah 7:10-15

Again the Lord spoke to Ahaz: Ask for a sign
from the Lord, your God; let it be deep as the
nether world, or high as the sky! But Ahaz answered, "I will not ask! I will not tempt the Lord!"
Then he said: Listen, O house of David! Is it not
enough for you to weary men, must you also weary
my God? Therefore the Lord himself will give you
this sign: the virgin shall be with child, and bear a
son, and shall name him Immanuel. He shall be
living on curds and honey by the time he learns to
reject the bad and choose the good.

RESPONSORY

Your light will come, Jerusalem;
the Lord will dawn on you in radiant beauty.
— Your light will come, Jerusalem;
the Lord will dawn on you in radiant beauty.

You will see his glory within you;
— the Lord will dawn on you in radiant beauty.

Glory to the Father . . .
— Your light will . . .

CANTICLE OF ZECHARIAH

Ant. The One who is coming after me is greater
than I; I am not worthy to untie the strap of
his sandals.

INTERCESSIONS

The Word of God humbled himself to dwell with us
so that we might see his glory. Rejoicing in hope,
let us call upon him:
*Emmanuel, be with us.*

Ruler, just and righteous,
— bring justice to the poor and the oppressed.
King of peace, you beat swords into plowshares and
   spears into pruning hooks,
— turn hatred into love and our grievances into forgiveness.
You do not judge by appearances,
— recognize those who are your own.
When you come with power and might upon the
   clouds,
— grant that we may come before you without shame.

Our Father . . .

CONCLUDING PRAYER

Lord our God,
grant that we may be ready
to receive Christ when he comes in glory
and to share in the banquet of heaven,
where he lives and reigns with you and the Holy
   Spirit,
one God, for ever and ever.

**Evening Prayer**

READING                                    1 Corinthians 4:5

Do not make any judgment before the appointed
time, until the Lord comes, for he will bring to light
what is hidden in darkness and will manifest the
motives of our hearts, and then everyone will receive praise from God.

RESPONSORY

Come and set us free, Lord God of power and might.
— Come and set us free, Lord God of power and
   might.

Let your face shine upon us and we shall be saved,
— Lord God of power and might.

Glory to the Father . . .
— Come and set . . .

CANTICLE OF MARY

Ant. The law will go forth from Zion; the word of the Lord from Jerusalem.

INTERCESSIONS

Let us pray to God the Father, who sent his Son to bring us endless peace:
   *Lord, your kingdom come.*
Father most holy, look kindly on your Church,
— come and visit this vine which your own right hand has planted.
Be mindful, Lord, of all the sons of Abraham,
— fulfill the promises you made to their fathers.
Merciful God, look kindly upon men and women of every race,
— may they honor you for your goodness.
Eternal Shepherd, visit the sheep of your flock,
— and gather them together into one fold.
Remember those who have gone forth from this world in your peace,
— lead them into glory with your Son.

Our Father . . .

CONCLUDING PRAYER

Lord our God,
grant that we may be ready
to receive Christ when he comes in glory
and to share in the banquet of heaven,
where he lives and reigns with you and the Holy Spirit,
one God, for ever and ever.

# THURSDAY

## Morning Prayer

READING                                    Isaiah 45:5-8

I am the Lord and there is no other,
  there is no God besides me.
It is I who arm you, though you know me not,
  so that toward the rising and the setting of the sun
  men may know that there is none besides me.
I am the Lord, there is no other;
  I form the light, and create the darkness,
I make well-being and create woe;
  I, the Lord, do all these things.
Let justice descend, O heavens, like dew from above,
  like gentle rain let the skies drop it down.
Let the earth open and salvation bud forth;
  let justice also spring up!
  I, the Lord, have created this.

RESPONSORY

Your light will come, Jerusalem;
the Lord will dawn on you in radiant beauty.
— Your light will come, Jerusalem;
the Lord will dawn on you in radiant beauty.

You will see his glory within you;
— the Lord will dawn on you in radiant beauty.

Glory to the Father . . .
— Your light will . . .

CANTICLE OF ZECHARIAH

Ant. I shall wait for my Lord and Savior and point
  him out when he is near, alleluia.

INTERCESSIONS

Christ is the wisdom and power of God, and his delight is to be with the children of men. With confidence let us pray:

*Draw near to us, Lord.*

Lord Jesus Christ, you have called us to your glorious kingdom,
— make us walk worthily, pleasing God in all we do.

You who stand unknown among us,
— reveal yourself to men and women.

You are nearer to us than we to ourselves,
— strengthen our faith and our hope of salvation.

You are the source of holiness,
— keep us holy and without sin now and until the day of your coming.

Our Father . . .

CONCLUDING PRAYER

Father,
we need your help.
Free us from sin and bring us to life.
Support us by your power.

Grant this through our Lord Jesus Christ, your Son, who lives and reigns with you and the Holy Spirit, one God, for ever and ever.

## Evening Prayer

READING					James 5:7-11

Be patient, therefore, brothers, until the coming of the Lord. See how the farmer waits for the precious fruit of the earth, being patient with it until it receives the early and the late rains. You too must be patient. Make your hearts firm, because the coming of the Lord is at hand. Do not complain, brothers, about one another, that you may not be judged. Behold, the Judge is standing before the gates. Take as an example of hardship and patience, brothers, the prophets who spoke in the name of the Lord. Indeed we call blessed those who have persevered. You have heard of the perseverance of Job, and you have seen the purpose of the Lord, because "the Lord is compassionate and merciful."

RESPONSORY

Come and set us free, Lord God of power and might.
— Come and set us free, Lord God of power and
  might.

Let your face shine upon us and we shall be saved,
— Lord God of power and might.

Glory to the Father . . .
— Come and set . . .

CANTICLE OF MARY

Ant. Blessed are you among women, and blessed is
    the fruit of your womb.

INTERCESSIONS

To Christ, the great light promised by the prophets to
    those who live in the shadow of death, let us raise
    our voices in prayer:
    Come, Lord Jesus!
Word of God, in the beginning you created all things
    and in the fullness of time assumed our nature,
— come and deliver us from death.
True light, shining on mankind,
— come and dispel our darkness.
Only-begotten Son, dwelling in the Father's heart,
— come and tell us of God's loving kindness.
Christ Jesus, you come among us as the Son of Man,
— transform those who know you into the sons of
  God.
You welcome all who call upon you in need,
— bring into your wedding feast those who beg at the
  door.

Our Father . . .

CONCLUDING PRAYER

Father,
we need your help.
Free us from sin and bring us to life.
Support us by your power.

Grant this through our Lord Jesus Christ, your Son, who lives and reigns with you and the Holy Spirit, one God, for ever and ever.

# FRIDAY

## Morning Prayer

READING                                    Jeremiah 30:21, 22

Thus says the Lord:
His leader shall be from Jacob
    and his ruler shall come from his kin.
When I summon him,
    he shall approach me.
You shall be my people,
    and I will be your God.

RESPONSORY

Your light will come, Jerusalem;
the Lord will dawn on you in radiant beauty.
— Your light will come, Jerusalem;
the Lord will dawn on you in radiant beauty.

You will see his glory within you;
— the Lord will dawn on you in radiant beauty.

Glory to the Father . . .
— Your light will . . .

CANTICLE OF ZECHARIAH

Ant. Our God comes, born as man of David's line, enthroned as king for ever, alleluia.

INTERCESSIONS

Through his Son, God the Father revealed his glory to men and women. Therefore, let our joyful cry resound:
    *Lord, may your name be glorified.*
Teach us, Lord, to love each other,
— as Christ loved us for God's glory.
Fill us with all joy and peace in faith,

— that we may walk in the hope and strength of the
   Holy Spirit.
Help all mankind, Lord, in your loving mercy,
— be near to those who seek you without knowing it.
You call and sanctify the elect,
— though we are sinners, crown us with eternal
   happiness.

Our Father . . .

CONCLUDING PRAYER

Jesus, our Lord,
save us from our sins.
Come, protect us from all dangers
and lead us to salvation,
for you live and reign with the Father and the Holy
   Spirit,
one God, for ever and ever.

## Evening Prayer

READING                                       2 Peter 3:8b-10

With the Lord one day is like a thousand years
and a thousand years like one day. The Lord does
not delay his promise, as some regard "delay," but
he is patient with you, not wishing that any should
perish but that all should come to repentance. But
the day of the Lord will come like a thief, and then
the heavens will pass away with a mighty roar and
the elements will be dissolved by fire, and the earth
and everything done on it will be found out.

RESPONSORY

Come and set us free, Lord God of power and might.
— Come and set us free, Lord God of power and
   might.

Let your face shine upon us and we shall be saved,
— Lord God of power and might.

Glory to the Father . . .
— Come and set . . .

Canticle of Mary

Ant. Out of Egypt I have called my Son; he will come to save his people.

Intercessions

With confidence let us call upon Christ, the shepherd and guardian of our souls:

*Lord, have mercy on us.*

Good shepherd of God's flock,
— gather all into your Church.

Lord Jesus, help the shepherds of your pilgrim people,
— until you come again may they zealously feed your flock.

Choose from among us heralds of your word,
— to proclaim your Gospel to the ends of the earth.

Take pity on all who struggle and fall along the way,
— may they find a friend to help them.

Show your glory in heaven,
— to those who listen to your voice on earth.

Our Father . . .

Concluding Prayer

Jesus, our Lord,
save us from our sins.
Come, protect us from all dangers
and lead us to salvation,
for you live and reign with the Father and the Holy Spirit,
one God, for ever and ever.

# SATURDAY
## Morning Prayer

Reading　　　　　　　　　　　　　　Isaiah 11:1-5

A shoot shall sprout from the stump of Jesse,
  and from his roots a bud shall blossom.
The spirit of the Lord shall rest upon him:
  a spirit of wisdom and understanding,

A spirit of counsel and of strength,
  a spirit of knowledge and of fear of the Lord,
    and his delight shall be the fear of the Lord.
Not by appearance shall he judge,
  nor by hearsay shall he decide,
But he shall judge the poor with justice,
  and decide aright for the land's afflicted.
He shall strike the ruthless with the rod of his mouth,
    and with the breath of his lips he shall slay the
      wicked.
Justice shall be the band around his waist,
  and faithfulness a belt upon his hips.

RESPONSORY

Your light will come, Jerusalem;
the Lord will dawn on you in radiant beauty.
— Your light will come, Jerusalem;
the Lord will dawn on you in radiant beauty.

You will see his glory within you;
— the Lord will dawn on you in radiant beauty.

Glory to the Father . . .
— Your light will . . .

CANTICLE OF ZECHARIAH

Ant. Banish your fears, O people of Zion; God, your
    own God, is coming to you, alleluia.

INTERCESSIONS

Let us pray to God our Father, who from of old has
    called his people to salvation:
    *Lord, protect your people.*
You promised to plant the seed of justice among
    your people,
— protect the holiness of your Church.
Lord, teach all men and women to listen to your
    word,
— and help believers to persevere in holiness.
Keep us in the love of your Spirit,
— that we may receive the mercy of your Son who is
    to come.

Father most merciful, strengthen us to the last,
— until the day of the coming of Jesus Christ our
  Lord.

Our Father . . .

CONCLUDING PRAYER

God our Father,
you loved the world so much
you gave your only Son to free us
from the ancient power of sin and death.
Help us who wait for his coming,
and lead us to true liberty.

We ask this through our Lord Jesus Christ, your Son,
who lives and reigns with you and the Holy Spirit,
one God, for ever and ever.

# DECEMBER 24

Invitatory antiphon, 19. Invitatory psalm, 22.

## Morning Prayer

HYMN, no. 65 or 64.

Ant. 1  Bethlehem in Judah's land, how glorious
        your future! The king who will rule my peo-
        ple comes from you.

Psalms and canticle from the current weekday.

Ant. 2  Lift up your heads and see; your redemp-
        tion is now at hand.

Ant. 3  The day has come at last when Mary will
        bring forth her firstborn Son.

Reading as on 376.

RESPONSORY

Tomorrow will be the day of your salvation,
the sinfulness of earth will be destroyed.
— Tomorrow will be the day of your salvation,
the sinfulness of earth will be destroyed.

The Savior of the world will be our king;
— the sinfulness of earth will be destroyed.

Glory to the Father . . .
— Tomorrow will be . . .

CANTICLE OF ZECHARIAH

Ant. The time has come for Mary to give birth to her firstborn Son.

INTERCESSIONS

To Jesus Christ, our Redeemer, who will come again in glory with great power, let us make our humble prayer:
*Come, Lord Jesus!*
Lord, Jesus, you will come with great power,
— look on our lowliness and make us worthy of your gifts.
You came to be the good news for mankind,
— may we always proclaim your saving work.
You are worthy of praise, for you have life and rule all things,
— help us to wait in joyful hope for the coming of your glory.
We long for the grace of your coming,
— console us with the gift of your own divine life.

Our Father. . .

CONCLUDING PRAYER

Come, Lord Jesus,
do not delay;
give new courage to your people who trust in your love.
By your coming, raise us to the joy of your kingdom,
where you live and reign with the Father and the Holy Spirit,
one God, for ever and ever.

## CHRISTMAS SEASON

For the Christmas Season, texts for the major feasts are given. For the weekdays after Christmas and Epiphany, see pages 392-395 and 399-402.

### December 25

### CHRISTMAS    Solemnity
### Evening Prayer I

HYMN, no. 75 or 76.

PSALMODY

Ant. 1   He comes in splendor, the King who is our peace; the whole world longs to see him.

#### Psalm 113

Praise, O servants of the Lord,
praise the name of the Lord!

May the name of the Lord be blessed
both now and for evermore!
From the rising of the sun to its setting
praised be the name of the Lord!

High above all nations is the Lord,
above the heavens his glory.
Who is like the Lord, our God,
who has risen on high to his throne
yet stoops from the heights to look down,
to look down upon heaven and earth?

From the dust he lifts up the lowly,
from his misery he raises the poor
to set him in the company of princes,—

yes, with the princes of his people.
To the childless wife he gives a home
and gladdens her heart with children.

Ant. 2  He sends forth his word to the earth, and his
command spreads swiftly through the land.

### Psalm 147:12-20

O praise the Lord, Jerusalem!
Zion, praise your God!

He has strengthened the bars of your gates,
he has blessed the children within you.
He established peace on your borders,
he feeds you with finest wheat.

He sends out his word to the earth
and swiftly runs his command.
He showers down snow white as wool,
he scatters hoar-frost like ashes.

He hurls down hailstones like crumbs.
The waters are frozen at his touch;
he sends forth his word and it melts them:
at the breath of his mouth the waters flow.

He makes his word known to Jacob,
to Israel his laws and decrees.
He has not dealt thus with other nations,
he has not taught them his decrees.

Ant. 3  The eternal Word, born of the Father before
time began, today emptied himself for our
sake and became man.

Canticle      Philippians 2:6-11

Though he was in the form of God,
Jesus did not deem equality with God
something to be grasped at.

Rather, he emptied himself
and took the form of a slave,
being born in the likeness of men.

He was known to be of human estate,
and it was thus that he humbled himself,
obediently accepting even death,
death on a cross!

Because of this,
God highly exalted him
and bestowed on him the name
above every other name,

So that at Jesus' name
every knee must bend
in the heavens, on the earth,
and under the earth,
and every tongue proclaim
to the glory of God the Father:
JESUS CHRIST IS LORD!

READING                            Galatians 4:3-7

In the same way we also, when we were not of age, were enslaved to the elemental powers of the world. But when the fullness of time had come, God sent his Son, born of a woman, born under the law, to ransom those under the law, so that we might receive adoption. As proof that you are children, God sent the spirit of his Son into our hearts, crying out, "Abba, Father!" So you are no longer a slave but a child, and if a child then also an heir, through God.

RESPONSORY

Today you will know the Lord is coming.
— Today you will know the Lord is coming.

And in the morning you will see his glory.
— The Lord is coming.

Glory to the Father . . .
— Today you will . . .

CANTICLE OF MARY

Ant. When the sun rises in the morning sky, you
    will see the King of kings coming forth from
    the Father like a radiant bridegroom from the
    bridal chamber.

INTERCESSIONS

Christ Jesus emptied himself and took the form of a
    slave. He was tested like us in all things and did
    not sin. Now let us worship him and pray to him
    with deep faith:
    *By the power of your birth, comfort those who are
    saved.*

You came into the world heralding the new age fore-
    told by the prophets,
— give your holy people the gift of renewal in every
    generation.

You once took on the weakness of our human condi-
    tion,
— be light now for those who do not see, strength for
    the wavering and comfort for the troubled of heart.

You were born into poverty and lowliness,
— look with favor on the poor and comfort them.

By your birth bring joy to all peoples with the
    promise of unending life,
— give joy to the dying through the hope of heavenly
    birth.

You came to earth to lead everyone into the kingdom,
— share your life of glory with those who have died.

Our Father . . .

CONCLUDING PRAYER

God our Father,
every year we rejoice
as we look forward to this feast of our salvation.
May we welcome Christ as our Redeemer,
and meet him with confidence when he comes to be
    our judge,

who lives and reigns with you and the Holy Spirit,
one God, for ever and ever.

### Alternative Prayer

God of endless ages, Father of all goodness,
we keep vigil for the dawn of salvation
and the birth of your Son.
With gratitude we recall his humanity,
the life he shared with the sons of men.
May the power of his divinity
help us to answer his call to forgiveness and life.

We ask this through Christ our Lord.

Night Prayer is said by those who do not participate in the Office of Readings and in the Mass at
midnight.

### Invitatory

Ant. Christ is born for us; come, let us adore him.

Invitatory psalm, as in the Ordinary, 22.

The plan of the hours demands that Morning
Prayer not be celebrated immediately after the
Mass at midnight, but in the morning.

### Morning Prayer

HYMN, no. 71 or 72.

Ant. 1 Tell us, shepherds, what have you seen?
        Who has appeared on earth? We have seen
        a newborn infant and a choir of angels
        praising the Lord, alleluia.

Psalms and canticle from Sunday, Week I, 43.

Ant. 2 The angel said to the shepherds: I proclaim
        to you a great joy; today the Savior of the
        world is born for you, alleluia.

Ant. 3  A little child is born for us today; little and
        yet called the mighty God, alleluia.

READING                                    Hebrews 1:1-4

In times past, God spoke in partial and various
ways to our ancestors through the prophets; in these
last days, he spoke to us through a son, whom he
made heir of all things and through whom he created
the universe,
    who is the refulgence of his glory,
        the very imprint of his being,
    and who sustains all things by his mighty word.
    When he had accomplished purification from sins,
    he took his seat at the right hand of the Majesty on
        high,
    as far superior to the angels
    as the name he has inherited is more excellent
        than theirs.

RESPONSORY

The Lord has made known, alleluia, alleluia.
— The Lord has made known, alleluia, alleluia.

His saving power,
— alleluia, alleluia.

Glory to the Father . . .
— The Lord has . . .

CANTICLE OF ZECHARIAH

Ant.  Glory to God in the highest, and peace to his
      people on earth, alleluia.

INTERCESSIONS

The Word of God existed before the creation of the
    universe yet was born among us in time. We praise
    and worship him as we cry out in joy:
    *Let the earth ring out with joy for you have come.*
You are the eternal Word of God who flooded the
    world with joy at your birth,
— fill us with joy by the continuous gift of your life.

You saved us and by your birth revealed to us the
  covenant faithfulness of the Lord,
— help us to be faithful to the promises of our baptism.
You are the King of heaven and earth who sent messengers to announce peace to all,
— let our lives be filled with your peace.
You are the true vine that brings forth the fruit of life,
— make us branches of the vine, bearing much fruit.

Our Father . . .

CONCLUDING PRAYER

Father,
we are filled with the new light
by the coming of your Word among us.
May the light of faith
shine in our words and actions.

Grant this through our Lord Jesus Christ, your Son,
who lives and reigns with you and the Holy Spirit,
one God, for ever and ever.

Alternative Prayer

Almighty God and Father of light,
a child is born for us and a son is given to us.
Your eternal Word leaped down from heaven
in the silent watches of the night,
and now your Church is filled with wonder
at the nearness of her God.
Open our hearts to receive his life
and increase our vision with the rising of dawn,
that our lives may be filled with his glory and his
  peace,
who lives and reigns for ever and ever.

## Evening Prayer II

HYMN, no. 70 or 74.

PSALMODY

Ant. 1  You have been endowed from your birth with princely gifts; in eternal splendor, before the dawn of light on earth, I have begotten you.

### Psalm 110:1-5, 7

The Lord's revelation to my Master:
"Sit on my right:
your foes I will put beneath your feet."

The Lord will wield from Zion
your scepter of power:
rule in the midst of all your foes.

A prince from the day of your birth
on the holy mountains;
from the womb before the dawn I begot you.

The Lord has sworn an oath he will not change.
"You are a priest for ever,
a priest like Melchizedek of old!"

The Master standing at your right hand
will shatter kings in the day of his great wrath.

He shall drink from the stream by the wayside
and therefore he shall lift up his head.

Ant. 2  With the Lord is unfailing love; great is his power to save.

### Psalm 130

Out of the depths I cry to you, O Lord,
Lord, hear my voice!
O let your ears be attentive
to the voice of my pleading.

If you, O Lord, should mark our guilt,
Lord, who would survive?
But with you is found forgiveness:
for this we revere you.

My soul is waiting for the Lord,
I count on his word.
My soul is longing for the Lord
more than watchman for daybreak.
Let the watchman count on daybreak
and Israel on the Lord.

Because with the Lord there is mercy
and fullness of redemption,
Israel indeed he will redeem
from all its iniquity.

Ant. 3   In the beginning, before time began, the
Word was God; today he is born, the Savior
of the world.

Canticle from Wednesday, Week I, 81.

READING                                    1 John 1:1-3

What was from the beginning,
what we have heard,
what we have seen with our eyes,
what we looked upon
and touched with our hands
concerns the Word of life—
for the life was made visible;
we have seen it and testify to it
and proclaim to you the eternal life
that was with the Father and was made visible to
   us—
what we have seen and heard
we proclaim now to you,
so that you too may have fellowship with us;
for our fellowship is with the Father
and with his Son, Jesus Christ.

RESPONSORY

The Word was made man, alleluia, alleluia.
— The Word was made man, alleluia, alleluia.

He lived among us,
— alleluia, alleluia.

Glory to the Father . . .
— The Word was made man, alleluia, alleluia.

CANTICLE OF MARY

Ant. Christ the Lord is born today; today, the Savior has appeared. Earth echoes songs of angel choirs, archangels' joyful praise. Today on earth his friends exult: Glory to God in the highest, alleluia.

INTERCESSIONS

At the birth of Jesus, angels proclaimed peace to the world. We worship him now with joy, and we pray with hearts full of faith:
*May your birth bring peace to all.*
Lord, fill your holy people with whatever good they need,
— let the mystery of your birth be the source of our peace.
You came as chief shepherd and guardian of our lives,
— let the pope and bishops be faithful channels of your many gifts of grace.
King from all eternity, you desired to be born within time and to experience the day-to-day life of men and women,
— share your gift of unending life with us, weak people, doomed to death.
Awaited from the beginning of the world, you came only in the fullness of time,
— now reveal your presence to those who are still expecting you.

You became man and gave new life to our human
    condition in the grip of death,
— now give the fullness of life to all who have died.

Our Father . . .

### CONCLUDING PRAYER

Lord God,
we praise you for creating man,
and still more for restoring him in Christ.
Your Son shared our weakness:
may we share his glory,
for he lives and reigns with you and the Holy Spirit,
one God, for ever and ever.

### Alternative Prayer

God of love, Father of all,
the darkness that covered the earth
has given way to the bright dawn of your Word
    made flesh.
Make us a people of this light.
Make us faithful to your Word,
that we may bring your life to the waiting world.

Grant this through Christ our Lord.

# Sunday in the Octave of Christmas

Psalter, Week I

## HOLY FAMILY

Feast

When Christmas occurs on Sunday, the feast of the Holy Family is celebrated on December 30 and there is no Evening Prayer I.

### Evening Prayer I

CANTICLE OF MARY

Ant. The child Jesus remained in Jerusalem, and his parents did not know it. They thought he was in the group of travelers and looked for him among their relatives and friends.

### Invitatory

Ant. Come, let us worship Christ, the Son of God, who was obedient to Mary and Joseph.

Invitatory psalm, as in the Ordinary, 22.

### Morning Prayer

CANTICLE OF ZECHARIAH

Ant. Lord, give us light through the example of your family and guide our feet into the way of peace.

CONCLUDING PRAYER

Father,
help us to live as the holy family,
united in respect and love.
Bring us to the joy and peace of your eternal home.

Grant this through our Lord Jesus Christ, your Son,
who lives and reigns with you and the Holy Spirit,
one God, for ever and ever.

## Alternative Prayer

Father in heaven, creator of all,
you ordered the earth to bring forth life
and crowned its goodness by creating the family of
   man.
In history's moment when all was ready,
you sent your Son to dwell in time,
obedient to the laws of life in our world.
Teach us the sanctity of human love,
show us the value of family life,
and help us to live in peace with all men
that we may share in your life for ever.

We ask this through Christ our Lord.

### Evening Prayer II

CANTICLE OF MARY

Ant. Son, why have you done this to us? Think what
     anguish your father and I have endured looking
     for you. But why did you look for me? Did you
     not know that I had to be in my Father's house?

---

# WEEKDAYS AFTER CHRISTMAS
## Invitatory

Ant. Christ is born for us; come, let us adore him.

Invitatory psalm, as in the Ordinary, 22.

## Morning Prayer

Hymn, antiphons, psalms and canticle, as in Morning Prayer of Christmas, 384.

READING                                        Isaiah 9:5-6

A child is born to us, a son is given us;
  upon his shoulder dominion rests.
They name him Wonder-Counselor, God-Hero,
  Father-Forever, Prince of Peace.
His dominion is vast
  and forever peaceful,
From David's throne, and over his kingdom,
  which he confirms and sustains
By judgment and justice,
  both now and forever.
The zeal of the Lord of hosts will do this!

RESPONSORY

The Lord has made known, alleluia, alleluia.
— The Lord has made known, alleluia, alleluia.
His saving power,
— alleluia, alleluia.
Glory to the Father . . .
— The Lord has . . .

CANTICLE OF ZECHARIAH

Ant. At the Lord's birth the choir of angels sang:
     Blessed be our God enthroned as King and
     blessed be the Lamb.

INTERCESSIONS

Let us pray to Christ, in whom the Father willed to
    make all things new:
    *Beloved Son of God, hear us.*
Son of God, you were with the Father in the begin-
    ning, and in the fullness of time you became a man,
— give us a brother's love for all people.
You became poor to make us rich; you emptied
    yourself that we might be lifted up by your lowli-
    ness and share in your glory,

— make us faithful ministers of your Gospel.
You shone on those who dwelt in darkness and the
   shadow of death,
— give us holiness, justice and peace.
Give us a heart that is upright and sincere, so that
   we may listen to your word,
— and bring it to perfection in ourselves and in the
   world for the sake of your glory.

Our Father . . .

CONCLUDING PRAYER

All-powerful God,
may the human birth of your Son
free us from our former slavery to sin
and bring us new life.

We ask this through our Lord Jesus Christ, your Son,
who lives and reigns with you and the Holy Spirit,
one God, for ever and ever.

## Evening Prayer

Hymns, antiphons, psalms and canticle, as in
Evening Prayer II of Christmas, 387.

READING                                    See 2 Peter 1:3-4

The divine power of Christ has bestowed on us
everything that makes for life and devotion,
through the knowledge of him who called us by his
own glory and power. Through these, he has bestowed on us the precious and very great promises,
so that through them you may come to share in the
divine nature, after escaping from the corruption
that is in the world because of evil desire.

RESPONSORY

The Word was made man, alleluia, alleluia.
— The Word was made man, alleluia, alleluia.

He lived among us,
— alleluia, alleluia.

Glory to the Father . . .
— The Word was made man, alleluia, alleluia.

CANTICLE OF MARY

Ant. We sing your praises, holy Mother of God: you gave birth to our Savior, Jesus Christ; watch over all who honor you.

INTERCESSIONS

Let us joyfully acclaim Christ, born at Bethlehem in Judea, for he gives nourishment and guidance to his holy people:
*Let your favor rest upon us, Lord.*
Christ the Savior, desired of the nations, spread your Gospel to places still deprived of the Word of life,
— draw every person to yourself.
Christ the Lord, let your Church grow and extend the boundaries of its homeland,
— until it embraces men and women of every language and race.
King of kings, direct the hearts and minds of rulers,
— to seek justice, peace and freedom for all nations.
Almighty ruler, strength of the weak, support those in temptation, lift up the fallen, protect those living in danger,
— console those who have been deceived, comfort the incurably ill, strengthen the faith of the anxious.
Consoler of the sorrowful, comfort the dying,
— and lead them to the fountains of living water.

Our Father . . .

CONCLUDING PRAYER

All-powerful God,
may the human birth of your Son
free us from our former slavery to sin
and bring us new life.

We ask this through our Lord . . . for ever and ever.

# MARY, MOTHER OF GOD

Solemnity

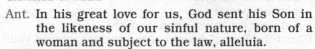

### Evening Prayer I

CANTICLE OF MARY

Ant. In his great love for us, God sent his Son in the likeness of our sinful nature, born of a woman and subject to the law, alleluia.

### Invitatory

Ant. Let us celebrate the motherhood of the Virgin Mary; let us worship her Son, Christ the Lord.

Invitatory psalm, as in the Ordinary, 22.

### Morning Prayer

CANTICLE OF ZECHARIAH

Ant. Marvelous is the mystery proclaimed today: man's nature is made new as God becomes man; he remains what he was and becomes what he was not. Yet each nature stays distinct and for ever undivided.

CONCLUDING PRAYER

God our Father,
may we always profit by the prayers
of the Virgin Mother Mary,
for you bring us life and salvation
through Jesus Christ her Son
who lives and reigns with you and the Holy Spirit,
one God, for ever and ever.

## Alternative Prayer

Father,
source of light in every age,
the virgin conceived and bore your Son
who is called Wonderful God, Prince of Peace.
May her prayer, the gift of a mother's love,
be your people's joy through all ages.
May her response, born of a humble heart,
draw your Spirit to rest on your people.

Grant this through Christ our Lord.

## Evening Prayer II

CANTICLE OF MARY

Ant. Blessed is the womb which bore you, O
Christ, and the breast that nursed you, Lord
and Savior of the world, alleluia.

---

# January 6 or the Sunday between January 2 and January 8

## EPIPHANY

Solemnity

CANTICLE OF MARY

Ant. Seeing the star, the wise men said: This must
signify the birth of some great king. Let us
search for him and lay our treasures at his
feet: gold, frankincense and myrrh.

## Invitatory

Ant. Christ has appeared to us; come, let us adore
him.

Invitatory psalm, as in the Ordinary, 22.

## Morning Prayer

CANTICLE OF ZECHARIAH

Ant. Today the Bridegroom claims his bride, the Church, since Christ has washed her sins away in Jordan's waters; the Magi hasten with their gifts to the royal wedding; and the wedding guests rejoice, for Christ has changed water into wine, alleluia.

CONCLUDING PRAYER

Father,
you revealed your Son to the nations
by the guidance of a star.
Lead us to your glory in heaven
by the light of faith.

We ask this through our Lord Jesus Christ, your Son, who lives and reigns with you and the Holy Spirit, one God, for ever and ever.

### Alternative Prayer

Father of light, unchanging God,
today you reveal to men of faith
the resplendent fact of the Word made flesh.
Your light is strong,
your love is near;
draw us beyond the limits which this world imposes,
to the life where your Spirit makes all life complete.

We ask this through Christ our Lord.

## Evening Prayer II

CANTICLE OF MARY

Ant. Three mysteries mark this holy day: today the star leads the Magi to the infant Christ; today water is changed into wine for the wedding feast; today Christ wills to be baptized by John in the river Jordan to bring us salvation.

# WEEKDAYS AFTER EPIPHANY

## Invitatory

Ant. Christ has appeared to us; come, let us adore
him.

Invitatory psalm, as in the Ordinary, 22.

## Morning Prayer

READING                                    Isaiah 4:2-3

On that day,
The branch of the Lord will be luster and glory,
    and the fruit of the earth will be honor and splendor
    for the survivors of Israel.
He who remains in Zion
    and he that is left in Jerusalem
Will be called holy:
    everyone marked down for life in Jerusalem.

RESPONSORY

All the kings of the earth will bow down in worship.
— All the kings of the earth will bow down in wor-
    ship.

Men and women of every nation will serve him.
— They will bow down in worship.

Glory to the Father . . .
— All the kings . . .

CANTICLE OF ZECHARIAH

Ant. The wise men offered gifts of gold, frankincense, and myrrh to the Lord, the Son of God
and King most high, alleluia.

INTERCESSIONS

Let us rejoice in the compassion of Christ, who came
to free mankind from the slavery of corruption and

to give us the freedom of the sons of God. Trusting in this divine compassion, we plead:
*By your birth, deliver us from evil.*

Lord, you existed before the ages, yet you entered into a new life,
— renew us continually through the mystery of your birth.

Without surrendering your divinity, you wondrously took on our humanity,
— grant that our lives may press on to a fuller participation in your divinity.

You came to be a light to the nations, the teacher of holiness,
— let your words be a light along our way.

Word of God made flesh in the womb of the Virgin Mary, you entered this world,
— live in our hearts always through faith.

Our Father . . .

CONCLUDING PRAYER

Father,
your Son became like us
when he revealed himself in our nature:
help us to become more like him,
who lives and reigns with you and the Holy Spirit,
one God, for ever and ever.

## Evening Prayer

READING                                          Ephesians 2:3b-5

We were by nature children of wrath, like the rest. But God, who is rich in mercy, because of the great love he had for us, even when we were dead in our transgressions, brought us to life with Christ (by grace you have been saved).

RESPONSORY

All peoples will be blessed in him, men and women of every race.

— All peoples will be blessed in him, men and
  women of every race.

All nations will acclaim his glory.
— Men and women of every race.

Glory to the Father . . .
— All peoples will be blessed in him, men and
  women of every race.

CANTICLE OF MARY

Ant. Christ, you are Light from Light; when you ap-
     peared on the earth, the wise men offered
     their gifts to you, alleluia.

INTERCESSIONS

United with all Christians in prayer and praise, we entreat the Lord:
   *Father, hear your children.*
Help those who do not know God but seek your presence in the shadows and projections of the human
   mind,
— make them new persons in the light of Christ.
Look with favor on all who adore you as the one true
   God and who await your coming in judgment on
   the last day,
— may they recognize your constant love for us.
Remember all those on whom you bestow life, light
   and all good things,
— let them never be far from you.
Watch over all travelers with angelic protection,
— and keep them from sudden and unforeseen death.
You revealed your truth to the dead while they were
   on earth,
— lead them to contemplate the beauty of your countenance.

Our Father . . .

CONCLUDING PRAYER

Father,
your Son became like us
when he revealed himself in our nature:
help us to become more like him,
who lives and reigns with you and the Holy Spirit,
one God, for ever and ever.

# The Sunday after January 6

# BAPTISM OF THE LORD

Feast

## Evening Prayer I

CANTICLE OF MARY

Ant. Our Savior came to be baptized, so that through the cleansing waters of baptism he might restore the old man to new life, heal our sinful nature, and clothe us with unfailing holiness.

## Invitatory

Ant. Come, let us worship Christ, the beloved Son in whom the Father was well pleased.

Invitatory psalm, as in the Ordinary, 22.

## Morning Prayer

CANTICLE OF ZECHARIAH

Ant. Christ is baptized, the world is made holy; he has taken away our sins. We shall be purified by water and the Holy Spirit.

CONCLUDING PRAYER

Almighty, eternal God,
when the Spirit descended upon Jesus
at his baptism in the Jordan,

403

you revealed him as your own beloved Son.
Keep us, your children born of water and the Spirit,
faithful to our calling.

We ask this through our Lord Jesus Christ, your Son,
who lives and reigns with you and the Holy Spirit,
one God, for ever and ever.

## Alternative Prayer

Father in heaven,
you revealed Christ as your Son
by the voice that spoke over the waters of the Jordan.
May all who share in the sonship of Christ
follow in his path of service to man,
and reflect the glory of his kingdom
even to the ends of the earth,
for he is Lord for ever and ever.

## Evening Prayer II

CANTICLE OF MARY

Ant.  Christ Jesus loved us, poured out his blood to
wash away our sins, and made us a kingdom
and priests for God our Father. To him be
glory and honor for ever.

## LENTEN SEASON

One week of texts is given for the Lenten Season. These texts may be repeated throughout the season. The hymns are indicated in the Liturgical Guide, **578**.

The hymns are indicated in the Liturgical Guide, **578**.

### INVITATORY

The antiphon for the invitatory psalm of Morning Prayer is:

Today if you hear the voice of the Lord,
harden not your hearts.

The psalms and canticle with their antiphon are from the current day in the Psalter.

## SUNDAY
### Evening Prayer I

READING                    2 Corinthians 6:1-4a

We appeal to you not to receive the grace of God in vain. For he says:

"In an acceptable time I heard you,
    and on the day of salvation I helped you."

Behold, now is a very acceptable time; behold, now is the day of salvation. We cause no one to stumble in anything, in order that no fault may be found with our ministry; on the contrary, in everything we commend ourselves as ministers of God.

RESPONSORY

Listen to us, O Lord, and have mercy, for we have sinned against you.
— Listen to us, O Lord, and have mercy, for we have sinned against you.

Christ Jesus, hear our humble petitions,
— for we have sinned against you.

405

Glory to the Father . . .
— Listen to us . . .

CANTICLE OF MARY

Ant. **Man cannot live on bread alone but by every word that comes from the mouth of God.**

INTERCESSIONS

Let us give glory to Christ the Lord, who became our teacher and example and our brother. Let us pray to him, saying:

*Lord, fill your people with your life.*

Lord Jesus, you became like us in all things but sin; teach us how to share with others their joy and sorrow,
— that our love may grow deeper every day.

Help us to feed you in feeding the hungry,
— and to give you drink in giving drink to the thirsty.

You raised Lazarus from the sleep of death,
— grant that those who have died the death of sin may rise again through faith and repentance.

Inspire many to follow you with greater zeal and perfection,
— through the example of the blessed Virgin Mary and the saints.

Let the dead rise in your glory,
— to enjoy your love for ever.

Our Father . . .

CONCLUDING PRAYER

Father,
through our observance of Lent,
help us to understand the meaning
of your Son's death and resurrection,
and teach us to reflect it in our lives.

Grant this through our Lord Jesus Christ, your Son,
who lives and reigns with you and the Holy Spirit,
one God, for ever and ever.

## Alternative Prayer

Lord our God,
you formed man from the clay of the earth
and breathed into him the spirit of life,
but he turned from your face and sinned.
In this time of repentance
we call out for your mercy.
Bring us back to you
and to the life your Son won for us
by his death on the cross,
for he lives and reigns for ever and ever.

## Morning Prayer

READING                                    See Nehemiah 8:9, 10

Today is holy to the Lord your God. Do not be
sad, and do not weep; for today is holy to our Lord.
Do not be saddened this day, for rejoicing in the
Lord must be your strength!

RESPONSORY

Christ, Son of the living God, have mercy on us.
— Christ, Son of the living God, have mercy on us.

You were wounded for our offenses,
— have mercy on us.

Glory to the Father . . .
— Christ, Son of . . .

CANTICLE OF ZECHARIAH

Ant. Jesus was led by the Spirit into the desert to be
tempted by the devil; and when he had fasted for
forty days and forty nights, he was hungry.

INTERCESSIONS

Let us praise our loving Redeemer, who gained for
us this season of grace, and pray to him, saying:
*Lord, create a new spirit in us.*
Christ, our life, through baptism we were buried
with you and rose to life with you,
— may we walk today in newness of life.

Lord, you have brought blessings to all mankind,
— bring us to share your concern for the good of all.
May we work together to build up the earthly city,
— with our eyes fixed on the city that lasts for ever.
Healer of body and soul, cure the sickness of our spirit,
— so that we may grow in holiness through your constant care.

Our Father . . .

<small>CONCLUDING PRAYER</small>

Father,
through our observance of Lent,
help us to understand the meaning
of your Son's death and resurrection,
and teach us to reflect it in our lives.

Grant this through our Lord Jesus Christ, your Son,
who lives and reigns with you and the Holy Spirit,
one God, for ever and ever.

## Alternative Prayer

Lord our God,
you formed man from the clay of the earth
and breathed into him the spirit of life,
but he turned from your face and sinned.
In this time of repentance
we call out for your mercy.
Bring us back to you
and to the life your Son won for us
by his death on the cross,
for he lives and reigns for ever and ever.

## Evening Prayer II

<small>READING</small>　　　　　　　　　　1 Corinthians 9:24-27

Do you not know that the runners in the stadium all run in the race, but only one wins the prize?

Run so as to win. Every athlete exercises discipline in every way. They do it to win a perishable crown, but we an imperishable one. Thus I do not run aimlessly; I do not fight as if I were shadowboxing. No, I drive my body and train it, for fear that, after having preached to others, I myself should be disqualified.

RESPONSORY

Listen to us, O Lord, and have mercy, for we have sinned against you.
— Listen to us, O Lord, and have mercy, for we have sinned against you.

Christ Jesus, hear our humble petitions,
— for we have sinned against you.

Glory to the Father . . .
— Listen to us . . .

CANTICLE OF MARY

Ant. Watch over us, eternal Savior; do not let the cunning tempter seize us. We place all our trust in your unfailing help.

INTERCESSIONS

All praise to God the Father who brought his chosen people to rebirth from imperishable seed through his eternal Word. Let us ask him as his children:
Lord, be gracious to your people.
God of mercy, hear the prayers we offer for all your people,
— may they hunger for your word more than for bodily food.
Give us a sincere and active love for our own nation and for all mankind,
— may we work always to build a world of peace and goodness.

Look with love on all to be reborn in baptism,
— that they may be living stones in your temple of
  the Spirit.
You moved Nineveh to repentance by the preaching
  of Jonah,
— in your mercy touch the hearts of sinners by the
  preaching of your word.
May the dying go in hope to meet Christ their
  judge,
— may they rejoice for ever in the vision of your
  glory.

Our Father . . .


CONCLUDING PRAYER

Father,
through our observance of Lent,
help us to understand the meaning
of your Son's death and resurrection,
and teach us to reflect it in our lives.

Grant this through our Lord Jesus Christ, your Son,
who lives and reigns with you and the Holy Spirit,
one God, for ever and ever.


Alternative Prayer

Lord our God,
you formed man from the clay of the earth
and breathed into him the spirit of life,
but he turned from your face and sinned.
In this time of repentance
we call out for your mercy.
Bring us back to you
and to the life your Son won for us
by his death on the cross,
for he lives and reigns for ever and ever.

# MONDAY

## Morning Prayer

READING                                    Exodus 19:4-6a

You have seen for yourselves how I bore you up on eagle wings and brought you here to myself. Therefore, if you hearken to my voice and keep my covenant, you shall be my special possession, dearer to me than all other people, though all the earth is mine. You shall be to me a kingdom of priests, a holy nation.

RESPONSORY

God himself will set me free, from the hunter's snare.
— God himself will set me free, from the hunter's snare.

From those who would trap me with lying words
— and from the hunter's snare.

Glory to the Father . . .
— God himself will . . .

CANTICLE OF ZECHARIAH

Ant. You have been blessed by my Father; come and receive the kingdom prepared for you from the foundation of the world.

INTERCESSIONS

Praise to Jesus, our Savior; by his death he has opened for us the way of salvation. Let us ask him:
*Lord, guide your people to walk in your ways.*
God of mercy, you gave us new life through baptism,
— make us grow day by day in your likeness.
May our generosity today bring joy to those in need,
— in helping them may we find you.
Help us to do what is good, right and true in your sight,
— and to seek you always with undivided hearts.

Forgive our sins against the unity of your family,
— make us one in heart and spirit.

Our Father . . .

CONCLUDING PRAYER

God our savior,
bring us back to you
and fill our minds with your wisdom.
May we be enriched by our observance of Lent.

Grant this through our Lord Jesus Christ, your Son,
who lives and reigns with you and the Holy Spirit,
one God, for ever and ever.

## Evening Prayer

READING                              Romans 12:1-2

I urge you, brothers, by the mercies of God, to offer
your bodies as a living sacrifice, holy and pleasing to
God, your spiritual worship. Do not conform yourself
to this age but be transformed by the renewal of your
mind, that you may discern what is the will of God,
what is good and pleasing and perfect.

RESPONSORY

To you, O Lord, I make my prayer for mercy.
— To you, O Lord, I make my prayer for mercy.

Heal my soul, for I have sinned against you.
— I make my prayer for mercy.

Glory to the Father . . .
— To you, O Lord . . .

CANTICLE OF MARY

Ant. Whatever you do for the least of my brothers,
      you do for me.

INTERCESSIONS

Our Lord Jesus Christ has saved us from our sins.
   As his people, let us call out to him:

*Jesus, Son of David, have mercy on us.*

Lord Christ, we pray for your holy Church; you gave yourself up to make it holy, cleansing it with water and the life-giving word,

— renew it constantly, and purify it by penance.

Good Master, show young people the way you have chosen for each of them,

— may they walk in it, and find fulfillment.

In your compassion you healed all forms of sickness; bring hope to the sick and raise them up,

— teach us to love and care for them.

Make us mindful of the dignity you gave us in baptism,

— may we live for you at every moment.

May the dead rise to glory in your peace,

— grant us with them a share in your kingdom.

Our Father . . .

CONCLUDING PRAYER

God our savior,
bring us back to you
and fill our minds with your wisdom.
May we be enriched by our observance of Lent.

Grant this through our Lord Jesus Christ, your Son, who lives and reigns with you and the Holy Spirit, one God, for ever and ever.

# TUESDAY
## Morning Prayer

READING                         Joel 2:12-13

Return to me with your whole heart,
    with fasting, and weeping, and mourning;
Rend your hearts, not your garments,
    and return to the Lord, your God.

For gracious and merciful is he,
  slow to anger, rich in kindness,
  and relenting in punishment.


RESPONSORY

God himself will set me free, from the hunter's snare.
— God himself will set me free, from the hunter's
  snare.

From those who would trap me with lying words
— and from the hunter's snare.

Glory to the Father . . .
— God himself will . . .


CANTICLE OF ZECHARIAH

Ant. Lord, teach us to pray as John taught his disciples.


INTERCESSIONS

Praise to Christ, who has given us himself as the
  bread from heaven. Let us pray to him, saying:
  *Jesus, you feed and heal our souls; come to
  strengthen us.*
Lord, feed us at the banquet of the eucharist,
— with all the gifts of your paschal sacrifice.
Give us a perfect heart to receive your word,
— that we may bring forth fruit in patience.
Make us eager to work with you in building a better
  world,
— so that it may listen to your Church and its
  gospel of peace.
We confess, Lord, that we have sinned,
— wash us clean by your gift of salvation.

Our Father . . .

CONCLUDING PRAYER

Father,
look on us, your children.
Through the discipline of Lent
help us to grow in our desire for you.

We ask this through our Lord Jesus Christ, your Son,
who lives and reigns with you and the Holy Spirit,
one God, for ever and ever.

## Evening Prayer

READING                           James 2:14-18

What good is it, my brothers, if someone says he
has faith but does not have works? Can that faith
save him? If a brother or sister has nothing to wear
and has no food for the day, and one of you says to
them, "Go in peace, keep warm, and eat well," but
you do not give them the necessities of the body,
what good is it? So also faith of itself, if it does not
have works, is dead.

Indeed someone might say, "You have faith and I
have works." Demonstrate your faith to me without
works, and I will demonstrate my faith to you from
my works.

RESPONSORY

To you, O Lord, I make my prayer for mercy.
— To you, O Lord, I make my prayer for mercy.

Heal my soul, for I have sinned against you.
— I make my prayer for mercy.

Glory to the Father . . .
— To you, O Lord . . .

CANTICLE OF MARY

Ant. When you wish to pray, go to your room, shut
the door, and pray to your Father in secret.

INTERCESSIONS

Christ our Lord has warned us to watch and pray to
    avoid temptation. With our whole heart let us
    pray to him:
    *Turn to us, Lord, and have mercy.*
Jesus, our Christ, you promised to be with those
    who pray in your name,
— help us always to pray with you to the Father in
    the Holy Spirit.
Bridegroom of the Church, cleanse her from every
    stain,
— teach her to walk in hope and in the power of the
    Holy Spirit.
Friend of the human race, teach us concern for our
    neighbor as you have commanded,
— that all may see you more clearly as the light of
    the world.
King of peace, give your peace to the world,
— that your presence may reveal your saving power
    in every place.
Open the door of eternal happiness to all the dead,
— welcome them into the glory of unending life.

Our Father . . .


CONCLUDING PRAYER

Father,
look on us, your children.
Through the discipline of Lent
help us to grow in our desire for you.

We ask this through our Lord Jesus Christ, your Son,
who lives and reigns with you and the Holy Spirit,
one God, for ever and ever.

# WEDNESDAY
## Morning Prayer

READING                                    Deuteronomy 7:6, 8-9

The Lord, your God, has chosen you from all the nations on the face of the earth to be a people peculiarly his own. It was because the Lord loved you and because of his fidelity to the oath he had sworn to your fathers, that he brought you out with his strong hand from the place of slavery, and ransomed you from the hand of Pharaoh, king of Egypt. Understand, then, that the Lord, your God, is God indeed, the faithful God who keeps his merciful covenant to the thousandth generation toward those who love him and keep his commandments.

RESPONSORY

God himself will set me free, from the hunter's snare.
— God himself will set me free, from the hunter's snare.

From those who would trap me with lying words
— and from the hunter's snare.

Glory to the Father . . .
— God himself will . . .

CANTICLE OF ZECHARIAH

Ant. This evil and faithless generation asks for a sign, but no sign will be given it except the sign of the prophet Jonah.

INTERCESSIONS

Blessed be God, the giver of salvation, who decreed that mankind should become a new creation in himself, when all would be made new. With great confidence let us ask him:

*Lord, renew us in your Spirit.*

Lord, you promised a new heaven and a new earth;
   renew us daily through your Spirit,
— that we may enjoy your presence for ever in the
   heavenly Jerusalem.

Help us to work with you to make this world alive
   with your Spirit,
— and to build on earth a city of justice, love and
   peace.

Free us from all negligence and sloth,
— and give us joy in your gifts of grace.

Deliver us from evil,
— and from slavery to the senses, which blinds us
   to goodness.

Our Father . . .

CONCLUDING PRAYER

Lord,
look upon us and hear our prayer.
By the good works you inspire,
help us to discipline our bodies
and to be renewed in spirit.

Grant this through our Lord Jesus Christ, your Son,
who lives and reigns with you and the Holy Spirit,
one God, for ever and ever.

## Evening Prayer

READING                          Philippians 2:12b-16

Work out your salvation with fear and trembling.
For God is the one who, for his good purpose,
works in you both to desire and to work. Do everything without grumbling or questioning, that you
may be blameless and innocent, children of God
without blemish in the midst of a crooked and perverse generation, among whom you shine like lights

in the world, as you hold on to the word of life, so that my boast for the day of Christ may be that I did not run in vain or labor in vain.

RESPONSORY

To you, O Lord, I make my prayer for mercy.
— To you, O Lord, I make my prayer for mercy.

Heal my soul, for I have sinned against you.
— I make my prayer for mercy.

Glory to the Father . . .
— To you, O Lord . . .

CANTICLE OF MARY

Ant. As Jonah was three days and three nights in the belly of the whale, so will the Son of Man spend three days and three nights in the heart of the earth.

INTERCESSIONS

Blessed be almighty God, who watches over us as a Father; he knows all our needs but wants us to seek first his kingdom. Let us cry out to him as his people:

*May your kingdom come, that justice may reign.*

Father of all holiness, you gave us Christ as the shepherd of our souls; stay with your shepherds and the flock entrusted to them, do not leave this flock without the loving care of its shepherd,
— do not leave your shepherds without an obedient flock to follow them.

Teach Christians to help the weak with loving care,
— and in serving them to serve your Son.

Gather into your Church those who do not yet believe,
— and help them to build it up by good deeds done for love of you.

Help us to turn to you for forgiveness,
— and, as you forgive us, reconcile us also with your Church.
May the dead pass from this world to eternal life,
— to be with you for ever.

Our Father . . .

CONCLUDING PRAYER

Lord,
look upon us and hear our prayer.
By the good works you inspire,
help us to discipline our bodies
and to be renewed in spirit.

Grant this through our Lord Jesus Christ, your Son, who lives and reigns with you and the Holy Spirit, one God, for ever and ever.

# THURSDAY

## Morning Prayer

READING                                    See 1 Kings 8:51-53a

We are your people and your inheritance. Thus may your eyes be open to the petition of your servant and to the petition of your people Israel. Hear us whenever we call upon you, because you have set us apart among all the peoples of the earth for your inheritance.

RESPONSORY

God himself will set me free, from the hunter's snare.
— God himself will set me free, from the hunter's snare.
From those who would trap me with lying words
— and from the hunter's snare.
Glory to the Father . . .
— God himself will . . .

C<small>ANTICLE OF</small> Z<small>ECHARIAH</small>

Ant. If you, evil as you are, know how to give your
children what is good, how much more will
your Father in heaven pour out his gifts on all
who pray to him.

I<small>NTERCESSIONS</small>

Christ our Lord came among us as the light of the
world, that we might walk in his light, and not in
the darkness of death. Let us praise him and cry
out to him:
*Let your word be a lamp to guide us.*
God of mercy, help us today to grow in your likeness,
— that we who sinned in Adam may rise again in
Christ.
Let your word be a lamp to guide us,
— that we may live the truth and grow always in
your love.
Teach us to be faithful in seeking the common
good for your sake,
— that your light may shine on the whole human
family by means of your Church.
Touch our hearts to seek your friendship more and
more,
— and to make amends for our sins against your
wisdom and goodness.

Our Father . . .

C<small>ONCLUDING</small> P<small>RAYER</small>

Father,
without you we can do nothing.
By your Spirit help us to know what is right
and to be eager in doing your will.

We ask this through our Lord Jesus Christ, your Son,
who lives and reigns with you and the Holy Spirit,
one God, for ever and ever.

## Evening Prayer

READING                                          James 4:7-10

Submit yourselves to God. Resist the devil, and he will flee from you. Draw near to God, and he will draw near to you. Cleanse your hands, you sinners, and purify your hearts, you of two minds. Begin to lament, to mourn, to weep. Let your laughter be turned into mourning and your joy into dejection. Humble yourselves before the Lord and he will exalt you.

RESPONSORY

To you, O Lord, I make my prayer for mercy.
— To you, O Lord, I make my prayer for mercy.

Heal my soul, for I have sinned against you.
— I make my prayer for mercy.

Glory to the Father . . .
— To you, O Lord . . .

CANTICLE OF MARY

Ant. Ask and you shall receive, seek and you shall find, knock and the door shall be opened to you.

INTERCESSIONS

Christ the Lord gave us a new commandment, of love for each other. Let us pray to him:
  *Lord, build up your people in love.*
Good Master, teach us to love you in our neighbor,
— and in serving them to serve you.
On the cross you asked pardon for your executioners,
— give us strength to love our enemies and pray for those who persecute us.
Through the mystery of your body and blood, deepen our love, our perseverance and our trust,
— strengthen the weak, console the sorrowful, and give hope to the dying.

Light of the world, you gave light to the man born
   blind when he had washed in the pool of Siloam,
— enlighten catechumens through the water of
   baptism and the word of life.
Give to the dead the perfect joy of your eternal love,
— and number us also among your chosen ones.

Our Father . . .

CONCLUDING PRAYER

Father,
without you we can do nothing.
By your Spirit help us to know what is right
and to be eager in doing your will.

We ask this through our Lord Jesus Christ, your Son,
who lives and reigns with you and the Holy Spirit,
one God, for ever and ever.

# FRIDAY

## Morning Prayer

READING                                Isaiah 53:11b-12

Through his suffering, my servant shall justify many,
   and their guilt he shall bear.
Therefore I will give him his portion among the great,
   and he shall divide the spoils with the mighty,
Because he surrendered himself to death
   and was counted among the wicked;
And he shall take away the sins of many
   and win pardon for their offenses.

RESPONSORY

God himself will set me free, from the hunter's snare.
— God himself will set me free, from the hunter's
   snare.

From those who would trap me with lying words
— and from the hunter's snare.

Glory to the Father . . .
— God himself will . . .

CANTICLE OF ZECHARIAH

Ant. If your virtue does not surpass that of the
scribes and Pharisees, you will never enter
the kingdom of heaven.

INTERCESSIONS

Thanks be to Christ the Lord, who brought us life
by his death on the cross. With our whole heart
let us ask him:
*By your death raise us to life.*
Teacher and Savior, you have shown us your fidelity
and made us a new creation by your passion,
— keep us from falling again into sin.
Help us to deny ourselves today,
— and not deny those in need.
May we receive this day of penance as your gift,
— and give it back to you through works of mercy.
Master our rebellious hearts,
— and teach us generosity.

Our Father . . .

CONCLUDING PRAYER

Lord,
may our observance of Lent
help to renew us and prepare us
to celebrate the death and resurrection of Christ,
who lives and reigns with you and the Holy Spirit,
one God, for ever and ever.

## Evening Prayer

READING                                James 5:16, 19-20

Confess your sins to one another and pray for one another, that you may be healed. The fervent prayer of a righteous person is very powerful.

My brothers, if anyone among you should stray from the truth and someone bring him back, he should know that whoever brings back a sinner from the error of his way will save his soul from death and will cover a multitude of sins.

RESPONSORY

To you, O Lord, I make my prayer for mercy.
— To you, O Lord, I make my prayer for mercy.

Heal my soul, for I have sinned against you.
— I make my prayer for mercy.

Glory to the Father . . .
— To you, O Lord . . .

CANTICLE OF MARY

Ant. If you are bringing your gift to the altar, and there you remember that your brother has something against you, leave your gift in front of the altar; go at once and make peace with your brother, and then come back and offer your gift.

INTERCESSIONS

The Lord Jesus sanctified his people with his blood. Let us cry out to him:
*Lord, have mercy on your people.*
Loving Redeemer, through your passion teach us self-denial, strengthen us against evil and adversity, and increase our hope,
— and so make us ready to celebrate your resurrection.

Grant that Christians, as your prophets, may make
  you known in every place,
— and bear witness to you with living faith and
  hope and love.
Give your strength to all in distress,
— and help us to raise them up through our loving
  concern.
Teach the faithful to see your passion in their sufferings,
— and show to others your power to save.
Author of life, remember those who have passed
  from this world,
— grant them the glory of your risen life.

Our Father . . .

<small>Concluding Prayer</small>

Lord,
may our observance of Lent
help to renew us and prepare us
to celebrate the death and resurrection of Christ,
who lives and reigns with you and the Holy Spirit,
one God, for ever and ever.

# SATURDAY

## Morning Prayer

<small>Reading</small>                              Isaiah 1:16-18

  Wash yourselves clean!
Put away your misdeeds from before my eyes;
  cease doing evil; learn to do good.
Make justice your aim; redress the wronged,
  hear the orphan's plea, defend the widow.
Come now, let us set things right,
  says the Lord:

Though your sins be like scarlet,
  they may become white as snow;
Though they be crimson red,
  they may become white as wool.

RESPONSORY

God himself will set me free, from the hunter's snare.
— God himself will set me free, from the hunter's
  snare.

From those who would trap me with lying words
— and from the hunter's snare.

Glory to the Father . . .
— God himself will . . .

CANTICLE OF ZECHARIAH

Ant. If you want to be true children of your heav-
     enly Father, then you must pray for those who
     persecute you and speak all kinds of evil
     against you, says the Lord.

INTERCESSIONS

To make us his new creation, Christ the Lord gave us
  the waters of rebirth and spread the table of his
  body and his word. Let us call upon him and say:
  *Lord, renew us in your grace.*
Jesus, meek and humble of heart, clothe us with
  compassion, kindness and humility,
— make us want to be patient with everyone.
Teach us to be true neighbors to all in trouble and
  distress,
— and so imitate you, the Good Samaritan.
May the Blessed Virgin, your Mother, pray for all
  those vowed to a life of virginity,
— that they may deepen their dedication to you and
  to the Church.

Grant us the gift of your mercy,
— forgive our sins and remit their punishment.

Our Father . . .

CONCLUDING PRAYER

Eternal Father,
turn our hearts to you.
By seeking your kingdom
and loving one another,
may we become a people who worship you
in spirit and truth.

Grant this through our Lord Jesus Christ, your Son,
who lives and reigns with you and the Holy Spirit,
one God, for ever and ever.

# PASSION SUNDAY
## (PALM SUNDAY)

## Evening Prayer I

HYMN, no. 39 or 101.

Psalms and canticle with proper antiphons from the current Sunday.

READING                                  1 Peter 1:18-21

Realize that you were ransomed from your futile conduct, handed on by your ancestors, not with perishable things like silver or gold but with the precious blood of Christ as of a spotless unblemished lamb. He was known before the foundation of the world but revealed in the final time for you, who through him believe in God who raised him from the dead and gave him glory, so that your faith and hope are in God.

RESPONSORY

We worship you, O Christ, and we praise you.
— We worship you, O Christ, and we praise you.

Because by your cross you have redeemed the world.
— We praise you.

Glory to the Father . . .
— We worship you . . .

CANTICLE OF MARY

Ant. Praise to our King, the Son of David, the Redeemer of the world; praise to the Savior whose coming had been foretold by the prophets.

INTERCESSIONS

Before his passion, Christ looked out over Jerusalem and wept for it, because it had not recog-
nized the hour of God's visitation. With sorrow
for our sins, let us adore him, and say:
*Lord, have mercy on your people.*

You longed to gather to yourself the people of Jerusalem, as the hen gathers her young,
— teach all peoples to recognize the hour of your
visitation.

Do not forsake those who have forsaken you,
— turn our hearts to you, and we will return to you,
our God.

Through your passion you gave grace to the world,
— help us to live always by your Spirit, given to us
in baptism.

By your passion, help us to deny ourselves,
— and so prepare to celebrate your resurrection.

You reign in the glory of the Father,
— remember those who have died today.

Our Father . . .

CONCLUDING PRAYER

Almighty, ever-living God,
you have given the human race Jesus Christ our
Savior
as a model of humility.
He fulfilled your will
by becoming man and giving his life on the cross.
Help us to bear witness to you
by following his example of suffering
and make us worthy to share in his resurrection.

We ask this through our Lord Jesus Christ, your Son,
who lives and reigns with you and the Holy Spirit,
one God, for ever and ever.

### Alternative Prayer

Almighty Father of our Lord Jesus Christ,
you sent your Son
to be born of woman and to die on a cross,
so that through the obedience of one man,
estrangement might be dissolved for all men.
Guide our minds by his truth
and strengthen our lives by the example of his death,
that we may live in union with you
in the kingdom of your promise.

Grant this through Christ our Lord.

## Morning Prayer

HYMN, no. 103 or 102.

Psalms and canticle with proper antiphons from
the current Sunday.

READING                                Zechariah 9:9

Rejoice heartily, O daughter Zion,
    shout for joy, O daughter Jerusalem!
See, your king shall come to you;
    a just savior is he,
Meek, and riding on an ass,
    on a colt, the foal of an ass.

RESPONSORY

By your own blood, Lord, you brought us back to
    God.
— By your own blood, Lord, you brought us back to
    God.

From every tribe, and tongue, and people and nation,
— you brought us back to God.

Glory to the Father . . .
— By your own . . .

CANTICLE OF ZECHARIAH

Ant. With palms let us welcome the Lord as he comes, with songs and hymns let us run to meet him, as we offer him our joyful worship and sing: Blessed be the Lord!

INTERCESSIONS

As Christ entered Jerusalem he was greeted as King and Messiah. Let us adore him, and joyfully praise him:

*Blessed is he who comes in the name of the Lord.*

Hosanna to you, Son of David, King of the ages,
— hosanna to you, victor over death and the powers of darkness.

You went up to Jerusalem to suffer and so enter into your glory,
— lead your Church into the paschal feast of heaven.

You made your cross the tree of life,
— grant its fruit to those reborn in baptism.

Savior of mankind, you came to save sinners,
— bring into your kingdom all who have faith, hope and love.

Our Father . . .

CONCLUDING PRAYER

Almighty, ever-living God,
you have given the human race Jesus Christ our Savior
as a model of humility.
He fulfilled your will
by becoming man and giving his life on the cross.
Help us to bear witness to you
by following his example of suffering
and make us worthy to share his resurrection.

We ask this through our Lord Jesus Christ, your Son,
who lives and reigns with you and the Holy Spirit,
one God, for ever and ever.

### Alternative Prayer

Almighty Father of our Lord Jesus Christ,
you sent your Son
to be born of woman and to die on a cross,
so that through the obedience of one man,
estrangement might be dissolved for all men.
Guide our minds by his truth
and strengthen our lives by the example of his death,
that we may live in union with you
in the kingdom of your promise.

Grant this through Christ our Lord.

## Evening Prayer II

HYMN, no. 104 or 39.

Psalms and canticle with proper antiphons from
the current Sunday.

READING                              Acts 13:26-30

My brothers, to us this word of salvation has been
sent. The inhabitants of Jerusalem and their leaders
failed to recognize Jesus, and by condemning him
they fulfilled the oracles of the prophets that are read
sabbath after sabbath. For even though they found no
grounds for a death sentence, they asked Pilate to
have him put to death, and when they had accomplished all that was written about him, they took him
down from the tree and placed him in a tomb. But
God raised him from the dead.

RESPONSORY

We worship you, O Christ, and we praise you.
— We worship you, O Christ, and we praise you.

Because by your cross you have redeemed the world.
— We praise you.

Glory to the Father . . .
— We worship you . . .

CANTICLE OF MARY

Ant. It is written: I will strike the shepherd and his flock shall be scattered. But when I have risen, I will go before you into Galilee. There you shall see me, says the Lord.

INTERCESSIONS

The Savior of mankind by dying destroyed death and by rising again restored life. Let us humbly ask him:

*Sanctify your people, redeemed by your blood.*

Redeemer of the world, give us a greater share of your passion through a deeper spirit of repentance,

— so that we may share the glory of your resurrection.

May your Mother, comfort of the afflicted, protect us,

— may we console others as you console us.

Look with love on those who suffer because of our indifference,

— come to their aid, and turn our uncaring hearts to works of justice and charity.

You humbled yourself by being obedient even to accepting death, death on a cross,

— give all who serve you the gifts of obedience and patient endurance.

Transform the bodies of the dead to be like your own in glory,

— and bring us at last into their fellowship.

Our Father . . .

CONCLUDING PRAYER

Almighty, ever-living God,
you have given the human race Jesus Christ our Savior
as a model of humility.
He fulfilled your will
by becoming man and giving his life on the cross.
Help us to bear witness to you

by following his example of suffering
and make us worthy to share in his resurrection.

We ask this through our Lord Jesus Christ, your Son,
who lives and reigns with you and the Holy Spirit,
one God, for ever and ever.

## Alternative Prayer

Almighty Father of our Lord Jesus Christ,
you sent your Son
to be born of woman and to die on a cross,
so that through the obedience of one man
estrangement might be dissolved for all men.
Guide our minds by his truth
and strengthen our lives by the example of his
    death,
that we may live in union with you
in the kingdom of your promise.

Grant this through Christ our Lord.

# EASTER TRIDUUM
# OF THE PASSION AND RESURRECTION
# OF THE LORD

## HOLY THURSDAY
### Evening Prayer

Evening Prayer is said only by those who do not participate in the evening Mass of the Lord's Supper.

HYMN, no. 108 or 107.

Psalms and canticle with the proper antiphons as in Week II, Thursday, 166.

READING                                        Hebrews 13:12-15

Jesus suffered outside the gate, to consecrate the people by his own blood. Let us then go to him outside the camp, bearing the reproach that he bore. For here we have no lasting city, but we seek the one that is to come. Through him [then] let us continually offer God a sacrifice of praise, that is, the fruit of lips that confess his name.

In place of the responsory the following is said:

Ant. For our sake Christ was obedient, accepting even death.

CANTICLE OF MARY

Ant. While they were at supper, Jesus took bread, said the blessing, broke the bread and gave it to his disciples.

INTERCESSIONS

At the Last Supper, on the night he was betrayed, our
    Savior entrusted to his Church the memorial of his
    death and resurrection, to be celebrated for ever.
    Let us adore him, and say:
    *Sanctify your people, redeemed by your blood.*
Redeemer of the world, give us a greater share of your
    passion through a deeper spirit of repentance,
— so that we may share the glory of your resurrec-
    tion.
May your Mother, comfort of the afflicted, protect us,
— may we console others as you console us.
In their trials enable your faithful people to share in
    your passion,
— and so reveal in their lives your saving power.
You humbled yourself by being obedient even to ac-
    cepting death, death on a cross,
— give all who serve you the gifts of obedience and
    patient endurance.
Transform the bodies of the dead to be like your own
    in glory,
— and bring us at last into their fellowship.

Our Father . . .

CONCLUDING PRAYER

Father,
for your glory and our salvation
you appointed Jesus Christ eternal High Priest.
May the people he gained for you by his blood
come to share in the power of his cross and resurrec-
    tion
by celebrating his memorial in this eucharist,
for he lives and reigns with you and the Holy Spirit,
one God, for ever and ever.

Night Prayer from Sunday, after Evening Prayer II,
333. In place of the responsory of Night Prayer the following is said:

Ant. For our sake Christ was obedient, accepting even death.

# GOOD FRIDAY

## Invitatory

Ant. Come, let us worship Christ, the Son of God, who redeemed us with his blood.

Invitatory psalm, as in the Ordinary, 22.

## Morning Prayer

HYMN, no. 104 or 107.

PSALMODY

Ant. 1 God did not spare his own Son, but gave him up to suffer for our sake.

### Psalm 51

Have mercy on me, God, in your kindness.
In your compassion blot out my offense.
O wash me more and more from my guilt
and cleanse me from my sin.

My offenses truly I know them;
my sin is always before me.
Against you, you alone, have I sinned;
what is evil in your sight I have done.

That you may be justified when you give sen-
    tence
and be without reproach when you judge.
O see, in guilt I was born,
a sinner was I conceived.

Indeed you love truth in the heart;
then in the secret of my heart teach me wisdom.
O purify me, then I shall be clean;
O wash me, I shall be whiter than snow.

Make me hear rejoicing and gladness,
that the bones you have crushed may revive.
From my sins turn away your face
and blot out all my guilt.

A pure heart create for me, O God,
put a steadfast spirit within me.
Do not cast me away from your presence,
nor deprive me of your holy spirit.

Give me again the joy of your help;
with a spirit of fervor sustain me,
that I may teach transgressors your ways
and sinners may return to you.

O rescue me, God, my helper,
and my tongue shall ring out your goodness.
O Lord, open my lips
and my mouth shall declare your praise.

For in sacrifice you take no delight,
burnt offering from me you would refuse,
my sacrifice, a contrite spirit.
A humbled, contrite heart you will not spurn.

In your goodness, show favor to Zion;
rebuild the walls of Jerusalem.
Then you will be pleased with lawful sacrifice,
holocausts offered on your altar.

Ant. 2   Jesus Christ loved us, and poured out his
         own blood for us to wash away our sins.

Canticle                        Habakkuk 3:2-4, 13a, 15-19

O Lord, I have heard your renown,
and feared, O Lord, your work.
In the course of the years revive it,
in the course of the years make it known;
in your wrath remember compassion!

God comes from Teman,
the Holy One from Mount Paran.
Covered are the heavens with his glory,
and with his praise the earth is filled.

His splendor spreads like the light;
rays shine forth from beside him,
where his power is concealed.
You come forth to save your people,
to save your anointed one.

You tread the sea with your steeds
amid the churning of the deep waters.
I hear, and my body trembles;
at the sound, my lips quiver.

Decay invades my bones,
my legs tremble beneath me.
I await the day of distress
that will come upon the people who attack us.

For though the fig tree blossom not
nor fruit be on the vines,
though the yield of the olive fail
and the terraces produce no nourishment,

Though the flocks disappear from the fold
and there be no herd in the stalls,
yet will I rejoice in the Lord
and exult in my saving God.

God, my Lord, is my strength;
he makes my feet swift as those of hinds
and enables me to go upon the heights.

Ant. 3  We worship your cross, O Lord, and we
praise and glorify your holy resurrection,
for the wood of the cross has brought joy to
the world.

## Psalm 147:12-20

O praise the Lord, Jerusalem!
Zion, praise your God!

He has strengthened the bars of your gates,
he has blessed the children within you.
He established peace on your borders,
he feeds you with finest wheat.

He sends out his word to the earth
and swiftly runs his command.
He showers down snow white as wool,
he scatters hoar-frost like ashes.

He hurls down hailstones like crumbs.
The waters are frozen at his touch;
he sends forth his word and it melts them:
at the breath of his mouth the waters flow.

He makes his word known to Jacob,
to Israel his laws and decrees.
He has not dealt thus with other nations;
he has not taught them his decrees.

READING                                    Isaiah 52:13-15

See, my servant shall prosper,
  he shall be raised high and greatly exalted.
Even as many were amazed at him—
  so marred was his look beyond that of man,
  and his appearance beyond that of mortals—
So shall he startle many nations,
  because of him kings shall stand speechless;
For those who have not been told shall see,
  those who have not heard shall ponder it.

In place of the responsory the following is said:

Ant. For our sake Christ was obedient, accepting
      even death, death on a cross.

CANTICLE OF ZECHARIAH

Ant. Over his head they hung their accusation:
    Jesus of Nazareth, King of the Jews.

INTERCESSIONS

For our sake our Redeemer suffered death and was
    buried, and rose again. With heartfelt love let us
    adore him, and pray:
    Lord, have mercy on us.
Christ our teacher, for our sake you were obedient
    even to accepting death,
— teach us to obey the Father's will in all things.
Christ our life, by your death on the cross you de-
    stroyed the power of evil and death,
— may we die with you, to rise with you in glory.
Christ our King, you became an outcast among us,
    a worm and no man,
— teach us the humility by which you saved the
    world.
Christ our salvation, you gave yourself up to death
    out of love for us,
— help us to show your love to one another.
Christ our Savior, on the cross you embraced all
    time with your outstretched arms,
— unite God's scattered children in your kingdom
    of salvation.

Our Father . . .

CONCLUDING PRAYER

Father,
look with love upon your people,
the love which our Lord Jesus Christ showed us
when he delivered himself to evil men
and suffered the agony of the cross,
for he lives and reigns with you and the Holy Spirit,
one God, for ever and ever.

## Evening Prayer

Evening Prayer is said only by those who do not participate in the celebration of the Lord's passion.

HYMN, no. 105 or 110.

PSALMODY

Ant. 1  Look well, all you peoples, and see my suffering.

### Psalm 116:10-19

I trusted, even when I said:
"I am sorely afflicted,"
and when I said in my alarm:
"No man can be trusted."

How can I repay the Lord
for his goodness to me?
This cup of salvation I will raise;
I will call on the Lord's name.

My vows to the Lord I will fulfill
before all his people.
O precious in the eyes of the Lord
is the death of his faithful.

Your servant, Lord, your servant am I;
you have loosened my bonds.
A thanksgiving sacrifice I make:
I will call on the Lord's name.

My vows to the Lord I will fulfill
before all his people,
in the courts of the house of the Lord,
in your midst, O Jerusalem.

Ant. 2  My soul is in anguish, my heart is in torment.

## Psalm 143:1-11

Lord, listen to my prayer:
turn your ear to my appeal.
You are faithful, you are just; give answer.
Do not call your servant to judgment
for no one is just in your sight.

The enemy pursues my soul;
he has crushed my life to the ground;
he has made me dwell in darkness
like the dead, long forgotten.
Therefore my spirit fails;
my heart is numb within me.

I remember the days that are past:
I ponder all your works.
I muse on what your hand has wrought
and to you I stretch out my hands.
Like a parched land my soul thirsts for you.

Lord, make haste and answer;
for my spirit fails within me.
Do not hide your face
lest I become like those in the grave.

In the morning let me know your love
for I put my trust in you.
Make me know the way I should walk:
to you I lift up my soul.

Rescue me, Lord, from my enemies;
I have fled to you for refuge.
Teach me to do your will—

for you, O Lord, are my God.
Let your good spirit guide me
in ways that are level and smooth.

For your name's sake, Lord, save my life;
in your justice save my soul from distress.

Ant. 3 When Jesus had taken the vinegar, he said: "It is accomplished." Then he bowed his head and died.

Canticle                    Philippians 2:6-11

Though he was in the form of God,
Jesus did not deem equality with God
something to be grasped at.

Rather, he emptied himself
and took the form of a slave,
being born in the likeness of men.

He was known to be of human estate,
and it was thus that he humbled himself,
obediently accepting even death,
death on a cross!

Because of this
God highly exalted him
and bestowed on him the name
above every other name,

So that at Jesus' name
every knee must bend
in the heavens, on the earth,
and under the earth,
and every tongue proclaim
to the glory of God the Father:
JESUS CHRIST IS LORD!

READING                      1 Peter 2:21-24

Christ suffered for you, leaving you an example that you should follow in his footsteps.

"He committed no sin,
and no deceit was found in his mouth."

When he was insulted, he returned no insult; when he suffered, he did not threaten; instead, he handed himself over to the one who judges justly. He himself bore our sins in his body upon the cross, so that, free from sin, we might live for righteousness. By his wounds you have been healed.

In place of the responsory the following is said:

Ant. For our sake Christ was obedient, accepting even death, death on a cross.

CANTICLE OF MARY

Ant. When we were his enemies, God reconciled us to himself by the death of his Son.

INTERCESSIONS

As intercessions the General Intercessions found in the Sacramentary for this day may be used. The prayers suggested here may be used as an alternative, or silent prayer may be offered for these intentions.

Today we lovingly remember the death of our Lord Jesus Christ, from which was born new life for the whole world. Let us turn to God the Father, and say:
   *By the merits of your Son's death, hear us, Lord.*
Give unity to your Church.
Protect N., our Pope.
Sanctify your people, both clergy and faithful, by your Spirit.
Increase faith and understanding in those under instruction.
Gather all Christians in unity.
Lead the Jewish people to the fullness of redemption.
Enlighten with your glory those who do not yet believe in Christ.
Show the marks of your love in creation to those who deny them.

Guide the minds and hearts of those who govern us.
Console all who are troubled.
Have pity on those who have died.

Our Father . . .

Father,
look with love upon your people,
the love which our Lord Jesus Christ showed us
when he delivered himself to evil men
and suffered the agony of the cross,
for he lives and reigns with you and the Holy Spirit,
one God, for ever and ever.

Night Prayer from Sunday, after Evening Prayer II,
333.

In place of the responsory the following is said:

Ant. For our sake Christ was obedient, accepting
even death, death on a cross.

# HOLY SATURDAY

## Invitatory

Ant. Come, let us worship Christ, who for our sake
suffered death and was buried.

Invitatory psalm, as in the Ordinary, 22.

## Morning Prayer

HYMN, no. 105.

PSALMODY

Ant. 1  Though sinless, the Lord has been put to death. The world is in mourning as for an only son.

### Psalm 64

Hear my voice, O God, as I complain,
guard my life from dread of the foe.
Hide me from the band of the wicked,
from the throng of those who do evil.

They sharpen their tongues like swords;
they aim bitter words like arrows
to shoot at the innocent from ambush,
shooting suddenly and recklessly.

They scheme their evil course;
they conspire to lay secret snares.
They say: "Who will see us?
Who can search out our crimes?"

He will search who searches the mind
and knows the depth of the heart.
God has shot them with his arrow
and dealt them sudden wounds.
Their own tongue has brought them to ruin
and all who see them mock.

Then will all men fear;
they will tell what God has done.
They will understand God's deeds.
The just will rejoice in the Lord
and fly to him for refuge.
All the upright hearts will glory.

Ant. 2  From the jaws of hell, Lord, rescue my soul.

Canticle                                    Isaiah 38:10-14, 17-20

Once I said,
"In the noontime of life I must depart!
To the gates of the nether world I shall be con-
    signed
for the rest of my years."

I said, "I shall see the Lord no more
in the land of the living.
No longer shall I behold my fellow men
among those who dwell in the world."

My dwelling, like a shepherd's tent,
is struck down and borne away from me;
you have folded up my life, like a weaver
who severs the last thread.

Day and night you give me over to torment;
I cry out until the dawn.
Like a lion he breaks all my bones;
day and night you give me over to torment.

Like a swallow I utter shrill cries;
I moan like a dove.
My eyes grow weak, gazing heaven-ward:
O Lord, I am in straits; be my surety!

You have preserved my life
from the pit of destruction,
when you cast behind your back
all my sins.

For it is not the nether world that gives you
    thanks,
nor death that praises you;
neither do those who go down into the pit
await your kindness.

The living, the living give you thanks,
as I do today.
Fathers declare to their sons,
O God, your faithfulness.

The Lord is our savior;
we shall sing to stringed instruments
in the house of the Lord
all the days of our life.

Ant. 3  I was dead, but now I live for ever, and I
hold the keys of death and of hell.

Psalm 150

Praise God in his holy place,
praise him in his mighty heavens.
Praise him for his powerful deeds,
praise his surpassing greatness.

O praise him with sound of trumpet,
praise him with lute and harp.
Praise him with timbrel and dance,
praise him with strings and pipes.

O praise him with resounding cymbals,
praise him with clashing of cymbals.
Let everything that lives and that breathes
give praise to the Lord.

READING                                    Hosea 5:15b—16:2

Thus says the Lord:
In their affliction, they shall look for me:
    "Come, let us return to the Lord,
For it is he who has rent, but he will heal us;
    he has struck us, but he will bind our wounds.
He will revive us after two days;
    on the third day he will raise us up,
    to live in his presence."

In place of the responsory the following is said:

Ant.  For our sake Christ was obedient, accepting
even death, death on a cross. Therefore God
raised him on high and gave him the name
above all other names.

## CANTICLE OF ZECHARIAH

Ant. Save us, O Savior of the world. On the cross you redeemed us by the shedding of your blood; we cry out for your help, O God.

## INTERCESSIONS

Our Redeemer suffered and was buried for us in order to rise again. With sincere love we adore him, and aware of our needs we cry out:

*Lord, have mercy on us.*

Christ our Savior, your sorrowing Mother stood by you at your death and burial,
— in our sorrows may we share your suffering.

Christ our Lord, like the seed buried in the ground, you brought forth for us the harvest of grace,
— may we die to sin and live for God.

Christ, the Good Shepherd, in death you lay hidden from the world,
— teach us to love a life hidden with you in the Father.

Christ, the new Adam, you entered the kingdom of death to release all the just since the beginning of the world,
— may all who lie dead in sin hear your voice and rise to life.

Christ, Son of the living God, through baptism we were buried with you,
— risen also with you in baptism, may we walk in newness of life.

Our Father . . .

## CONCLUDING PRAYER

All-powerful and ever-living God,
your only Son went down among the dead
and rose again in glory.
In your goodness
raise up your faithful people,
buried with him in baptism,

to be one with him
in the eternal life of heaven,
where he lives and reigns with you and the Holy
  Spirit,
one God, for ever and ever.

## Evening Prayer

HYMN, no. 98 or 113.

PSALMODY

Ant. 1 Death, you shall die in me; hell, you shall
       be destroyed by me.

### Psalm 116:10-19

I trusted, even when I said:
"I am sorely afflicted,"
and when I said in my alarm:
"No man can be trusted."

How can I repay the Lord
for his goodness to me?
The cup of salvation I will raise;
I will call on the Lord's name.

My vows to the Lord I will fulfill
before all his people.
O precious in the eyes of the Lord
is the death of his faithful.

Your servant, Lord, your servant am I;
you have loosened my bonds.
A thanksgiving sacrifice I make:
I will call on the Lord's name.

My vows to the Lord I will fulfill
before all his people,
in the courts of the house of the Lord,
in your midst, O Jerusalem.

Ant. 2 As Jonah was three days and three nights
       in the belly of the whale, so will the Son of
       Man be three days and three nights in the
       heart of the earth.

## Psalm 143:1-11

Lord, listen to my prayer:
turn your ear to my appeal.
You are faithful, you are just; give answer.
Do not call your servant to judgment
for no one is just in your sight.

The enemy pursues my soul;
he has crushed my life to the ground;
he has made me dwell in darkness
like the dead, long forgotten.
Therefore my spirit fails;
my heart is numb within me.

I remember the days that are past:
I ponder all your works.
I muse on what your hand has wrought
and to you I stretch out my hands.
Like a parched land my soul thirsts for you.

Lord, make haste and answer;
for my spirit fails within me.
Do not hide your face
lest I become like those in the grave.

In the morning let me know your love
for I put my trust in you.
Make me know the way I should walk:
to you I lift up my soul.

Rescue me, Lord, from my enemies;
I have fled to you for refuge.
Teach me to do your will
for you, O Lord, are my God.
Let your good spirit guide me
in ways that are level and smooth.

For your name's sake, Lord, save my life;
in your justice save my soul from distress.

Ant. 3  **Destroy this temple, says the Lord, and in three days I will rebuild it. He was speaking of the temple of his body.**

Canticle                              Philippians 2:6-11

Though he was in the form of God,
Jesus did not deem equality with God
something to be grasped at.

Rather, he emptied himself
and took the form of a slave,
being born in the likeness of men.

He was known to be of human estate,
and it was thus that he humbled himself,
obediently accepting even death,
death on a cross!

Because of this,
God highly exalted him
and bestowed on him the name
above every other name,

So that at Jesus' name
every knee must bend
in the heavens, on the earth,
and under the earth,
and every tongue proclaim
to the glory of God the Father:
JESUS CHRIST IS LORD!

READING                              1 Peter 1:18-21

Realize that you were ransomed from your futile conduct, handed on by your ancestors, not with perishable things like silver or gold but with the precious blood of Christ as of a spotless unblemished lamb. He was known before the foundation of the world but revealed in the final time for you, who through him believe in God who raised him from the dead and gave him glory, so that your faith and hope are in God.

In place of the responsory the following is said:

Ant. For our sake Christ was obedient, accepting even death, death on a cross. Therefore God raised him on high and gave him the name above all other names.

CANTICLE OF MARY

Ant. Now the Son of Man has been glorified and God has been glorified in him.

INTERCESSIONS

For our sake our Redeemer suffered death and was buried, and rose again. With heartfelt love let us adore him, and pray:
  *Lord, have mercy on us.*
Lord Jesus, when your side was pierced, there flowed out blood and water, the marvelous symbol of the whole Church,
— through your death, burial and resurrection, bring life to your bride, the Church.
Lord Jesus, you remembered those who did not remember your promise of resurrection,
— remember those without hope, who do not know that you have risen.
Lamb of God, you were offered for all as our paschal sacrifice,
— draw all mankind to yourself.
God of all the world, you encompass the universe but were pleased to be laid in a tomb,
— free the human race from the powers of darkness, and grant it the gift of immortal glory.
Christ, Son of the living God, you opened the gates of paradise to the repentant thief,
— gather all who have shared your death and burial into the glory of your resurrection.

**Our Father . . .**

CONCLUDING PRAYER

All-powerful and ever-living God,
your only Son went down among the dead
and rose again in glory.
In your goodness
raise up your faithful people,
buried with him in baptism,
to be one with him
in the eternal life of heaven,
where he lives and reigns with you and the Holy
Spirit,
one God, for ever and ever.

Night Prayer from Sunday, after Evening Prayer
II, 333.

In place of the responsory the following is said:

Ant. For our sake Christ was obedient, accepting
even death, death on a cross. Therefore God
raised him on high and gave him the name
above all other names.

# EASTER SUNDAY

The beginning of the Easter Season

## Invitatory

On Easter Sunday the Invitatory is always said at the beginning of Morning Prayer.

Ant.  The Lord is risen, alleluia.

Invitatory psalm, as in the Ordinary, 22.

## Morning Prayer

HYMN, no. 117 or 118-123, 14.

Ant. 1  The splendor of Christ risen from the dead has shone on the people redeemed by his blood, alleluia.

Psalms and canticle from Sunday, Week I, 43.

Ant. 2  Our Redeemer has risen from the tomb; let us sing a hymn of praise to the Lord our God, alleluia.

Ant. 3  Alleluia, the Lord is risen as he promised, alleluia.

READING                                    Acts 10:40-43

God raised Jesus [on] the third day and granted that he be visible, not to all the people, but to us, the witnesses chosen by God in advance, who ate and drank with him after he rose from the dead. He commissioned us to preach to the people and testify that he is the one appointed by God as judge of the living and the dead. To him all the prophets

bear witness, that everyone who believes in him
will receive forgiveness of sins through his name.

In place of the responsory the following is said:

Ant. This is the day the Lord has made; let us rejoice and be glad, alleluia.

CANTICLE OF ZECHARIAH

Ant. Very early on the morning after the Sabbath,
when the sun had just risen, they came to the
tomb, alleluia.

INTERCESSIONS

Christ is the Lord of life, raised up by the Father; in
his turn he will raise us up by his power. Let us
pray to him, saying:
*Christ our life, save us.*
Lord Jesus, light shining in the darkness, you lead
your people into life, and give our mortal nature
the gift of holiness,
— may we spend this day in praise of your glory.
Lord, you walked the way of suffering and crucifix-
ion,
— may we suffer and die with you, and rise again to
share your glory.
Son of the Father, our master and our brother, you
have made us a kingdom of priests for our God,
— may we offer you our joyful sacrifice of praise.
King of glory, we look forward to the great day of
your coming in splendor,
— that we may see you face to face, and be transformed in your likeness.

Our Father . . .

CONCLUDING PRAYER

God our Father,
by raising Christ your Son
you conquered the power of death
and opened for us the way to eternal life.

Let our celebration today
raise us up and renew our lives
by the Spirit that is within us.

Grant this through our Lord Jesus Christ, your Son,
who lives and reigns with you and the Holy Spirit,
one God, for ever and ever.

### Alternative Prayer

God our Father, creator of all,
today is the day of Easter joy.
This is the morning on which the Lord appeared to
  men
who had begun to lose hope
and opened their eyes to what the scriptures foretold:
that first he must die, and then he would rise
and ascend into his Father's glorious presence.
May the risen Lord
breathe on our minds and open our eyes
that we may know him in the breaking of bread,
and follow him in his risen life.

Grant this through Christ our Lord.

The following dismissal is said:

Go in peace, alleluia, alleluia.
— Thanks be to God, alleluia, alleluia.

## Evening Prayer

HYMN, no. 98 or 112-116.

PSALMODY

Ant. 1  Mary Magdalene and the other Mary came
        to see the Lord's tomb, alleluia.

### Psalm 110:1-5, 7

The Lord's revelation to my Master:
"Sit on my right:
your foes I will put beneath your feet."

The Lord will wield from Zion
your scepter of power:
rule in the midst of all your foes.

A prince from the day of your birth
on the holy mountains;
from the womb before the dawn I begot you.

The Lord has sworn an oath he will not change.
"You are a priest for ever,
a priest like Melchizedek of old."

The Master standing at your right hand
will shatter kings in the day of his great wrath.

He shall drink from the stream by the wayside
and therefore he shall lift up his head.

Ant. 2  Come and see the place where the Lord was
buried, alleluia.

### Psalm 114

When Israel came forth from Egypt,
Jacob's sons from an alien people,
Judah became the Lord's temple,
Israel became his kingdom.

The sea fled at the sight:
the Jordan turned back on its course,
the mountains leapt like rams
and the hills like yearling sheep.

Why was it, sea, that you fled,
that you turned back, Jordan, on your course?
Mountains, that you leapt like rams,
hills, like yearling sheep?

Tremble, O earth, before the Lord,
in the presence of the God of Jacob,
who turns the rock into a pool
and flint into a spring of water.

Ant. 3  **Jesus said: Do not be afraid. Go and tell my brothers to set out for Galilee; there they will see me, alleluia.**

The following canticle is said with the **Alleluia** when Evening Prayer is sung; when the office is recited, the **Alleluia** may be said at the beginning and end of each strophe.

Canticle                    See Revelation 19:1-7

Alleluia.
Salvation, glory, and power to our God:
(℟. Alleluia.)
his judgments are honest and true.
℟. Alleluia (alleluia).

Alleluia.
Sing praise to our God, all you his servants,
(℟. Alleluia.)
all who worship him reverently, great and small.
℟. Alleluia (alleluia).

Alleluia.
The Lord our all-powerful God is King;
(℟. Alleluia.)
let us rejoice, sing praise, and give him glory.
℟. Alleluia (alleluia).

Alleluia.
The wedding feast of the Lamb has begun,
(℟. Alleluia.)
and his bride is prepared to welcome him.
℟. Alleluia (alleluia).

READING                      Hebrews 10:12-14

Jesus offered one sacrifice for sins, and took his seat forever at the right hand of God; now he waits until his enemies are made his footstool. For by one offering he has made perfect forever those who are being consecrated.

In place of the responsory the following is said:

Ant. **This is the day the Lord has made; let us rejoice and be glad, alleluia.**

CANTICLE OF MARY

Ant. **On the evening of the first day of the week, the disciples were gathered together behind locked doors; suddenly, Jesus stood among them and said: Peace be with you, alleluia.**

INTERCESSIONS

With joy in our hearts, let us call upon Christ the Lord, who died and rose again, and lives always to intercede for us:
*Victorious King, hear our prayer.*

Light and salvation of all peoples,
— send into our hearts the fire of your Spirit, as we proclaim your resurrection.

Let Israel recognize in you her longed-for Messiah,
— and the whole earth be filled with the knowledge of your glory.

Keep us in the communion of your saints,
— and grant us rest from our labors in their company.

You have triumphed over death, your enemy; destroy in us the power of death,
— that we may live only for you, victorious and immortal Lord.

Savior Christ, you were obedient even to accepting death, and you were raised up to the right hand of the Father,
— in your goodness welcome your brothers and sisters into the kingdom of your glory.

Our Father . . .

CONCLUDING PRAYER

God our Father,
by raising Christ your Son

you conquered the power of death
and opened for us the way to eternal life.
Let our celebration today
raise us up and renew our lives
by the Spirit that is within us.

Grant this through our Lord Jesus Christ, your Son,
who lives and reigns with you and the Holy Spirit,
one God, for ever and ever.

## Alternative Prayer

God our Father, creator of all,
today is the day of Easter joy.
This is the morning on which the Lord appeared to
    men
who had begun to lose hope
and opened their eyes to what the scriptures foretold:
that first he must die, and then he would rise
and ascend into his Father's glorious presence.
May the risen Lord
breathe on our minds and open our eyes
that we may know him in the breaking of bread,
and follow him in his risen life.

Grant this through Christ our Lord.

The following dismissal is said:

Go in peace, alleluia, alleluia.
— Thanks be to God, alleluia, alleluia.

The Easter Triduum ends with the conclusion of
Evening Prayer.

During the octave of Easter and on the Second Sunday of Easter, Morning Prayer and Evening Prayer
of Easter Sunday may be used.

During the octave of Easter, Night Prayer is said
each day from either of the Night Prayers for Sunday, 330 or 333.

# EASTER SEASON

One week of texts is provided for the Easter Season. These texts may be repeated throughout the season. The hymns for Easter Season are indicated in the Liturgical Guide, **578**.

INVITATORY

The antiphon for the invitatory psalm of Morning Prayer is:

Before Ascension: **The Lord is risen, alleluia.**

After Ascension: **Alleluia, come let us worship Christ the Lord as he ascends into heaven, alleluia.**

The psalms and canticle with their antiphons are from the current day in the Psalter.

## SUNDAY
### Evening Prayer I

READING                                 1 Peter 2:9-10

You are "a chosen race, a royal priesthood, a holy nation, a people of his own, so that you may announce the praises" of him who called you out of darkness into his wonderful light.

Once you were "no people"
    but now you are God's people;
you "had not received mercy"
    but now you have received mercy.

RESPONSORY

The disciples rejoiced, alleluia, alleluia.
— The disciples rejoiced, alleluia, alleluia.

When they saw the risen Lord,
— alleluia, alleluia.

Glory to the Father . . .
— The disciples rejoiced . . .

CANTICLE OF MARY

Ant. I will ask the Father and he will give you another Paraclete to remain with you for ever, alleluia.

464

INTERCESSIONS

In rising from the dead, Christ destroyed death and
   restored life. Let us cry out to him, saying:
   *Lord Jesus, you live for ever; hear our prayer.*
You are the stone rejected by the builders which became the chief cornerstone,
   — make us living stones in the temple of your
   Church.
You are the faithful and true witness, the firstborn
   from the dead,
   — make your Church bear constant witness to yourself.
You alone are the Bridegroom of the Church, born
   from your wounded side,
   — make us reveal to the world the love of Bridegroom
   and Bride.
You are the first and the last, you were dead and are
   alive,
   — keep those who have been baptized faithful until
   death, that they may receive the crown of victory.
Light and lamp of God's holy city,
   — shine on our friends who have died, that they may
   reign for ever.

Our Father . . .

CONCLUDING PRAYER

Ever-living God,
help us to celebrate our joy
in the resurrection of the Lord
and to express in our lives
the love we celebrate.

Grant this through our Lord Jesus Christ, your Son,
who lives and reigns with you and the Holy Spirit,
one God, for ever and ever.

Alternative Prayer

God our Father, maker of all,
the crown of your creation was the Son of Man,
born of a woman, but without beginning;

he suffered for us but lives for ever.
May our mortal lives be crowned with the ultimate joy
of rising with him,
who is Lord for ever and ever.

### Invitatory

Ant. The Lord is risen, alleluia.

Invitatory psalm, 22.

### Morning Prayer

READING                                      Acts 10:40-43

God raised Jesus [on] the third day and granted
that he be visible, not to all the people, but to us,
the witnesses chosen by God in advance, who ate
and drank with him after he rose from the dead. He
commissioned us to preach to the people and testify that he is the one appointed by God as judge of
the living and the dead. To him all the prophets
bear witness, that everyone who believes in him
will receive forgiveness of sins through his name.

RESPONSORY

Christ, Son of the living God, have mercy on us, alleluia, alleluia.
— Christ, Son of the living God, have mercy on us,
alleluia, alleluia.

You have risen from the dead,
— alleluia, alleluia.

Glory to the Father . . .
— Christ, Son of . . .

CANTICLE OF ZECHARIAH

Ant. As the Father has loved me, so I have loved
you; live on in my love, alleluia.

INTERCESSIONS

God the almighty Father raised Jesus as the first-
born from the dead, and made him our savior. Let
us call upon him, saying:

*Give us, Lord, the glory of your Son.*

All-holy Father, you brought your beloved Son Jesus from the darkness of death into the splendor of your glory,
— bring us also into your marvelous light.

You have given us faith to save us,
— may we live today by the faith of our baptism.

You command us to seek the things that are above, where Christ is seated at your right hand,
— do not let us be deceived by the allurements of sin.

May our life, hidden with Christ in you, our Father, shine before the world,
— foreshadowing a new heaven and a new earth.

Our Father . . .

CONCLUDING PRAYER

Ever-living God,
help us to celebrate our joy
in the resurrection of the Lord
and to express in our lives
the love we celebrate.

Grant this through our Lord Jesus Christ, your Son,
who lives and reigns with you and the Holy Spirit,
one God, for ever and ever.

Alternative Prayer

God our Father, maker of all,
the crown of your creation was the Son of Man,
born of a woman, but without beginning;
he suffered for us but lives for ever.

May our mortal lives be crowned with the ultimate joy
of rising with him,
who is Lord for ever and ever.

## Evening Prayer II

READING                          Hebrews 10:12-14

Jesus offered one sacrifice for sins, and took his seat forever at the right hand of God; now he waits until his enemies are made his footstool. For by one offering he has made perfect forever those who are being consecrated.

RESPONSORY

The Lord is risen, alleluia, alleluia.
— The Lord is risen, alleluia, alleluia.

He has appeared to Simon,
— alleluia, alleluia.

Glory to the Father . . .
— The Lord is . . .

CANTICLE OF MARY

Ant. If anyone loves me he will keep my word, and my Father will love him. We will come to him and make our home with him, alleluia.

INTERCESSIONS

God the Father raised Christ from the dead and exalted him at his right hand. Let us pray to the Father, saying:
   *Through Christ in glory, watch over your people, Lord.*
Righteous Father, you lifted Jesus above the earth through the triumph of the cross,
— may all things be lifted up in him.
Through your Son in glory send the Holy Spirit upon the Church,
— that it may be the sacrament of unity for the whole human race.
You have brought a new family into being through water and the Holy Spirit,

— keep them faithful to their baptism, and bring
   them to everlasting life.
Through your exalted Son help those in distress,
   free those in captivity, heal the sick,
— and by your blessings give joy to the world.
You nourished our deceased brothers and sisters
   with the body and blood of the risen Christ,
— raise them up at the last day.

Our Father . . .

CONCLUDING PRAYER

Ever-living God,
help us to celebrate our joy
in the resurrection of the Lord
and to express in our lives
the love we celebrate.

Grant this through our Lord Jesus Christ, your Son,
who lives and reigns with you and the Holy Spirit,
one God, for ever and ever.

## Alternative Prayer

God our Father, maker of all,
the crown of your creation was the Son of Man,
born of a woman, but without beginning;
he suffered for us but lives for ever.
May our mortal lives be crowned with the ultimate
   joy
of rising with him,
who is Lord for ever and ever.

# MONDAY
## Morning Prayer

READING                                    Romans 10:8b-10

   "The word is near you,
      in your mouth and in your heart"

(that is, the word of faith that we preach), for, if you
confess with your mouth that Jesus is Lord and be-

lieve in your heart that God raised him from the dead, you will be saved. For one believes with the heart and so is justified, and one confesses with the mouth and so is saved.

RESPONSORY

The Lord is risen from the tomb, alleluia, alleluia.
— The Lord is risen from the tomb, alleluia, alleluia.

He hung upon the cross for us,
— alleluia, alleluia.

Glory to the Father . . .
— The Lord is . . .

CANTICLE OF ZECHARIAH

Ant. By raising Jesus Christ from the dead, God has given us a new birth to a living hope in the promise of an inheritance that will last for ever, alleluia.

INTERCESSIONS

God the Father was glorified in the death and resurrection of his Son. Let us pray to him with confidence, saying:
    *Lord, enlighten our minds.*
Father of lights, you bathed the world in splendor when Christ rose again in glory,
— fill our minds today with the light of faith.
Through the resurrection of your Son you opened for us the way to eternal life,
— as we work today sustain us with the hope of glory.
Through your risen Son you sent the Holy Spirit into the world,
— set our hearts on fire with spiritual love.
May Jesus Christ, who was crucified to set us free,
— be today our salvation and redemption.

Our Father . . .

CONCLUDING PRAYER

God of mercy,
may our celebration of your Son's resurrection
help us to experience its effect in our lives.

We ask this through our Lord Jesus Christ, your Son,
who lives and reigns with you and the Holy Spirit,
one God, for ever and ever.

## Evening Prayer

READING                                    Hebrews 8:1b-3a

We have such a high priest, who has taken his seat
at the right hand of the throne of the Majesty in
heaven, a minister of the sanctuary and of the true
tabernacle that the Lord, not man, set up. Now every
high priest is appointed to offer gifts and sacrifices.

RESPONSORY

The disciples rejoiced, alleluia, alleluia.
— The disciples rejoiced, alleluia, alleluia.

When they saw the risen Lord,
— alleluia, alleluia.

Glory to the Father . . .
— The disciples rejoiced . . .

CANTICLE OF MARY

Ant. The Spirit of truth who proceeds from the
     Father will be my witness, and you will also
     bear witness to me, alleluia.

INTERCESSIONS

Let us pray to Christ the Lord, who bathed the
     world in glory through his resurrection. With joy-
     ful hearts let us say:
     *Christ, our life, hear our prayer.*
Lord Jesus Christ, you walked with your disciples
     on the way,

— be with your Church on its pilgrimage through life.
Do not let us be slow to believe,
— but ready to proclaim you as victor over death.
Look with kindness on those who do not recognize
    your presence,
— reveal yourself to them, so that they may welcome
    you as Savior.
Through the cross you have brought reconciliation to
    mankind in your body,
— grant unity and peace to all nations.
Judge of the living and the dead,
— forgive the sins of the faithful departed.

Our Father . . .

CONCLUDING PRAYER

God of mercy,
may our celebration of your Son's resurrection
help us to experience its effect in our lives.

We ask this through our Lord Jesus Christ, your Son,
who lives and reigns with you and the Holy Spirit,
one God, for ever and ever.

# TUESDAY

## Morning Prayer

READING                                    Acts 13:30-33

God raised Jesus from the dead, and for many
days he appeared to those who had come up with
him from Galilee to Jerusalem. These are [now] his
witnesses before the people. We ourselves are proclaiming this good news to you that what God
promised our ancestors he has brought to fulfillment for us, [their] children, by raising up Jesus,
as it is written in the second psalm, "You are my
son; this day I have begotten you."

## RESPONSORY

The Lord is risen from the tomb, alleluia, alleluia.
— The Lord is risen from the tomb, alleluia, alleluia.

He hung upon the cross for us,
— alleluia, alleluia.

Glory to the Father . . .
— The Lord is . . .

## CANTICLE OF ZECHARIAH

Ant. In a little while the world will no longer see me,
but you will see me, for I live and you will live,
alleluia.

## INTERCESSIONS

The spotless Lamb of God takes away the sins of the
world. Let us give thanks to the Father, and say:
*Source of all life, raise us to life.*
Source of all life, remember the death and resurrection of the Lamb slain on the cross,
— listen to his voice as he lives for ever, making intercession for us.
Now that the old leaven of wickedness and evil is destroyed,
— may we always feed on the unleavened bread of
sincerity and truth.
Grant that today we may put aside all friction and
jealousy,
— and show greater concern for the needs of others.
Send into our hearts the spirit of the Gospel,
— that we may walk in the way of your commandments, today and for ever.

Our Father . . .

## CONCLUDING PRAYER

God our Father,
may we look forward with hope to our resurrection,

for you have made us your sons and daughters,
and restored the joy of our youth.

We ask this through our Lord Jesus Christ, your Son,
who lives and reigns with you and the Holy Spirit,
one God, for ever and ever.

## Evening Prayer

READING                                        1 Peter 2:4-5

Come to the Lord, a living stone, rejected by
human beings but chosen and precious in the sight
of God, and, like living stones, let yourselves be
built into a spiritual house to be a holy priesthood
to offer spiritual sacrifices acceptable to God
through Jesus Christ.

RESPONSORY

The disciples rejoiced, alleluia, alleluia.
— The disciples rejoiced, alleluia, alleluia.

When they saw the risen Lord,
— alleluia, alleluia.

Glory to the Father . . .
— The disciples rejoiced . . .

CANTICLE OF MARY

Ant. Believe me, it is for your own good that I am
    going. If I do not go, the Paraclete will not
    come, alleluia.

INTERCESSIONS

By his resurrection Christ has given sure hope to
    his people. Let us ask him with our whole hearts:
    *Lord Jesus, you live for ever; hear our prayer.*
Lord Jesus, from your wounded side flowed blood
    and water,
— make the Church your spotless bride.
Chief shepherd, after your resurrection you made

Peter shepherd of your flock when he professed
his love for you,
— increase from day to day the love and devotion of
N., our Pope.

You showed your disciples how to make a great
catch of fish,
— send others to continue their work as fishers of
men.

At the lakeside you prepared bread and fish for
your disciples,
— grant that we may never allow others to die of
hunger.

Jesus, the new Adam and life-giving spirit, transform the dead into your own likeness,
— that the fullness of your joy may be theirs.

Our Father . . .

CONCLUDING PRAYER

God our Father,
may we look forward with hope to our resurrection,
for you have made us your sons and daughters,
and restored the joy of our youth.

We ask this through our Lord Jesus Christ, your Son,
who lives and reigns with you and the Holy Spirit,
one God, for ever and ever.

# WEDNESDAY
## Morning Prayer

READING                              Romans 6:8-11

If we have died with Christ, we believe that we shall
also live with him. We know that Christ, raised from
the dead, dies no more; death no longer has power
over him. As to his death, he died to sin once and for
all; as to his life, he lives for God. Consequently, you
too must think of yourselves as [being] dead to sin
and living for God in Christ Jesus.

RESPONSORY

The Lord is risen from the tomb, alleluia, alleluia.
— The Lord is risen from the tomb, alleluia, alleluia.

He hung upon the cross for us,
— alleluia, alleluia.

Glory to the Father . . .
— The Lord is . . .

CANTICLE OF ZECHARIAH

Ant. I have many more things to tell you, but they
     would be too much for you now. When the
     Spirit of truth comes he will guide you to all
     truth, alleluia.

INTERCESSIONS

By the gift of the Father, the risen Christ was seen by
     the apostles. Let us pray to the Father, and say:
     *Give us, Lord, the glory of your Son.*
Father of lights, today we offer you our thanks and
     praise for calling us into your marvelous light,
— to receive your mercy.
May the efforts of mankind to make the world more
     human,
— be purified and strengthened by the power of your
     Spirit.
May we be so dedicated to the service of others,
— that the whole human family may become a pleas-
     ing sacrifice in your honor.
At the dawn of a new day, fill us with your mercy,
— that the whole day may be a day of joy and praise.

Our Father . . .

CONCLUDING PRAYER

Lord,
as we celebrate your Son's resurrection,
so may we rejoice with all the saints

when he returns in glory,
who lives and reigns with you and the Holy Spirit,
one God, for ever and ever.

## Evening Prayer

READING                                       Hebrews 7:24-27

Jesus, because he remains forever, has a priesthood that does not pass away. Therefore, he is always able to save those who approach God through him, since he lives forever to make intercession for them.

It was fitting that we should have such a high priest: holy, innocent, undefiled, separated from sinners, higher than the heavens. He has no need, as did the high priests, to offer sacrifice day after day, first for his own sins and then for those of the people; he did that once for all when he offered himself.

RESPONSORY

The disciples rejoiced, alleluia, alleluia.
— The disciples rejoiced, alleluia, alleluia.

When they saw the risen Lord,
— alleluia, alleluia.

Glory to the Father . . .
— The disciples rejoiced . . .

CANTICLE OF MARY

Ant. The Spirit will glorify me, for he will proclaim to you all that he has received from me, alleluia.

INTERCESSIONS

In his Son, risen from the dead, God has opened for us the way to everlasting life. Let us ask the Father:
*Through the victory of Christ, save the people he has redeemed.*
God of our fathers, you raised your Son Jesus from the dead and clothed him in glory; move our hearts to complete repentance,

— that we may walk in newness of life.
You have led us back to the shepherd and bishop of
    our souls,
— keep us faithful under the guidance of the shep-
    herds of the Church.
You chose the firstfruits of Christ's disciples from
    the Jewish people,
— reveal to the children of Israel the fulfillment of the
    promise made to their forefathers.
Remember the lonely, the orphaned and the widowed,
— and do not abandon those who have been recon-
    ciled with you by the death of your Son.
You called Stephen to your presence when he bore
    witness to Jesus, standing at your right hand,
— welcome our deceased brothers and sisters who in
    faith and love hoped for the vision of your glory.

Our Father . . .

CONCLUDING PRAYER

Lord,
as we celebrate your Son's resurrection,
so may we rejoice with all the saints
when he returns in glory,
who lives and reigns with you and the Holy Spirit,
one God, for ever and ever.

# THURSDAY

## Morning Prayer

READING                                        Romans 8:10-11

If Christ is in you, although the body is dead because of sin, the spirit is alive because of righteousness. If the Spirit of the one who raised Jesus from the dead dwells in you, the one who raised Christ from the dead will give life to your mortal bodies also, through his Spirit that dwells in you.

RESPONSORY

The Lord is risen from the tomb, alleluia, alleluia.
— The Lord is risen from the tomb, alleluia, alleluia.

He hung upon the cross for us,
— alleluia, alleluia.

Glory to the Father . . .
— The Lord is . . .

CANTICLE OF ZECHARIAH

Ant. In a little while you will no longer see me, says the Lord; then a little while later you will see me again, since I am going to the Father, alleluia.

INTERCESSIONS

God the Father has given us his Son for the resurrection of his people. Let us turn with confidence to the Father, and say:
  *May the Lord Jesus be our very life.*
As a pillar of fire, you lighted the way for your people in the desert,
— through his resurrection may Christ be today the light of our life.
Through the voice of Moses you taught your people from the mountain,

— through his resurrection may Christ be today the
  light of our life.
You fed your pilgrim people with your gift of manna,
— through his resurrection may Christ be today the
  light of our life.
You gave your people water from the rock,
— through his resurrection may Christ be today the
  light of our life.

Our Father . . .

CONCLUDING PRAYER

Father,
may we always give you thanks
for raising Christ our Lord to glory,
because we are his people
and share the salvation he won,
for he lives and reigns with you and the Holy Spirit,
one God, for ever and ever.

## Evening Prayer

READING                                          1 Peter 3:18, 22

Christ suffered for sins once, the righteous for the
sake of the unrighteous, that he might lead you to
God. Put to death in the flesh, he was brought to life
in the spirit. He has gone into heaven and is at the
right hand of God, with angels, authorities, and powers subject to him.

RESPONSORY

The disciples rejoiced, alleluia, alleluia.
— The disciples rejoiced, alleluia, alleluia.
When they saw the risen Lord,
— alleluia, alleluia.
Glory to the Father . . .
— The disciples rejoiced . . .

CANTICLE OF MARY

Ant. Your sorrow will be turned into joy, and that
     joy no one will take from you, alleluia.

INTERCESSIONS

The Father has established in Christ the foundation of all our hope and the principle of our resurrection. Let us rejoice in Christ, and cry out to him, saying:

*King of glory, hear our prayer.*

Lord Jesus, through your resurrection you entered the sanctuary of heaven to offer the blood of your own sacrifice,
— lead us with you into the glory of the Father.

Through your resurrection you confirmed the faith of your disciples and sent them out into the world,
— make all bishops and priests faithful preachers of the Gospel.

Through your resurrection you became our peace and reconciliation,
— unite the baptized in perfect communion of faith and love.

Through your resurrection the crippled man was healed at the gate of the temple,
— look on the sick and reveal in them the power of your glory.

You became the firstborn from the dead, the first-fruits of the resurrection,
— grant to the dead who hoped in you a share in your glory.

Our Father . . .

CONCLUDING PRAYER

Father,
may we always give you thanks
for raising Christ our Lord to glory,
because we are his people
and share the salvation he won,
for he lives and reigns with you and the Holy Spirit,
one God, for ever and ever.

# FRIDAY

## Morning Prayer

READING                                    Acts 5:30-32

The God of our ancestors raised Jesus, though
you had him killed by hanging him on a tree. God
exalted him at his right hand as leader and savior
to grant Israel repentance and forgiveness of sins.
We are witnesses of these things, as is the holy
Spirit that God has given to those who obey him.

RESPONSORY

The Lord is risen from the tomb, alleluia, alleluia.
— The Lord is risen from the tomb, alleluia, alleluia.

He hung upon the cross for us,
— alleluia, alleluia.

Glory to the Father . . .
— The Lord is . . .

CANTICLE OF ZECHARIAH

Ant. My commandment is this: love one another as
      I have loved you, alleluia.

INTERCESSIONS

Let us pray to God the Father, who gave us new life
      through the risen Christ:
      *Give us the glory of your Son.*
Lord our God, your mighty works have revealed
      your eternal plan: you created the earth, and you
      are faithful in every generation,
— hear us, Father of mercy.
Purify our hearts with your truth, and guide them
      in the way of holiness,
— so that we may do what is pleasing in your sight.
Let your face shine upon us,
— that we may be freed from sin and filled with
      your plenty.

You gave the apostles the peace of Christ,
— grant peace to your people and to the whole world.

Our Father . . .

CONCLUDING PRAYER

Eternal Father,
you gave us the Easter mystery
as our covenant of reconciliation.
May the new birth we celebrate
show its effects in the way we live.

We ask this through our Lord Jesus Christ, your Son,
who lives and reigns with you and the Holy Spirit,
one God, for ever and ever.

# Evening Prayer

READING                                                    Hebrews 5:8-10

Son though he was, Christ learned obedience
from what he suffered; and when he was made perfect, he became the source of eternal salvation for
all who obey him, declared by God high priest according to the order of Melchizedek.

RESPONSORY

The disciples rejoiced, alleluia, alleluia.
— The disciples rejoiced, alleluia, alleluia.
When they saw the risen Lord,
— alleluia, alleluia.
Glory to the Father . . .
— The disciples rejoiced . . .

CANTICLE OF MARY

Ant. There is no greater love than to lay down your
life for your friends, alleluia.

INTERCESSIONS

Christ is the way, the truth and the life. Let us
praise him, and say:
   *Son of the living God, bless your people.*
We pray to you, Lord Jesus, for all ministers of
your Church,
— as they break for us the bread of life, may they
themselves receive nourishment and strength.
We pray for the whole Christian people, that all may
be worthy of their calling,
— and safeguard their unity in the Spirit by the
bond of peace.
We pray for those who govern us, that they may
temper justice with mercy,
— and promote harmony and peace throughout the
world.
We pray for ourselves, that our hearts may be purified to sing your praises in the communion of
saints,
— may we be reunited with our deceased brothers
and sisters, whom we commend to your loving
kindness.

Our Father . . .


CONCLUDING PRAYER

Eternal Father,
you gave us the Easter mystery
as our covenant of reconciliation.
May the new birth we celebrate
show its effects in the way we live.

We ask this through our Lord Jesus Christ, your Son,
who lives and reigns with you and the Holy Spirit,
one God, for ever and ever.

# SATURDAY

## Morning Prayer

READING                                      Romans 14:7-9

None of us lives for oneself, and no one dies for oneself. For if we live, we live for the Lord, and if we die, we die for the Lord; so then, whether we live or die, we are the Lord's. For this is why Christ died and came to life, that he might be Lord of both the dead and the living.

RESPONSORY

The Lord is risen from the tomb, alleluia, alleluia.
— The Lord is risen from the tomb, alleluia, alleluia.

He hung upon the cross for us,
— alleluia, alleluia.

Glory to the Father . . .
— The Lord is . . .

CANTICLE OF ZECHARIAH

Ant. Christ died and rose from the dead, that he might be the Lord of the living and the dead, alleluia.

INTERCESSIONS

Christ is the bread of life; he will raise up on the last day all who share the table of his word and his body. In our joy let us pray:
*Lord, give us peace and joy.*
Son of God, you were raised from the dead to lead us into life,
— bless and sanctify all the children of your Father.
You give peace and joy to all who believe in you,
— grant that we may walk as children of the light, rejoicing in your victory.

Build up the faith of your pilgrim Church on earth,
— that it may bear witness to your resurrection before the whole world.
You suffered and so entered into the glory of the Father,
— change the tears of the sorrowful into joy.

Our Father . . .

CONCLUDING PRAYER

Father of love,
by the outpouring of your grace
you increase the number of those who believe in you.
Watch over your chosen family.
Give undying life to all
who have been born again in baptism.

Grant this through our Lord Jesus Christ, your Son, who lives and reigns with you and the Holy Spirit, one God, for ever and ever.

# ASCENSION
Solemnity

## Evening Prayer I

Ant. Father, I have made known your name to the men you have given me; now I am praying for them and not for the world, because I am coming to you, alleluia.

## Invitatory

Ant. Alleluia, come, let us worship Christ the Lord as he ascends into heaven, alleluia.

Invitatory psalm, as in the Ordinary, 22.

## Morning Prayer

Canticle of Zechariah

Ant. I am ascending to my Father and your Father, to my God and your God, alleluia.

Concluding Prayer

God our Father,
make us joyful in the ascension of your Son Jesus Christ.
May we follow him into the new creation,
for his ascension is our glory and our hope.

We ask this through our Lord Jesus Christ, your Son,
who lives and reigns with you and the Holy Spirit,
one God, for ever and ever.

### Alternative Prayer

Father in heaven,
our minds were prepared for the coming of your
   kingdom
when you took Christ beyond our sight
so that we might seek him in his glory.
May we follow where he has led
and find our hope in his glory,
for he is Lord for ever.

# Evening Prayer II

CANTICLE OF MARY

Ant.  O Victor King, Lord of power and might, today
you have ascended in glory above the heavens.
Do not leave us orphans, but send us the
Father's promised gift, the Spirit of truth, alleluia.

# PENTECOST

Solemnity

## Evening Prayer I

HYMN, no. 127 or 21.

PSALMODY

Ant. 1 On the day of Pentecost they had all gathered together in one place, alleluia.

Psalm 113

Praise, O servants of the Lord,
praise the name of the Lord!
May the name of the Lord be blessed
both now and for evermore!
From the rising of the sun to its setting
praised be the name of the Lord!

High above all nations is the Lord,
above the heavens his glory.
Who is like the Lord, our God,
who has risen on high to his throne
yet stoops from the heights to look down,
to look down upon heaven and earth?

From the dust he lifts up the lowly,
from his misery he raises the poor
to set him in the company of princes,
yes, with the princes of his people.
To the childless wife he gives a home
and gladdens her heart with children.

Ant. 2  Tongues as of fire appeared before the
        apostles, and the Holy Spirit came upon
        each of them, alleluia.

### Psalm 147:1-11

Praise the Lord for he is good;
sing to our God for he is loving:
to him our praise is due.

The Lord builds up Jerusalem
and brings back Israel's exiles,
he heals the broken-hearted,
he binds up all their wounds.
He fixes the number of the stars;
he calls each one by its name.

Our Lord is great and almighty;
his wisdom can never be measured.
The Lord raises the lowly;
he humbles the wicked to the dust.
O sing to the Lord, giving thanks;
sing psalms to our God with the harp.

He covers the heavens with clouds;
he prepares the rain for the earth,
making mountains sprout with grass
and with plants to serve man's needs.
He provides the beasts with their food,
and young ravens that call upon him.

His delight is not in horses
nor his pleasure in warriors' strength.
The Lord delights in those who revere him,
in those who wait for his love.

Ant. 3  The Spirit who comes from the Father will
        glorify me, alleluia.

Canticle                          Revelation 15:3-4

Mighty and wonderful are your works,
Lord God Almighty!
Righteous and true are your ways,
O King of the nations!

Who would dare refuse you honor,
or the glory due your name, O Lord?

Since you alone are holy,
all nations shall come
and worship in your presence.
Your mighty deeds are clearly seen.

READING                            Romans 8:9-11

You are not in the flesh; on the contrary, you are in
the spirit, if only the Spirit of God dwells in you. Whoever does not have the Spirit of Christ does not belong
to him. But if Christ is in you, although the body is
dead because of sin, the spirit is alive because of righteousness. If the Spirit of the one who raised Jesus
from the dead dwells in you, the one who raised
Christ from the dead will give life to your mortal bodies also, through his Spirit that dwells in you.

RESPONSORY

The Holy Spirit is the Paraclete, alleluia, alleluia.
— The Holy Spirit is the Paraclete, alleluia, alleluia.

He will teach you all things,
— alleluia, alleluia.

Glory to the Father . . .
— The Holy Spirit . . .

CANTICLE OF MARY

Ant.  Come, Holy Spirit, fill the hearts of all believ-
      ers and set them on fire with your love.
      Though they spoke many different languages,
      you united the nations in professing the same
      faith, alleluia.

INTERCESSIONS

When the days of Pentecost were complete, God sent
the Holy Spirit upon the apostles. As we celebrate
this great feast with joy and faith, let us cry out:
*Send forth your Spirit and make the whole world
new.*

In the beginning you created heaven and earth, and
in the fullness of time you renewed all things in
Christ,
— through your Spirit go on renewing the world
with the gift of salvation.

You breathed the breath of life into Adam,
— send your Spirit into your Church to be its life
and vigor, that it may bring new life to the whole
world.

By the light of your Spirit, enlighten the world and
dispel the darkness of our times,
— turn hatred into love, sorrow into joy and war
into the peace we so desire.

Water flowed from the side of Christ as the fountain
of your Spirit,
— may it flow over all the earth and bring forth
goodness.

You bring life and glory to mankind through the
Holy Spirit,
— through the Spirit lead the departed into the love
and joy of heaven.

Our Father . . .

CONCLUDING PRAYER

Almighty and ever-living God,
you fulfilled the Easter promise
by sending us your Holy Spirit.
May that Spirit unite the races and nations on earth
to proclaim your glory.

Grant this through our Lord Jesus Christ, your Son,
who lives and reigns with you and the Holy Spirit,
one God, for ever and ever.

### Alternative Prayer

Father in heaven,
fifty days have celebrated the fullness
of the mystery of your revealed love.
See your people gathered in prayer,
open to receive the Spirit's flame.
May it come to rest in our hearts
and disperse the divisions of word and tongue.
With one voice and one song
may we praise your name in joy and thanksgiving.
Grant this through Christ our Lord.

## Invitatory

Ant. Alleluia, the Spirit of the Lord has filled the
whole world; come, let us worship him, alleluia.

Invitatory psalm, as in the Ordinary, 22.

## Morning Prayer

HYMN, no. 21 or 130.

Ant. 1  O Lord, how good and gentle is your Spirit
in us, alleluia.

Psalms and canticle from Sunday, Week I, 43.

Ant. 2  Let streams and rivers and all creatures that
live in the waters sing praise to God, alleluia.

Ant. 3  The apostles preached in different tongues,
and proclaimed the great works of God, alleluia.

READING                                    Acts 5:30-32

The God of our ancestors raised Jesus, though
you had him killed by hanging him on a tree. God
exalted him at his right hand as leader and savior
to grant Israel repentance and forgiveness of sins.
We are witnesses of these things, as is the holy
Spirit that God has given to those who obey him.

RESPONSORY

All were filled with the Holy Spirit, alleluia, alleluia.
— All were filled with the Holy Spirit, alleluia, alleluia.
They began to speak,
— alleluia, alleluia.
Glory to the Father . . .
— All were filled . . .

CANTICLE OF ZECHARIAH

Ant.  Receive the Holy Spirit; the sins of those you forgive shall be forgiven, alleluia.

INTERCESSIONS

Christ the Lord has gathered his Church in unity through the Spirit. With sure hope let us ask him: *Lord, make the whole world new.*
Lord Jesus, when you were raised high upon the cross, streams of living water flowed from your pierced side,
— pour out on us your life-giving Spirit.
In glory at the right hand of God, you gave the Gift of the Father to your disciples,
— send forth your Spirit to renew the world.
You gave your Spirit to the apostles, with the power to forgive sins,
— destroy all sin in the world.
You promised us the Holy Spirit, to teach us all things and remind us of all you had said,
— send us your Spirit to enlighten our minds in faith.
You promised to send the Spirit of truth, to bear witness to yourself,
— send forth your Spirit to make us your faithful witnesses.

Our Father . . .

CONCLUDING PRAYER

God our Father,
let the Spirit you sent on your Church
to begin the teaching of the gospel
continue to work in the world
through the hearts of all who believe.

We ask this through our Lord Jesus Christ, your Son,
who lives and reigns with you and the Holy Spirit,
one God, for ever and ever.

### Alternative Prayer

Father of light, from whom every good gift comes,
send your Spirit into our lives
with the power of a mighty wind,
and by the flame of your wisdom
open the horizons of our minds.
Loosen our tongues to sing your praise
in words beyond the power of speech,
for without your Spirit
man could never raise his voice in words of peace
or announce the truth that Jesus is Lord,
who lives and reigns with you and the Holy Spirit,
one God, for ever and ever.

### Evening Prayer II

HYMN, no. 127 or 21.

Ant. 1   The Spirit of the Lord has filled the whole
world, alleluia.

Psalms and canticle from Sunday, Week I, 48.

Ant. 2   Send us your strength, O God, from your
holy temple in Jerusalem, and perfect your
work in us, alleluia.

Ant. 3   All were filled with the Holy Spirit, and they
began to speak, alleluia.

READING                                    Ephesians 4:3-6

Strive to preserve the unity of the spirit through
the bond of peace: one body and one Spirit, as you
were also called to the one hope of your call; one
Lord, one faith, one baptism; one God and Father of
all, who is over all and through all and in all.

RESPONSORY

The Spirit of the Lord has filled the whole world, alleluia, alleluia.
— The Spirit of the Lord has filled the whole world,
   alleluia, alleluia.

He sustains all creation and knows every word that
   is spoken,
— alleluia, alleluia.

Glory to the Father . . .
— The Spirit of . . .

CANTICLE OF MARY

Ant. Today we celebrate the feast of Pentecost, al-
     leluia; on this day the Holy Spirit appeared be-
     fore the apostles in tongues of fire and gave
     them his spiritual gifts. He sent them out to
     preach to the whole world, and to proclaim
     that all who believe and are baptized shall be
     saved, alleluia.

INTERCESSIONS

God the Father has gathered his Church in unity
   through Christ. With joy in our hearts let us ask
   him:
   *Send your Holy Spirit into the Church.*

You desire the unity of all Christians through one
     baptism in the Spirit,
— make all who believe one in heart and soul.
You desire the whole world to be filled with the Spirit,
— help all mankind to build a world of justice and
     peace.
Lord God, Father of all mankind, you desire to gather
     together your scattered children in unity of faith,
— enlighten the world by the grace of the Holy Spirit.
Through the Spirit you make all things new,
— heal the sick, comfort the distressed, give salva-
     tion to all.
Through the Spirit you raised your Son from the
     dead,
— raise up the bodies of the dead into everlasting life.

Our Father . . .

CONCLUDING PRAYER

God our Father,
let the Spirit you sent on your Church
to begin the teaching of the gospel
continue to work in the world
through the hearts of all who believe.

We ask this through our Lord Jesus Christ, your Son,
who lives and reigns with you and the Holy Spirit,
one God, for ever and ever.

## Alternative Prayer

Father of light, from whom every good gift comes,
send your Spirit into our lives
with the power of a mighty wind,
and by the flame of your wisdom
open the horizons of our minds.
Loosen our tongues to sing your praise
in words beyond the power of speech,
for without your Spirit
man could never raise his voice in words of peace
or announce the truth that Jesus is Lord,

who lives and reigns with you and the Holy Spirit, one God, for ever and ever.

The following dismissal is said:

Go in peace, alleluia, alleluia.
— Thanks be to God, alleluia, alleluia.

The Easter Season ends with the conclusion of Evening Prayer.

# FEASTS OF THE LORD
# IN ORDINARY TIME
## Sunday after Pentecost
## TRINITY SUNDAY
### Solemnity
## Evening Prayer I

CANTICLE OF MARY

Ant. We give you thanks, O God; we give you
thanks, Trinity one and true, Divinity one and
most high, Unity one and holy.

## Morning Prayer

CANTICLE OF ZECHARIAH

Ant. O holy, undivided Trinity, Creator and Ruler of
all that exists, may all praise be yours now, for
ever, and for ages unending.

CONCLUDING PRAYER

Father,
you sent your Word to bring us truth
and your Spirit to make us holy.
Through them we come to know the mystery of
    your life.
Help us to worship you, one God in three Persons,
by proclaiming and living our faith in you.

Grant this through our Lord Jesus Christ, your Son,
who lives and reigns with you and the Holy Spirit,
one God, for ever and ever.

### Alternative Prayer

God, we praise you:
Father all-powerful, Christ Lord and Savior, Spirit
    of Love,

drawing us to share in your life and your love.
One God, three Persons,
be near to the people formed in your image,
close to the world your love brings to life.

We ask you this, Father, Son, and Holy Spirit,
one God, true and living, for ever and ever.

## Evening Prayer II

CANTICLE OF MARY

Ant. With our whole heart and voice we acclaim you,
    O God; we offer you our praise and worship, un-
    begotten Father, only-begotten Son, Holy Spirit,
    constant friend and guide; most holy and undi-
    vided Trinity, to you be glory for ever.

# Thursday after Trinity Sunday

# THE BODY AND BLOOD OF CHRIST

## CORPUS CHRISTI

### Solemnity

Where the solemnity of Corpus Christi is not observed as a holy day, it is assigned to the Sunday
after Trinity Sunday, which is then considered its
proper day in the calendar.

## Evening Prayer I

CANTICLE OF MARY

Ant. How kind and gentle you are, O Lord. You
    showed your goodness to your sons by giving
    them bread from heaven. You filled the hungry
    with good things, and the rich you sent away
    empty.

## Morning Prayer

CANTICLE OF ZECHARIAH

Ant. I am the living bread come down from heaven; anyone who eats this bread will live for ever, alleluia.

CONCLUDING PRAYER

Lord Jesus Christ,
you gave us the eucharist
as the memorial of your suffering and death.
May our worship of this sacrament of your body
    and blood
help us to experience the salvation you won for us
and the peace of the kingdom
where you live with the Father and the Holy Spirit,
one God, for ever and ever.

### Alternative Prayer

Lord Jesus Christ,
we worship you living among us
in the sacrament of your body and blood.
May we offer to our Father in heaven
a solemn pledge of undivided love.
May we offer to our brothers and sisters
a life poured out in loving service of that kingdom
where you live with the Father and the Holy Spirit,
one God, for ever and ever.

## Evening Prayer II

CANTICLE OF MARY

Ant. How holy this feast in which Christ is our food; his passion is recalled; grace fills our hearts; and we receive a pledge of the glory to come, alleluia.

# Friday After the Second Sunday After Pentecost

## SACRED HEART    Solemnity

### Evening Prayer I

CANTICLE OF MARY

Ant. I have come to cast fire upon the earth; how I
long to see the flame leap up.

## Morning Prayer

CANTICLE OF ZECHARIAH

Ant. With tender compassion, our God has come to
his people and set them free.

CONCLUDING PRAYER

Father,
we rejoice in the gifts of love
we have received from the heart of Jesus your Son.
Open our hearts to share his life
and continue to bless us with his love.

We ask this through our Lord Jesus Christ, your Son,
who lives and reigns with you and the Holy Spirit,
one God, for ever and ever.

### Alternative Prayer

Father,
we honor the heart of your Son
broken by man's cruelty,
yet symbol of love's triumph,
pledge of all that man is called to be.
Teach us to see Christ in the lives we touch,
to offer him living worship
by love-filled service to our brothers and sisters.

We ask this through Christ our Lord.

### Evening Prayer II

CANTICLE OF MARY

Ant. The Lord has lifted us up and drawn us to his
heart, for he has remembered his promise of
mercy, alleluia.

## ORDINARY TIME

### FIRST WEEK IN ORDINARY TIME

Psalter, Week I

The feast of the Baptism of the Lord, **403**, takes the place of the First Sunday in Ordinary Time.

CONCLUDING PRAYER

Father of love,
hear our prayers.
Help us to know your will
and to do it with courage and faith.

Grant this through our Lord Jesus Christ, your Son, who lives and reigns with you and the Holy Spirit, one God, for ever and ever.

# SECOND SUNDAY IN ORDINARY TIME

Psalter, Week II

## Evening Prayer I

CANTICLE OF MARY

Ant. **Behold the Lamb of God, behold him who takes away the sins of the world.**

## Morning Prayer

CANTICLE OF ZECHARIAH

Ant. **The disciples came to see where Jesus lived, and all that day they stayed with him.**

CONCLUDING PRAYER

Father of heaven and earth,
hear our prayers,
and show us the way to peace in the world.

Grant this through our Lord Jesus Christ, your Son,
who lives and reigns with you and the Holy Spirit,
one God, for ever and ever.

## Alternative Prayer

Almighty and ever-present Father,
your watchful care reaches from end to end
and orders all things in such power
that even the tensions and the tragedies of sin
cannot frustrate your loving plans.
Help us to embrace your will,
give us the strength to follow your call,
so that your truth may live in our hearts
and reflect peace to those who believe in your love.

We ask this in the name of Jesus the Lord.

## Evening Prayer II

CANTICLE OF MARY

Ant. **There was a wedding in Cana of Galilee, and Jesus was there with Mary his mother.**

# THIRD SUNDAY IN ORDINARY TIME

Psalter, Week III

## Evening Prayer I

CANTICLE OF MARY

Ant. Jesus preached the Gospel of the kingdom and cured those who were in need of healing.

## Morning Prayer

CANTICLE OF ZECHARIAH

Ant. Come, follow me, says the Lord; I will make you fishers of men.

CONCLUDING PRAYER

All-powerful and ever-living God,
direct your love that is within us,
that our efforts in the name of your Son
may bring mankind to unity and peace.

We ask this through our Lord Jesus Christ, your Son,
who lives and reigns with you and the Holy Spirit,
one God, for ever and ever.

### Alternative Prayer

Almighty Father,
the love you offer
always exceeds the furthest expression of our
  human longing,
for you are greater than the human heart.
Direct each thought, each effort of our life,
so that the limits of our faults and weaknesses
may not obscure the vision of your glory
or keep us from the peace you have promised.

We ask this through Christ our Lord.

## Evening Prayer II

CANTICLE OF MARY

Ant. The Spirit of the Lord rests upon me; he has sent me to preach the good news to the poor.

# FOURTH SUNDAY IN ORDINARY TIME

Psalter, Week IV

## Evening Prayer I

CANTICLE OF MARY

Ant. When Jesus saw the crowds, he went up the mountain; his disciples came and gathered around him, and he opened his mouth and began to teach them.

## Morning Prayer

CANTICLE OF ZECHARIAH

Ant. Everyone heard with amazement what Jesus taught, for he spoke with such authority.

CONCLUDING PRAYER

Lord our God,
help us to love you with all our hearts
and to love all men as you love them.

Grant this through our Lord Jesus Christ, your Son,
who lives and reigns with you and the Holy Spirit,
one God, for ever and ever.

### Alternative Prayer

Father in heaven,
from the days of Abraham and Moses
until this gathering of your Church in prayer,
you have formed a people in the image of your Son.
Bless this people with the gift of your kingdom.
May we serve you with our every desire
and show love for one another
even as you have loved us.

Grant this through Christ our Lord.

## Evening Prayer II

CANTICLE OF MARY

Ant. They all marveled at the words that came forth from the mouth of God.

# FIFTH SUNDAY IN ORDINARY TIME

Psalter, Week I

## Evening Prayer I

CANTICLE OF MARY

Ant. You are the light of the world. Let your light shine before men, that they may see your good works and give glory to your heavenly Father.

## Morning Prayer

CANTICLE OF ZECHARIAH

Ant. Jesus rose early in the morning and went out to a place of solitude, and there he prayed.

CONCLUDING PRAYER

Father,
watch over your family
and keep us safe in your care,
for all our hope is in you.

Grant this through our Lord Jesus Christ, your Son, who lives and reigns with you and the Holy Spirit, one God, for ever and ever.

## Alternative Prayer

In faith and love we ask you, Father,
to watch over your family gathered here.
In your mercy and loving kindness
no thought of ours is left unguarded,
no tear unheeded, no joy unnoticed.
Through the prayer of Jesus
may the blessings promised to the poor in spirit
lead us to the treasures of your heavenly kingdom.

We ask this in the name of Jesus the Lord.

## Evening Prayer II

CANTICLE OF MARY

Ant. Master, we have worked all night and have caught nothing; but if you say so, I will lower the nets again.

# SIXTH SUNDAY IN ORDINARY TIME

Psalter, Week II

## Evening Prayer I

CANTICLE OF MARY

Ant. If you are bringing your gift to the altar, and there you remember that your brother has something against you, leave your gift in front of the altar; go at once and make peace with your brother, and then come back and offer your gift.

## Morning Prayer

CANTICLE OF ZECHARIAH

Ant. Lord, if you will, you can make me clean. And Jesus said: I do will it; you are made clean.

CONCLUDING PRAYER

God our Father,
you have promised to remain for ever
with those who do what is just and right.
Help us to live in your presence.

We ask this through our Lord Jesus Christ, your Son,
who lives and reigns with you and the Holy Spirit,
one God, for ever and ever.

### Alternative Prayer

Father in heaven,
the loving plan of your wisdom took flesh in Jesus
    Christ
and changed mankind's history
by his command of perfect love.
May our fulfillment of his command reflect your
    wisdom
and bring your salvation to the ends of the earth.

We ask this through Christ our Lord.

## Evening Prayer II

CANTICLE OF MARY

Ant. Blessed are you who are poor, for the kingdom of God is yours. And blessed are you who hunger now; you shall be satisfied.

# SEVENTH SUNDAY IN ORDINARY TIME

Psalter, Week III

## Evening Prayer I

CANTICLE OF MARY

Ant. If you want to be true children of your heavenly Father, then you must pray for those who persecute you and speak all kinds of evil against you, says the Lord.

## Morning Prayer

CANTICLE OF ZECHARIAH

Ant. The paralyzed man picked up the bed on which he was lying, and gave praise to God; all who saw it gave glory to God.

CONCLUDING PRAYER

Father,
keep before us the wisdom and love
you have revealed in your Son.
Help us to be like him
in word and deed,
for he lives and reigns with you and the Holy Spirit,
one God, for ever and ever.

### Alternative Prayer

Almighty God,
Father of our Lord Jesus Christ,

faith in your word is the way to wisdom,
and to ponder your divine plan is to grow in the
   truth.
Open our eyes to your deeds,
our ears to the sound of your call,
so that our every act may increase our sharing
in the life you have offered us.

Grant this through Christ our Lord.

### Evening Prayer II

CANTICLE OF MARY

Ant. Do not judge others, and you will not be
      judged, for as you have judged them, so God
      will judge you.

# EIGHTH SUNDAY IN ORDINARY TIME

Psalter, Week IV

### Evening Prayer I

CANTICLE OF MARY

Ant. Seek first the kingdom of God and his justice,
      and all the rest will be given to you as well, al-
      leluia.

### Morning Prayer

CANTICLE OF ZECHARIAH

Ant. No one pours new wine into old wineskins;
      new wine should be put in new wineskins.

CONCLUDING PRAYER

Lord,
guide the course of world events
and give your Church the joy and peace
of serving you in freedom.

We ask this through our Lord Jesus Christ, your Son, who lives and reigns with you and the Holy Spirit, one God, for ever and ever.

### Alternative Prayer

Father in heaven,
form in us the likeness of your Son
and deepen his life within us.
Send us as witnesses of gospel joy
into a world of fragile peace and broken promises.
Touch the hearts of all men with your love
that they in turn may love one another.

We ask this through Christ our Lord.

## Evening Prayer II

CANTICLE OF MARY

Ant. A good tree cannot bear bad fruit, nor a bad tree good fruit.

# NINTH SUNDAY IN ORDINARY TIME

Psalter, Week I

## Evening Prayer I

CANTICLE OF MARY

Ant. Not everyone who says: "Lord, Lord," will enter the kingdom of heaven, but the one who does the will of my heavenly Father will certainly enter it.

## Morning Prayer

CANTICLE OF ZECHARIAH

Ant. The sabbath was made for man, not man for the sabbath.

CONCLUDING PRAYER

Father,
your love never fails.
Hear our call.
Keep us from danger
and provide for all our needs.

Grant this through our Lord Jesus Christ, your Son,
who lives and reigns with you and the Holy Spirit,
one God, for ever and ever.

## Alternative Prayer

God our Father,
teach us to cherish the gifts that surround us.
Increase our faith in you
and bring our trust to its promised fulfillment
in the joy of your kingdom.

Grant this through Christ our Lord.

## Evening Prayer II

CANTICLE OF MARY

Ant. Lord, I am not worthy to have you enter my
house; just say the word and my servant will
be healed.

# TENTH SUNDAY IN ORDINARY TIME

Psalter, Week II

## Evening Prayer I

CANTICLE OF MARY

Ant. I desire mercy and not sacrifice. I did not come to call the virtuous but sinners.

## Morning Prayer

CANTICLE OF ZECHARIAH

Ant. Whoever does the will of God, he is my brother, and my sister, and my mother.

CONCLUDING PRAYER

God of wisdom and love,
source of all good,
send your Spirit to teach us your truth
and guide our actions
in your way of peace.

We ask this through our Lord Jesus Christ, your Son,
who lives and reigns with you and the Holy Spirit,
one God, for ever and ever.

### Alternative Prayer

Father in heaven,
words cannot measure the boundaries of love
for those born to new life in Christ Jesus.
Raise us beyond the limits this world imposes,
so that we may be free to love as Christ teaches
and find our joy in your glory.

We ask this through Christ our Lord.

## Evening Prayer II

CANTICLE OF MARY

Ant. A great prophet has risen up among us and God has visited his people.

# ELEVENTH SUNDAY IN ORDINARY TIME

Psalter, Week III

## Evening Prayer I

CANTICLE OF MARY

Ant. Go, preach the good news of the kingdom;
freely you have received, freely give, alleluia.

## Morning Prayer

CANTICLE OF ZECHARIAH

Ant. The kingdom of heaven is like a mustard seed,
the smallest of all seeds; yet when full-grown
it is the largest of shrubs.

CONCLUDING PRAYER

Almighty God,
our hope and our strength,
without you we falter.
Help us to follow Christ
and to live according to your will.

We ask this through our Lord Jesus Christ, your Son,
who lives and reigns with you and the Holy Spirit,
one God, for ever and ever.

### Alternative Prayer

God our Father,
we rejoice in the faith that draws us together,
aware that selfishness can drive us apart.
Let your encouragement be our constant strength.
Keep us one in the love that has sealed our lives,
help us to live as one family
the gospel we profess.

We ask this through Christ our Lord.

## Evening Prayer II

CANTICLE OF MARY

Ant. Jesus said to the woman: Your faith has saved
you, go in peace.

# TWELFTH SUNDAY IN ORDINARY TIME

Psalter, Week IV

## Evening Prayer I

CANTICLE OF MARY

Ant. If anyone bears witness to me before men, I will praise him in the presence of my Father.

## Morning Prayer

CANTICLE OF ZECHARIAH

Ant. Help us, O Lord, for we are troubled; give the command, O God, and bring us peace.

CONCLUDING PRAYER

Father,
guide and protector of your people,
grant us an unfailing respect for your name,
and keep us always in your love.

Grant this through our Lord Jesus Christ, your Son,
who lives and reigns with you and the Holy Spirit,
one God, for ever and ever.

## Alternative Prayer

God of the universe,
we worship you as Lord.
God, ever close to us,
we rejoice to call you Father.
From this world's uncertainty we look to your covenant.
Keep us one in your peace, secure in your love.
We ask this through Christ our Lord.

## Evening Prayer II

CANTICLE OF MARY

Ant. Whoever wishes to come after me must deny himself, take up his cross and follow me.

# THIRTEENTH SUNDAY IN ORDINARY TIME

Psalter, Week I

## Evening Prayer I

CANTICLE OF MARY

Ant. Those who welcome you are welcoming me, and those who welcome me are welcoming him who sent me.

## Morning Prayer

CANTICLE OF ZECHARIAH

Ant. Jesus, turning, saw the woman and said: Take courage, daughter; your faith has saved you, alleluia.

CONCLUDING PRAYER

Father,
you call your children
to walk in the light of Christ.
Free us from darkness
and keep us in the radiance of your truth.

We ask this through our Lord Jesus Christ, your Son,
who lives and reigns with you and the Holy Spirit,
one God, for ever and ever.

### Alternative Prayer

Father in heaven,
the light of Jesus
has scattered the darkness of hatred and sin.
Called to that light
we ask for your guidance.
Form our lives in your truth, our hearts in your love.

We ask this through Christ our Lord.

## Evening Prayer II

CANTICLE OF MARY

Ant. The Son of Man did not come to condemn men but to save them.

# FOURTEENTH SUNDAY IN ORDINARY TIME

Psalter, Week II

## Evening Prayer I

CANTICLE OF MARY

Ant. **My yoke is easy and my burden is light, says the Lord.**

## Morning Prayer

CANTICLE OF ZECHARIAH

Ant. **Many who heard the teaching of Jesus were astonished and said: Where did he get all this? Is he not the carpenter, the son of Mary?**

CONCLUDING PRAYER

Father,
through the obedience of Jesus,
your servant and your Son,
you raised a fallen world.
Free us from sin
and bring us the joy that lasts for ever.

We ask this through our Lord Jesus Christ, your Son,
who lives and reigns with you and the Holy Spirit,
one God, for ever and ever.

### Alternative Prayer

Father,
in the rising of your Son
death gives birth to new life.
The sufferings he endured restored hope to a fallen
    world.
Let sin never ensnare us
with empty promises of passing joy.
Make us one with you always,
so that our joy may be holy,
and our love may give life.

We ask this through Christ our Lord.

## Evening Prayer II

CANTICLE OF MARY

Ant. So great a harvest, and so few to gather it in;
pray to the Lord of the harvest; beg him to
send out laborers for his harvest.

# FIFTEENTH SUNDAY IN ORDINARY TIME

Psalter, Week III

## Evening Prayer I

CANTICLE OF MARY

Ant. The seed is the word of God; the sower is
Christ; all who listen to his words will live for
ever.

## Morning Prayer

CANTICLE OF ZECHARIAH

Ant. The disciples went out and preached repentance. They anointed many sick people with
oil, and healed them.

CONCLUDING PRAYER

God our Father,
your light of truth
guides us to the way of Christ.
May all who follow him
reject what is contrary to the gospel.

We ask this through our Lord Jesus Christ, your Son,
who lives and reigns with you and the Holy Spirit,
one God, for ever and ever.

### Alternative Prayer

Father,
let the light of your truth
guide us to your kingdom
through a world filled with lights contrary to your
own.
Christian is the name and the gospel we glory in.

May your love make us what you have called us to be.
We ask this through Christ our Lord.

## Evening Prayer II

CANTICLE OF MARY

Ant. Teacher, what is the greatest commandment
in the law? Jesus said to him: You shall love
the Lord your God with your whole heart.

# SIXTEENTH SUNDAY IN ORDINARY TIME

Psalter, Week IV

## Evening Prayer I

CANTICLE OF MARY

Ant. The kingdom of heaven is like yeast which a
woman took and kneaded into three measures
of flour until all the dough had risen.

## Morning Prayer

CANTICLE OF ZECHARIAH

Ant. He saw the great crowd and had pity on them,
for they were like sheep without a shepherd.

CONCLUDING PRAYER

Lord, be merciful to your people.
Fill us with your gifts
and make us always eager to serve you
in faith, hope, and love.

Grant this through our Lord Jesus Christ, your Son,
who lives and reigns with you and the Holy Spirit,
one God, for ever and ever.

### Alternative Prayer

Father,
let the gift of your life
continue to grow in us,
drawing us from death to faith, hope, and love.

Keep us alive in Christ Jesus.
Keep us watchful in prayer
and true to his teaching
till your glory is revealed in us.

Grant this through Christ our Lord.

## Evening Prayer II

CANTICLE OF MARY

Ant. Mary has chosen the better part, and it shall
not be taken from her.

# SEVENTEENTH SUNDAY IN ORDINARY TIME

Psalter, Week I

## Evening Prayer I

CANTICLE OF MARY

Ant. The kingdom of heaven is like a merchant in
search of fine pearls; when he found one of
great value, he sold everything he had and
bought it.

## Morning Prayer

CANTICLE OF ZECHARIAH

Ant. When those men saw the signs Jesus performed, they said: Surely this is the Prophet
who is to come into the world.

CONCLUDING PRAYER

God our Father and protector,
without you nothing is holy,
nothing has value.
Guide us to everlasting life
by helping us to use wisely
the blessings you have given to the world.

We ask this through our Lord Jesus Christ, your Son,
who lives and reigns with you and the Holy Spirit,
one God, for ever and ever.

### Alternative Prayer

God our Father,
open our eyes to see your hand at work
in the splendor of creation,
in the beauty of human life.
Touched by your hand our world is holy.
Help us to cherish the gifts that surround us,
to share your blessings with our brothers and sisters,
and to experience the joy of life in your presence.

We ask this through Christ our Lord.

## Evening Prayer II

CANTICLE OF MARY

Ant. Ask and you will receive, seek and you will find,
knock and the door will be opened to you.

# EIGHTEENTH SUNDAY IN ORDINARY TIME

Psalter, Week II

## Evening Prayer I

CANTICLE OF MARY

Ant. A great crowd gathered around Jesus, and they
had nothing to eat. He called his disciples and
said: I have compassion on all these people.

## Morning Prayer

CANTICLE OF ZECHARIAH

Ant. Do not work for food that will perish, but for
food that lasts to eternal life.

CONCLUDING PRAYER

Father of everlasting goodness,
our origin and guide,
be close to us
and hear the prayers of all who praise you.

Forgive our sins and restore us to life.
Keep us safe in your love.

Grant this through our Lord Jesus Christ, your Son,
who lives and reigns with you and the Holy Spirit,
one God, for ever and ever.

### Alternative Prayer

God our Father,
gifts without measure flow from your goodness
to bring us your peace.
Our life is your gift.
Guide our life's journey,
for only your love makes us whole.
Keep us strong in your love.

We ask this through Christ our Lord.

## Evening Prayer II

CANTICLE OF MARY

Ant. Brothers, if you desire to be truly rich, set
your heart on true riches.

# NINETEENTH SUNDAY IN
# ORDINARY TIME

Psalter, Week III

## Evening Prayer I

CANTICLE OF MARY

Ant. Lord, bid me walk across the waters. Jesus
reached out to take hold of Peter, and said: O
man of little faith, why did you falter?

## Morning Prayer

CANTICLE OF ZECHARIAH

Ant. Amen, amen I say to you: Whoever believes in
me will live for ever, alleluia.

CONCLUDING PRAYER

Almighty and ever-living God,
your Spirit made us your children,
confident to call you Father.
Increase your Spirit within us
and bring us to our promised inheritance.

Grant this through our Lord Jesus Christ, your Son,
who lives and reigns with you and the Holy Spirit,
one God, for ever and ever.

## Alternative Prayer

Father,
we come, reborn in the Spirit,
to celebrate our sonship in the Lord Jesus Christ.
Touch our hearts,
help them grow toward the life you have promised.
Touch our lives,
make them signs of your love for all men.

Grant this through Christ our Lord.

### Evening Prayer II

CANTICLE OF MARY

Ant.  Where your treasure is, there is your heart,
      says the Lord.

# TWENTIETH SUNDAY IN ORDINARY TIME

Psalter, Week IV

### Evening Prayer I

CANTICLE OF MARY

Ant.  Woman, great is your faith; what you ask, I
      give to you.

## Morning Prayer

<small>CANTICLE OF ZECHARIAH</small>

Ant. I am the living bread come down from heaven. Anyone who eats this bread will live for ever, alleluia.

<small>CONCLUDING PRAYER</small>

God our Father,
may we love you in all things and above all things
and reach the joy you have prepared for us
beyond all our imagining.

We ask this through our Lord Jesus Christ, your Son,
who lives and reigns with you and the Holy Spirit,
one God, for ever and ever.

### Alternative Prayer

Almighty God, ever-loving Father,
your care extends beyond the boundaries of race and nation
to the hearts of all who live.
May the walls, which prejudice raises between us,
crumble beneath the shadow of your outstretched arm.

We ask this through Christ our Lord.

## Evening Prayer II

<small>CANTICLE OF MARY</small>

Ant. I have come to cast fire upon the earth; how I long to see the flame leap up!

# TWENTY-FIRST SUNDAY
# IN ORDINARY TIME

Psalter, Week I

## Evening Prayer I

CANTICLE OF MARY

Ant. You are Christ, the Son of the living God. Blessed are you, Simon, son of John.

## Morning Prayer

CANTICLE OF ZECHARIAH

Ant. Lord, to whom shall we go? You have the words of eternal life. We believe and we are convinced that you are Christ, the Son of God, alleluia.

CONCLUDING PRAYER

Father,
help us to seek the values
that will bring us lasting joy in this changing world.
In our desire for what you promise
make us one in mind and heart.

Grant this through our Lord Jesus Christ, your Son,
who lives and reigns with you and the Holy Spirit,
one God, for ever and ever.

## Alternative Prayer

Lord our God,
all truth is from you,
and you alone bring oneness of heart.
Give your people the joy
of hearing your word in every sound
and of longing for your presence more than for life
    itself.
May all the attractions of a changing world
serve only to bring us
the peace of your kingdom which this world does
    not give.

Grant this through Christ our Lord.

## Evening Prayer II

CANTICLE OF MARY

Ant. Many shall come from the east and the west, and they shall sit down with Abraham and Isaac and Jacob in the kingdom of heaven.

# TWENTY-SECOND SUNDAY IN ORDINARY TIME

Psalter, Week II

## Evening Prayer I

CANTICLE OF MARY

Ant. Of what use is it to a man to gain the whole world, if he pays for it by losing his soul?

### Morning Prayer

CANTICLE OF ZECHARIAH

Ant. Listen and understand the instructions the Lord has given to you.

CONCLUDING PRAYER

Almighty God,
every good thing comes from you.
Fill our hearts with love for you,
increase our faith,
and by your constant care
protect the good you have given us.

We ask this through our Lord Jesus Christ, your Son,
who lives and reigns with you and the Holy Spirit,
one God, for ever and ever.

Alternative Prayer

Lord God of power and might,
nothing is good which is against your will,
and all is of value which comes from your hand.

Place in our hearts a desire to please you
and fill our minds with insight into love,
so that every thought may grow in wisdom
and all our efforts may be filled with your peace.

We ask this through Christ our Lord.

### Evening Prayer II

CANTICLE OF MARY

Ant. When you are invited to a wedding, go to the
lowest place, so that the one who invited you
can say: Friend, go up higher. Then you will
be honored in the eyes of all who are at table
with you.

# TWENTY-THIRD SUNDAY
# IN ORDINARY TIME

Psalter, Week III

### Evening Prayer I

CANTICLE OF MARY

Ant. Where two or three are gathered together in my
name, I am there among them, says the Lord.

### Morning Prayer

CANTICLE OF ZECHARIAH

Ant. He has done all things well: he has made the
deaf hear and the mute speak, alleluia.

CONCLUDING PRAYER

God our Father,
you redeem us
and make us your children in Christ.
Look upon us,
give us true freedom
and bring us to the inheritance you promised.

Grant this through our Lord Jesus Christ, your Son, who lives and reigns with you and the Holy Spirit, one God, for ever and ever.

Alternative Prayer

Lord our God,
in you justice and mercy meet.
With unparalleled love you have saved us from death
and drawn us into the circle of your life.
Open our eyes to the wonders this life sets before us,
that we may serve you free from fear
and address you as God our Father.

We ask this in the name of Jesus the Lord.

### Evening Prayer II

CANTICLE OF MARY

Ant. Whoever refuses to take up his cross and follow me cannot be my disciple, says the Lord.

## TWENTY-FOURTH SUNDAY IN ORDINARY TIME

Psalter, Week IV

### Evening Prayer I

CANTICLE OF MARY

Ant. Jesus said to Peter: I do not tell you to forgive only seven times, but seventy times seven.

### Morning Prayer

CANTICLE OF ZECHARIAH

Ant. He who loses his life because of me and for the sake of the Gospel shall save it, says the Lord.

CONCLUDING PRAYER

Almighty God,
our creator and guide,
may we serve you with all our heart
and know your forgiveness in our lives.

We ask this through our Lord Jesus Christ, your Son,
who lives and reigns with you and the Holy Spirit,
one God, for ever and ever.

### Alternative Prayer

Father in heaven, Creator of all,
look down upon your people in their moments of
    need,
for you alone are the source of our peace.
Bring us to the dignity which distinguishes the
    poor in spirit
and show us how great is the call to serve,
that we may share in the peace of Christ
who offered his life in the service of all.

We ask this through Christ our Lord.

### Evening Prayer II

CANTICLE OF MARY

Ant. I say to you: there is great rejoicing among the
    angels of God over one repentant sinner.

# TWENTY-FIFTH SUNDAY IN
# ORDINARY TIME

Psalter, Week I

### Evening Prayer I

CANTICLE OF MARY

Ant. Go into my vineyard, and I will pay you a just
    wage.

### Morning Prayer

CANTICLE OF ZECHARIAH

Ant. The greatest among you will be your servant,
    says the Lord; for I will lift up in glory the man
    who humbles himself.

CONCLUDING PRAYER

Father,
guide us, as you guide creation
according to your law of love.
May we love one another
and come to perfection
in the eternal life prepared for us.

Grant this through our Lord Jesus Christ, your Son,
who lives and reigns with you and the Holy Spirit,
one God, for ever and ever.

### Alternative Prayer

Father in heaven,
the perfection of justice is found in your love
and all mankind is in need of your law.
Help us to find this love in each other
that justice may be attained
through obedience to your law.

We ask this through Christ our Lord.

## Evening Prayer II

CANTICLE OF MARY

Ant.  No servant can obey two masters: you cannot
serve God and the love of money at the same
time.

# TWENTY-SIXTH SUNDAY IN
# ORDINARY TIME

Psalter, Week II

## Evening Prayer I

CANTICLE OF MARY

Ant.  Not everyone who says: "Lord, Lord," will
enter the kingdom of heaven, but the one who
does the will of my heavenly Father, alleluia.

## Morning Prayer

CANTICLE OF ZECHARIAH

Ant. Whoever gives you a cup of water in my name
because you are a follower of Christ shall not
go unrewarded, says the Lord.

CONCLUDING PRAYER

Father,
you show your almighty power
in your mercy and forgiveness.
Continue to fill us with your gifts of love.
Help us to hurry toward the eternal life you
   promise
and come to share in the joys of your kingdom.

Grant this through our Lord Jesus Christ, your Son,
who lives and reigns with you and the Holy Spirit,
one God, for ever and ever.

### Alternative Prayer

Father of our Lord Jesus Christ,
in your unbounded mercy
you have revealed the beauty of your power
through your constant forgiveness of our sins.
May the power of this love be in our hearts
to bring your pardon and your kingdom to all we
   meet.

We ask this through Christ our Lord.

## Evening Prayer II

CANTICLE OF MARY

Ant. Son, remember the good things you received
in your lifetime and the bad things Lazarus received in his.

# TWENTY-SEVENTH SUNDAY IN ORDINARY TIME

## Evening Prayer I

CANTICLE OF MARY

Ant. He will bring those evil men to an evil end and entrust his vineyard to other tenants who will give him the harvest at the proper season.

## Morning Prayer

CANTICLE OF ZECHARIAH

Ant. Let the little children come to me, for they are at home in my Father's kingdom.

CONCLUDING PRAYER

Father,
your love for us
surpasses all our hopes and desires.
Forgive our failings,
keep us in your peace
and lead us in the way of salvation.

We ask this through our Lord Jesus Christ, your Son,
who lives and reigns with you and the Holy Spirit,
one God, for ever and ever.

## Alternative Prayer

Almighty and eternal God,
Father of the world to come,
your goodness is beyond what our spirit can touch
and your strength is more than the mind can bear.
Lead us to seek beyond our reach
and give us the courage to stand before your truth.

We ask this through Christ our Lord.

## Evening Prayer II

CANTICLE OF MARY

Ant. Tell yourselves: We are useless servants, for we did only what we should have done.

# TWENTY-EIGHTH SUNDAY IN ORDINARY TIME

Psalter, Week IV

## Evening Prayer I

CANTICLE OF MARY

Ant. A certain man held a banquet and invited many; when it was time for the banquet to begin, he sent his servant to call his guests, for now the feast was ready, alleluia.

## Morning Prayer

CANTICLE OF ZECHARIAH

Ant. You have left everything to follow me; you will have it all returned a hundredfold and will inherit eternal life.

CONCLUDING PRAYER

Lord,
our help and guide,
make your love the foundation of our lives.
May our love for you express itself
in our eagerness to do good for others.

Grant this through our Lord Jesus Christ, your Son,
who lives and reigns with you and the Holy Spirit,
one God, for ever and ever.

## Alternative Prayer

Father in heaven,
the hand of your loving kindness
powerfully yet gently guides all the moments of our
   day.
Go before us in our pilgrimage of life,
anticipate our needs and prevent our falling.
Send your Spirit to unite us in faith,
that sharing in your service,
we may rejoice in your presence.

We ask this through Christ our Lord.

## Evening Prayer II

CANTICLE OF MARY

Ant. One of them, realizing that he had been cured, returned praising God in a loud voice, alleluia.

# TWENTY-NINTH SUNDAY IN ORDINARY TIME

Psalter, Week I

## Evening Prayer I

CANTICLE OF MARY

Ant. Give to Caesar what belongs to Caesar, but to God what belongs to God, alleluia.

## Morning Prayer

CANTICLE OF ZECHARIAH

Ant. The Son of Man did not come to be served but to serve, and to give his life as a ransom for many.

CONCLUDING PRAYER

Almighty and ever-living God,
our source of power and inspiration,
give us strength and joy
in serving you as followers of Christ,
who lives and reigns with you and the Holy Spirit,
one God, for ever and ever.

## Alternative Prayer

Lord our God, Father of all,
you guard us under the shadow of your wings
and search into the depths of our hearts.
Remove the blindness that cannot know you
and relieve the fear that would hide us from your sight.
We ask this through Christ our Lord.

## Evening Prayer II

CANTICLE OF MARY

Ant. When the Son of Man comes to earth, do you
think he will find faith in men's hearts?

# THIRTIETH SUNDAY IN ORDINARY TIME

Psalter, Week II

## Evening Prayer I

CANTICLE OF MARY

Ant. Teacher, what is the greatest commandment in
the law? Jesus said to him: You shall love the
Lord your God with your whole heart, alleluia.

## Morning Prayer

CANTICLE OF ZECHARIAH

Ant. Son of David, have pity on me. What do you
want me to do for you? Lord, restore my sight.

CONCLUDING PRAYER

Almighty and ever-living God,
strengthen our faith, hope, and love.
May we do with loving hearts
what you ask of us
and come to share the life you promise.

We ask this through our Lord Jesus Christ, your Son,
who lives and reigns with you and the Holy Spirit,
one God, for ever and ever.

## Alternative Prayer

Praised be you, God and Father of our Lord Jesus
Christ.
There is no power for good
which does not come from your covenant,
and no promise to hope in
that your love has not offered.

Strengthen our faith to accept your covenant
and give us the love to carry out your command.

We ask this through Christ our Lord.

## Evening Prayer II

CANTICLE OF MARY

Ant. The publican went home at peace with God, for
everyone who exalts himself shall be humbled,
and whoever humbles himself shall be exalted.

# THIRTY-FIRST SUNDAY IN ORDINARY TIME

Psalter, Week III

## Evening Prayer I

CANTICLE OF MARY

Ant. You have one teacher, and he is in heaven:
Christ your Lord.

## Morning Prayer

CANTICLE OF ZECHARIAH

Ant. Love the Lord your God with all your heart
and love your neighbor as yourself. There is
no greater commandment than these.

CONCLUDING PRAYER

God of power and mercy,
only with your help
can we offer you fitting service and praise.
May we live the faith we profess
and trust your promise of eternal life.

Grant this through our Lord Jesus Christ, your Son,
who lives and reigns with you and the Holy Spirit,
one God, for ever and ever.

Alternative Prayer

Father in heaven, God of power and Lord of mercy,
from whose fullness we have received,
direct our steps in our everyday efforts.
May the changing moods of the human heart
and the limits which our failings impose on hope
never blind us to you, source of every good.
Faith gives us the promise of peace
and makes known the demands of love.
Remove the selfishness that blurs the vision of faith.

Grant this through Christ our Lord.

## Evening Prayer II

CANTICLE OF MARY

Ant. The Son of Man came to seek out and to save
those who were lost.

# THIRTY-SECOND SUNDAY IN
# ORDINARY TIME

Psalter, Week IV

## Evening Prayer I

CANTICLE OF MARY

Ant. At midnight a cry was heard: Behold, the
Bridegroom comes, go out to meet him.

## Morning Prayer

CANTICLE OF ZECHARIAH

Ant. That poor widow gave more than anyone, because in her poverty she gave all she had.

CONCLUDING PRAYER

God of power and mercy,
protect us from all harm.

Give us freedom of spirit
and health in mind and body
to do your work on earth.

We ask this through our Lord Jesus Christ, your Son,
who lives and reigns with you and the Holy Spirit,
one God, for ever and ever.

### Alternative Prayer

Almighty Father,
strong is your justice and great is your mercy.
Protect us in the burdens and challenges of life.
Shield our minds from the distortion of pride
and enfold our desire with the beauty of truth.
Help us to become more aware of your loving design
so that we may more willingly give our lives in ser-
    vice to all.

We ask this through Christ our Lord.

## Evening Prayer II

CANTICLE OF MARY

Ant. He is not a God of the dead, but of the living:
    for to him all things are alive, alleluia.

## THIRTY-THIRD SUNDAY IN
## ORDINARY TIME

Psalter, Week I

## Evening Prayer I

CANTICLE OF MARY

Ant. Well done, my good and faithful servant, you
    have been trustworthy in small things. Now
    share your master's joy.

## Morning Prayer

CANTICLE OF ZECHARIAH

Ant. They will see the Son of Man coming in the
    clouds with great glory and majesty.

CONCLUDING PRAYER

Father of all that is good,
keep us faithful in serving you,
for to serve you is our lasting joy.

We ask this through our Lord Jesus Christ, your Son,
who lives and reigns with you and the Holy Spirit,
one God, for ever and ever.

### Alternative Prayer

Father in heaven,
ever-living source of all that is good,
from the beginning of time you promised man salvation
through the future coming of your Son, our Lord
Jesus Christ.
Help us to drink of his truth
and expand our hearts with the joy of his promises,
so that we may serve you in faith and in love
and know for ever the joy of your presence.

We ask this through Christ our Lord.

## Evening Prayer II

CANTICLE OF MARY

Ant. By your trusting acceptance of trials, you will
gain your life, says the Lord.

# THIRTY-FOURTH WEEK IN
ORDINARY TIME

The feast of Christ the King, 540, takes the place
of the Thirty-Fourth Sunday in Ordinary Time.

Psalter, Week II

CONCLUDING PRAYER

Lord,
increase our eagerness to do your will
and help us to know the saving power of your love.

Grant this through our Lord Jesus Christ, your Son,
who lives and reigns with you and the Holy Spirit,
one God, for ever and ever.

## Last Sunday in Ordinary Time

## CHRIST THE KING

Solemnity

### Evening Prayer I

CANTICLE OF MARY

Ant. The Lord God will give him the throne of David, his ancestor; he will rule in the house of Jacob for ever and his kingdom will have no end, alleluia.

### Morning Prayer

CANTICLE OF ZECHARIAH

Ant. He fashioned us into a kingdom for the glory of his God and Father; he is the firstborn of the dead and the leader of all the kings of the earth, alleluia.

CONCLUDING PRAYER

Almighty and merciful God,
you break the power of evil
and make all things new
in your Son Jesus Christ, the King of the universe.
May all in heaven and earth proclaim your glory
and never cease to praise you.

We ask this through our Lord Jesus Christ, your Son,
who lives and reigns with you and the Holy Spirit,
one God, for ever and ever.

### Evening Prayer II

CANTICLE OF MARY

Ant. All authority in heaven and on earth has been given to me, says the Lord.

# PROPER OF SAINTS

The section contains a selection of texts so that the major feasts of the Proper of Saints may be taken into account when any office is celebrated. The full variety of sanctoral texts will be found in *The Liturgy of the Hours* and *Christian Prayer.*

Unless otherwise indicated, the Psalmody is as given in the Four-Week Psalter. The hymn is to be chosen from the Liturgical Guide for Hymns, 578-582.

## February 2

## PRESENTATION OF THE LORD

Feast

If this feast falls on Sunday, Evening Prayer I is said.

### Evening Prayer I

CANTICLE OF MARY

Ant. The old man carried the child, but the child was the old man's Lord. The Virgin gave birth to the child yet remained a virgin for ever. She knelt in worship before her child.

### Invitatory

Ant. Come, let us worship the Lord of creation; he enters his holy temple.

Invitatory psalm, as in the Ordinary, 22.

### Morning Prayer

CANTICLE OF ZECHARIAH

Ant. When the parents of Jesus brought him into the temple, Simeon took him in his arms and gave thanks to God.

CONCLUDING PRAYER

All-powerful Father,
Christ your Son became man for us
and was presented in the temple.
May he free our hearts from sin
and bring us into your presence.

We ask this through our Lord Jesus Christ, your Son,
who lives and reigns with you and the Holy Spirit,
one God, for ever and ever.

## Evening Prayer II

CANTICLE OF MARY

Ant. Today the Blessed Virgin Mary presented the
Child Jesus in the temple; and Simeon, inspired by the Holy Spirit, took him in his
arms, and gave thanks to God.

## March 19

# JOSEPH, HUSBAND OF MARY

Solemnity

## Evening Prayer I

CANTICLE OF MARY

Ant. This is the faithful and prudent steward whom
the Lord has set over his household (alleluia).

## Invitatory

Ant. Let us praise Christ the Lord as we celebrate
the feast of Saint Joseph (alleluia).

Invitatory psalm, as in the Ordinary, 22.

## Morning Prayer

CANTICLE OF ZECHARIAH

Ant. Joseph lived in the town of Nazareth to fulfill
what the prophets had foretold of Christ: He
will be called a Nazarean (alleluia).

CONCLUDING PRAYER

Father,
you entrusted our Savior to the care of Saint Joseph.
By the help of his prayers
may your Church continue to serve its Lord, Jesus
Christ,

who lives and reigns with you and the Holy Spirit,
one God, for ever and ever.

## Evening Prayer II

CANTICLE OF MARY

Ant. When Jesus began his ministry, he was about
thirty years old, and was thought to be the
son of Joseph (alleluia).

**March 25**

## ANNUNCIATION

Solemnity

## Evening Prayer I

CANTICLE OF MARY

Ant. The Holy Spirit will come upon you, Mary, and
the power of the Most High will overshadow
you (alleluia).

## Invitatory

Ant. The Word was made flesh; come, let us worship him (alleluia).

Invitatory psalm, as in the Ordinary, 22.

## Morning Prayer

CANTICLE OF ZECHARIAH

Ant. In his great love for us, God sent his Son in
the likeness of our sinful nature (alleluia).

CONCLUDING PRAYER

God our Father,
your Word became man and was born of the Virgin
    Mary.
May we become more like Jesus Christ,
whom we acknowledge as our redeemer, God and
    man.
We ask this through our Lord Jesus Christ, your Son,
who lives and reigns with you and the Holy Spirit,
one God, for ever and ever.

## Evening Prayer II

CANTICLE OF MARY

Ant. The angel Gabriel said to Mary in greeting:
     Hail, full of grace, the Lord is with you;
     blessed are you among women (alleluia).

## June 24

# BIRTH OF JOHN
# THE BAPTIST

### Solemnity

## Evening Prayer I

CANTICLE OF MARY

Ant. Zechariah entered the temple of the Lord, and
     the angel Gabriel appeared to him, standing
     on the right of the altar of incense.

CONCLUDING PRAYER

All-powerful God,
help your people to walk the path to salvation.
By following the teaching of John the Baptist,
may we come to your Son, our Lord Jesus Christ,

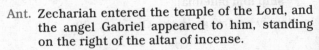

who lives and reigns with you and the Holy Spirit,
one God, for ever and ever.

## Invitatory

Ant. Come, let us worship the Lord, the Lamb of
God, proclaimed by John.

Invitatory psalm, as in the Ordinary, 22.

## Morning Prayer

CANTICLE OF ZECHARIAH

Ant. The mouth of Zechariah was opened, and he
spoke this prophecy: Blessed be the Lord, the
God of Israel.

CONCLUDING PRAYER

God our Father,
you raised up John the Baptist
to prepare a perfect people for Christ the Lord.
Give your Church joy in spirit
and guide those who believe in you
into the way of salvation and peace.

We ask this through our Lord Jesus Christ, your Son,
who lives and reigns with you and the Holy Spirit,
one God, for ever and ever.

## Evening Prayer II

CANTICLE OF MARY

Ant. This child, born to us, is greater than any
prophet; the Savior said of him: There is no man
born of women greater than John the Baptist.

Prayer as in Morning Prayer.

**June 29**

# PETER AND PAUL,
# APOSTLES

Solemnity

## Evening Prayer I

CANTICLE OF MARY

Ant. How glorious are the apostles of Christ; in life they loved one another; in death they rejoice together for ever.

CONCLUDING PRAYER

Lord our God,
encourage us through the prayers of Saints Peter and Paul.
May the apostles who strengthened the faith of the infant Church
help us on our way of salvation.
We ask this through our Lord Jesus Christ, your Son,
who lives and reigns with you and the Holy Spirit,
one God, for ever and ever.

## Invitatory

Ant. Come, let us worship the Lord, the king of apostles.

Invitatory psalm, as in the Ordinary, 22.

## Morning Prayer

CANTICLE OF ZECHARIAH

Ant. Simon Peter said: Lord, to whom shall we go? You have the words of eternal life; and we believe and we are convinced that you are the Christ, the Son of God, alleluia.

548

Concluding Prayer

God our Father,
today you give us the joy
of celebrating the feast of the apostles Peter and Paul.
Through them your Church first received the faith.
Keep us true to their teaching.

Grant this through our Lord Jesus Christ, your Son,
who lives and reigns with you and the Holy Spirit,
one God, for ever and ever.

## Evening Prayer II

Canticle of Mary

Ant. Peter the apostle and Paul the teacher of the
Gentiles taught us your law, O Lord.

Prayer as in Morning Prayer.

## August 6

# TRANSFIGURATION
## Evening Prayer I
(when this feast occurs on Sunday)

Canticle of Mary

Ant. Christ Jesus, you are the splendor of the
Father and the perfect image of his being; you
sustain all creation with your powerful word
and cleanse us of all our sins. On this day you
were exalted in glory upon the high mountain.

## Invitatory

Ant. Come, let us worship the King of glory, exalted on high.

Invitatory psalm, as in the Ordinary, 22.

## Morning Prayer

Canticle of Zechariah

Ant. A voice spoke from the cloud: This is my
beloved Son in whom I am well pleased; listen
to him.

CONCLUDING PRAYER

God our Father,
in the transfigured glory of Christ your Son,
you strengthen our faith
by confirming the witness of your prophets,
and show us the splendor of your beloved sons and
   daughters.
As we listen to the voice of your Son,
help us to become heirs to eternal life with him
who lives and reigns with you and the Holy Spirit,
one God, for ever and ever.

## Evening Prayer II

CANTICLE OF MARY

Ant.  When they heard the voice from the cloud, the
      disciples fell on their faces, overcome with
      fear; Jesus came up to them, touched them
      and said: Stand up. Do not be afraid.

## August 15

# ASSUMPTION

Solemnity

## Evening Prayer I

CANTICLE OF MARY

Ant.  All generations will call me blessed: the Al-
      mighty has done great things for me, alleluia.

CONCLUDING PRAYER

Almighty God,
you gave a humble virgin
the privilege of being the mother of your Son,
and crowned her with the glory of heaven.
May the prayers of the Virgin Mary
bring us to the salvation of Christ
and raise us up to eternal life.

We ask this through our Lord Jesus Christ, your Son,
who lives and reigns with you and the Holy Spirit,
one God, for ever and ever.

## Invitatory

Ant. Come let us worship the King of kings; on this
day his Virgin Mother was taken up to heaven.

Invitatory psalm, as in the Ordinary, 22.

## Morning Prayer

CANTICLE OF ZECHARIAH

Ant. This daughter of Jerusalem is lovely and beautiful as she ascends to heaven like the rising
sun at daybreak.

CONCLUDING PRAYER

All-powerful and ever-living God,
you raised the sinless Virgin Mary,
mother of your Son,
body and soul to the glory of heaven.
May we see heaven as our final goal
and come to share her glory.

We ask this through our Lord Jesus Christ, your Son,
who lives and reigns with you and the Holy Spirit,
one God, for ever and ever.

### Evening Prayer II

CANTICLE OF MARY

Ant. Today the Virgin Mary was taken up to heaven;
rejoice, for she reigns with Christ for ever.

Prayer as in Morning Prayer.


## September 14

# TRIUMPH OF THE CROSS

### Feast
### Evening Prayer I
(when this feast occurs on Sunday)

CANTICLE OF MARY

Ant. It was ordained that Christ should suffer, and
on the third day rise from the dead.

### Invitatory

Ant. Come, let us worship Christ the King who was
lifted up on the cross for our sake.

Invitatory psalm, as in the Ordinary, 22.

### Morning Prayer

CANTICLE OF ZECHARIAH

Ant. We worship your cross, O Lord, and we praise
and glorify your holy resurrection, for the wood
of the cross has brought joy to the world.

CONCLUDING PRAYER

God our Father,
in obedience to you
your only Son accepted death on the cross
for the salvation of mankind.
We acknowledge the mystery of the cross on earth.
May we receive the gift of redemption in heaven.

We ask this through our Lord Jesus Christ, your Son,
who lives and reigns with you and the Holy Spirit,
one God, for ever and ever.

### Evening Prayer II

CANTICLE OF MARY

Ant. O cross, you are the glorious sign of our victory. Through your power may we share in the triumph of Christ Jesus.

## November 1

## ALL SAINTS
Solemnity

### Evening Prayer I

CANTICLE OF MARY

Ant. The glorious company of apostles praises you, the noble fellowship of prophets praises you,

the white-robed army of martyrs praises you,
all the saints together sing your glory, O Holy
Trinity, one God.

## Invitatory

Ant. Come, let us worship God whose praises are
sung in the assembly of the saints.

Invitatory psalm, as in the Ordinary, 22.

## Morning Prayer

CANTICLE OF ZECHARIAH

Ant. The saints will shine like the sun in the kingdom of their Father, alleluia.

CONCLUDING PRAYER

Father, all-powerful and ever-living God,
today we rejoice in the holy men and women
of every time and place.
May their prayers bring us your forgiveness and
love.

We ask this through our Lord Jesus Christ, your Son,
who lives and reigns with you and the Holy Spirit,
one God, for ever and ever.

## Evening Prayer II

CANTICLE OF MARY

Ant. How glorious is that kingdom where all the
saints rejoice with Christ; clothed in white
robes, they follow the Lamb wherever he goes.

## November 2

## ALL SOULS

When November 2 occurs on Sunday, even though the Mass for All Souls Day may be celebrated, the office is taken from the current Sunday in Ordinary Time; the Office for the Dead is not said. However, when Morning Prayer and Evening Prayer are celebrated with the people, these hours may be taken from the Office for the Dead.

As in the Office for the Dead, 559.

## November 9

## DEDICATION OF SAINT JOHN LATERAN

### Feast

### Evening Prayer I

CANTICLE OF MARY

Ant. All you who love Jerusalem, rejoice with her for ever (alleluia).

### Invitatory

Ant. Come, let us worship Christ, the Bridegroom of his Church (alleluia).

Or: Come, let us worship Christ, who has shown his love for the Church (alleluia).

Invitatory psalm, as in the Ordinary, 22.

### Morning Prayer

CANTICLE OF ZECHARIAH

Ant. Zacchaeus, hurry down, I mean to stay with you today. He hurried down and welcomed Christ

with joy, for this day salvation had come to his
house (alleluia).

CONCLUDING PRAYER

God our Father,
from living stones, your chosen people,
you built an eternal temple to your glory.
Increase the spiritual gifts you have given to your
  Church
that your faithful people may continue to grow
into the new and eternal Jerusalem.

We ask this through our Lord Jesus Christ, your Son,
who lives and reigns with you and the Holy Spirit,
one God, for ever and ever.

Or:

Father,
you called your people to be your Church.
As we gather together in your name,
may we love, honor, and follow you
to eternal life in the kingdom you promise.

Grant this through our Lord Jesus Christ, your Son,
who lives and reigns with you and the Holy Spirit,
one God, for ever and ever.

## Evening Prayer II

CANTICLE OF MARY

Ant. This is God's dwelling place and he has made
    it holy; here we call on his name, for Scripture
    says: There you will find me (alleluia).

# December 8

## IMMACULATE CONCEPTION
### Solemnity

### Evening Prayer I

<small>CANTICLE OF MARY</small>

Ant. All generations will call me blessed: the Almighty has done great things for me.

### Invitatory

Ant. Come, let us celebrate the Immaculate Conception of the Virgin Mary; let us worship her Son, Christ the Lord.

Invitatory psalm, as in the Ordinary, 22.

### Morning Prayer

<small>CANTICLE OF ZECHARIAH</small>

Ant. The Lord God said to the serpent: I will make you enemies, you and the woman, your offspring and her offspring; she will crush your head, alleluia.

<small>CONCLUDING PRAYER</small>

Father,
you prepared the Virgin Mary
to be the worthy mother of your Son.
You let her share beforehand
in the salvation Christ would bring by his death,

and kept her sinless from the first moment of her
  conception.
Help us by her prayers
to live in your presence without sin.

We ask this through our Lord Jesus Christ, your Son,
who lives and reigns with you and the Holy Spirit,
one God, for ever and ever.

### Evening Prayer II

CANTICLE OF MARY

Ant.  Hail Mary, full of grace; the Lord is with you;
      blessed are you among women, and blessed is
      the fruit of your womb, alleluia.

# OFFICE FOR THE DEAD

During the Easter Season the **Alleluia** may be used at the end of the antiphons, verses and responsories.

## Invitatory

Ant. Come, let us worship the Lord, all things live for him.

Invitatory psalm, as in the Ordinary, 22.

## Morning Prayer

HYMN, no. 120 or 114.

PSALMODY

Ant. 1  The bones that were crushed shall leap for joy before the Lord.

Psalm 51

Have mercy on me, God, in your kindness.
In your compassion blot out my offense.
O wash me more and more from my guilt
and cleanse me from my sin.

My offenses truly I know them;
my sin is always before me.
Against you, you alone, have I sinned;
what is evil in your sight I have done.

That you may be justified when you give sentence
and be without reproach when you judge,
O see, in guilt I was born,
a sinner was I conceived.

Indeed you love truth in the heart;
then in the secret of my heart teach me wisdom.
O purify me, then I shall be clean;
O wash me, I shall be whiter than snow.

Make me hear rejoicing and gladness,
that the bones you have crushed may revive.
From my sins turn away your face
and blot out all my guilt.

A pure heart create for me, O God,
put a steadfast spirit within me.
Do not cast me away from your presence,
nor deprive me of your holy spirit.

Give me again the joy of your help;
with a spirit of fervor sustain me,
that I may teach transgressors your ways
and sinners may return to you.

O rescue me, God, my helper,
and my tongue shall ring out your goodness.
O Lord, open my lips
and my mouth shall declare your praise.

For in sacrifice you take no delight,
burnt offering from me you would refuse,
my sacrifice, a contrite spirit.
A humbled, contrite heart you will not spurn.

In your goodness, show favor to Zion:
rebuild the walls of Jerusalem.
Then you will be pleased with lawful sacrifice,
holocausts offered on your altar.

Ant. 2  At the very threshold of death, rescue me,
Lord.

Canticle                              Isaiah 38:10-14, 17-20

Once I said
"In the noontime of life I must depart!
To the gates of the nether world I shall be con-
signed
for the rest of my years."

I said, "I shall see the Lord no more
in the land of the living.
No longer shall I behold my fellow men
among those who dwell in the world."

My dwelling, like a shepherd's tent,
is struck down and borne away from me;
you have folded up my life, like a weaver
who severs the last thread.

Day and night you give me over to torment;
I cry out until the dawn.
Like a lion he breaks all my bones;
day and night you give me over to torment.

Like a swallow I utter shrill cries;
I moan like a dove.
My eyes grow weak, gazing heaven-ward:
O Lord, I am in straits; be my surety!

You have preserved my life
from the pit of destruction,
when you cast behind your back
all my sins.

For it is not the nether world that gives you
thanks,
nor death that praises you;
neither do those who go down into the pit
await your kindness.

The living, the living give you thanks,
as I do today.
Fathers declare to their sons,
O God, your faithfulness.
The Lord is our savior;
we shall sing to stringed instruments
in the house of the Lord
all the days of our life.

Ant. 3  I will praise my God all the days of my life.

## Psalm 146

My soul, give praise to the Lord;
I will praise the Lord all my days,
make music to my God while I live.

Put no trust in princes,
in mortal men in whom there is no help.
Take their breath, they return to clay
and their plans that day come to nothing.

He is happy who is helped by Jacob's God,
whose hope is in the Lord his God,
who alone made heaven and earth,
the seas and all they contain.

It is he who keeps faith for ever,
who is just to those who are oppressed.
It is he who gives bread to the hungry,
the Lord, who sets prisoners free,

the Lord, who gives sight to the blind,
who raises up those who are bowed down,
the Lord, who protects the stranger
and upholds the widow and orphan.

It is the Lord who loves the just
but thwarts the path of the wicked.
The Lord will reign for ever,
Zion's God, from age to age.

---

Or:

Ant. 3   Let everything that breathes give praise to
         the Lord.

## Psalm 150

Praise God in his holy place,
praise him in his mighty heavens.
Praise him for his powerful deeds,
praise his surpassing greatness.

O praise him with sound of trumpet,
praise him with lute and harp.
Praise him with timbrel and dance,
praise him with strings and pipes.

O praise him with resounding cymbals,
praise him with clashing of cymbals.
Let everything that lives and breathes
give praise to the Lord.

READING                           1 Thessalonians 4:14

If we believe that Jesus died and rose, so too will
God, through Jesus, bring with him those who have
fallen asleep.

RESPONSORY

I will praise you, Lord, for you have rescued me.
— I will praise you, Lord, for you have rescued me.

You turned my sorrow into joy,
— for you have rescued me.

Glory to the Father . . .
— I will praise . . .

CANTICLE OF ZECHARIAH

Ant. I am the Resurrection, I am the Life; to believe
in me means life, in spite of death, and all who
believe and live in me shall never die.

Or, during the Easter Season:

Ant. The splendor of Christ risen from the dead
has shone on the people redeemed by his
blood, alleluia.

INTERCESSIONS

Let us pray to the all-powerful Father who raised
Jesus from the dead and gives new life to our
mortal bodies, and say to him:

*Lord, give us new life in Christ.*

Father, through baptism we have been buried with your Son and have risen with him in his resurrection,

—grant that we may walk in newness of life so that when we die, we may live with Christ for ever.

Provident Father, you have given us the living bread that has come down from heaven and which should always be eaten worthily,

—grant that we may eat this bread worthily and be raised up to eternal life on the last day.

Lord, you sent an angel to comfort your Son in his agony,

—give us the hope of your consolation when death draws near.

You delivered the three youths from the fiery furnace,

—free your faithful ones from the punishment they suffer for their sins.

God of the living and the dead, you raised Jesus from the dead,

—raise up those who have died and grant that we may share eternal glory with them.

Our Father . . .

CONCLUDING PRAYER

Lord, hear our prayers.
By raising your Son from the dead, you have given us faith.
Strengthen our hope that N., our brother (sister),
will share in his resurrection.

We ask this through our Lord Jesus Christ, your Son, who lives and reigns with you and the Holy Spirit, one God, for ever and ever.

Or:

Lord God,
you are the glory of believers
and the life of the just.

Your Son redeemed us
by dying and rising to life again.
Our brother (sister) N. was faithful
and believed in our own resurrection.
Give to him (her) the joy and blessings
of the life to come.

We ask this through our Lord Jesus Christ, your Son,
who lives and reigns with you and the Holy Spirit,
one God, for ever and ever.

Or, during the Easter Season:

Almighty and merciful God,
may our brother (sister) N. share the victory of Christ
who loved us so much that he died and rose again
to bring us new life.

We ask this through our Lord Jesus Christ, your Son,
who lives and reigns with you and the Holy Spirit,
one God, for ever and ever.

For several people:

God, our creator and redeemer,
by your power Christ conquered death
and returned to you in glory.
May all your people (N. and N.), who have gone be-
    fore us in faith,
share his victory
and enjoy the vision of your glory for ever,
where Christ lives and reigns with you and the Holy
    Spirit,
one God, for ever and ever.

For relatives, friends, and benefactors:

Father,
source of forgiveness and salvation for all mankind,
hear our prayer.
By the prayers of the ever-virgin Mary,
may our friends, relatives, and benefactors

who have gone from this world
come to share eternal happiness with all your saints.

We ask this through our Lord Jesus Christ, your Son,
who lives and reigns with you and the Holy Spirit,
one God, for ever and ever.

### Evening Prayer

HYMN, no. 184 or 185, 172, 113.

PSALMODY

Ant. 1   The Lord will keep you from all evil. He will
            guard your soul.

#### Psalm 121

I lift up my eyes to the mountains:
from where shall come my help?
My help shall come from the Lord
who made heaven and earth.

May he never allow you to stumble!
Let him sleep not, your guard.
No, he sleeps not nor slumbers,
Israel's guard.

The Lord is your guard and your shade;
at your right side he stands.
By day the sun shall not smite you
nor the moon in the night.

The Lord will guard you from evil,
he will guard your soul.
The Lord will guard your going and coming
both now and for ever.

Ant. 2   If you kept a record of our sins, Lord, who
            could escape condemnation?

Psalm 130

Out of the depths I cry to you, O Lord,
Lord, hear my voice!
O let your ears be attentive
to the voice of my pleading.

If you, O Lord, should mark our guilt,
Lord, who would survive?
But with you is found forgiveness:
for this we revere you.

My soul is waiting for the Lord,
I count on his word.
My soul is longing for the Lord
more than watchman for daybreak.
Let the watchman count on daybreak
and Israel on the Lord.

Because with the Lord there is mercy
and fullness of redemption,
Israel indeed he will redeem
from all its iniquity.

Ant. 3  As the Father raises the dead and gives them
life, so the Son gives life to whom he wills.

Canticle    Philippians 2:6-11

Though he was in the form of God,
Jesus did not deem equality with God
something to be grasped at.

Rather, he emptied himself
and took the form of a slave,
being born in the likeness of men.

He was known to be of human estate,
and it was thus that he humbled himself,
obediently accepting even death,
death on a cross!

Because of this,
God highly exalted him
and bestowed on him the name
above every other name,

so that at Jesus' name
every knee must bend
in the heavens, on the earth,
and under the earth,
and every tongue proclaim
to the glory of God the Father:
JESUS CHRIST IS LORD!

READING              1 Corinthians 15:55-57

"Where, O death, is your victory?
Where, O death, is your sting?"

The sting of death is sin, and the power of sin is the law. But thanks be to God who gives us the victory through our Lord Jesus Christ.

RESPONSORY

In you, Lord, is our hope. We shall never hope in vain.
— In you, Lord, is our hope. We shall never hope in vain.

We shall dance and rejoice in your mercy.
— We shall never hope in vain.

Glory to the Father . . .
— In you, Lord . . .

Or:

Lord, in your steadfast love, give them eternal rest.
— Lord, in your steadfast love, give them eternal rest.

You will come to judge the living and the dead.
— Give them eternal rest.

Glory to the Father . . .
— Lord, in your . . .

CANTICLE OF MARY

Ant. All that the Father gives me will come to me, and whoever comes to me I shall not turn away.

Or, during the Easter Season:

Ant. **Our crucified and risen Lord has redeemed us, alleluia.**

INTERCESSIONS

We acknowledge Christ the Lord through whom we hope that our lowly bodies will be made like his in glory, and we say:

*Lord, you are our life and resurrection.*

Christ, Son of the living God, who raised up Lazarus, your friend, from the dead,

— raise up to life and glory the dead whom you have redeemed by your precious blood.

Christ, consoler of those who mourn, you dried the tears of the family of Lazarus, of the widow's son, and the daughter of Jairus,

— comfort those who mourn for the dead.

Christ, Savior, destroy the reign of sin in our earthly bodies, so that just as through sin we deserved punishment,

— so through you we may gain eternal life.

Christ, Redeemer, look on those who have no hope because they do not know you,

— may they receive faith in the resurrection and in the life of the world to come.

You revealed yourself to the blind man who begged for light of his eyes,

— show your face to the dead who are still deprived of your light.

When at last our earthly home is dissolved,

— give us a home, not of earthly making, but built of eternity in heaven.

Our Father . . .

Concluding Prayer, as in Morning Prayer.

## Night Prayer

All as on Sunday, 333.

# MEMORIAL OF THE BLESSED VIRGIN MARY ON SATURDAY

On Saturdays in Ordinary Time on which an optional memorial is permitted, the optional memorial of the Blessed Virgin Mary may be chosen.

## Invitatory

Ant. Come, let us worship Christ, the Son of Mary.

Or: Let us sing to the Lord as we keep this day in memory of the Blessed Virgin Mary.

Invitatory psalm, as in the Ordinary, 22.

## Morning Prayer

The hymn is taken from one of those given for the common of the Blessed Virgin Mary, 582.

The antiphons and psalms are from the current Saturday.

The reading with its responsory may be chosen from the following:

READING                                          Galatians 4:4-5

When the fullness of time had come, God sent his Son, born of a woman, born under the law, to ransom those under the law, so that we might receive adoption.

RESPONSORY

After the birth of your son, you remained a virgin.
— After the birth of your son, you remained a virgin.

Mother of God, intercede for us;
— you remained a virgin.

Glory to the Father . . .
— After the birth . . .

---

Alternative:

READING
See Isaiah 61:10

I rejoice heartily in the Lord,
    in my God is the joy of my soul;
For he has clothed me with a robe of salvation,
    and wrapped me in a mantle of justice,
    like a bride bedecked with her jewels.

RESPONSORY

The Lord has chosen her,
his loved one from the beginning.
— The Lord has chosen her,
his loved one from the beginning.

He has taken her to live with him,
— his loved one from the beginning.

Glory to the Father . . .
— The Lord has . . .

---

Alternative:

READING
Revelation 12:1

A great sign appeared in the sky, a woman
clothed with the sun, with the moon under her feet,
and on her head a crown of twelve stars.

RESPONSORY

Hail, Mary, full of grace; the Lord is with you.
— Hail, Mary, full of grace; the Lord is with you.

Blessed are you among women, and blessed is the
    fruit of your womb.
— The Lord is with you.

Glory to the Father . . .
— Hail, Mary, full . . .

---

CANTICLE OF ZECHARIAH

One of the following antiphons may be chosen:

1 Let us celebrate with great devotion this day in memory of the Blessed Virgin Mary; may she intercede for us with the Lord Jesus Christ.

2 The Lord God Most High has blessed you, Virgin Mary, above all the women on the earth.

3 Through you, sinless Virgin, the life we had lost was restored to us; from heaven you received a child, and you gave birth to the Savior of the world.

4 Hail, Mary, full of grace; the Lord is with you; blessed are you among women, alleluia.

5 Holy and sinless Virgin Mary, how shall I find words to praise you, for through you we have received our Redeemer, Jesus Christ, the Lord!

6 You are the glory of Jerusalem, the joy of Israel; you are the fairest honor of our race.

---

INTERCESSIONS

Let us glorify our Savior, who chose the Virgin Mary for his mother. Let us ask him:
  *May your mother intercede for us, Lord.*
Sun of Justice, the immaculate Virgin was the white dawn announcing your rising,
— grant that we may always live in the light of your coming.
Eternal Word, you chose Mary as the uncorrupted ark of your dwelling place,
— free us from the corruption of sin.
Savior of mankind, your mother stood at the foot of your cross,
— grant, through her intercession, that we may rejoice to share in your passion.

With ultimate generosity and love, you gave Mary as
    a mother to your beloved disciple,
— help us to live as worthy sons of so noble a
    mother.

Or:

Let us glorify our Savior, who chose the Virgin
    Mary for his mother. Let us ask him:
    *May your mother intercede for us, Lord.*
Savior of the world, by your redeeming might you
    preserved your mother beforehand from all stain
    of sin,
— keep watch over us, lest we sin.
You are our redeemer, who made the immaculate
    Virgin Mary your purest home and the sanctuary
    of the Holy Spirit,
— make us temples of your Spirit for ever.
Eternal Word, you taught your mother to choose
    the better part,
— grant that in imitating her we may seek the food
    that brings life everlasting.
King of kings, you lifted up your mother, body and
    soul, into heaven,
— help us to fix our thoughts on things above.
Lord of heaven and earth, you crowned Mary and
    set her at your right hand as queen,
— make us worthy to share this glory.

Our Father . . .

CONCLUDING PRAYER

The prayer is chosen from one of the following:

Lord God,
give to your people the joy
of continual health in mind and body.
With the prayers of the Virgin Mary to help us,
guide us through the sorrows of this life
to eternal happiness in the life to come.

Grant this through our Lord Jesus Christ, your Son,
who lives and reigns with you and the Holy Spirit,
one God, for ever and ever.

Or:

Lord,
take away the sins of your people.
May the prayers of Mary the mother of your Son help
    us,
for alone and unaided we cannot hope to please you.

We ask this through our Lord Jesus Christ, your Son,
who lives and reigns with you and the Holy Spirit,
one God, for ever and ever.

Or:

God of mercy,
give us strength.
May we who honor the memory of the Mother of God
rise above our sins and failings with the help of her
    prayers.

Grant this through our Lord Jesus Christ, your Son,
who lives and reigns with you and the Holy Spirit,
one God, for ever and ever.

Or:

Lord,
may the prayers of the Virgin Mary
bring us protection from danger
and freedom from sin
that we may come to the joy of your peace.

We ask this through our Lord Jesus Christ, your Son,
who lives and reigns with you and the Holy Spirit,
one God, for ever and ever.

Or:

Lord,
as we honor the glorious memory of the Virgin Mary,
we ask that by the help of her prayers
we too may come to share the fullness of your grace.

Grant this through our Lord Jesus Christ, your Son,
who lives and reigns with you and the Holy Spirit,
one God, for ever and ever.

Or:

All-powerful God,
we rejoice in the protection of the holy Virgin Mary.
May her prayers help to free us from all evils here
    on earth
and lead us to eternal joy in heaven.

Grant this through our Lord Jesus Christ, your Son,
who lives and reigns with you and the Holy Spirit,
one God, for ever and ever.

# HYMNS

# LITURGICAL GUIDE FOR HYMNS

## PROPER OF SEASONS

No.

### ADVENT

| 54 | On Jordan's bank |
| 55 | Maranatha |
| 56 | Come, thou long-expected Jesus |
| 57 | Be consoled, my people |
| 58 | Hear the herald voice |
| 59 | The King of glory |
| 60 | Wake, awake, the night is dying |
| 61 | Creator of the stars of night |
| 62 | You heavens |
| 63 | O come, O come, Emmanuel |
| 64 | The coming of our God |
| 65 | Behold a Virgin bearing him |
| 66 | The night is ending (Song of Salvation) |
| 67 | Behold, a rose of Judah |

### CHRISTMAS

| 68 | Unto us a child is born (A child is born) |
| 69 | From heaven high |
| 70 | Go tell it on the mountain |
| 71 | O come, all ye faithful |
| 72 | Songs of praise the angels sang |
| 73 | Virgin-born, we bow before you |
| 74 | What child is this? |
| 75 | A child is born in Bethlehem |
| 76 | Unto us a child is given |

### HOLY FAMILY

| 77 | Sing of Mary, pure and lowly |
| 78 | Joseph |

No.

### MARY, MOTHER OF GOD

| 73 | Virgin-born, we bow before you |
| 79 | Joy to you |
| 80 | O Mary, of all women |

### EPIPHANY

| 3 | Sion, sing |
| 11 | All you nations |
| 81 | As with gladness men of old |
| 84 | Songs of thankfulness |

### BAPTISM OF THE LORD

| 82 | Sing praise to our Creator |
| 83 | When Jesus comes to be baptized |
| 84 | Songs of thankfulness |

### LENT

| 53 | The Master came |
| 85 | Now let us all with one accord |
| 86 | Creator of the earth and skies |
| 87 | Lord, your glory in Christ we have seen |
| 88 | Praise to the holiest |
| 89 | The glory of these forty days |
| 90 | Grant to us |
| 91 | With hearts renewed |
| 92 | Take up your cross |
| 93 | For forty years |
| 94 | Lord who throughout these forty days |
| 95 | This is our accepted time |
| 96 | Draw near, O Lord |

No.

**ORDINARY TIME**

**Morning Prayer**

| | |
|---|---|
| 1 | On this day, the first of days (Sunday only) |
| 2 | Brightness of the Father's glory |
| 3 | Sion, sing |
| 4 | Morning has broken |
| 5 | Darkness has faded |
| 6 | When morning fills the sky |
| 7 | Lord whose love in humble service |
| 8 | Praise, my soul, the King of heaven |
| 9 | Sing with all the sons of glory |
| 10 | I sing the mighty power of God |
| 11 | All you nations |
| 12 | This day God gives me |
| 13 | God Father, praise and glory |
| 14 | All creatures of our God |
| 15 | O God of light |
| 16 | We turn to you, O God |
| 17 | Christ is the world's light |
| 19 | From all that dwell |
| 20 | From all that dwell |
| 24 | Help us, O Lord |
| 25 | Lord of all hopefulness |
| 26 | Lord of all being throned afar |
| 29 | Lord God and Maker of all things |
| 82 | Sing praise to our Creator |
| 91 | With hearts renewed |
| 131 | All hail, adored Trinity |
| 132 | Holy, holy, holy |
| 151 | Praise the Lord, ye heavens, adore him |

No.

**Evening Prayer**

| | |
|---|---|
| 27 | Almighty ruler, God of truth |
| 28 | Firmly I believe and truly |
| 32 | Now thank we all our God |
| 33 | O Christ, you are the light and day |
| 34 | Lord Jesus Christ, abide with us |
| 35 | The setting sun |
| 36 | O Father, whose creating hand |
| 37 | For the fruits of his creation |
| 38 | When, in his own image |
| 39 | At the name of Jesus |
| 40 | Love divine all loves excelling |
| 41 | Now fades all earthly splendor |
| 42 | Day is done |
| 43 | O worship the King |
| 44 | For to those who love God |
| 45 | Let all things now living |
| 46 | Father, we thank thee |
| 47 | We plough the fields and scatter |
| 182 | O God, our help in ages past |
| 184 | O radiant light, O sun divine |

**Night Prayer**

| | |
|---|---|
| 33 | O Christ, you are the light and day |
| 34 | Lord Jesus Christ, abide with us |
| 42 | Day is done |
| 48 | We praise you, Father, for your gifts |
| 49 | Holy God, we praise thy name |

No.

| No. | |
|---|---|
| 50 | This world, my God |
| 51 | Now at the daylight's ending |
| 52 | All praise to you, O God |
| 53 | The Master came |
| 99 | When from the darkness |
| 152 | They come, God's messengers of love |
| 153 | You holy angels bright |
| 184 | O radiant Light, O Sun divine |

**SOLEMNITIES OF THE LORD IN ORDINARY TIME**

**Trinity Sunday**

| | |
|---|---|
| 1 | On this day, the first of days |
| 13 | God Father, praise and glory |
| 30 | Most ancient of all mysteries |
| 31 | Faith of our Fathers |
| 82 | Sing praise to our Creator |
| 131 | All hail, adored Trinity |
| 132 | Holy, holy, holy |
| 133 | Come, thou almighty King |

**Corpus Christi**

| | |
|---|---|
| 46 | Father, we thank thee |

No.

| No. | |
|---|---|
| 108 | I shall praise the Savior's glory |
| 113 | We who once were dead (in the Midst of Death) |
| 114 | I am the bread of life |
| 121 | Alleluia! Sing of Jesus |
| 134 | Lord, who at your first Eucharist did pray |
| 135 | God with hidden majesty |

**Sacred Heart**

| | |
|---|---|
| 40 | Love divine all loves excelling |
| 136 | O Christ, Redeemer of mankind |
| 137 | Heart of Christ |
| 138 | To Christ, the Prince of peace |
| 139 | Come to me |
| 140 | Shepherd of souls |

**Christ the King**

| | |
|---|---|
| 101 | Crown him with many crowns |
| 102 | Hail, Redeemer, King divine |
| 141 | To Jesus Christ, our sov'reign King |

# PROPER OF SAINTS

**Immaculate Conception (Dec. 8)**

| | |
|---|---|
| 156 | Mary, crowned with living light |
| 157 | Mary Immaculate, star of the morning |
| 158 | Holy Mary, now we crown you |

**Presentation (Feb. 2)**

| | |
|---|---|
| 3 | Sion, sing |
| 143 | Hail to the Lord who comes |
| 144 | When Mary bought her treasure |

**Solemnity of Joseph (March 19)**

| | |
|---|---|
| 78 | Joseph |
| 145 | Look down to us |
| 183 | Who would true valor see |

**Annunciation (March 25)**

| | |
|---|---|
| 159 | Mother of Christ |
| 160 | Hail, this festival day |
| 161 | Rejoice, O Virgin Mary |

**Birth of John the Baptist (June 24)**

| | |
|---|---|
| 57 | Be consoled, my people |
| 146 | The great forerunner |

## MEMORIAL OF THE BLESSED VIRGIN MARY

## OFFICE FOR THE DEAD

# On This Day, the First of Days

Melody: Gott Sei Dank
(Lübeck) 77.77

Music: Freylinghausen's *Gesangbuch*, 1704
Text: *Le Mans Breviary*, 1748
Translator: Henry W. Baker, 1821-1877, alt.

**1**

On this day, the first of days
God the Father's name we praise;
Who, creation's Lord and spring
Did the world from darkness bring.

**2**

On this day the eternal Son
Over death his triumph won;
On this day the Spirit came
With his gifts of living flame.

**3**

Father, who didst fashion man
Godlike in thy loving plan
Fill us with that love divine,
And conform our wills to thine.

**4**

Word made flesh, all hail to thee!
Thou from sin hast set us free.
And with thee we die and rise
Unto God in sacrifice.

**5**

Holy Spirit, you impart
Gifts of love to every heart;
Give us light and grace, we pray
Fill our hearts this holy day.

**6**

God, the blessed Three in One,
May thy holy will be done.
In thy word our souls are free.
And we rest this day with thee.

# Brightness of the Father's Glory

Melody: Halton Holgate 87.87

Music: Later form of tune by
William Boyce, c. 1710-1779
Text: Mount Saint Bernard Abbey

**1**

Brightness of the Father's glory
Springing from eternal light
Source of light by light engendered,
Day enlightening every day,

**2**

In your ever-lasting radiance
Shine upon us, Christ, true sun,
Bringing life to mind and body
Through the Holy Spirit's pow'r.

**3**

Father of unfading glory
Rich in grace and strong to save,
Hear our prayers and come to save us,
Keep us far from sinful ways.

**4**

Dawn is drawing ever nearer,
Dawn that brings us all we seek,
Son who dwells within the Father
Father uttering one Word.

**5**

Glory be to God the Father,
Glory to his Only Son,
Glory now and through all ages,
To the Spirit Advocate.

583

**3**

# Sion, Sing

Melody: Sion, Sing
Irregular with Antiphon

Music. Lucien Deiss, C.S.Sp.
Text: Lucien Deiss, C.S.Sp.

Antiphon:    Sion, sing, break into song!
             For within you is the Lord
             With his saving power.

### 1

Rise and shine forth, for your light has
    come,
And upon you breaks the glory of the
    Lord;
For the darkness covers the earth,
And the thick clouds, the people.
*Antiphon*

### 2

But upon you the Lord shall dawn,
And in you his splendor shall be re-
    vealed;
Your light shall guide the Gentiles on
    their path,
And kings shall walk in your brightness.
*Antiphon*

### 3

Wonder and thanksgiving shall fill your
    heart,
As the wealth of nations enriches you;
You shall be called the City of the Lord,
Dear to the Holy One of Israel.
*Antiphon*

### 4

You who were desolate and alone,
A place unvisited by men
Shall be the pride of ages untold,
And everlasting joy to the nations.
*Antiphon*

### 5

No more shall the sun be your light by
    day,
Nor the moon's beam enlighten you by
    night;
The Lord shall be your everlasting light,
And your God shall be your glory.
*Antiphon*

### 6

No more for you the setting of suns,
No more the waning of moons;
The Lord shall be your everlasting light
And the days of your mourning shall
    come to an end.
*Antiphon*

**4**

# Morning Has Broken

Melody: Bunessan 55.54.D

Music: Old Gaelic Melody
Text: Eleanor Farjeon, 1881-1965

### 1

Morning has broken
Like the first morning,
Blackbird has spoken
Like the first bird.
Praise for the singing!
Praise for the morning!
Praise for them, springing
Fresh from the Word!

### 2

Sweet the rains new fall
Sunlit from heaven,
Like the first dew fall
On the first grass.
Praise for the sweetness
Of the wet garden,
Sprung in completeness
Where his feet pass.

### 3

Mine is the sunlight!
Mine is the morning,
Born of the one light
Eden saw play!

Praise with elation,
Praise every morning,
God's re-creation
Of the new day!

584

# Darkness Has Faded

Melody: Christe Sanctorum
11.11.11.5

Music: *Paris Antiphoner*, 1681
Text: James Quinn, S.J.

**1**

Darkness has faded, night gives way to morning;
Sleep has refreshed us, now we thank our Maker,
Singing his praises, lifting up to heaven
Hearts, minds and voices.

**2**

Father of mercies, bless the hours before us;
While there is daylight may we work to please you,
Building a city fit to be your dwelling,
Home for all nations.

**3**

Daystar of heaven, Dawn that ends our darkness,
Sun of salvation, Lord enthroned in splendor,
Stay with us, Jesus; let your Easter glory
Fill all creation.

**4**

Flame of the Spirit, fire with love's devotion
Hearts love created, make us true apostles
Give us a vision wide as heav'n's horizon,
Bright with your promise.

**5**

Father in heaven, guide your children homewards;
Jesus, our Brother, walk beside us always.
Joy-giving Spirit, make the world one people,
Sign of God's Kingdom.

# 6

# When Morning Fills the Sky

Melody: O Seigneur 667.667.D

Music: Louis Bourgeois, 1500-1561
Text: E. Caswell, 1814-1878, alt.

**1**

When morning fills the sky,
Our hearts awaking cry:
May Jesus Christ be praised.
In all our works and prayer
His Sacrifice we share:
May Jesus Christ be praised.
The night becomes as day,
When from our hearts we say:
May Jesus Christ be praised.
The powers of darkness fear
When this glad song they hear:
May Jesus Christ be praised.

**2**

In heav'n our joy will be
To sing eternally:
May Jesus Christ be praised.
Let earth and sea and sky
From depth to height reply:
May Jesus Christ be praised.
Let all the earth now sing
To our eternal King:
May Jesus Christ be praised.
By this the eternal song,
Through ages all along:
May Jesus Christ be praised.

# 7

## Lord Whose Love in Humble Service

Melody: In Babilone 87.87.D

Music: Traditional Dutch Melody
Text: Albert Bayly, 1901-

**1**

Lord, whose love in humble service
Bore the weight of human need,
Who did on the Cross, forsaken,
Show us mercy's perfect deed:
We, your servants, bring the worship
Not of voice alone, but heart;
Consecrating to your purpose
Every gift which you impart.

**2**

As we worship, grant us vision,
Till your love's revealing light,
Till the height and depth and greatness
Dawns upon our human sight;
Making known the needs and burdens
Your compassion bids us bear,
Stirring us to faithful service,
Your abundant life to share.

**3**

Called from worship into service
Forth in your great name we go,
To the child, the youth, the aged,
Love in living deals to show.
Hope and health, goodwill and comfort,
Counsel, aid, and peace we give
That your children, Lord, in freedom,
May your mercy know, and live.

# 8

## Praise, My Soul, the King of Heaven

Melody: Lauda Anima 87.87.87

Music: John Goss, 1869
Based on *Psalm 102*, H. F. Lyte 1834, alt.

**1**

Praise, my soul, the King of heaven;
To his feet your tribute bring;
Ransomed, healed, restored, forgiven,
Evermore his praises sing;
Alleluia! Alleluia!
Praise the everlasting King.

Father-like he tends and spares us;
Well our feeble frame he knows;
In his hand he gently bears us,
Rescues us from all our foes.
Alleluia! Alleluia!
Widely yet his mercy flows.

**2**

Praise him for his grace and favor
To his children in distress;
Praise him still the same as ever
Slow to chide and swift to bless:
Alleluia! Alleluia!
Glorious in his faithfulness.

**4**

Angels, help us to adore him;
You beheld him face to face;
Sun and moon, bow down before him,
Join the praises of our race:
Alleluia! Alleluia!
Praise with us the God of grace.

586

# Sing with All the Sons of Glory

# 9

Melody: Hymn To Joy (Beethoven) 87.87.D
Music: Arr. from
Ludwig von Beethoven, 1770-1827, by Edward Hodges, 1796-1867
Text: Based on 1 Corinthians 15:20, William J. Irons, 1812-1883

### 1

Sing with all the sons of glory,
Sing the resurrection song!
Death and sorrow, earth's dark story,
To the former days belong.
All around the clouds are breaking,
Soon the storms of time shall cease;
In God's likeness man awaking,
Knows the everlasting peace.

### 2

O what glory, far exceeding
All that eye has yet perceived!
Holiest hearts for ages pleading,
Never that full joy conceived.
God has promised, Christ prepares it,
There on high our welcome waits;
Every humble spirit shares it,
Christ has passed the eternal gates.

### 3

Life eternal! heaven rejoices:
Jesus lives who once was dead.
Join, O man, the deathless voices;
Child of God, lift up thy head!
Patriarchs from the distant ages
Saints all longing for their heaven,
Prophets, psalmists, seers, and sages,
All await the glory given.

### 4

Life eternal! O what wonders
Crowd on faith; what joy unknown,
When, amidst earth's closing thunders
Saints shall stand before the throne!
O to enter that bright portal,
See that glowing firmament
Know, with thee, O God immortal
"Jesus Christ whom thou hast sent!"

# I Sing the Mighty Power of God

Melody: Ellacombe C.M.D.
Music: *Würtemburg Gesangbuch*, 1784,
adapted in the *Mainz Gesangbuch*, 1833,
and further adapted in the *Saint Gall Gesangbuch*, 1863
Text: Isaac Waats, 1715

### 1

I sing the mighty power of God,
That made the mountains rise;
That spread the flowing seas abroad,
And built the lofty skies.
I sing the wisdom that ordained
The sun to rule the day.
The moon shines full at his command,
And all the stars obey.

### 2

I sing the goodness of the Lord,
That filled the earth with food.
He formed the creatures with his word,
And then pronounced them good.
Lord, how your wonders are displayed
Where e'er I turn my eye:
If I survey the ground I tread,
Or gaze upon the sky!

### 3

There's not a plant or flower below,
But makes your glories known;
And clouds arise, and tempests blow,
By order from your throne;

While all that borrows life from you
Is ever in your care,
And everywhere that man can be,
You, God, are present there.

# All You Nations

Melody: All You Nations
Irregular with Antiphon

Music: Lucien Deiss, C.S.Sp.
Text: Lucien Deiss, C.S.Sp.

Antiphon:
All you nations, sing out your joy to the
    Lord:
Alleluia, alleluia!

1

Joyfully shout, all you on earth,
give praise to the glory of God;
And with a hymn, sing out his glorious
    praise:
Alleluia!

Antiphon

2

Let all the earth kneel in his sight,
extolling his marvelous fame;
Honor his name, in highest heaven give
    praise:
Alleluia!                    Antiphon

3

Come forth and see all the great works
that God has brought forth by his might;
Fall on your knees before his glorious
    throne:
Alleluia!                    Antiphon

4

Glory and thanks be to the Father;
honor and praise to the Son;
And to the Spirit, source of life and of love:
Alleluia!                    Antiphon

# 12

# This Day God Gives Me

Melody: Bunessan 55.54.D

Music: Old Gaelic Melody
Text: James Quinn, S.J.

1

This day God gives me
Strength of high heaven,
Sun and moon shining,
    Flame in my hearth,
Flashing of lightning
Wind in its swiftness,
Deeps of the ocean,
    Firmness of earth.

2

This day God sends me
Strength as my steersman,
Might to uphold me,
    Wisdom as guide.
Your eyes are watchful,
Your ears are listening,
Your lips are speaking,
    Friend at my side.

3

God's way is my way,
God's shield is round me,
God's host defends me,
    Saving from ill.
Angels of heaven,
Drive from me always
All that would harm me,
    Stand by me still.

4

Rising, I thank you,
Mighty and strong one
King of creation,
    Giver of rest,
Firmly confessing
Threeness of persons,
Oneness of Godhead,
    Trinity blest.

## God Father, Praise and Glory

Melody: Gott Vater! Sei Gepriesen
76.76 with Refrain

Music: *Mainz Gesangbuch*, 1813
Text: Anon.
Translator: John Rothensteiner, 1936, alt.

**1**

God Father, praise and glory
Your children come to sing.
Good will and peace to mankind,
The gifts your kingdom brings.

Refrain:
O most Holy Trinity,
Undivided Unity;
Holy God, Mighty God,
God Immortal, be adored.

**2**

And you, Lord Coeternal,
God's sole begotten Son,
O Jesus, King anointed,
You have redemption won. Refrain

**3**

O Holy Ghost, Creator,
The Gift of God most high;
Life, love and holy wisdom,
Our weakness now supply.
Refrain

## All Creatures of our God and King

Melody: Lasst Uns Enfreuen
(Vigiles et Sancti) 88.44.88
with Alleluias

Music: *Geistliche Kirchengesange*,
Cologne, 1623
Text: Saint Francis of Assisi, 1182-1226
Translator: William H. Draper, 1855-1933

**1**

All creatures of our God and King,
Lift up your voice and with us sing Al-
leluia, alleluia!
Thou burning sun with golden beam,
Thou silver moon with softer gleam:

Refrain:
O praise him, O praise him, Alleluia,
alleluia, alleluia!

**2**

Thou rushing winds that are so strong,
Ye clouds that sail in heaven along,
O praise him, alleluia!
Thou rising morn, in praise rejoice,
Ye lights of evening, find a voice:
Refrain

## O God of Light

Melody: Danby, L.M.

Music: Traditional English
Text: James Quinn, S.J.

**1**

O God of light, the dawning day
Gives us new promise of your love.
Each fresh beginning is your gift,
Like gentle dew from heav'n above.

**2**

Your blessings, Father, never fail:
Your Son, who is our daily Bread,
The Holy Spirit of your love,
By whom each day your sons are led.

**3**

Make us the servant of your peace,
Renew our strength, remove all fear;
Be with us, Lord, throughout this day,
For all is joy if you are near.

**4**

To Father, Son and Spirit blest,
One only God, we humbly pray:
Show us the splendor of your light
In death, the dawn of perfect day.

**16**

# We Turn to You, O God

Melody: Intercessor 11.10.11.10

Music: C. H. H. Parry
Text: Fred Kaan, 1929-

**1**

We turn to you, O God of every nation,
Giver of life and origin of good;
Your love is at the heart of all creation,
Your hurt is people's broken brother-
hood.

**2**

We turn to you that we may be forgiven
For crucifying Christ on earth again;
We know that we have never wholly
striven,
Forgetting self, to love the other man.

**3**

Free every heart from pride and self-
reliance,
Our ways of thought inspire with simple
grace;
Break down among us barriers of
defiance,
Speak to the soul of all the human race.

**4**

Teach us, good Lord, to serve the need
of others,
Help us to give and not to count the
cost.
Unite us all for we are born as brothers;
Defeat our Babel with your Pentecost.

**17**

# Christ is the World's Light

Melody: Christe Sanctorum 11.11.11.5

Music: *Paris Antiphoner*, 1681
Text: F. Pratt Green, 1903-

**1**

Christ is the world's Light, he and
none other;
Born in our darkness, he became our
brother.
If we have seen him, we have seen the
Father:
Glory to God on high.

**2**

Christ is the world's Peace, he and
none other;
No man can serve him and despise his
brother.
Who else unites us, one in God the
Father?
Glory to God on high.

**3**

Christ is the world's Life, he and none
other;
Sold, once for silver, murdered here,
our brother.
He, who redeems us, reigns with God
the Father:
Glory to God on high.

**4**

Give God the glory, God and none
other;
Give God the glory, Spirit, Son and
Father;
Give God the glory, God in man my
brother.
Glory to God on high.

590

# Breathe on Me, Breath of God

Melody: Yattendon 46 S.M.

Music: H. E. Wooldridge, 1845-1917
Text: Edwin Hatch, 1835-1889,
adapted by Anthony G. Petti

**18**

### 1
Breathe on me, breath of God,
Fill me with life anew,
That I may love the things you love,
And do what you would do.

### 2
Breathe on me, breath of God,
Until my heart is pure,
Until with you I have one will,
To live and to endure.

### 3
Breathe on me, breath of God,
My soul with grace refine,
Until this earthly part of me
Glows with your fire divine.

### 4
Breathe on me, breath of God
So I shall never die,
But live with you the perfect life
In your eternity.

**19** **20**

# From All That Dwell Below the Skies

Melody: Erschienen Ist Der
Herrliche Tag L.M. with Hallelujah

Music: Nikolaus Hermann 1560
Text: Isaac Watts 1719

Melody: Eisenach L.M.

Music: Johann H. Schein, 1583-1630
Text: Isaac Watts, 1719

### 1
From all that dwell below the skies
Let the Creator's praise arise:
Let the Redeemer's name be sung
Through every land, by every tongue,
Hallelujah!

### 2
Eternal are thy mercies, Lord;
Eternal truth attends thy word:
Thy praise shall sound from shore to
shore,
Till suns shall rise and set no more:
Hallelujah!

# Father, Lord of Earth and Heaven

**21**

Melody: Drakes Boughton 87.87

Music: E. Elgar, 1857-1934
Text: James Quinn, S.J.

### 1
Father, Lord of earth and heaven,
King to whom all gifts belong,
Give your greatest Gift, your Spirit,
God the holy, God the strong.

### 2
Son of God, enthroned in Glory,
Send your promised Gift of grace
Make your Church your holy Temple,
God the Spirit's dwelling-place.

### 3
Spirit, come, in peace descending
As at Jordan, heav'nly Dove
Seal your Church as God's anointed
Set our hearts on fire with love.

### 4
Stay among us, God the Father,
Stay among us, God the Son,
Stay among us, Holy Spirit:
Dwell within us, make us one.

591

## 22. Holy Spirit, Come Confirm Us

Melody: Laus Deo (Redhead 46)
87.87

Music: Richard Redhead,
1820-1901
Text: Brian Foley

**1**

Holy Spirit, come, confirm us
In the truth that Christ makes known;
We have faith and understanding
Through your helping gifts alone.

**2**

Holy Spirit, come, console us,
Come as Advocate to plead,
Loving Spirit from the Father,
Grant in Christ the help we need.

**3**

Holy Spirit, come, renew us,
Come yourself to make us live:
Holy through your loving presence,
Holy through the gifts you give.

**4**

Holy Spirit, come, possess us,
You the Love of Three in One,
Holy Spirit of the Father,
Holy Spirit of the Son.

## 23. Come, Holy Ghost, Who Ever One

Melody: O Jesu Mi
Dulcissime L.M.

Music: *Clausener Gesangbuch*, 1653
Text: Attributed to Saint Ambrose, c. 340-397
Translator: J. H. Newman, 1801-1890

**1**

Come Holy Ghost, who ever one
Art with the Father and the Son,
Come, Holy Ghost, our souls possess
With thy full flood of holiness.

**2**

In will and deed, in heart and tongue,
With all the powers, thy praise be sung;
And love light up our mortal frame
Till others catch the living flame.

**3**

Almighty Father, hear our cry
Through Jesus Christ, our Lord most high,
Who with the Holy Ghost and thee
Doth live and reign eternally.

## 24. Help Us, O Lord

Melody: Franconia S.M.

Music: J. B. Konig, 1691-1758
adapted by W. Havergal, 1793-1870
Text: W. W. Reid, 1923-

**1**

Help us, O Lord, to learn
The truths thy Word imparts:
To study that thy laws may be
Inscribed upon our hearts.

**2**

Help us, O Lord, to live
The faith which we proclaim
That all our thoughts and words and
deeds
May glorify your name.

**3**

Help us, O Lord, to teach
The beauty of your ways,
That yearning souls may find the Christ,
And sing aloud his praise.

# Lord of All Hopefulness

**25**

Melody: Slane 10.11.11.12

Music: Traditional Irish Melody
Text: Jan Struther, 1901-1953

**1**

Lord of all hopefulness, Lord of all joy,
Whose trust, ever childlike, no cares
could destroy,
Be there at our waking, and give us, we
pray,
Your bliss in our hearts, Lord, at the
break of the day.

**2**

Lord of all eagerness, Lord of all faith,
Whose strong hands were skilled at the
plane and the lathe,
Be there at our labors, and give us, we
pray,
Your strength in our hearts, Lord, at the
noon of the day.

**3**

Lord of all kindliness, Lord of all grace,
Your hand swift to welcome, your arms
to embrace,
Be there at our homing, and give us, we
pray,
Your love in our hearts, Lord, at the eve
of the day.

**4**

Lord of all gentleness, Lord of all calm,
Whose voice is contentment, whose
presence is balm,
Be there at our sleeping, and give us,
we pray,
Your peace in our hearts, Lord, at the
end of the day.

# Lord of All Being Throned Afar

**26**

Melody: Uffingham L.M.

Music: Jeremiah Clarke, c. 1659-1707
Text: Oliver Wendell Holmes, 1809-1894

**1**

Lord of all being, throned afar,
Your glory flames from sun and star;
Center and soul of every sphere,
And yet to loving hearts how near.

**2**

Sun of our life, your living ray
Sheds on our path the glow of day;
Star of our hope, your gentle light
Shall ever cheer the longest night.

**3**

Lord of all life, below, above
Whose light is truth, whose warmth is
love;
Before the brilliance of your throne
We ask no luster of our own.

**4**

Give us your grace to make us true,
And kindling hearts that burn for you,
Till all your living altars claim
One holy light, one heavenly flame.

# Almighty Ruler, God of Truth

**27**

Melody: Ballerma C.M.

Music: F. Barthélémon, 1741-1808
Text: Ralph Wright, O.S.B.

**1**

Almighty Ruler, God of truth
Who guide and master all,
The rays with which you gild the dawn
With noonday heat now fall.

**2**

O quench the fires of hatred, Lord,
Of anger and of strife;
Bring health to every mind and heart
That peace may enter life.

**3** Most holy Father, grant our prayer
Through Christ your only Son,
That in your Spirit we may live
And praise you ever one.

# 28 Firmly I Believe and Truly

Melody: Halton Holgate 87.87

Music: Later form of tune by
William Boyce, c. 1710-1779

Text: John H. Newman, 1801-1890, adapted by Anthony G. Petti

**1**

Firmly I believe and truly
God is three and God is one;
And I next acknowledge duly
Manhood taken by the Son.

**2**

And I trust and hope most fully
In that manhood crucified;
And I love supremely, solely
Christ who for my sins has died.

**3**

And I hold in veneration,
For the love of him alone,
Holy Church as his creation,
And her teachings as his own.

**4**

Praise and thanks be ever given
With and through the angel host,
To the God of earth and heaven,
Father, Son and Holy Ghost.

# 29 Lord God and Maker of All Things

Melody: Auctoritate Saeculi L.M.

Music: *Poitiers Antiphoner*, 1746
Text: Stanbrook Abbey

**1**

Lord God and Maker of all things,
Creation is upheld by you.
While all must change and know
  decay,
You are unchanging, always new.

To God the Father and the Son
And Holy Spirit render praise,

**2**

You are man's solace and his shield,
His rock secure on which to build,
You are the spirit's tranquil home
In you alone is hope fulfilled.

**3** Blest Trinity, from age to age
The strength of all our living days.

# 30 Most Ancient of All Mysteries

Melody: Saint Flavian C.M.

Music: Adapted from *Psalm 132*,
John Day's *Psalter*, 1562
Text: Frederick William Faber, 1814-1863,
adapted by Geoffrey Laycock

**1**

Most ancient of all mysteries,
Before your throne we lie;
Have mercy now, most merciful,
Most holy Trinity.

**2**

When heaven and earth were still un-
  made,
When time was yet unknown,
You in your radiant majesty
Did live and love alone.

Most ancient of all mysteries,
Before your throne we lie;

**3**

You were not born, there was no source
From which your Being flowed;
There is no end which you can reach,
For you are simply God.

**4**

How wonderful creation is,
The work which you did bless,
What then must you be like, dear God,
Eternal loveliness!

**5** Have mercy now and evermore,
Most holy Trinity.

594

# Faith of Our Fathers

Melody: Saint Catherine L.M.
with Refrain

Music: Henry F. Hemy, 1818-1888
and James G. Walton, 1821-1905
Text: Frederick William Faber, 1814-1863

**1**

Faith of our fathers! faith and prayer
Shall win all nations unto thee;
And through the truth that comes from God
Mankind shall then indeed be free.

**2**

Faith of our fathers! we will love
Both friend and foe in all our strife:
And preach thee too, as love knows how
By kindly deeds and virtuous life.

Refrain: Faith of our fathers, holy faith!
We will be true to thee till death.

# Now Thank We All Our God

Melody: Nun Danket 67.67.66.66
Text: Based on *Ecclesiasticus* 50:22-24. Martin Rinkart, 1586-1649
Music: Johann Crüger, 1598-1662
Translator: Catherine Winkworth, 1829-1878

**1**

Now thank we all our God
With heart and hands and voices,
Who wondrous things has done,
In whom his world rejoices;
Who from our mothers' arms
Has blessed us on our way
With countess gifts of love
And still is ours today.

All praise and thanks to God
The Father now be given
The Son and Spirit blest,
Who reigns in highest heaven;

**2**

O may this gracious God
Through all our life be near us,
With ever joyful hearts,
And blessed peace to cheer us;
Preserve us in his grace,
And guide us in distress,
And free us from all sin,
Till heaven we possess.

3 Eternal, Triune God,
Whom earth and heaven adore;
For thus it was, is now,
And shall be ever more.

# O Christ, You Are the Light and Day

Melody: Saint Anne C.M.

Music: William Croft, 1708
Text: *Christe qui Lux es et Dies*
Translator: Rev. M. Quinn, O.P. et al., 1965

**1**

O Christ, you are the light and day
Which drives away the night,
The ever shining Sun of God
And pledge of future light.

**2**

As now the ev'ning shadows fall
Please grant us, Lord, we pray,

A quiet night to rest in you
Until the break of day.

**3**

Remember us, poor mortal men
We humbly ask, O Lord,
And may your presence in our souls,
Be now our great reward.

# 34 Lord Jesus Christ, Abide With Us

Melody:
Old 100th L.M.

Music: Attr. to Louis Bourgeois 1510-1561; melody
of Psalm 134 in the *Genevan Psalter* 1551 with
English (1563) form of rhythm in last line
Text: *Mane Nobiscum Domine*, paraphrased by
Jerome Leaman, 1967.

1
Lord Jesus Christ, abide with us,
Now that the sun has run its course;
Let hope not be obscured by night,
But may faith's darkness be as light.

2
Lord Jesus Christ, grant us your peace,
And when the trials of earth shall
cease,
Grant us the morning light of grace,
The radiant splendor of your face.

3
Immortal, Holy, Threefold Light,
Yours be the kingdom, pow'r, and might;
All glory be eternally
To you, life giving Trinity!

# 35 The Setting Sun

Melody:
Angelus L.M.

Music: Melody by Georg Joseph, 1657, arr. in *Cantica
Spiritualis*, 1847, slightly adapted by G. Laycock
Text: *Jam sol recedit igneus*
Translator: G. Laycock; translation based on
version in *Primer*, 1706

1
The setting sun now dies away,
And darkness comes at close of day;
Your brightest beams, dear Lord, im-
part,
And let them shine within our heart.

2
We praise your name with joy this night:
Please watch and guide us till the
light;
Joining the music of the blest,
O Lord, we sing ourselves to rest.

3
To God the Father, God the Son,
And Holy Spirit, Three in One,
Trinity blest, whom we adore,
Be praise and glory evermore.

# 36 O Father, Whose Creating Hand

Melody: Melita 88.88.88

Music: John B. Dykes, 1823-1876
Text: Donald Hughes, 1911-1967

1
O Father, whose creating hand
Brings harvest from the fruitful land,
Your providence we gladly own,
And bring our hymns before your throne
To praise you for the living bread
On which our lives are daily fed.

2
O Lord, who in the desert fed
The hungry thousands in their need,
Where want and famine still abound
Let your relieving love be found,
And in your name may we supply
Your hungry children when they cry.

3

O Spirit your revealing light
Has led our questing souls aright;
Source of our science, you have taught

The marvels human minds have wrought
So that the barren deserts yield
The bounty by your love revealed.

# For the Fruits of His Creation

Melody: East Acklam 84.84.88.84

Music: Francis Jackson
Text: F. Pratt Green, 1903-

1

For the fruits of his creation
  Thanks be to God;
For the gifts to every nation,
  Thanks be to God;
For the ploughing, sowing, reaping,
Silent growth while men are sleeping,
Future needs in earth's safe keeping,
  Thanks be to God.

2

In the just reward of labor,
  God's will is done;
In the help we give our neighbor,
  God's will is done;
In our world-wide task of caring
For the hungry and despairing,
In the harvests men are sharing,
  God's will is done.

3

For the harvests of his spirit, Thanks be to God;
For the good all men inherit, Thanks be to God;
For the wonders that astound us,
For the truths that still confound us,
Most of all, that love has found us, Thanks be to God.

# When, in His Own Image

Melody: King's Weston
65.65.D

Music: R. Vaughan Williams, 1872-1958
Text: Fred Kaan, 1929-

1

When, in his own image,
God created man,
He included freedom
In creation's plan.
For he loved us even
From before our birth;
By his grace he made us
Freemen of this earth.

2

God to man entrusted
Life as gift and aim.
Sin became our prison,
Turning hope to shame.
Man against his brother
Lifted hand and sword,
And the Father's pleading
Went unseen, unheard.

3

Then in time, our maker
Chose to intervene,
Set his love in person
In the human scene.
Jesus broke the circle
Of repeated sin,
So that man's devotion
Newly might begin.

4

Choose we now in freedom
Where we should belong,
Let us turn to Jesus,
Let our choice be strong.
May the great obedience
Which in Christ we see
Perfect all our service:
Then we shall be free!

597

# 39

# At the Name of Jesus

Melody: King's Weston
65.65.D

Music: R. Vaughan Williams, 1872-1958
Text: C. Noel, d. 1877, alt.

**1**

At the name of Jesus
Ev'ry knee shall bow,
Ev'ry tongue confess him
King of glory now;
'Tis the Father's pleasure,
We should call him Lord,
Who from the beginning
Was the mighty Word.

**2**

Humbled for a season,
To receive a name
From the lips of sinners,
Unto whom he came,
Faithfully he bore it,
Spotless to the last,
Brought it back victorious,
When from death he passed.

**3**

Bore it up triumphant,
With its human light,
Through all ranks of creatures,
To the central height,

To the throne of Godhead,
To the Father's breast;
Filled it with the glory
Of that perfect rest.

**4**

In your hearts enthrone him;
There, let him subdue
All that is not holy,
All that is not true;
May your voice entreat him
In temptation's hour;
Let his will enfold you
In its light and power.

**5**

Brothers, this Lord Jesus
Shall return again,
With his Father's glory,
O'er the earth to reign;
He is God the Savior,
He is Christ the Lord,
Ever to be worshiped,
Always blest, adored.

# Love Divine All Loves Excelling

Melody: Hyfrydol 87.87.D

Music: Rowland H. Prichard, 1811-1887
Text: Charles Wesley, 1707-1788,
adapted by C. T. Andrews

**1**

Love divine, all loves excelling,
Joy of heaven to earth come down,
And impart to us, here dwelling,
Grace and mercy all around.
Jesus, source of all compassion,
Pure, unbounded love you share;
Grant us many choicest blessings,
Keep us in your loving care.

**2**

Come, oh source of inspiration,
Pure and spotless let us be:
Let us see your true salvation,
Perfect in accord with thee.
Praising Father for all glory
With the Spirit and the Son;
Everlasting thanks we give thee,
Undivided, love, in one.

# Now Fades All Earthly Splendor

Melody: Ewing 76.76.D

Music: Alexander Ewing, 1830-1895
Text: James Quinn, S.J.

**1**

Now fades all earthly splendor,
The shades of night descend;
The dying of the daylight
Foretells creation's end.
Though noon gives place to sunset,
Yet dark gives place to light:
The promise of tomorrow
With dawn's new hope is bright.

**2**

The silver notes of morning
Will greet the rising sun,
As once the Easter glory
Shone round the Risen One.
So will the night of dying
Give place to heaven's day,
And hope of heaven's vision,
Will light our pilgrim way.

**3**

So will the new creation
Rise from the old reborn
To splendor in Christ's glory
And everlasting morn.
All darkness will be ended
As faith gives place to sight
Of Father, Son and Spirit,
One God, in heaven's light.

# Day Is Done

Melody: Ar Hyd Y Nos
84.84.88.84

Music: Traditional Welsh Melody
Text: James Quinn, S.J.

**1**

Day is done, but Love unfailing
    Dwells ever here;
Shadows fall, but hope, prevailing,
    Calms every fear.
Loving Father, none forsaking,
Take our hearts, of Love's own mak-
    ing,
Watch our sleeping, guard our waking,
    Be always near.

**2**

Dark descends, but Light unending
    Shines through our night;
You are with us, ever lending
    New strength to sight;
One in love, your truth confessing,
One in hope of heaven's blessing,
May we see, in love's possessing,
    Love's endless light!

**3**

Eyes will close, but you, unsleeping,
    Watch by our side;
Death may come: in Love's safe
    keeping
    Still we abide.
God of love, all evil quelling,
Sin forgiving, fear dispelling,
Stay with us, our hearts indwelling;
    This eventide.

# O Worship the King

Melody: Hanover 55.55.65.55

Music: William Croft, 1682-1727
Text: Robert Grant, 1779-1838

### 1
O worship the king, all glorious above;
O gratefully sing his power and his love;
Our Shield and Defender, the ancient of days,
Pavilioned in splendor, and girded with praise.

### 2
O tell of his might, O sing of his grace;
Whose robe is the light, whose canopy space;
His chariots of wrath the deep thunderclouds form,
And dark is his path on the wings of the storm.

### 3
This earth, with its store of wonders untold,
Almighty, thy power hath founded of old;
Hath 'stablished it fast by a changeless decree,
And round it has cast, like a mantle, the sea.

### 4
Thy bountiful care what tongue can recite?
It breathes in the air, it shines in the light;
It streams from the hills, it descends to the plain,
And sweetly distills in the dew and the rain.

### 5
Frail children of dust, and feeble as frail,
In thee do we trust, nor find thee to fail;
Thy mercies how tender, how firm to the end,
Our Maker, Defender, Redeemer, and Friend.

### 6
O measureless Might, ineffable Love,
While angels delight to hymn thee above,
Thy humbler creation, though feeble their lays,
With true adoration shall sing to thy praise.

# 44

# Romans VIII

Melody: Romans VIII
Irregular with Antiphon

Music: Enrico Garzilli, 1970
Text: Enrico Garzilli. 1970

Refrain:
For to those who love God,
Who are called in his plan,
Everything works out for good.
And God himself chose them
To bear the likeness of his Son
That he might be the first of many, many brothers.

Who is able to condemn? Only Christ who died for us;
Christ who rose for us, Christ who prays for us.

Refrain

In the face of all this, what is there left to say?
For if God is for us, who can be against us?

Refrain

Who can separate us from the love of
Christ?
Neither trouble, nor pain, nor perse-
cution.

Refrain

What can separate us from the love of
Christ?
Not the past, the present, nor the fu-
ture.

Refrain

# Let All Things Now Living

**45**

Melody: The Ash Grove
6.6.11.6.6.11.D

Music: Traditional Welsh Melody
Text: Anon.

### 1

Let all things now living a song of
thanksgiving
To God our Creator triumphantly raise;
Who fashioned and made us, pro-
tected and stayed us,
Who guideth us on to the end of our
days.
His banners are o'er us, his light goes
before us,
A pillar of fire shining forth in the
night:
Till shadows have vanished and dark-
ness is banished,
As forward we travel from light into
Light.

### 2

His law he enforces, the stars in their
courses,
The sun in his orbit obediently shine,
The hills and the mountains, the rivers
and fountains,
The depths of the ocean proclaim him
divine.
We, too, should be voicing our love and
rejoicing;
With glad adoration, a song let us raise:
Till all things now living unite in thanks-
giving,
To God in the highest, hosanna and
praise.

# Father, We Thank Thee

**46**

Melody: Rendez à Dieu 98.98.D

Music: Louis Bourgeois, 1543
Text: *Didache*, c. 110
Translator: F. Bland Tucker

### 1

Father, we thank thee who hast
planted
Thy holy Name within our hearts.
Knowledge and faith and life immortal
Jesus, thy Son, to us imparts.
Thou, Lord, didst make all for thy
pleasure,
Didst give man food for all his days,
Giving in Christ the Bread eternal;
Thine is the power, be thine the
praise.

### 2

Watch o'er thy Church, O Lord, in
mercy,
Save it from evil, guard it still;
Perfect it in thy love, unite it,
Cleansed and conformed unto thy will.
As grain, once scattered on the hill-
sides,
Was in this broken bread made one,
So from all lands thy Church be gath-
ered
Into thy kingdom by thy Son.

601

**47**

# We Plough the Fields and Scatter

Melody: Wir Pflügen
76.76.D with Refrain

Music: Attr. to Johann A. P. Schultz. 1747-1800
Text: *Wir Pflügen und wir streuen,*
M. Claudius, 1740-1815
Translator: Jane M. Campbell, alt.

1

We plough the fields and scatter
The good seed on the land,
But it is fed and watered
By God's almighty hand;
He sends the snow in winter,
The warmth to swell the grain;
The breezes and the sunshine,
And soft refreshing rain:

Refrain
All good gifts around us
Are sent from heav'n above,
Then thank the Lord,
O thank the Lord, for all his love.

2

He only is the maker
Of all things near and far;

He paints the wayside flower,
He lights the ev'ning star.
The winds and waves obey him,
By him the birds are fed:
Much more to us, his children,
He gives our daily bread:

Refrain

3

We thank you then, dear Father,
For all things bright and good:
The seedtime and the harvest,
Our life, our health, our food.
And all that we can offer
Your boundless love imparts,
The gifts to you most pleasing
Are humble, thankful hearts:

Refrain

**48**

# We Praise You, Father, for Your Gifts

Melody: Te Lucis Ante Terminum
(plainchant) L.M.

Music: Gregorian, Mode VIII
Text: West Malling Abbey

1

We praise you, Father, for your gifts
Of dusk and nightfall over earth,
Foreshadowing the mystery
Of death that leads to endless day.

Your glory may we ever seek
In rest, as in activity,

2

Within your hands we rest secure;
In quiet sleep our strength renew;
Yet give your people hearts that wake
In love to you, unsleeping Lord.

3    Until its fullness is revealed,
O source of life, O Trinity.

**49**

# Holy God, We Praise Thy Name

Melody: Grosser
Gott (Te Deum)
78.78.77

Music: *Katholisches Gesangbuch,* Vienna, c. 1774
Text: Ignaz Franz, 1719-1790
Translator: Clarence Walworth, 1820-1900

1

Holy God, we praise thy Name!
Lord of all, we bow before thee!
All on earth thy scepter claim,
All in heaven above adore thee!
Infinite thy vast domain,
Everlasting is thy reign.

2

Hark the loud celestial hymn
Angel choirs above are raising;
Cherubim and Seraphim,
In unceasing chorus praising.
Fill the heavens with sweet accord:
Holy, Holy, Holy Lord!

3  Holy Father, Holy Son,
   Holy Spirit, Three we name thee,
   While in essence only One,
   Undivided God we claim thee;
   And adoring bend the knee,
   While we own the mystery.

# This World, My God

**50**

Melody: In Manus Tuas 10.10.10.10

Music: Herbert Howells
Text: Hamish Swanston

1

This world, my God, is held within your hand,
Though we forget your love and stead-fast might
And in the changing day uncertain stand,
Disturbed by morning, and afraid of night.

2

From youthful confidence to careful age,
Help us each one to be your loving friend,
Rewarded by the faithful servant's wage,
God in three persons, reigning without end.

# Now at the Daylight's Ending

**51**

Melody: Christus Der Ist Mein Leben
76.76

Music: Melchior Vulpius, 1609
Text: James Quinn, S.J.

1

Now at the daylight's ending
We turn, O God, to you:
Send forth your Holy Spirit,
Our spirit now renew.

2

To you in adoration,
In thankfulness and praise,
In faith and hope and gladness,
Our loving hearts we raise.

3

The gift you gave at daylight
This night you take away,
To leave within our keeping
The blessings of this day.

4

Take all its joy and sorrow,
Take all that love can give,
But all that needs forgiveness,
Dear Father, now forgive.

5

With watchful eyes, O Shepherd,
Look down upon your sheep.
Stretch forth your hands in healing
And close our eyes in sleep.

6

Come down, O Holy Spirit,
To be our loving Guest;
Be near us, holy angels,
And guard us as we rest.

7

We praise you, heav'nly Father:
From you all light descends;
You give us heaven's glory
When life's brief daylight ends.

8

We praise you, Jesus, Savior,
The light of heav'n above;
We praise you, Holy Spirit,
The living flame of love.

# 52

# All Praise to You, O God, This Night

Melody: Illsley L.M.

Music: J. Bishop, c. 1665-1737
Text: Thomas Ken, 1709, alt.

**1**

All praise to you, O God, this night
For all the blessings of the light;
Keep us, we pray, O King of kings,
Beneath your own almighty wings.

**2**

Forgive us, Lord, through Christ your Son,
Whatever wrong this day we've done;
Your peace give to the world, O Lord,
That man might live in one accord.

**3**

Enlighten us, O blessed Light,
And give us rest throughout this night.
O strengthen us, that for your sake,
We all may serve you when we wake.

# 53

# The Master Came

Melody: Ich Glaub' An Gott
87.87 with Refrain

Music: *Mainz Gesangbuch*, 1870
Text: Gabriel Huck, 1965

**1**

The Master came to bring good news,
The news of love and freedom,
To heal the sick and seek the poor,
To build the peaceful kingdom.

Refrain:
Father, forgive us! Through Jesus, hear us!
As we forgive one another.

**2**

Through Jesus Christ the Law's fulfilled,
The man who lived for others.
The law of Christ is love alone,
To serve now all our brothers.

Refrain

**3**

To seek the sinners Jesus came,
To live among the friendless,
To show them love that they might share
The kingdom that is endless.

Refrain

**4**

Forgive us, Lord, as we forgive
And seek to help each other.
Forgive us, Lord, and we shall live
To pray and work together.

Refrain

# 54

# On Jordan's Bank

Melody: Winchester New L.M.

Music: *Musikalisches Handbuch*, Hamburg 1690
Text: *Iordanis ora praevia*, Charles Coffin, 1736
Translator: John Chandler, 1837, alt.

**1**

On Jordan's bank the Baptist's cry
Announces that the Lord is nigh;
Awake and hearken, for he brings
Glad tidings of the King of kings.

**2**

Then cleansed be ev'ry heart from sin,
Make straight the way of God within;
O let us all our hearts prepare
For Christ to come and enter there.

3
For you are man's salvation, Lord,
Our refuge and our great reward;
Once more upon your people shine,
And fill the world with love divine.

4
To God the Son all glory be,
Whose advent set all nations free,
Whom with the Father we adore,
And Holy Spirit ever more.

# Maranatha

**55**

Melody: Maranatha
Irregular with Antiphon

Music: Lucien Deiss. C.S.Sp.
Text: Lucien Deiss. C.S.Sp.

Antiphon

Maranatha! Come, O Christ the Lord!

1

I am the Root of Jesse and David's
    Son,
The radiant Star of morning and God's
    own Light.

Antiphon

2

The Spirit and the Bride say: "Come!"
Let him who hears their voices say:
    "Come!"

Antiphon

3

He who has thirst, let him come,
and he who has desire, let him drink
the waters of everlasting life.

Antiphon

4

"Yes, I come very soon!"
Amen!
Come, O Lord Jesus!

Antiphon

# Come Thou Long-Expected Jesus

**56**

Melody: Stuttgart 87.87

Music: C. F. Witt, 1660-1716
Text: Charles Wesley, 1707-1788

1

Come, thou long-expected Jesus,
Born to set thy people free;
From our fears and sins release us,
Let us find our rest in thee.

2

Israel's strength and consolation,
Hope of all the earth thou art;
Dear desire of every nation,
Joy of every longing heart.

3

Born thy people to deliver,
Born a child, and yet a king,
Born to reign in us for ever,
Now thy gracious kingdom bring.

4

By thine own eternal Spirit
Rule in all our hearts alone;
By thine all-sufficient merit
Raise us to thy glorious throne.

605

# 57

# Be Consoled, My People

Melody: Be Consoled, My People
Irregular with Refrain

Music: Tom Parker 1968
Text: Tom Parker, 1968

**Refrain**

Be consoled, my people;
take courage, O fair Jerusalem,
for your slav'ry has come to an end.

**1**

Speak to the heart of Jerusalem
and call to her that her slav'ry has
ended,
her sin is forgiven and her punishment
over and done.

*Refrain*

**2**

A voice cries "Prepare in the wilderness
a way for our God and make a straight
highway
for the Lord 'cause he's cumin'
to rescue our desert land."

*Refrain*

**3**

Let every valley be filled in,
every mountain made low
and let ev'ry cliff become a plain,
let nothing hinder our God.

*Refrain*

**4**

Then the glory of Yahweh shall be revealed
and all mankind shall see it;
it is I your God who have spoken.

*Refrain*

# 58

# Hear the Herald Voice Resounding

Melody: Merton 87.87

Music: W. H. Monk, 1823-1889
Text: *Vox clara ecce intonat*
Translator: Edward Caswall, 1814-1878,
adapted by Anthony G. Petti

**1**

Hear the herald voice resounding:
"Christ is near," it seems to say,
"Cast away the dreams of darkness,
Welcome Christ, the light of day!"

**2**

Wakened by this solemn warning,
Let the earthbound soul arise;
Christ her sun, all sloth dispelling,
Shines upon the morning skies.

**3**

See the Lamb so long expected,
Comes with pardon down from heav'n;
Hasten now, with tears of sorrow,
One and all to be forgiv'n.

**4**

So when next he comes with glory,
Shrouding all the earth in fear,
May he then as our defender
On the clouds of heav'n appear.

**5**     Honor, glory, virtue, merit,
To the Father and the Son,
With the co-eternal Spirit,
While eternal ages run.

# The King of Glory

Melody: The King of Glory
12.12 with Refrain

Music: Traditional Israeli Folksong
Text: Rev. W. P. Jabusch, 1967

Refrain:

The King of glory comes, the nation rejoices;
Open the gates before him, lift up your voices.
In all of Galilee, in city or village,
He goes among his people curing their illness.

1

Who is the king of glory;
how shall we call him?
He is Emmanuel, the promised of ages.

Refrain

2

Sing then of David's Son,
our Savior and brother;
In all of Galilee was never another.

Refrain

3

He gave his life for us,
the lamb of salvation,
He took upon himself the sins of the nation.

Refrain

4

He conquered sin and death,
he truly has risen,
And he will share with us his heavenly vision.

Refrain

# Wake, Awake, the Night Is Dying

Melody: Wachet auf
898.898.664.448

Music: Philip Nicolai, 1599
adapted and harmonized by J. S. Bach, 1685-1750
Text: Philip Nicolai, 1556-1608
Translator: Melvin Farrell, S.S.

1

Wake, awake, the night is dying,
And prophets from of old are crying:
Awake, ye children of the light!
Lo, the Dawn shall banish sadness,
The Rising Sun shall bring us gladness,
And all the blind shall see aright.

Refrain:

Rejoice, the King is near,
Our praises he will hear,
Alleluia!
But we must be
Prepared to see
The Brightness of eternity.

2

We shell heed the prophets' warning,
And rise to greet the Prince of Morning:
His gentle rule shall bring us peace.
Love and mercy are his treasure,
The seas and skies obey his pleasure:
His mighty rule shall never cease.

Refrain

3

Let the shadows be forsaken:
The time has come for us to waken,
And to the Day our lives entrust.
Search the sky for heaven's portal:
The clouds shall rain the Light Immortal,
And earth will soon bud forth the Just.

Refrain

## 61

# Creator of the Stars of Night

Melody: Creator alme siderum
L.M

Music: Sarum plainsong, Mode IV
Text: Anon., 7th century
Translator: J. M. Neale et al., alt.

### 1

Creator of the stars of night,
Your people's everlasting light,
Jesus, Redeemer, save us all,
And hear your servants when they call.

### 2

Now, grieving that the ancient curse
Should doom to death a universe,
You heal all men who need your grace
To save and heal a ruined race.

### 3

At whose great name, majestic now,
All knees must bend, all hearts must bow;
All things in heaven and earth adore,
And own thee King for evermore.

### 4

To God the Father, God the Son,
And God the Spirit, Three in One,
Praise, honor, might, and glory be
From age to age eternally.

## 62

# You Heavens, Open From Above

Melody: Rorate Coeli
Irregular with Refrain

Music: P. Bourget (?), first published, Paris, 1634
Text: Rorate Coeli, Paris, 1634
Translator: Melvin Farrell, S.S.

Refrain:
You heavens, open from above, that
clouds may rain the Just One.

### 1

Do not be angry, Lord our God,
No longer be mindful that we have
sinned before you.
See how Zion, your city, now is left
abandoned.
Zion is left unguarded now, Jerusalem
now is desolate:
City that claimed your loving blessing
and worked for your glory,
City where our fathers sang your
praises.

Refrain

### 2

We know our sin, and we are burdened
as with some loathsome thing,
And have fallen down just like leaves in
the blast of winter:
And the sins we have committed just
like winds have blown us all
about.
You have taken from us your brightness
and comfort,

And you have broken us by laying the
debt of our sins upon us.

Refrain

### 3

Lord, now turn to us and see your chosen people's affliction
And send down him who is to come,
The One promised, Lamb and yet Lord
of all lands,
From the rock in the desert to the
mount of Zion, your daughter,
That he may bring pardon, freeing us
captives of our burden.

Refrain

### 4

Be you comforted, be you comforted,
hear me, my people:
Soon shall come to you Christ, your
Savior.
Why do you give way to sorrowing:
Has this grieving ended your sadness?
Your Savior comes, do not be fearful,
for it is I, your God and your
mighty Ruler,
Zion's Holy One and your Redeemer.

Refrain

608

# O Come, O Come, Emmanuel

Melody: Veni, Veni Emmanuel
L.M. with Refrain

Music: Thomas Helmore, 1811-1890,
adapted from a first Mode Responsory
in a 15th century French *Processional*
Text: *Veni, Veni Emmanuel,* a paraphrase
of the Latin 12th-13th century
"Great O Antiphons" in *Psalteriolum
Cantionum Catholicarum,* 1770
Translator: J. M. Neale, 1818-1886, et al.

**1**
O come, O come, Emmanuel,
And ransom captive Israel,
That mourns in lonely exile here
Until the Son of God appear.

**Refrain**
Rejoice! Rejoice! O Israel,
To thee shall come Emmanuel!

**2**
O come, thou wisdom, from on high,
And order all things far and nigh;
To us the path of knowledge show,
And teach us in her ways to go.

Refrain

**3**
O come, O come, thou Lord of might,
Who to thy tribes on Sinai's height
In ancient times did give the law,
In cloud, and majesty, and awe.

Refrain

**4**
O come, thou rod of Jesse's stem,
From ev'ry foe deliver them
That trust thy mighty power to save,
And give them vict'ry o'er the grave.

Refrain

**5**
O come, thou key of David, come,
And open wide our heav'nly home,
Make safe the way that leads on high,
That we no more have cause to sigh.

Refrain

**6**
O come, thou Dayspring from on high,
And cheer us by thy drawing nigh;
Disperse the gloomy clouds of night
And death's dark shadow put to flight.

Refrain

**7**
O come, Desire of nations, bind
In one the hearts of all mankind;
Bid every strife and quarrel cease
And fill the world with heaven's peace.

Refrain

# 64

# The Coming of Our God

Melody: Saint Thomas (Williams)
S.M.

Music: Aaron Williams, 1763
Text: *Instantis Adventum Dei*,
Charles Coffin, 1736
Translator: Roger Nachtwey, 1974

1 The coming of our God
We seek in ardent prayer;
In joy we'll meet him on the way
And sing our praises there.

2 The everlasting Son
Comes down to Mary's womb;
He bears our human servitude
To save us from our doom.

3 O Zion, rise in haste
To meet the meek and mild;
Throw wide your arms; embrace the
peace
Brought by this holy child.

4 As Judge, on glist'ning clouds,
The Victor comes again
To take his members back in joy
With him to heaven then.

5 Let dark and evil deeds
Retreat before his dawn;
Our new life must advance in grace;
The old one must be gone.

6 We praise your Father blest;
Your Spirit, too, we praise;
Emancipator, Christ, our Lord
We'll praise you all our days!

# 65

# Behold a Virgin Bearing Him

Melody: O Heyland Reiss Die
Himmel Auff L.M.

Music: *Rheinfels Gesangbuch*, 1666
Text: Michael Gannon

**1**

Behold a Virgin bearing him
Who comes to save us from our sin;
The prophets cry: prepare his way!
Make straight his paths to Christmas
Day.

**2**

Behold our Hope and Life and Light,
The promise of the holy night;
We lift our prayer and bend our knee
To his great love and majesty.

# 66

# Song of Salvation Drawing Near

Melody: Song of Salvation
Irregular with Refrain

Music: Bernard Huijbers, 1970
Text: Huub Oosterhuis, 1970

Antiphon

The night now is ending,
the day is drawing near!

**1**

People who live in darkness,
soon will know who their savior is,
who unexpected comes from far
the son of man, the morning star.

Antiphon

**2**

Signs in the stars, in sun and moon,
say that the day is coming soon.
Hear the Lord speak: rise up, be free,
for your salvation's soon to be.

Antiphon

**3**

When the sea roars and floods the
land,
striking your life out of your hand,
know in your fear and dying pain
that you will rise and live again.

Antiphon

610

# Behold, a Rose of Judah

Melody: Es Ist Ein'Ros
76.76.676

Music: Traditional Melody from
*Alte catholische geistliche Kirchengesang,*
Cologne, 1599
Text: *Es ist ein' Ros' entsprungen,* 15th cent.
Translator: Composite

**67**

**1**

Behold, a rose of Judah
From tender branch has sprung,
From Jesse's lineage coming,
As men of old have sung.
It came a flower bright
Amid the cold of winter,
When half spent was the night.

**2**

Isaiah has foretold it
In words of promise sure,
And Mary's arms enfold it,
A virgin meek and pure.
Through God's eternal will
She bore for men a savior
At midnight calm and still.

# A Child Is Born

**68**

Melody: A Child Is Born
Irregular with Antiphon

Music: Lucien Deiss, C.S.Sp.
Text: Lucien Deiss, C.S.Sp.

Antiphon:  Unto us a Child is born, unto us a Son is given.
Eternal is his sway.

**1**

The people who walk in darkness have
seen a great light;
For men abiding in the land of death,
a new splendor has appeared;
To them you have brought abundant
joy; before you they rejoice,
As with the joy at harvest, as men rejoice when dividing spoils.

Antiphon

**3**

For to us a Child is born, to our race a
Son is given;
His shoulders will bear the scepter of
his reign, and his name shall be
called:
Counselor of marvelous deeds, Mighty
Warrior of God, everlasting
Father of nations,
And royal Prince of Peace.

Antiphon

**2**

For the yoke of his burden and the bar
on his shoulder
And the rod of the oppressor you have
broken, as on the day of Ma-
dian;
For ev'ry boot that tramped in battle,
for every cloak that rolled in
blood,
Will be set aside, will go to feed the
blazing fire.

Antiphon

**4**

Ever wider shall his dominion be over
his kingdom;
Upon the throne of David, in a peace
that never ends.
He has established it and made it firm,
based on justice and on right;
Both now and forever the Lord of
hosts will do these mighty
deeds.

Antiphon

611

## 69 From Heaven High

Melody: Vom Himmel Hoch
L.M.

Music: *Geistliche Lieder*, Leipzig, 1539
Text: *Vom Himmel hoch*,
Martin Luther, 1483-1546
Translator: Winfred Douglas, 1867-1944

**1**

From heaven high I come to you,
I bring you tidings good and new;
Good tidings of great joy I bring;
Thereof will I both say and sing:

**2**

For you a little child is born
Of God's own chosen maid this morn,
A fair and tender baby bright,
To be your joy and your delight.

**3**

Lo, he is Christ, the Lord indeed,
Our God to guide you in your need,

And he will be your Savior, strong
To cleanse you from all sin and wrong.

## 70 Go Tell It on the Mountain

Melody: Go Tell It On The Mountain
Irregular with Refrain

Music: Negro Spiritual
Text: Anon.

Refrain:

Go tell it on the mountain
Over the hills and everywhere,
Go tell it on the mountain,
Our Jesus Christ is born.

**1**

When I was a learner,
I sought both night and day;
I asked the Lord to help me,
And he showed me the way.

Refrain

**2**

While shepherds kept their watching
O'er wand'ring flocks at night;
Behold from out the heavens
There came a holy light.

Refrain

**3**

Lo, when they had seen it,
They all bowed down and prayed;
They traveled on together
To where the babe was laid.

Refrain

## 71 O Come, All Ye Faithful

Melody: Adeste Fideles
Irregular with Refrain

Music: J. F. Wade, 1711-1786
Text: J. F. Wade, *Adeste Fideles*,
Latin, 18th century
Translator: Frederick Oakeley, 1841, et al.

**1**

O come, all ye faithful, joyful and triumphant,
O come ye, O come ye to Bethlehem;
Come and behold him, born the King
of angels:

Refrain:

O come, let us adore him,
O come, let us adore him,
O come, let us adore him,
Christ the Lord.

## 2

Sing, choirs of angels, sing in exulta-
    tion,
Sing, all ye citizens of heaven above;
Glory to God, in the highest glory:

*Refrain*

## 3

Savior, we greet thee, born this happy
    morning,
Jesus, to thee be all glory giv'n;
Word of the Father, now in flesh ap-
    pearing:

*Refrain*

# Songs of Praise the Angels Sang

**72**

Melody: Lands 77.77

Music: John Wilson
Text: James Montgomery, 1771-1854,
    adapted by Anthony G. Petti

## 1

Songs of praise the angels sang,
Heav'n with alleluias rang,
When creation was begun,
When God spoke and it was done.

## 2

Songs of praise awoke the morn
When the Prince of Peace was born;
Songs of praise arose when he
Captive led captivity.

## 3

Heav'n and earth must pass away,
Songs of praise shall crown that day;
God will make new heav'n and earth,
Songs of praise shall hail their birth.

## 4

And will voice of man be dumb
Till that glorious kingdom come?
No, the Church delights to raise
Psalms and hymns and songs of praise.

## 5

Saints below, with hearts and voice,
Still in songs of praise rejoice,
Learning here, by faith and love,
Songs of praise to sing above.

## 6

Borne upon their final breath,
Songs of praise shall conquer death;
Then, amidst eternal joy,
Songs of praise their powers employ.

# Virgin-Born, We Bow Before You

**73**

Melody: Mon Dieu, Prete Moi
L'Oreille 88.77.D

Music: *Genevan Psalter*, 1543
Text: Reginald Heber, 1783-1826, alt.

## 1

Virgin-born, we bow before you;
Blessed was the womb that bore you;
Mary, Mother meek and mild,
Blessed was she in her Child.
Blessed was the maid that fed you;
Blessed was the hand that led you;
Blessed was the parent's eye
That watched your slumbering infancy.

## 2

Blessed she by all creation,
Who brought forth the world's salva-
    tion;
And blessed they forever blest,
Who love you most and serve you best.
Virgin-born, we bow before you:
Blessed was the womb that bore you;
Mary, Mother meek and mild,
Blessed was she in her Child.

## 74   What Child Is This?

Melody: Greensleeves
87.87.68.67

Music: 16th Century English Melody
Text: William Chatterton Dix, 1837-1898

**1**

What child is this, who, laid to rest,
On Mary's lap is sleeping?
Whom angels greet with anthems sweet,
While shepherds watch are keeping?
This, this is Christ the King.
Whom shepherds guard and angels sing;
Haste, haste to bring him laud,
The Babe, the Son of Mary.

**2**

Why lies he in such mean estate,
Where ox and ass are feeding?
Good Christian, fear, for sinners here

The silent Word is pleading.
Nails, spear, shall pierce him through,
The cross be borne for me, for you.
Hail, hail, the Word made flesh,
The Babe, the Son of Mary!

**3**

So bring him incense, gold and myrrh,
Come, peasant, king, to own him;
The King of Kings salvation brings,
Let loving hearts enthrone him.
Raise, raise the song on high,
The virgin sings her lullaby;
Joy, joy, for Christ is born,
The Babe, the Son of Mary!

## 75   A Child Is Born in Bethlehem

Melody: Puer Natus In Bethlehem
88 with Alleluias and Refrain

Music: Gregorian Mode I
Text: *Puer Natus In Bethlehem*,
14th century
Translator: Anon.

**1**

A Child is born in Bethlehem, alleluia;
O come, rejoice Jerusalem, alleluia, alleluia.

Refrain:
Let grateful hearts now sing,
A song of joy and holy praise
To Christ the new-born King.

**2**

Though found within a manger poor, alleluia,
His Kingdom shall for e'er endure, alleluia, alleluia.   Refrain

**3**

As brother in the flesh he came, alleluia,
Our King whose name we now proclaim, alleluia, alleluia.   Refrain

## 76   Unto Us a Child Is Given

Melody: Drakes Boughton 87.87

Music: E. Elgar, 1857-1934
Text: Stanbrook Abbey

**1**

Unto us a Child is given,
Christ our Savior bring release;
Counselor, Eternal Father,
God made man, and Prince of Peace.

**2**

Born of Mary, gentle virgin,
By the Spirit of the Lord;
From eternal ages spoken:
This the mighty Father's Word.

**3**

Love and truth in him shall flower,
From his strength their vigor take.
Branches that are bare shall blossom;
Joy that slept begins to wake.

**4**

Praise the everlasting Father,
And the Word, his only Son;
Praise them with the holy Spirit,
Perfect Trinity in One.

# Sing of Mary, Pure and Lowly

**77**

Melody: Pleading Savior 87.87.D

Music: Joshua Leavitt's
*The Christian Lyre*, 1830-1831
Text: Roland F. Palmer, 1938,
based on a 1914 Poem

**1**

Sing of Mary, pure and lowly,
Virgin mother undefiled,
Sing of God's own Son most holy
Who became her little child.
Fairest child of fairest mother,
God the Lord, who came to earth,
Word made flesh, our very brother,
Takes our nature by his birth.

**2**

Sing of Jesus, son of Mary,
In the home at Nazareth.
Toil and labor cannot weary
Love enduring unto death.
Constant was the love he gave her,
Though he went forth from her side,
Forth to preach and heal and suffer,
Till on Calvary he died.

**3**

Glory be to God the Father,
Glory be to God the Son:
Glory be to God the Spirit,
Glory to the Three in One.
From the heart of blessed Mary,
From all saints the song ascends,
And the Church the strain re-echoes
Unto earth's remotest ends.


# Joseph of Nazareth

**78**

Melody: Joseph 10.10.10.6

Music: Stephen Somerville, 1972
Text: Stephen Somerville, 1971

**1**

Joseph of Nazareth, you are the man
Last in the line that rose from David,
    King,
Down through the royal generations
    ran,
And ends with Jesus Christ.

**2**

Gabriel from heaven came to Mary's
    side,
Came with the joyful promise of a
    King,
Came to you also, Joseph, to confide
That God conceived this Child.

**3**

Guardian and foster-father of the Christ,
Honor to you, so chosen by our God!
Husband of Virgin Mary, you are first
To show us Christian love.

615

# 79

# Joy To You

Melody: Joy To You
Irregular with Antiphon

Music: Lucien Deiss, C.S.Sp.
Text: Lucien Deiss, C.S.Sp.

**Antiphon**

Joy to you, O Virgin Mary, Mother of
the Lord!

**1**

Humble maiden of Nazareth town,
Betrothed to the carpenter Joseph,
You became the mother of God.

**Antiphon**

**2**

You are the handmaid of God;
You found favor with him;
Full of grace, the Lord is with you.

**Antiphon**

**3**

Lovely Mother of Abraham's Son,
Praised Mother of David's Son,
Holy Mother of Jesus, the Lord:

**Antiphon**

**4**

You are blessed among all women;
Blessed is the fruit of your womb;
You are praised by all generations.

**Antiphon**

**5**

Your Son you bore in a manger,
Angels sang: "Glory to God,
On earth, peace to men of good will!"

**Antiphon**

**6**

You showed your child to the wise
men,
You brought him up to the temple,
You brought joy to Simeon's old age.

**Antiphon**

**7**

Chosen Mother of the Messiah,
Virgin and daughter of Zion,
Joy and glory of God's holy people.

**Antiphon**

# 80

# O Mary, of All Women

Melody: Au Fort De Ma Detresse
76.76.D

Music. Flemish Melody,
17th century, alt.
Text: Michael Gannon

**1**

O Mary, of all women,
You are the chosen one,
Who ancient prophets promised,
Would bear God's only Son;
All Hebrew generations
Prepared the way to thee,
That in your womb the God-man
Might come to set man free.

**2**

O Mary, you embody
All God taught to our race,
For you are first and foremost
In fullness of his grace;
We praise this wondrous honor
That you gave birth to him
Who from you took his manhood
And saved us from our sin.

616

# As with Gladness Men of Old

Melody:
Dix 77.77.77

Music: Adapted by William H. Monk, 1823-1889,
from a chorale by Conrad Kocher, 1786-1872
Text: W. Chatterton Dix, 1837-1898

**1**

As with gladness men of old,
Did the guiding star behold,
As with joy they hailed its light,
Leading onwards, beaming bright,
So, most gracious God, may we
Evermore be led to thee.

**2**

As with joyful steps they sped
To that lowly manger-bed,
There to bend the knee before
Him whom heaven and earth adore,
So may we with willing feet
Ever seek thy mercy-seat.

**3**

As they offered gifts most rare
At that manger rude and bare,
So may we with holy joy,
Pure, and free from sin's alloy,
All our costliest treasures bring,
Christ, to thee our heavenly king.

**4**

In the heavenly country bright
Need they no created light;
Thou its light, its joy, its crown,
Thou its sun which goes not down:
There for ever may we sing
Alleluias to our king.

# Sing Praise to Our Creator

Melody: Gott Vater! Sei Gepriesen
76.76 with Refrain

Music: Mainz Gesangbuch, 1833
Text: Omer Westendorf, 1961

**1**

Sing praise to our Creator,
O sons of Adam's race;
God's children by adoption,
Baptized into his grace.

**Refrain:**

Praise the holy Trinity
Undivided Unity;
Holy God, Mighty God,
God Immortal, be adored.          Refrain

**2**

To Jesus Christ give glory,
God's coeternal Son;
As members of his Body
We live in him as one.          Refrain

**3**

Now praise the Holy Spirit
Poured forth upon the earth
Who sanctifies and guides us,
Confirmed in our rebirth.          Refrain

# When Jesus Comes To Be Baptized

Melody: Saint Venantius
L.M.

Music: Clausener Gesangbuch, 1653
Text: Stanbrook Abbey

**1**

When Jesus comes to be baptized,
He leaves the hidden years behind,
The years of safety and of peace,
To bear the sins of all mankind.

**2**

The Spirit of the Lord comes down,
Anoints the Christ to suffering,
To preach the word, to free the bound,
And to the mourner, comfort bring.

**3**

He will not quench the dying flame,
And what is bruised he will not break,
But heal the wound injustice dealt,
And out of death his triumph make.

**4**

Our everlasting Father, praise,
With Christ, his well-beloved Son,
Who with the Spirit reigns serene,
Untroubled Trinity in One.

617

**84**

# Songs of Thankfulness and Praise

Melody: Salzburg 77.77

Music: Jakob Hintze, 1678, alt.
Text: Christopher Wordsworth, alt.

1

Songs of thankfulness and praise,
Jesus, Lord, to thee we raise,
Manifested by the star
To the wise men from afar;
Branch of royal David's stem
In thy birth at Bethlehem;
Praises be to thee addressed,
God in man made manifest.

2

Manifest at Jordan's stream,
Prophet, Priest, and King supreme;
And at Cana, wedding guest,
In thy Godhead manifest;
Manifest in power divine,
Changing water into wine;
Praises be to thee addressed,
God in man made manifest.

3

Grant us grace to see thee, Lord,
Mirrored in thy holy Word;
May we imitate thee now,
And be pure, as pure art thou;
That we like to thee may be
At thy great Epiphany;
And may praise thee, ever blessed,
God in man made manifest.

**85**

# Now Let Us All with One Accord

Melody: Truth From Above
L.M.

Music: Grenoble Antiphoner, 1868,
as adapted in Recueil Noté, Lyon, 1871
Text: Ex more docti, attributed to
Saint Gregory the Great, 540-604
Translators: Editors of Praise the Lord

1

Now let us all with one accord
In fellowship with ages past,
Keep vigil with our heav'nly Lord,
In his temptation and his fast.

2

The covenant, so long revealed
To faithful men in former time,
Christ by his own example sealed,
The Lord of love, in love sublime.

3

This love, O Lord, we sinful men
Have not returned, but falsified;
Author of mercy, turn again
And see our sorrow for our pride.

4

Remember, Lord, though frail we be,
By your own kind hand were we made;
And help us, lest our frailty
Cause your great name to be betrayed.

5

Therefore we pray you, Lord, forgive
So when our wanderings here shall
cease,
We may with you for ever live,
In love and unity and peace.

6

Hear us, O Trinity sublime,
And undivided unity;
So let this consecrated time
Bring forth its fruit abundantly.

618

# Creator of the Earth and Skies

# 86

Melody: Uffingham L.M.

Music: J. Clarke, c. 1659-1707
Text: Donald Hughes

**1**
Creator of the earth and skies,
To whom all truth and power belong,
Grant us your truth to make us wise;
Grant us your power to make us strong.

**2**
We have not known you: to the skies
Our monuments of folly soar,
And all our self-wrought miseries
Have made us trust ourselves the more.

**3**
We have not loved you: far and wide
The wreckage of our hatred spreads,
And evils wrought by human pride
Recoil on unrepentant heads.

**4**
We long to end this worldwide strife:
How shall we follow in your way?
Speak to mankind your words of life,
Until our darkness turns to day.

# Lord, Your Glory in Christ We Have Seen

# 87

Melody: Dieu, Nous Avons Vu Ta Gloire

Music: Jean Langlais
Irregular with Antiphon  Text: *Dieu, nous avons vu ta gloire*, Didier Rimaud
Translator: Anthony G. Petti

Antiphon:
Lord, your glory in Christ we have seen,
Full of goodness and full of grace:
In Christ let us live anew,
Fill us with his love,
And all men shall see the Fruits of your
victory.

**1**
The Almighty has planted his Seed in
the earth:
He tended well the grain, and he waits
for rebirth.

*Antiphon*

**2**
The Almighty has ground all the grain
for the feast:
He made it into flour, and he waits for
the yeast.

*Antiphon*

**3**
The Almighty has given his body for
man:
He broke for us the bread, and he waits
like a lamb.

*Antiphon*

**4**
The Almighty was given a crown made
of thorn:
It pierced him till he bled, and he waits:
do we mourn?

*Antiphon*

**5**
The Almighty did suffer and evil destroy:
He died to ease our pain, and he waits
for our joy.

*Antiphon*

# 88

## Praise to the Holiest

Melody: Billing C.M.

Music: Richard R. Terry, 1865-1938
Text: J. H. Newman, 1801-1890

### 1

Praise to the holiest in the height,
And in the depth be praise,
In all his words most wonderful,
Most sure in all his ways.

### 2

O loving wisdom of our God!
When all was sin and shame,
A second Adam to the fight
And to the rescue came.

### 3

O wisest love! that flesh and blood
Which did in Adam fail,
Should strive afresh against the foe,
Should strive and should prevail;

### 4

And that a higher gift than grace
Should flesh and blood refine,
God's presence and his very self
And essence all divine.

### 5

O generous love! that he, who smote
In man for man the foe,
The double agony in man
For man should undergo;

### 6

And in the garden secretly,
And on the cross on high,
Should teach his brethren, and inspire
To suffer and to die.

### 7

Praise to the holiest in the height,
And in the depth be praise,
In all his words most wonderful,
Most sure in all his ways.

# 89

## The Glory of These Forty Days

Melody: Erhalt'uns,
Herr (Spires) L. M.

Music: J. Klug's Geistliche Lieder, 1547
Text: Latin, 6th century
Translator: Maurice F. Bell, 1906, alt.

### 1

The glory of these forty days
We celebrate with songs of praise;
For Christ, by whom all things were made,
Himself has fasted and has prayed.

### 2

Alone and fasting Moses saw
The loving God who gave the law;
And to Elijah, fasting, came
The steeds and chariots of flame.

### 3

So Daniel trained his mystic sight,
Deliver'd from the lions' might.
And John, the Bridegroom's friend, became
The herald of Messiah's name.

### 4

Then grant us, Lord, like them to do
Such things as bring great praise to you;
Our spirits strengthen with your grace
And give us joy to see your face.

### 5

O Father, Son, and Spirit blest,
To you be every prayer addressed
And by all mankind be adored,
From age to age, the only Lord.

# Grant to Us

# 90

Melody: Grant to Us
Irregular with Antiphon

Music Lucien Deiss, C.S.Sp.
Text: Lucien Deiss, C.S.Sp.

Antiphon: Grant to us, O Lord a heart renewed;
Recreate in us your own Spirit, Lord!

**1**

Behold, the days are coming, says the
Lord our God,
When I will make a new covenant with
the house of Israel.   Antiphon

**2**

Deep within their being I will implant
my law,
I will write it in their hearts.   Antiphon

**3**

I will be their God, and they shall be
my people.   Antiphon

**4**

And for all their faults I will grant for-
giveness;
Never more will I remember their sins.
Antiphon

# With Hearts Renewed

# 91

Melody: Frankfort
887.887.48.48

Music: P. Nicolai, 1599, arranged by J. S. Bach, 1730
Text: Jack May, S.J.

**1**

With hearts renewed by living faith,
We lift our thoughts in grateful prayer
To God our gracious Father
Whose plan it was to make us sons
Through his own Son's redemptive
death,
That rescued us from darkness.
Lord, God, Savior,
Give us strength to mold our hearts in
your true likeness.
Sons and servants of our Father.

**2**

So rich God's grace in Jesus Christ,
That we are called as sons of light
To bear the pledge of glory.
Through him in whom all fullness
dwells,
We offer God our gift of self
In union with the Spirit.
Lord, God, Savior,
Give us strength to mold our hearts in
your true likeness.
Sons and servants of our Father.

# Take Up Your Cross

Melody: Breslau L.M.

Music: *As Hymnodus Sacer*, 1625,
adapted and harmonized by F. Men-
delssohn-Bartholdy 1807-1847
Text: Charles William Everest, 1814-
1877, adapted by Anthony G. Petti

**1**

Take up your cross, the Savior said,
If you would my disciple be;
Deny yourself, the world forsake,
And humbly follow after me.

**2**

Take up your cross, let not its weight
Fill your weak spirit with alarm;
His strength shall bear your spirit up,
Shall brace your heart and nerve your
arm.

**3**

Take up your cross then in his strength,
And ev'ry danger calmly brave,
To guide you to a better home,
And vict'ry over death and grave.

**4**

Take up your cross and follow Christ,
Nor think till death to lay it down;
For only he who bears the cross
May hope to wear the glorious crown.

**5**

To you, great Lord, the One in three,
All praise for evermore ascend;
O grant us here below to see
The heav'nly life that knows no end.

# For Forty Years

Melody: Toronto 12.12.12.12
with Refrain

Music: Stephen Somerville
Text: Stephen Somerville

**1**

For forty years God's people lived in
desert land.
For forty days Elijah trudged the wilderness.
Our Lord was tempted, prayed and
fasted forty days;
Now we his Church observe the sacred
time of Lent.

Refrain

Have mercy on your people, Lord, have
mercy.

**2**

Lord, make us understand the desert of
this life;
The misery, the sin, the death that all
must face:
That we will conquer only if we turn to
you,
With prayer and fasting and almsgiving
in this Lent.

Refrain

**3**

Teach us to spurn the pomps of Satan
in our path,
Lead us to glimpse the promised land,
the Mount of God,
With eyes of faith and hope that pierce
the worldly gloom,
With heart of charity your Holy Spirit
gives.

Refrain

**4**

And when we celebrate the Paschal
Triduum,
The holy days you suffered, died, and
rose again;
Live in us, Lord, these sad and glorious
mysteries,
Until the Last Day when eternal Easter
dawns.

Refrain

**5**

May all your Church acclaim you, Jesus, Lord and Christ,
And praise the heav'nly Father's power that conquered death;
Confess the Holy Spirit you have poured on us,
Through Lent, through life and death, and through eternity. Refrain

# Lord Who Throughout These Forty Days

Melody: Saint Flavian C.M.

Music: Adapted from *Psalm 132*,
John Day's *Psalter* 1562
Text: Claudia Hernaman, 1838-1898. alt.

**1**

Lord, who throughout these forty days
For us did fast and pray,
Teach us with you to mourn our sins,
And close by you to stay.

**2**

As you with Satan did contend
And did the vict'ry win,
O give us strength in you to fight,
In you to conquer sin.

**3**

As you did hunger and did thirst,
So teach us, gracious Lord,
To die to self and so to live
By your most holy word.

**4**

Abide with us, that through this life
Of suff'ring and of pain
An Easter of unending joy
We may at last attain.

# This Is Our Accepted Time

Melody: Weimar 76.76.D

Music: Melchior Vulpius, 1609
Text: Michael Gannon, alt.

**1**

This is our accepted time,
This is our salvation;
Prayer and fasting are our hope,
Penance, our vocation.
God of pardon and of love,
Mercy past all measure,
You alone can grant us peace,
You, our holy treasure.

**2**

Lord, look down upon your sons,
Look upon their yearning;
Man is dust, and unto dust
He shall be returning.
Lift him up, O Lord of life,
Flesh has gained him sadness,
Hear his plea, bestow on him
Everlasting gladness.

# Draw Near, O Lord

Melody: Attende Domine
11.11.11 with Refrain

Music: *Paris Processional*, 1824
Text: *Attende Domine*
Translator: Melvin Farrell, S.S.

**Refrain**

Draw near, O Lord, our God, graciously
      hear us,
guilty of sinning before you.

**1**

O King exalted, Savior of all nations,
See how our grieving lifts our eyes to
      heaven;
Hear us, Redeemer, as we beg for-
      giveness.

      *Refrain*

**2**

Might of the Father, Keystone of God's
      temple,
Way of salvation, Gate to heaven's
      glory;
Sin has enslaved us; free your sons
      from bondage.

      *Refrain*

**3**

We pray you, O God, throned in
      strength and splendor,
Hear from your kingdom this, our song
      of sorrow:
Show us your mercy, pardon our of-
      fenses.

      *Refrain*

**4**

Humbly confessing countless sins
      committed,
Our hearts are broken, laying bare
      their secrets;
Cleanse us, Redeemer, boundless in
      compassion.

      *Refrain*

**5**

Innocent captive, unresisting victim,
Liars denounced you, sentenced for
      the guilty;
Once you redeemed us: now renew us,
      Jesus.

      *Refrain*

# When I Survey the Wondrous Cross

Melody: Rockingham L.M.

Music: Adapted by E. Miller, 1731-1807
Text: Isaac Watts, 1674-1748, slightly adapted
from A. Williams' *A Second Supplement to Psalmody
in Miniature*, Oxford, c. 1780

1 When I survey the wondrous cross
On which the Prince of glory died,
My richest gain I count but loss,
And pour contempt on all my pride.

2 Forbid it, Lord, that I should boast,
Save in the death of Christ my God;
The vain delights that charm me
most:
I sacrifice them to his blood.

3 See, from his head, his hands, his
feet
What grief and love flow mingling
down;
Did e'er such love and sorrow meet,
Or thorns compose so rich a crown?

4 Were all the realm of nature mine,
That were a present far too small;
Love so amazing, so divine,
Demands my soul, my life, my all.

# 98

# Keep in Mind

Melody: Keep in Mind
Irregular with Antiphon

Music: Lucien Deiss, C.S. Sp.
Text: Lucien Deiss, C.S.Sp.

Antiphon:
Keep in mind that Jesus Christ has died
for us
and is risen from the dead.
He is our saving Lord,
he is joy for all ages.

1
If we die with the Lord,
we shall live with the Lord.
Antiphon:

2
If we endure with the Lord,
we shall reign with the Lord. Antiphon:

3
In him all our sorrow,
in him all our joy. Antiphon:

4
In him hope of glory,
in him all our love. Antiphon:

5
In him our redemption,
in him all our grace. Antiphon:

6
In him our salvation,
in him all our peace. Antiphon:

# 99

# When from the Darkness

Melody: Courtney 89.89.4

Music: Colin Mawby
Text: Brendan McLaughlin

1
When from the darkness comes no
light,
When from the weeping comes no
laughter,
When in the day we hope for night
nor any comfort coming after:
Grant us your peace.

2
When in our confidence our fears
Clutch at the heart and make us
tremble;
When in our joy we weep cold tears,
And in our frankness we dissemble:
Grant us your light.

3
When in our love there is not care,
And in our yearning we are dullness;
When what we know we cannot dare,
And we are nothing that is fullness:
Grant us your truth.

# Let All Mortal Flesh Keep Silence

**100**

Melody: Picardy 87.87.87

Music: *Chansons Populaires des Provinces de France,* 1860
Text: *Liturgy of Saint James,* 5th century
Translator: Gerard Moultrie, 1864, alt.

1  Let all mortal flesh keep
And with fear and trembling stand;
Ponder nothing earthly-minded,
For with blessing in his hand
Christ our Lord to earth descends now,
Our full homage to demand.

2  Rank on rank the host of heaven
Spreads its vanguard on the way,
As the Light of Light descends now
From the realms of endless day,
That the powers of hell may vanish
As the darkness clears away.

# Crown Him with Many Crowns

**101**

Melody: Diademata S.M.D.

Music: George J. Elvey, 1816-1893
Text: st. 1, Matthew Bridges, 1800-1894;
sts. 2 & 3, Godfrey Thring, 1823-1903

1
Crown him with many crowns,
The lamb upon his throne;
Hark! how the heav'nly anthem drowns
All music but its own:
Awake, my soul, and sing
Of him who died for thee,
And hail him as thy matchless King
Through all eternity.

2
Crown him the Lord of Lords,
Who over all doth reign,
Who once on earth, the incarnate Word,
For ransomed sinners slain,
Now lives in realms of light,
Where saints with angels sing
Their songs before him day and night
Their God, Redeemer, King.

3
Crown him the Lord of heav'n,
Enthroned in worlds above;
Crown him the King, to whom is giv'n
The wondrous name of Love.
Crown him with many crowns,
As thrones before him fall,
Crown him, ye kings, with many crowns,
For he is King of all.

# Hail, Redeemer, King Divine

**102**

Melody: Hail, Redeemer
(St. George's Windsor) 77.77.D

Music: George J. Elvey, 1816-1895
Text: Patrick Brennan, C.SS.R., alt.

1  Hail, Redeemer, King divine!
Priest and Lamb, the throne is thine;
King whose reign shall never cease,
Prince of everlasting peace. Refrain

2  Christ, thou King of truth and might,
Be to us eternal light,
Till in peace each nation rings
With thy praises, King of kings.
Refrain

Refrain  Angels, saints, and nations sing:
"Praise be Jesus Christ, our King;
Lord of earth and sky and sea
King of love on Calvary."

## 103  All Glory, Praise, and Honor

Melody: Saint Theodulph,
76.76.D

Music: Melchior Teschner, pub. 1615
Text: *Gloria, Laus et Honor*
Theodulph of Orleans, c. 820
Translator: John Mason Neale, 1851, alt.

**Refrain**
All glory, praise, and honor
To you, Redeemer, King!
To whom the lips of children
Made glad hosannas ring.

**1**
You are the King of Israel,
And David's royal Son,
Who in the Lord's Name comest,
The King and Blessed One. **Refrain**

**2**
The company of angels
Are praising you on high;
And mortal men and all things
Created make reply. **Refrain**

**3**
The people of the Hebrews
With palms before you went:
Our praise and prayers and anthems
Before you we present. **Refrain**

**4**
To you before your Passion
They sang their hymns of praise:
To you, now high exalted,
Our melody we raise. **Refrain**

**5**
As once you did accept their praise,
Accept the praise we bring,
You who rejoice in ev'ry good,
Our good and gracious King. **Refrain**

## 104  O Sacred Head, Surrounded

Melody: Passion Chorale
76.76.D

Music: Hans Leo Hassler, 1601
Text: St. 1, Sir W. H. Baker, 1821-1877,
alt., st. 2, Melvin Farrell, S.S., 1961

**1**
O Sacred Head, surrounded
By crown of piercing thorn.
O Bleeding Head, so wounded,
Reviled and put to scorn.
Our sins have marred the glory
Of thy most holy Face,
Yet angel hosts adore thee,
And tremble as they gaze.

**2**
The Lord of every nation
Was hung upon a tree;
His death was our salvation,
Our sins, his agony.
O Jesus, by thy Passion,
Thy Life in us increase;
Thy death for us did fashion
Our pardon and our peace.

## 105  Were You There?

Melody: Were You There?
10.10 with Refrain

Music: Negro Spiritual
Text: Traditional, Anon.

1  Were you there when they crucified my Lord?
Were you there when they crucified my Lord?
Oh! . . . Sometimes it causes me to tremble, tremble, tremble.
Were you there when they crucified my Lord?

2  Were you there when they nailed him to the tree?
Were you there when they nailed him to the tree?
Oh! . . . Sometimes it causes me to tremble, tremble, tremble.
Were you there when they nailed him to the tree?

3 Were you there when they laid him in the tomb?
Were you there when they laid him in the tomb?
Oh! . . . Sometimes it causes me to tremble, tremble, tremble.
Were you there when they laid him in the tomb?

4 Were you there when they rolled the stone away?
Were you there when they rolled the stone away?
Oh! . . Sometimes it causes me to tremble, tremble, tremble.
Were you there when they rolled the stone away?

# John 15

**106**

Melody: John 15
Irregular with Antiphon

Music: Enrico Garzilli, 1970
Text: Enrico Garzilli, 1970

Antiphon

This I ask: that you love each other
as I have loved you.
I look on you as friends, as friends.

1

Don't be distressed;
let your hearts be free,
for I leave with you my peace, my word.
Antiphon

2

If you really love me,
be glad, have hope,
for I leave with you my Spirit to guide
you.

Antiphon

3

When the end is near
I still am with you,
for I will never leave you alone.
Antiphon

# Have Mercy, O Lord

**107**

Melody Have Mercy, O Lord
Irregular with Antiphon

Music: Lucien Deiss, C.S. Sp.
Text: Lucien Deiss, C.S. Sp.

Antiphon: Have mercy, O Lord, have mercy on us!

1

O Lord Jesus Christ,
At prayer in the Garden of Olives,
Weeping with sadness and fear,
Comforted by an Angel.
Antiphon

2

O Lord Jesus Christ,
Betrayed by the kiss of Judas,
Abandoned by your apostles,
Delivered over to sinners.
Antiphon

3

O Lord Jesus Christ,
Buffeted, covered with spittle,
Bruised by the blows of soldiers,
Condemned to die on the cross.
Antiphon

4

O Lord Jesus Christ,
Scourged and crowned with thorns,
Clothed in a robe of purple,
Covered with scorn and shame.
Antiphon

627

**Antiphon: Have mercy, O Lord, have mercy on us!**

5

O Lord Jesus Christ,
Burdened with your cross,
Mounting even to Calvary,
Bearing the weight of our sins.

Antiphon

7

O Lord Jesus Christ,
Forgiving your executioners,
Confiding your holy Mother
To your beloved disciple.

Antiphon

6

O Lord Jesus Christ,
Stripped of your garments,
Given gall in your thirst,
Crucified with thieves.

Antiphon

8

O Lord Jesus Christ,
Breathing forth your spirit
Into the hands of your Father,
Dying for all sinners.

Antiphon

---

## 108 I Shall Praise the Savior's Glory

Melody: Pange Lingua
87.87.87

Music: Mode III Vatican Plainsong
Text: *Pange Lingua*, Saint Thomas Aquinas,
c. 1225-1274
Translator: Edward Caswall, 1814-1878,
adapted by Anthony G. Petti

1

I shall praise the Savior's glory,
Of his flesh the mystery sing,
And the blood, all price excelling,
Shed by our immortal King:
God made man for our salvation,
Who from Virgin pure did spring.

2

Born for us, and for us given,
Born a man like us below,
Christ as man with man residing,
Lived the seed of truth to sow,
Suffered bitter death unflinching,
And immortal love did show.

3

On the night before he suffered,
Seated with his chosen band,
Jesus, when they all had feasted,
Faithful to the law's command,
Far more precious food provided:
Gave himself with his own hand.

4

Word made flesh, true bread of
heaven,
By his word made flesh to be,
From the wine his blood is taken,
Though our senses cannot see,
Faith alone which is unshaken
Shows pure hearts the mystery.

5

Therefore we, before him falling,
This great sacrament revere;
Ancient forms are now departed,
For new acts of grace are here,
Faith our feeble senses aiding,
Makes the Savior's presence clear.

6

To the everlasting Father
And his Son who reigns on high,
With the Holy Ghost proceeding
Forth from each eternally,
Be all honor, glory, blessing,
Power and endless majesty.

# The Word of God Proceeding Forth

# 109

Melody:
Rockingham L.M.

Music: Adapted by Edward Miller, 1731-1807 from
A. Williams' *A Second Supplement to Psalmody
in Miniature*, Oxford, c. 1873
Text: Thomas Aquinas, c. 1225-1274
Translator: Sts. 1 and 5, John M. Neale, 1818-1866, Edward Caswall,
1814-1878, et al.; sts. 2-4, Gerard Manley Hopkins, 1844-1889

### 1
The word of God, proceeding forth
Yet leaving not his Father's side,
And going to his work on earth
Had reached at length life's eventide.

### 2
Soon by his own false friend betrayed,
Given to his foes, to death went he;
His own true self, in form of bread,
He gave his friends, their life to be.

### 3
A double gift his love did plan,
His flesh to feed, his blood to cheer,
That flesh and blood, the whole of
man,
Might find its own fulfillment here.

### 4
The manger, Christ their equal made;
That upper room, their souls' repast;
The cross, their ransom dearly paid,
And heaven, their high reward at last.

### 5
All praise and thanks to thee ascend
For evermore, blest one in three.
O grant us life that shall not end
In our true native land with thee.

# My Loving Savior

# 110

Melody: Herzliebster Jesu
11.11.11.5

Music: Johannes Crüger, 1597-1662,
adapted and harmonized by J. S. Bach, 1685-1750
Text: *Herzliebster Jesu* by Johann Heermann, 1585-1647
Trans.: Anthony G. Petti, based on the
translation of Robert Bridges, 1844-1930

### 1
My loving Savior, how have you of-
fended,
That such a hate in man on you de-
scended?
Both mocked and scorned, you suf-
fered our rejection
In deep affliction.

### 2
It was my guilt brought all these things
upon you,
Through all my sins was this injustice
done you.
Lord Jesus, it was I that did deny you
And crucify you.

### 3
So now the Shepherd for the sheep is
offered,
Mankind is guilty, but the Son has suf-
fered.
For man's atonement, which man never
heeded,
God interceded.

### 4
For us, dear Jesus, was your incarna-
tion,
Your bitter death and shameful cruci-
fixion,
Your burial and your glorious resurrec-
tion:
For our salvation.

### 5
Although, good Jesus, we cannot repay you,
We shall adore you and shall ever praise you,
For all your kindness and your love unswerving,
Not our deserving.

629

# 11    Christ, Victim for the Sins of Men

Melody: Erhalt' uns,
Herr (Spires) L.M.

Music: J. Klug's *Geistliche Lieder*, 1547
Text: *O salutaris hostia*, pare. by Brian Foley

**1**

Christ, victim for the sins of men,
Your death brings hope to our despair;
With your new life we live again,
Your heav'nly joy is ours to share.

Lord God, eternal Trinity,
We praise you for yourself alone;

**2**

Yet still in many things we fail,
And fall again in sin and shame;
Let not our sinfulness prevail,
Let not your saving be in vain.

**3**

And pray that we may ever be
Blest in that kingdom of your own.

# 12    Alleluia! The Strife Is O'er

Melody: Victory 8.8.8
with Alleluias

Music: G. P. da Palestrina, 1588,
ad. with alleluias by W. H. Monk, 1861
Text: *Symphonia Sirenum Selectarum*, Cologne, 1695
Translator: Francis Pott, 1861, alt.

**1**

Alleluia! Alleluia! Alleluia!
The strife is o'er, the battle done;
Now is the Victor's triumph won:
O let the song of praise be sung.
Alleluia!

Alleluia! Alleluia! Alleluia!
O risen Lord, all praise to thee,

**2**

Alleluia! Alleluia! Alleluia!
On the third morn he rose again,
Glorious in majesty to reign:
O let us swell the joyful strain:
Alleluia!

**3**

Who from our sin has set us free,
That we may live eternally:
Alleluia!

# 113    In the Midst of Death

Melody: In the Midst of Death
56.56.5

Music: Rik Veelenturf
Text: Muus Jacobse, David Smith

**1**

We who once were dead
Now live fully knowing
Jesus as our head.
Life is overflowing
When he breaks the bread.

**2**

We were lost in night,
But you sought and found us.
Give us strength to fight.
Death is all around us.
Jesus, be our light.

**3**

He became our bread;
Jesus died to save us.
On him we are fed,
Eating what he gave us,
Rising from the dead.

**4**

Let us share the pain
You endured in dying.
We shall then remain
Living, death defying,
We shall rise again.

**5**

Jesus, you were dead,
But you rose and living,
Made yourself our bread,

In your goodness giving
Life though we were dead.

630

# I Am the Bread of Life

**114**

Melody: I Am The Bread Of Life
Irregular with Refrain

Music: S. Suzanne Toolan, 1970
Text. S. Suzanne Toolan, 1970

**1**

I am the bread of Life. He who comes to
me shall not hunger;
He who believes in me shall not thirst.
No one can come to me unless the
Father draw him.

Refrain:
And I will raise him up,
And I will raise him up,
And I will raise him up on the last day.

**2**

I am the resurrection, I am the life.
He who believes in me
Even if he die, he shall live for ever.

Refrain

**3**

Yes, lord, I believe that you are the
Christ,
The Son of God,
The Son of God, who has come into the
world.

Refrain

**4**

I am the way and the truth; I am the
life.
No one comes to the Father,
Except he come through me, except he
come through me.

Refrain

# Christ Jesus Lay in Death's Strong Bands

**115**

Melody: Christ Lag In
Todesbanden 87.87.78.74
with Alleluia

Music: Walther's *Gesangbuchlein*, 1524
Text: Martin Luther, 1483-1546,
based on *Victimae Paschali laudes*
Translator: Richard Massie, 1800-1887, ad. by Anthony G. Petti

**1**

Christ Jesus lay in death's strong
bands
For our offenses given:
But now at God's right hand he stands
And brings us life from heaven;
Therefore let us joyful be,
And praise the Father thankfully
With songs of Alleluia.
Alleluia.

**2**

How long and bitter was the strife
When life and death contended,
The victory remained with life,
The reign of death was ended:
Stripped of power, no more it reigns,
And empty form alone remains.
Death's sting is lost for ever.
Alleluia.

**3**

So let us keep this festival
To which Our Lord invites us,
The Savior who is joy of all,
The Sun that warms and lights us:
By his grace he shall impart
Eternal sunshine to the heart,
The night of sin has ended. Alleluia.

# 116

# At the Lamb's High Feast

Melody: Salzburg 77.77.D

Music: Jakob Hintze, 1622-1702
Text: *Ad regias Agni dapes*
Translator: Robert Campbell, 1814-1868, adapted by Geoffrey Laycock

**1**

At the Lamb's high feast we sing
Praise to our victorious King,
Who has washed us in the tide
Flowing from his wounded side;
Praise the Lord, whose love divine
Gives his sacred blood for wine,
Gives his body for the feast,
Christ the victim, Christ the priest.

**2**

Where the Paschal blood is poured,
Death's dark angel sheathes his sword;
Israel's hosts in triumph go
Through the waves that drown the foe.
Christ the Lamb whose blood was shed,
Paschal victim, Paschal bread;
Let us with a fervent love
Taste the manna from above.

**3**

Mighty victim from on high,
Pow'rs of hell now vanquished lie;
Sin is conquered in the fight:
You have brought us life and light;
Your resplendent banners wave,
You have risen from the grave;
Christ has opened Paradise,
And in him all men shall rise.

**4**

Easter triumph, Easter joy,
Sin alone can this destroy;
Souls from sin and death set free
Glory in their liberty.
Hymns of glory, hymns of praise
Father, unto you we raise;
Risen Lord, for joy we sing:
Let our hymns through heaven ring.

# The Day of Resurrection

Melody: Ellacombe 76.76.D

Music: *Würtemburg Gesangbuch*, 1784,
adapted in the *Mainz Gesangbuch*,
1833, and further adapted in the
*St. Gall Gesangbuch*, 1863
Text: John Mason Neale, 1818-1866, adapted by Anthony G. Petti

**1**

The day of resurrection!
Earth spread the news abroad;
The Paschal feast of gladness,
The Paschal feast of God.
From death to life eternal,
From earth to heaven's height
Our Savior Christ has brought us,
The glorious Lord of Light.

**2**

Our hearts be free from evil
That we may see aright
The Savior resurrected
In his eternal light;
And hear his message plainly,
Delivered calm and clear:
"Rejoice with me in triumph,
Be glad and do not fear."

**3**

Now let the heav'ns be joyful,
And earth her song begin,
The whole world keep high triumph
And all that is therein;
Let all things in creation
Their notes of gladness blend,
For Christ the Lord has risen,
Our joy that has no end.

# Jesus Christ Is Ris'n Today

Melody: Easter Hymn 7.7.7.7.
with Alleluias

Music: Lyra Davidica, 1708
Text: st. 1, *Surrexit Christus hodie*, Latin
Carol, pare. in *Lyra Davidica*, 1708 alt.; sts.
2, 3, *The Compleat Psalmodist*, 1749, alt.;
st. 4, William Reynolds, 1860

### 1

Jesus Christ is ris'n today, Alleluia!
Our triumphant holy day, Alleluia!
Who did once upon the cross, Alleluia!
Suffer to redeem our loss, Alleluia!

### 2

Hymns of praise then let us sing,
  Alleluia!
Unto Christ, our heav'nly King, Alleluia!
Who endured the cross and grave,
  Alleluia!
Sinners to redeem and save, Alleluia!

### 3

But the pains which He endured,
  Alleluia!
Our salvation have procured, Alleluia!
Now He rules eternal King, Alleluia!
Where the angels ever sing, Alleluia!

### 4

Praise to God the Father sing, Alleluia.
Praise to God the Son, our King,
  Alleluia.
Praise to God the Spirit be, Alleluia.
Now and through eternity, Alleluia.

# Ye Sons and Daughters

Melody: O Filii Et Filiae,
8.8.8. with Alleluias

Music: 17th cent. French Proper Melody
Text: *O filii et filiae*, Jean Tisserand. d 1474
Translator: John Mason Neale, 1818-1866, alt.

### 1

Alleluia, alleluia, alleluia.
Ye sons and daughters, let us sing!
The King of heav'n, the glorious King,
O'er death today rose triumphing.
  Alleluia!

### 2

Alleluia, alleluia, alleluia.
That Easter morn, at break of day,
The faithful women went their way
To seek the tomb where Jesus lay.
  Alleluia!

### 3

Alleluia, alleluia, alleluia.
An angel clad in white they see,
Who sat, and spoke unto the three,
"Your Lord doth go to Galilee."
  Alleluia!

### 4

Alleluia, alleluia, alleluia.
On this most holy day of days,
To God your hearts and voices raise,
In laud and jubilee and praise.
  Alleluia!

### 5

Alleluia, alleluia, alleluia.
And we with Holy Church unite,
As evermore is just and right,
In glory to the King of light.
  Alleluia!

# Christ the Lord Is Risen Today

Melody: Llanfair 7.7. 7.7
with Alleluias

Music: Attributed to Robert Williams, 1781-1821
Text: Charles Wesley, 1707-1788, alt.

**1**

Christ the Lord is risen today, Alleluia!
Sons of men and angels say: Alleluia!
Raise your joys and triumphs high;
Alleluia!
Sing, ye heavens, and earth reply,
Alleluia!

**2**

Vain the stone, the watch, the seal;
Alleluia!
Christ has burst the gates of hell:
Alleluia!
Death in vain forbids his rise; Alleluia
Christ hath opened paradise, Alleluia!

**3**

Lives again our glorious King; Alleluia!
Where, O death, is now thy sting?
Alleluia!
Once he died, our souls to save;
Alleluia!
Where thy victory, O grave? Alleluia!

**4**

Hail, the Lord of earth and heaven!
Alleluia!
Praise to thee by both be given;
Alleluia!
Thee we greet triumphant now;
Alleluia!
Hail, the resurrection Thou! Alleluia!

# Alleluia! Sing to Jesus

Melody: Hyfrydol 87.87.D

Music: Rowland H. Prichard, 1811-1887
Text: William Chatterton Dix, 1837-1898

**1**

Alleluia! sing to Jesus!
His the scepter, his the throne;
Alleluia! his the triumph,
His the victory alone:
Hark! the songs of peaceful Sion
Thunder like a mighty flood;
Jesus, out of ev'ry nation
Has redeemed us by his Blood.

**2**

Alleluia! not as orphans
Are we left in sorrow now;
Alleluia! he is near us,
Faith believes nor questions how:
Though the cloud from sight received
him,
When the forty days were o'er
Shall our hearts forget his promise,
"I am with you evermore"?

**3**

Alleluia! Bread of angels,
Thou on earth our food, our stay;
Alleluia! here the sinful
Flee to thee from day to day:
Intercessor, friend of sinners,
Earth's Redeemer, plead for me,
Where the songs of all the sinless
Sweep across the crystal sea.

**4**

Alleluia! King eternal,
Thee the Lord of Lords we own;
Alleluia! born of Mary
Earth thy footstool, heav'n thy throne:
Thou within the veil hast entered,
Robed in flesh, our great High Priest;
Thou on earth both Priest and Victim
In the Eucharistic feast.

# Hail Thee, Festival Day

Melody: Salve Festa Dies
Irregular with Refrain

Music: R. Vaughan Williams, 1906
Text: Venantius Honorius Fortunatus, 530-609
Translator: Maurice F. Bell, 1862-1947

### Refrain for Easter

Hail thee, festival day!
Blest day that art hallowed for ever;
Day whereon Christ arose,
Breaking the kingdom of death.

### Refrain for Ascension

Hail thee, festival day!
Blest day that art hallowed for ever;
Day when the Christ ascends,
High in the heavens to reign.

### Refrain for Pentecost

Hail thee, festival day!
Blest day that art hallowed for ever;
Day whereon God from heav'n
Shone in the world with his grace.

**1**

Lo, the fair beauty of earth,
From the death of the winter arising!
Ev'ry good gift of the year
Now with its Master returns:
*Refrain*

**2**

He who was nailed to the cross
Is Lord and the ruler of all men;
All things created on earth
Sing to the glory of God:
*Refrain*

**3**

Daily the loveliness grows,
Adorned with the glory of blossom;
Heaven her gates unbars,
Flinging her increase of light:
*Refrain*

**4**

Rise from the grave now, O Lord,
Who art author of life and creation
Treading the pathway of death,
Life thou bestowest on man:
*Refrain*

**5**

God the All-Father, the Lord,
Who rulest the earth and the heavens,
Guard us from harm without,
Cleanse us from evil within:
*Refrain*

**6**

Jesus the health of the world,
Enlighten our minds, thou Redeemer,
Son of the Father supreme,
Only begotten of God:
*Refrain*

**7**

Spirit of life and of power,
Now flow in us, fount of our being,
Light that dost lighten all,
Life that in all dost abide:
*Refrain*

**8**

Praise to the Giver of good!
Thou Love who art author of concord,
Pour out thy balm on our souls,
Order our ways in thy peace:
*Refrain*

635

# 123

## Christ the Lord Is Ris'n Today

Melody: Victimae Paschali Laudes
77.77.D

Music: Traditional, alt.
Text: *Victimae Paschali Laudes*,
ascribed to Wipo of Burgundy, d. c. 1050
Translator: Jane E. Leeson, 1807-1882, alt.

**1**

Christ the Lord is ris'n today;
Christians, haste your vows to pay;
Offer you your praises meet
At the Paschal Victim's feet.
For the sheep the Lamb has bled,
Sinless in the sinner's stead;
Christ, the Lord, is ris'n on high,
Now he lives no more to die!

**2**

Christ, the Victim undefiled,
Man to God has reconciled;
When in strange and awful strife
Met together death and life;
Christians, on this happy day
Haste with joy your vows to pay.
Christ, the Lord, is ris'n on high,
Now he lives no more to die!

**3**

Christ, who once for sinners bled,
Now the firstborn from the dead,
Throned in endless might and power,
Lives and reigns for ever more
Hail, eternal Hope on high!
Hall, our King of Victory!
Hall, our Prince of life adored!
Help and save us, gracious Lord.

# 124

## Let the Earth Rejoice and Sing

Melody: Llanfair 7.7.7.7
with Alleluias

Music: Attributed to Robert Williams, 1781-1821
Text: Melvin Farrell, S.S.

**1**

Let the earth rejoice and sing, alleluia!
At the triumph of our King, alleluia!
He ascends from mortal sight, alleluia!
Reigns now at our Father's right,
alleluia!

**2**

He who died upon a tree, alleluia!
Now shall reign eternally, alleluia!
He who saved our fallen race, alleluia!
Takes in heav'n his rightful place,
alleluia!

**3**

Jesus, Lord, all hail to thee, alleluia!
On this day of victory, alleluia!
Thou didst shatter Satan's might,
alleluia!
Rising glorious from the fight, alleluia!

**4**

Jesus, Victor, hear our prayer, alleluia!
In thy triumph let us share, alleluia!
Lift our minds and hearts above,
alleluia!
Strengthen all men in thy love, alleluia!

**5**

While in heaven thou dost gaze, alleluia!
On thy Church who sings thy praise, alleluia!
Fasten all our hope in thee, alleluia!
Till thy face unveiled we see, alleluia!

636

# Praise Him As He Mounts the Skies

# 125

Melody: Llanfair 7.7.7.7
with Alleluias

Music: Attributed to R. Williams, 1781-1821
Text: James Quinn, S.J.

**1**

Praise him as he mounts the skies,
  Alleluia!
Christ, the Lord of Paradise! Alleluia!
Cry hosanna in the height, Alleluia!
As he rises out of sight! Alleluia!

**2**

Now at last he takes his throne,
  Alleluia!
From all ages his alone! Alleluia!
With his praise creation rings: Alleluia!
"Lord of lords and King of kings!"
  Alleluia!

**3**

Hands and feet and side reveal!
  Alleluia!
Wounds of love, high priesthood's
  seal! Alleluia!
Advocate, for us he pleads; Alleluia!
Heavenly Priest, he intercedes!
  Alleluia!

**4**

Christians, raise your eyes above!
  Alleluia!
He will come again in love, Alleluia!
On that great and wondrous day,
  Alleluia!
When this world will pass away!
  Alleluia!

**5**   At his word new heavens and earth, Alleluia!
  Will in glory spring to birth! Alleluia!
  Joy of angels, joy of men, Alleluia!
  Come, Lord Jesus, come again! Alleluia!

# The Head That Once Was Crowned with Thorns

Melody: Saint Magnus
(Nottingham) C.M.

Music: Attr. to Jeremiah Clarke, 1659-1707
Text: Thomas Kelly, 1769-1854, slightly adap.

**1**

The head that once was crowned with
  thorns
Is crowned with glory now:
A royal diadem adorns
The mighty victor's brow.

**2**

The highest place that heav'n affords
Is surely his by right:
The King of kings and Lord of lords,
And heav'n's eternal light.

**3**

The joy he is of all above,
The joy to all below:
To ev'ryone he shows his love,
And grants his name to know.

**4**

To them the cross, with all its shame,
With all its grace, is giv'n:
Their name an everlasting name.
Their joy the joy of heav'n.

**5**   The cross he bore is life and health,
  Though shame and death to him;
  His people's hope, his people's wealth,
  Their everlasting theme.

# Come, Holy Ghost, Creator, Come

Melody: Tallis' Ordinal C.M.

Music: Thomas Tallis, c. 1510-1585
Text: Attr. to Rabanus Maurus, 766-856
Translator: Anon., *Hymns for the Year*, 1876

**1**

Come, Holy Ghost, Creator, come
From thy bright heavenly throne,
Come, take possession of our souls
And make them all thy own.

**2**

Thou who art called the Paraclete,
Best gift of God above,
The living spring, the living fire,
Sweet unction and true love.

**3**

Thou who art sevenfold in thy grace,
Finger of God's right hand;
His promise, teaching little ones
To speak and understand.

**4**

O guide our minds with thy blest light,
With love our hearts inflame;
And with thy strength, which ne'er decays,
Confirm our mortal frame.

**5**

Far from us drive our deadly foe;
True peace unto us bring;
And from all perils lead us safe
Beneath thy sacred wing.

**6**

Through thee may we the Father know,
Through thee th'eternal Son,
And thee the Spirit of them both,
Thrice-blessed Three in One.

**7**   All glory to the Father be,
     With his co-equal Son:

The same to thee, great Paraclete,
While endless ages run.

# 128

# The Spirit of God

Melody: The Spirit Of God
Irregular with Antiphon

Music: Lucien Deiss, C.S.Sp.
Text: Lucien Deiss, C.S.Sp.

**Antiphon**
The Spirit of God rests upon me,
The Spirit of God consecrates me,
The Spirit of God bids me go forth to
proclaim his peace, his joy.

**1**

The Spirit of God sends me forth,
Called to witness the kingdom of Christ
among all the nations;
Called to proclaim the good news of
Christ to the poor.
My spirit rejoices in God, my Savior.
*Antiphon*

**2**

The Spirit of God sends me forth,
Called to witness the kingdom of Christ
among all the nations;
Called to console the hearts overcome
with great sorrow.
My spirit rejoices in God, my Savior.
*Antiphon*

**3**

The Spirit of God sends me forth,
Called to witness the kingdom of Christ
among all the nations;
Called to comfort the poor who mourn
and who weep.
My spirit rejoices in God, my Savior.
*Antiphon*

**4**

The Spirit of God sends me forth,
Called to witness the kingdom of Christ
among all the nations;
Called to announce the grace of salvation to men.
My spirit rejoices in God, my Savior.
*Antiphon*

638

# Holy Spirit, God of Light

Melody: Veni Sancte Spiritus
7.7.7.D

Music: Samuel Webbe, 1740-1816,
slightly adapted by Geoffrey Laycock
Text: *Veni, Sancte Spiritus*, ascribed
to Stephen Langton, c. 1150-1228
freely translated by Anthony G. Petti

**1**

Holy Spirit God of light,
Fill us with your radiance bright;
Gentle father of the poor,
Make us, by your help, secure;
Come, your boundless grace impart,
Bring your love to ev'ry heart.

**2**

Lord of consolation, come,
Warm us when our hearts are numb;
Great consoler, come and heal,
To our souls your strength reveal;
Cool, refreshing comfort pour,
And our peace of mind restore.

**5**

Give to ev'ry faithful soul
Gifts of grace to make us whole;
Help us when we come to die,

**3**

Light immortal, fire divine,
With your love our hearts refine;
Come, our inmost being fill,
Make us all to do your will;
Goodness you alone can give,
Grant that in your grace we live.

**4**

Come, our lukewarm hearts inspire,
Mold our wills to your desire;
In our weakness make us strong,
And amend our every wrong;
Guide us when we go astray,
Wash our stain of guilt away.

So that we may live on high;
Ever let your love descend,
Give us joys that never end.

# Splendor of Creation

Melody: Splendor of Creation
Irregular with Antiphon

Music: Lucien Deiss, C.S.Sp.
Text: Lucien Deiss, C.S.Sp.

**Antiphon:** Send forth your Spirit, O Lord,
That the face of the earth be renewed.

**1**

O my soul, arise and bless the Lord God,
O Lord, in majesty,
Enrobed with pow'r and eternal might.
*Antiphon*

**2**

You are clothed with splendor and with
beauty,
O God, and heav'nly light
Is like a cloud that conceals your face.
*Antiphon*

**3**

You have built your palace on the waters;
On wings of winds and fire

You reign in heav'n, rule supreme on
earth.
*Antiphon*

**4**

Like the winds your angels fly before
you;
As fire and flaming light,
Your ministers stand before your
throne.
*Antiphon*

**5**

Praise to God, the Father, Son, and
Spirit,
To God who gives us life,
Our thanks return, now and ever more.
*Antiphon*

639

# 131

# All Hail, Adored Trinity

Melody:
Old 100th L.M.

Music: Attr. to Louis Bourgeois, 1510-1561. Melody
of *Psalm 134* in the *Genevan Psalter*, 1551, with
English (1583) form of rhythm in last line
Texts: Sts. 1, 2, 3, *Ave, colenda Trinitas*, anon. be-
fore 11th century: st. 4, *Praise God*, Thomas Ken, 1709
Translator: J. D. Chambers, 1805-1893, cento, alt.

**1**

All hail, adored Trinity:
All praise, eternal Unity:
O God the Father, God the Son,
And God the Spirit, ever One.

**2**

Three Persons praise we evermore,
And thee the Eternal One adore:
In thy sure mercy, ever kind,
May we our true protection find.

**3**

O Trinity, O Unity,
Be present as we worship thee;
And to the angels' songs in light
Our prayers and praises now unite.

**4**

Praise God, from whom all blessings
flow;
Praise him, all creatures here below;
Praise him above, ye heav'nly host:
Praise Father, Son, and Holy Ghost.

# 132

# Holy, Holy, Holy

Melody: Nicaea 11.12.12.10

Music: John B. Dykes, 1823-1876
Text: Reginald Heber, 1783-1826, alt.

**1**

Holy, holy, holy! Lord God Almighty!
Early in the morning our song shall rise
to thee:
Holy, holy, holy! Merciful and mighty,
God in three persons, blessed Trinity.

**2**

Holy, holy, holy! All the saints adore
thee,
Though the eye of sinful man thy glory
may not see;
Only thou art holy; there is none beside
thee,
Which were, and are, and ever more
shall be.

**3**

Holy, holy, holy! Lord God Almighty!
All thy works shall praise thy name, in
earth, and sky, and sea;
Holy, holy, holy! Merciful and mighty,
God in three persons, blessed Trinity.

# Come, Thou Almighty King

Melody: Italian Hymn
(Moscow) 664.6664

Music: Felice de Giardini, 1716-1796
Text: Anon., c. 1757, alt.

**1**

Come, thou almighty King,
Help us thy Name to sing;
Help us to praise:
Father, all glorious,
O'er all victorious,
Come, and reign over us,
Ancient of Days.

**2**

Come, thou incarnate Word,
Gird on thy mighty sword;
Our prayer attend;
Come, and thy people bless,
And give thy word success;
Spirit of holiness,
On us descend.

**3**

Come, holy Comforter,
Thy sacred witness bear
In this glad hour!
Thou who almighty art,
Now rule in ev'ry heart,
And ne'er from us depart,
Spirit of pow'r.

**4**

To the great One in Three,
Eternal praises be
Hence evermore!
His sov'reign majesty
May we in glory see,
And to eternity
Love and adore.

# Lord, Who at Your First Eucharist Did Pray

Melody: Unde Et Memores
10.10.10.10.10.10

Music: William H. Monk, 1875, alt.
Text: William Harry Turton, 1881, alt.

**1**

Lord, who at your first Eucharist did
pray
That all your Church might be for ever
one,
Grant us at every Eucharist to say
With longing heart and soul, "Your will
be done."
O may we all one bread, one body be,
Through this blest Sacrament of Unity.

**2**

For all your Church, O Lord, we inter-
cede;
O make our lack of charity to cease;
Draw us the nearer each to each we
plead,
By drawing all to you, O Prince of
Peace;
Thus may we all one bread, one body
be,
Through this blest Sacrament of Unity.

**3**

We pray then, too, for wand'rers from
your fold;
O bring them back, good Shepherd of
the sheep,
Back to the faith which saints believed
of old,
Back to the Church which still that faith
does keep;
Soon may we all one bread, one body
be,
Through this blest Sacrament of Unity.

**4**

So, Lord, at length when sacraments
shall cease,
May we be one with all your Church
above,
One with your saints in one unending
peace,
One with your saints in one unbounded
love;
More blessed still in peace and love to
be
One with the Trinity in Unity.

641

# 135

# God with Hidden Majesty

Melody: Adoro Te 75.75.D

Music: *Paris Processional*, 1697
Text: *Adoro te devote*, Saint Thomas Aquinas,
c. 1225-1274, para. by Anthony G. Petti

1

God, with hidden majesty, lies in presence here,
I, with deep devotion, my true God revere:
Whom this outward shape and form secretly contains,
Christ in his divinity manhood still retains.

2

All my other senses cannot now perceive,
But my hearing, taught by faith, always will believe:
I accept whatever God the Son has said:
Those who hear the word of God by the truth are fed.

3

God lay stretched upon the cross, only man could die,
Here upon the altar God and man both lie;
This I firmly hold as true, this is my belief,
And I seek salvation, like the dying thief.

4

Wounds that doubting Thomas saw I could never see,
But I still acknowledge you my true God to be;
Grant that I shall always keep strong in faith and trust,
Guided by my Savior, merciful and just.

5   Blest reminder of the death suffered for mankind,
Sacrament of living bread, health to every mind,
Let my soul approach you, live within your grace,
Let me taste the perfect joys time shall not efface.

# O Christ, Redeemer of Mankind

Melody: Saint Flavian C.M.

Music: Adapted from *Psalm 132*,
John Day's *Psalter*, 1562
Text: National Office of the Apostleship of Prayer
and of the Eucharistic Crusade, Dindigul, India

1

O Christ, Redeemer of mankind,
Creator of our earth,
Light of Light and God of God,
Son of eternal birth!

2

Love forced you to become a man
That pardon you could win,
As second Adam could restore
What Adam lost by sin.

3

That love which of your bounty made
The earth and sky and sea
Had mercy on our parents' fall,
Broke bonds and set us free.

4

May wondrous love in endless flood
Flow from your wounded side;
May nations win your saving grace,
And, Lord, with you abide.

5

For this you bore the lance's thrust
And scourge and thorns and pains,
That blood and water from your Heart
Might wash away our stains.

6

Glory be to Jesus Christ
Whose Heart does graces send;
To Father and the Spirit too
For ages without end.

# Heart of Christ

Melody: Stuttgart 87.87

Music: C. F. Witt, 1660-1716
Text: Melvin Farrell, S.S.

1
Heart of Christ, we sing thy praises,
Wellspring of eternal life!
Through the sorrows of thy Passion
We find refuge from our strife.

2
Heart of Christ, thou dost embody
All the wonder of God's love!
Thou dost tell the tender mercies
Showered from our God above!

3
Heart of Christ, who bringest healing
To the lowly and the weak,
Let us know thy loving kindness,
Show thyself to all who seek!

# To Christ, the Prince of Peace

# 138

Melody: Narenza S.M.

Music: Melody in Leisentritt's *Catholicum Hymnologium Germanicum*, 1584, adap. by W. H. Havergal, 1793-1870
Text: *Summi parentis filio*
Translator: Edward Caswall, 1814-1878, adap. by A. G. Petti

1 To Christ, the prince of peace,
And Son of God most high,
The Father of the world to come,
Sing we with holy joy.

2 Deep in his heart for us
The wound of love he bore:
A love inspiring all the hearts
That Christ their Lord adore.

3 Dear Jesus, victim blest,
What else but love divine
Could thee persuade to sacrifice
That sacred heart of thine?

4 Pure fount of endless life,
Cool spring of water clear,
Great flame celestial, cleansing all
Who unto thee draw near.

5 Take us to thy dear heart,
For there we long to be,
To find thy grace and after death
Thine immortality.

6 Praise to the Father be,
And sole-begotten Son;
Praise, holy Paraclete, to thee
While endless ages run.

# Come to Me

# 139

Melody: Come To Me
Irregular with Antiphon

Music: Gregory Norbert, O.S.B.
Text: Gregory Norbert, O.S.B.

Antiphon
Come to me, all who labor and are
heavy burdened,
And I shall give you rest.
Take up my yoke and learn from me,
For I am meek and humble of heart.
And you'll find rest for your souls.
Yes, my yoke is easy
And my burden is light.

1
The Lord is my shepherd,
I shall never be in need.
Fresh and green are the meadows
Where he gives me rest.
Antiphon

## 140

# Shepherd of Souls, in Love Come, Feed Us

Melody: Du Meiner Seelen
98.98.88

Music: Hungarian chorale melody,
16th century
Text: Omer Westendorf

**1**

Shepherd of souls, in love come, feed
us,
Life-giving Bread for hungry hearts!
To those refreshing waters lead us
Where dwells that peace your grace
imparts.
May we, the wayward in your fold,
By our forgiveness rest consoled.

**2**

Life-giving vine, come, feed and nour-
ish,
Strengthen each branch with life di-
vine;
Ever in you O may we flourish,
Fruitful the branches on the vine.
Lord, may our souls be purified
So that in Christ may we abide.

**3**

Sinful is man who kneels before you,
Worthy of you are you alone;
Yet in your name do we implore you,
Rich are the mercies you have shown.
Say but the word, O Lord divine,
Then are our hearts made pure like thine.

## 141

# To Jesus Christ, Our Sovereign King

Melody: Ich Glaub' An Gott
87.87 with Refrain

Music: Mainz Gesangbuch, 1870
Text: Msgr. Martin B. Hellriegel,
1941, alt.

**1**

To Jesus Christ, our sov'reign King,
Who is the world's Salvation,
All praise and homage do we bring
And thanks and adoration.

**Refrain**

Christ Jesus, Victor!
Christ Jesus, Ruler!
Christ Jesus, Lord and Redeemer!

**2**

Your reign extend, O King benign,
To ev'ry land and nation;
For in your kingdom, Lord divine,
Alone we find salvation.

Refrain

**3**

To you and to your Church, great King,
We pledge our hearts' oblation;
Until before your throne we sing
In endless jubilation.

Refrain

644

## Great Saint Andrew  142

Melody: Contemplation
87.87.D

Music: Felix Mendelssohn, 1809-1847
Text: Frederick Oakeley, 1802-1880,
adapted by Anthony G. Petti

1 Great Saint Andrew, friend of Jesus,
Lover of his glorious cross,
Quickly, at the Master's bidding,
Called from ease to pain and loss;
Strong Saint Andrew, Simon's brother,
Like him started life anew,
Gladly spread the holy gospel
Which from Word of God he drew.

2 Blest Saint Andrew, noble herald,

True apostle, martyr bold,
Who by deeds his words confirming
Sealed with blood the truth he told.
Never was a crown more glorious,
Never prize to heart so dear,
As to him the cross of Jesus
When its promised joys drew near.

## Hail to the Lord Who Comes  143

Melody: Psalm 32 66.66

Music: Henry Lawes, 1595-1662
Text: John Ellerton, 1826-1893, alt.

1 Hail to the Lord who comes,
Comes to his temple gate,
Not with his angel hosts,
Not in his kingly state;

2 But borne upon the throne
Of Mary's gentle breast,
Thus to this Father's house
He comes, a humble guest.

3 The world's true light draws near
All darkness to dispel,
The flame of faith is lit
And dies the power of hell.

4 Our bodies and our souls
Are temples now for him,
For we are born of grace—
God lights our souls within.

5 O light of all the earth!
We light our lives with thee;
The chains of darkness gone,
All sons of God are free.

## When Mary Brought Her Treasure  144

Melody: Allons, Suivons
Les Mages 76.76.676

Music: Trad. French Carol Melody
Text: Jan Struther, 1901-

1 When Mary brought her treasure
Unto the holy place,
No eye of man could measure
The joy upon her face.
He was but six weeks old,
Her plaything and her pleasure,
Her silver and her gold.

2 Then Simeon, on him gazing
With wonder and with love,
His aged voice upraising
Gave thanks to God above:
"Now welcome sweet release!
For I, my Savior praising,
May die at last in peace."

3 As by the sun in splendor
The flags of night are furled,
So darkness shall surrender
To Christ who lights the world,
To Christ the star of day,
Who once was small and tender,
A candle's gentle ray.

645

## 145

# Look Down to Us, Saint Joseph

Melody: Look Down To Us,
Saint Joseph 76.76.D

Music: Holland, 1539
Text: Michael Gannon

**1**

Look down to us, Saint Joseph,
Protector of Our Lord,
Who followed you through deserts,
And gave you blessed reward;
Our foes are yet about us,
Be strength now at our side;
Be light against the darkness:
Saint Joseph, be our guide!

**2**

We venerate your justice,
The gospels praise your name;
You are the saint all humble,
Who gained eternal fame;
In your devoted family
Our souls in trust confide;
Direct our way to heaven:
Saint Joseph, be our guide!

## 146

# The Great Forerunner of the Morn

Melody: Sedulius L.M.

Music: Nürnbergisches Gesangbuch, 1676
Text: The Venerable Bede, 673-735
Translator: J. M. Neale, 1818-1866

**1**

The great forerunner of the morn,
The herald of the Word, is born;
And faithful hearts shall never fail
With thanks and praise his light to
hail.

**2**

With heavenly message Gabriel came,
That John should be that herald's
name,
And with prophetic utterance told
His actions great and manifold.

**3**

John, still unborn, yet gave aright
His witness to the coming light;
And Christ, the Sun of all the earth,
Fulfilled that witness at his birth.

**4**

Of woman-born shall never be
A greater prophet than was he,
Whose mighty deeds exalt his fame
To greater than a prophet's name.

**5**

All praise to God the Father be,
All praise, eternal Son, to thee,
Whom with the Spirit we adore
For ever and for evermore.

# What Fairer Light?

# 147

Melody: Decora Lux 12.12.D

Music: Samuel Webbe, 1740-1816
Text Attr. to Elphis, ?-493, wife of Boethius
Translator: R. A. Knox, 1888-1957

**1**

What fairer light is this than time itself
doth own,
The golden day with beams more radiant brightening?
The princes of God's Church this feast
day doth enthrone,
To sinners heavenward bound their burden lightening?

**2**

One taught mankind its creed, one
guards the heavenly gate,
Founders of Rome, they bind the world
in loyalty;
One by the sword achieved, one by the
cross his fate;
With laurelled brows they hold eternal
royalty.

**3**

Rejoice, O Rome, this day; thy walls
they once did sign
With princely blood, who now their
glory share with thee.
What city's vesture glows with crimson
deep as thine?
What beauty else has earth that may
compare with thee?

**4**

To God the three in one eternal homage
be,
All honor, all renown, all songs victorious,
Who rules both heaven and earth by
one divine decree
To everlasting years in empire glorious.

# O Raise Your Eyes on High and See

# 148

Melody: This Endris Nyght C.M.

Music: Ancient English Carol,
15th century
Text: Ralph Wright, O.S.B.

**1**

O raise your eyes on high and see
There stands our sovereign Lord,
His glory is this day revealed,
His Word a two-edged sword.

**2**

We glimpse the splendor and the
power
Of him who conquered death,
The Christ in whom the universe
Knows God's creating breath.

**3**

Of every creed and nation King,
In him all strife is stilled;
The promise made to Abraham
In him has been fulfilled.

**4**

The prophets stand and with great joy
Give witness as they gaze;
The Father with a sign has sealed
Our trust, our hope, our praise.

**5**

This glory that today our eyes
Have glimpsed of God's own Son
Will help us ever sing with love
Of Three who are but One.

## 149   'Tis Good, Lord, To Be Here

Melody: Narenza S.M.

Music: Melody in Leisentritt's
*Catholicum Hymnologium Germanicum,*
1584, adapted by W. H. Havergal, 1814-1878
Text: J. A. Robinson. 1858-1933

1 'Tis good, Lord, to be here!
   Thy glory fills the night;
   Thy face and garments, like the sun,
   Shine with unborrowed light.

2 'Tis good, Lord, to be here,
   Thy beauty to behold,
   Where Moses and Elijah stand,
   Thy messengers of old.

3 Fulfiller of the past!
   Promiser of things to be!
   We hail thy body glorified,
   And our redemption see.

4 Before we taste of death,
   We see thy kingdom come;
   Before us keep thy vision bright,
   And make this place our home.

## 150   O Cross of Christ, Immortal Tree

Melody: Saint Flavian C.M.

Music: Adapted from *Psalm 132,*
John Day's *Psalter,* 1562   Text: Stanbrook Abbey

**1**

O Cross of Christ, immortal tree
On which our Savior died,
The world is sheltered by your arms
That bore the Crucified.

**2**

From bitter death and barren wood
The tree of life is made;
Its branches bear unfailing fruit
And leaves that never fade.

**3**

O faithful Cross, you stand unmoved
While ages run their course;
Foundation of the universe,
Creation's binding force.

**4**

Give glory to the risen Christ
And to his Cross give praise,
The sign of God's unfathomed love,
The hope of all our days.

## 151   Praise the Lord, Ye Heavens, Adore Him

Melody: Austria 87.87 D

Music: Franz Joseph Haydn, 1797
Text: Stanzas 1 and 2, *Foundling
Hospital Collection,* c. 1801; st. 3, E. Osler 1836, alt.

**1**

Praise the Lord, ye heavens, adore
   him;
Praise him, angels in the height;
Sun and moon, rejoice before him;
Praise him, all ye stars of light.
Praise the Lord for he has spoken;
Worlds his mighty voice obeyed;
Laws which never shall be broken,
For their guidance he has made.

**3**

Worship, honor, glory, blessing,
Lord, we offer unto thee;
Young and old, thy praise expressing,
In glad homage bend the knee.

**2**

Praise the Lord, for he is glorious,
Never shall his promise fail;
God has made his saints victorious,
Sin and death shall not prevail.
Praise the God of our salvation;
Hosts on high his power proclaim;
Heaven and earth and all creation,
Praise and magnify his name.

All the saints in heaven adore thee,
We would bow before thy throne;
As thine angels serve before thee,
So on earth thy will be done.

# They Come, God's Messengers of Love

# 152

Melody: Saint Botolph L.M.

Music: Gordon Slater, 1896-
Text: Robert Campbell, 1814-1868

### 1
They come, God's messengers of love,
They come from realms of peace
above,
From homes of never-fading light,
From blissful mansions ever bright.

### 2
They come to watch around us here,
To soothe our sorrow, calm our fear:
Ye heavenly guides, speed not away,
God willeth you with us to stay.

### 3
But chiefly at its journey's end
'Tis yours the spirit to befriend,
And whisper to the willing heart,
"O Christian soul, in peace depart."

### 4
To us the zeal of angels give,
With love to serve thee while we live;
To us an angel-guard supply,
When on the bed of death we lie.

### 5
To God the Father, God the Son,
And God the Spirit, Three in One,
From all above and all below
Let joyful praise unceasing flow.

# You Holy Angels Bright

# 153

Melody: Darwall's 148th
66.66.44.44

Music: John Darwall, 1731-1789
Text: J. Hampden Gurney, 1802-1862,
from a poem by Richard Baxter,
1615-1691, adap. by Anthony G. Petti

### 1
You holy angels bright,
Who wait at God's right hand,
Or through the realms of light
Fly at your Lord's command,
Assist our song,
For else the theme
Too high will seem
For mortal tongue.

### 2
You blessed souls at rest,
Who ran this earthly race,
And now, from sin released,
Behold the Savior's face;
His praises sound,
As in his sight
With sweet delight
You all abound.

### 3
Let us who toil below
Adore our heav'nly King,
And onward as we go
Our joyful anthem sing.
With one accord,
Through good or ill,
We praise him still,
Eternal Lord.

### 4
My soul, now take your part,
Acclaiming God above:
And with a well-tuned heart
Sing out the songs of love.
Let all your days
Till life shall end,
What e'er he send,
Be filled with praise.

649

# 154 Christ Is Made Our Sure Foundation

Melody: Belville (Westminster Abbey)
87.87.87

Music Adap. by Ernest Hawkins,
1802-1868, from an anthem by
Henry Purcell, 1659-1695
Text: *Urbs beata Jerusalem*, c 7th cent.
Translator: John Mason Neale,
1818-1866, adap. by Anthony G. Petti

### 1
Christ is made our sure foundation,
Christ is head and Cornerstone;
Chosen of the Lord and precious,
Binding all the Church in one,
Holy Zion's help for ever,
And her confidence alone.

### 2
To this temple, we implore you,
Come, great Lord of Hosts, today;
Come with all your loving kindness,
Hear your servants as they pray,
And your fullest benediction
Shed in all its brightest ray.

### 3
Grant, we pray, to all your people,
All the grace they ask to gain;
What they gain from you for ever
With the blessed to retain,
And hereafter in your glory
Evermore with you to reign.

### 4
Praise and honor to the Father,
Praise and honor to the Son,
Praise and honor to the Spirit,
Ever Three and ever One:
Unified in power and glory,
While unending ages run.

# 155 The Church's One Foundation

Melody: Aurelia 76.76.D

Music: Samuel Sebastian Wesley, 1864
Text: Samuel John Stone, 1839-1900

### 1
The Church's one foundation
Is Jesus Christ her Lord;
She is his new creation
By water and the word:
From heav'n he came and sought her
To be his holy bride;
With his own blood he bought her,
And for her life he died.

### 2
Elect from ev'ry nation,
Yet one o'er all the earth,
Her charter of salvation,
One Lord, one faith, one birth;
One holy Name she blesses,
Partakes one holy food,
And to one hope she presses,
With ev'ry grace endued.

### 3
Though with a scornful wonder
Men see her sore opprest,
By schisms rent asunder,
By heresies distrest;
Yet saints their watch are keeping,
Their cry goes up, "How long?"
And soon the night of weeping
Shall be the morn of song.

650

# Mary, Crowned with Living Light

# 156

Melody: Glorification 75.75.D

Music: *Gossner's Choralbuch*,
Leipzig, 1832
Text: Stanbrook Abbey

### 1
Mary, crowned with living light,
Temple of the Lord,
Place of peace and holiness,
Shelter of the Word.
Mystery of sinless life
In our fallen race,
Free from shadow, you reflect
Plenitude of grace.

### 2
Virgin-Mother of our God,
Lift us when we fall,
Who were named upon the Cross
Mother of us all.
Father, Son and Holy Ghost,
Heaven sings your praise;
Mary magnifies your name
Through eternal days.

# Mary Immaculate, Star of the Morning

# 157

Melody: Liebster Immanuel
11.10.11.10

Music: Melody from *Himmels-Lust*,
1675, adap. and harmonized by
J. S. Bach, 1685-1750
Text: F. W. Weatherell

### 1
Mary immaculate, star of the morning,
Chosen before the creation began,
Chosen to bring, for thy bridal adorning,
Woe to the serpent and rescue to man.

### 2
Here, in an orbit of shadow and sadness,
Veiling thy splendor, thy course thou hast run;
Now thou art throned in all glory and gladness,
Crowned by the hand of the Savior and Son.

### 3
Sinners, we worship thy sinless perfection;
Fallen and weak, for thy pity we plead;
Grant us the shield of thy sovereign protection,
Measure thine aid by the depth of our need.

### 4
Bend from thy throne at the voice of our crying,
Bend to this earth which thy footsteps have trod;
Stretch out thine arms to us, living and dying,
Mary immaculate, Mother of God.

## 158

# Holy Mary, Now We Crown You

Melody: Steiner 87.87
with Refrain

Music: J. L. Steiner, 1735, alt.
Text: Melvin Farrell, S.S.

Refrain:
Holy Mary, now we crown you
Honored Queen of all our race;
Noble Virgin, may our tribute
Win your love and gain us grace.

### 1

On this day we sing your praises,
Purest Maid of all the earth:
While the beauty of the springtime
Tells your joy at Jesus' birth.
*Refrain*

### 2

Glorious Queen, look down in kindness
While before your throne we stand:
Bring God's blessing to your children;
Watch our homes and guard our land.
*Refrain*

### 3

Gate of Heaven, you were Mother
To the King of heav'n and earth:
Now be Mother to your subjects,
In our souls give Jesus birth.
*Refrain*

### 4

Queen of Mankind, while creation
Speaks the grandeur of God's love,
Mold our hearts to seek his glory
Till we reach our home above.
*Refrain*

## 159

# Mother of Christ

Melody: Farley Castle
10.10.10.10

Music: Henry Lawes, 1596-1662
Text: James Quinn, S.J.

### 1

Mother of Christ, our hope, our Patroness,
Star of the sea, our beacon in distress,
Guide to the shores of everlasting day
God's holy people on their pilgrim way.

### 2

Virgin by vow but Mother of all grace,
Chosen by God to be his dwelling-place,
Blessed are you: God's word you did believe,
Your "Yes" undid the "No" of sinful Eve.

### 3

Daughter of God, who bore his holy One,
Dearest of all, the Christ, your loving Son,
Show us his face, O Mother, as on earth,
Loving us all, you gave our Savior birth.

# 160

# Hail, This Festival Day

Melody: Salve Festa Dies
Irregular with Antiphon

Music: Ralph Vaughan Williams,
1872-1958
Text: John Dunn

Refrain:

Hail, this festival day!
Blest day to be hallowed for ever
When we in Mary's praise
Our joyful anthem raise.

**1**

Ave Maria, the maid
Who bore for us the Redeemer;
Blest is she by all creation;
Blest is she in her child.

Refrain

**2**

Ave Maria, the Virgin Mother,
Pray for us sinners.
Hail Mary, full of grace,
Mother of mercy and love.

Refrain

**3**

Star of the ocean most fair,
O lead us to Christ, our brother;
Pray God defend us, ever guide us
Show us his loving care.

Refrain

**4**

Sing out her praises, ye choirs of angels,
Sing all ye peoples.
Heavenly hosts rejoice;
Sing to her glory and praise.

Refrain

# Rejoice, O Virgin Mary

Melody: Rejoice, O Virgin Mary
Irregular with Antiphon

Music: Lucien Deiss, C.S.Sp.
Text: Lucien Deiss, C.S.Sp.

Refrain

Rejoice, O Virgin Mary,
Rejoice, O full of grace.

**1**

For within you is the Lord,
Rejoice, full of grace.
Do not fear, you have found favor in God's sight,
Rejoice, full of grace.          Refrain

**2**

You will bear a child in joy,
Rejoice, full of grace,
Jesus is the name that you will give to him,
Rejoice, full of grace.          Refrain

**3**

He is Son of God most high,
Rejoice full of grace.
God will give him David's throne as he foretold,
Rejoice, full of grace.          Refrain

**4**

At the head of Jacob's race,
Rejoice, full of grace.
He will reign throughout the ages without end,
Rejoice, full of grace.          Refrain

**5**

God the Spirit comes to you,
Rejoice, full of grace.
With his strength the Lord will overshadow you,
Rejoice, full of grace.          Refrain

**6**

This is why the Holy Child,
Rejoice, full of grace.
Who is born of you will be the Son of God,
Rejoice, full of grace.          Refrain

**7**

Glory be to God, on high,
Rejoice, full of grace.
He has made you mother of his only Son,
Rejoice, full of grace.          Refrain

# Hail, Holy Queen

Melody: Hail Holy Queen
Irregular with Antiphon

Music: Lucien Deiss, C.S.Sp.
Text: Lucien Deiss, C.S.Sp.

Hail, holy Queen of the Heavens.
Hail, holy Queen of the Angels.
Hail, Root of Jesse.
Hail, Gate of Heaven.
By you the Light has entered the world.
Rejoice, glorious Virgin,
Beautiful among all women.
Hail, radiant Splendor,
Intercede with Christ for us.

# The God Whom Earth and Sea and Sky

Melody: Eisenach L.M.

Music: Johann H. Schein, 1586-1630
Text: Venantius Fortunatus, c. 530-609
Trans.: John Mason Neale, 1618-1866, alt.

1

The God whom earth and sea and sky
Adore and laud and magnify,
Whose might they own, whose praise they tell,
In Mary's body deigned to dwell.

2

O Mother blest! the chosen shrine
Wherein the Architect divine,
Whose hand contains the earth and sky,
Vouchsafed in hidden guise to lie:

3

Blest in the message Gabriel brought;
Blest in the work the Spirit wrought;
Most blest, to bring to human birth
The long desired of all the earth.

4

O Lord, the Virgin born, to thee
Eternal praise and glory be,
Whom with the Father we adore
And Holy Ghost for ever more.

# Mother of Holy Hope

Melody: Mother of Holy Hope
Irregular with Antiphon

Music: Lucien Deiss, C.S.Sp.
Text: Lucien Deiss, C.S.Sp.

Antiphon:     Mother of holy hope and of love everlasting,
O pray for us.

**1**

At the dawning of time I was known by
the Lord
and his command he gave to me.
He chose the land where I should establish my tent.          Antiphon

**2**

In the city of God he has given me
rest,
and my body he placed therein.
For ever more I shall rule the city of
God.          Antiphon

**3**

As a tree that is planted beside flowing streams,
a cedar strong, lifted on high,
so I took root in the holy people of
God.          Antiphon

**4**

As the odor of spice or the fragrance
of balm,
or choicest myrrh, is my perfume.
As fragrant incense I lift my praise to
the Lord.          Antiphon

**5**

Come to me, all who yearn to be filled
with my fruits,
and you will yet hunger for more.
For all who try me will find my memory
sweet.          Antiphon

**6**

Of a virgin was born Jesus, Lord, whom
we pray.
Glory and praise be to his name.
May every age call his Mother holy
and blest.          Antiphon

# Mary the Dawn

# 165

Melody: Mary the Dawn
Irregular

Music: Paul Cross, 1949
Text: Paul Cross slightly alt.

**1**

Mary the Dawn, Christ the Perfect Day;
Mary the Gate, Christ the Heavenly
Way!

**2**

Mary the Root, Christ the Mystic Vine;
Mary the Grape, Christ the Sacred
Wine!

**3**

Mary the Wheat, Christ the Living-
Bread;
Mary the Stem, Christ the Rose blood-
red!

**4**

Mary the Font, Christ the Cleansing
Flood;
Mary the Cup, Christ the Saving Blood!

**5**

Mary the Temple, Christ the Temple's
Lord;
Mary the Shrine, Christ the God adored!

**6**

Mary the Beacon, Christ the Haven's
Rest;
Mary the Mirror, Christ the Vision Blest!

**7**

Mary the Mother, Christ the Mother's
Son
By all things blest while endless ages
run. Amen.

## 166
# Praise to Mary, Heaven's Gate

Melody Gott Sei Dank
(Lübeck) 77.77

Music: Freylinghausen's *Gesangbuch*, 1704
Text: *Ave, Maris Stella*, c. 9th cent.
Trans.: Rev. M. Quinn, O.P., et al. and adap.

1 Praise to Mary, Heaven's Gate,
Guiding Star of Christians' way,
Mother of our Lord and King,
Light and hope to souls astray.

2 When you heard the call of God
Choosing to fulfill his plan,
By your perfect act of love
Hope was born in fallen man.

3 Help us to amend our ways,
Halt the devil's strong attack,
Walk with us the narrow path,
Beg for us the grace we lack.

4 Mary, show your motherhood,
Bring your children's prayers to
Christ,
Christ, your son, who ransomed man,
Who, for us, was sacrificed.

5 Virgin chosen, singly blest,
Ever faithful to God's call,
Guide us in this earthly life,
Guard us lest, deceived, we fall.

6 Mary, help us live our faith
So that we may see your son;
Join our humble prayers to yours,
Till life's ceaseless war is won.

7 Praise toe Father, praise the Son,
Praise the holy Paraclete;
Offer all through Mary's hands,
Let her make our prayers complete.

## 167
# Queen of Heaven

Melody: Queen of Heaven
Irregular with Antiphon

Music: Lucien Deiss, C.S.Sp.
Text: Lucien Deiss, C.S.Sp.

Queen of heaven, rejoice, Alleluia!
For the Lord whom you were worthy to bear, Alleluia!
Has risen as he said, Alleluia!
Pray for us to God, Alleluia!

## 168
# The Eternal Gifts of Christ the King

Melody: Deo Gratias L.M.

Music: English Melody, 15th cent.
Text: Saint Ambrose, d. c. 397
Trans.: John Mason Neale 1818-1866 and
compilers of *Hymns Ancient and Modern*

**1**
The eternal gifts of Christ the King,
The apostles' glory, let us sing,
And all with hearts of gladness, raise
Due hymns of thankful love and praise.

**2**
Their faith in Christ, the Lord, prevailed;
Their hope, a light that never failed;
Their love ablaze o'er pathways trod
To lead them to the eternal God.

**3**
In them the Father's glory shone,
In them the will of God the Son,
In them exults the Holy Ghost,
Through them rejoice the heav'nly host.

**4**
To thee, Redeemer, now we cry,
That thou wouldst join to them on high
Thy servants, who this grace implore,
For ever and for ever more.

# Now Let the Heav'ns Resound with Praise

# 169

Melody: Rex Gloriose Martyrum
L.M.

Music: *Catholische Geistliche Gesange*, Andernach, 1608
Text: *Exultet Caelum Laudibus*, 10th cent.
Translator: Peter Scagnelli, 1972

**1**

Now let the heav'ns resound with praise
And all on earth their voices raise
In song to honor solemnly
The great apostles' victory.

**2**

Just judges of the world we praise,
True lights for earth through endless days;
The homage of our hearts we pay;
O hear your people as they pray.

**3**

The gates of heav'n your word obey
To welcome in or send away.
We pray: Command our sins to flee;
From bonds of guilt your brothers free.

**4**

Disease and health bow down to you.
Respond as you command them to:
O heal us of our sickness now,
With virtue's light our souls endow.

**5**

So, when the world is at its end
And Christ for judgment shall descend,
May he grant answer to our prayer
And bid us: "Come," your joys to share.

**6**

All glory be to God above;
He sent apostles in his love,
Whose teaching broke the clouds of night
And leads us on to heaven's light.

# Christ, in Whose Passion Once Was Sown

Melody: Mein' Seel', O Gott,
Muss Loben Dich L.M.

Music: M. Praetorius, 1571-1621
Text: Walter Shewring

**1**

Christ, in whose passion once was sown
All virtue of all saints to be,
For the white field of these thy own
We praise the seed and sower, thee.

**2**

Thine was the first and holiest grain
To die and quicken and increase;
And then came these, and died again,
That spring and harvest should not cease.

**3**

From thee the martyrs, we from those,
Each in thy grace's measure, spring;
Their strength upon our weakness flows
And guides us to the goal we sing.

**4**

These were thy great ones: we, thy least,
One in desire and faith with them,
Called by the Lord to keep one feast,
Journey to one Jerusalem.

# A Mighty Fortress Is Our God

Melody: Ein' Feste Burg
87.87.66.667

Music: Martin Luther, 1483-1546
Text: Martin Luther
Translator: Frederick Henry Hedge, 1852

**1**

A mighty fortress is our God,
A bulwark never failing;
Our helper he amid the flood
Of mortal ills prevailing:
For still our ancient foe
Does seek to work us woe;
His craft and power are great
And, armed with cruel hate,
On earth is not his equal.

**2**

Did we in our own strength confide,
Our striving would be losing;
Were not the right man on our side,
The man of God's own choosing:
You ask who that may be?
Christ Jesus, it is he;
Lord Sabaoth his Name,
From age to age the same,
And he must win the battle.

**3**

And tho' this world, with devils filled,
Should threaten to undo us;
We will not fear, for God has willed
His truth to triumph through us:
The prince of darkness grim,
We tremble not for him;
His rage we can endure,
For lo! his doom is sure,
One little word shall fell him.

# For All the Saints

Melody: Sine Nomine
10.10.10 with Alleluias

Music: Ralph Vaughan Williams,
1872-1958
Text: William W. How, 1823-1897

**1**

For all the saints who from their labors
rest,
Who thee by faith before the world con-
fessed,
Thy name, O Jesus, be for ever blest:
Alleluia, alleluia!

**2**

Thou wast their rock, their fortress and
their might;
Thou, Lord, their captain in the well-
fought fight;
Thou in the darkness drear their one
true light:
Alleluia, alleluia!

**3**

O blest communion, fellowship divine!
We feebly struggle, they in glory shine;
Yet all are one in thee, for all are thine:
Alleluia, alleluia!

**4**

But, lo, there breaks a yet more glori-
ous day;
The saints triumphant rise in bright
array;
The King of glory passes on his way:
Alleluia, alleluia!

## Amazing Grace

Melody: Amazing Grace C.M.

Music: Trad. American Melody
Text: John Newton, 1725-1807

1

Amazing grace! how sweet the sound,
That saved a wretch like me!
I once was lost, but now am found,
Was blind, but now I see.

2

'Twas grace that taught my heart to fear,
And grace my fears relieved;
How precious did that grace appear
The hour I first believed!

3   Through many dangers, toils and snares,
I have already come;
'Tis grace hath brought me safe thus far,
And grace will lead me home.

## Loving Shepherd of Thy Sheep

# 174

Melody: Buckland 77.77

Music: Leighton Hayne, 1836-1883
Text: Jane E. Leeson, 1807-1882

1   Loving shepherd of thy sheep,
Keep thy lamb, in safety keep;
Nothing can thy power withstand,
None can pluck me from thy hand.

2   I would bless thee every day,
Gladly all they will obey,
Like thy blessed ones above,
Happy in thy precious love.

3   Loving Shepherd, ever near,
Teach thy lamb thy voice to hear;
Suffer not my steps to stray
From the straight and narrow way.

4   Where thou leadest I would go,
Walking in thy steps below,
Till before my Father's throne
I shall know as I am known.

## The King of Love My Shepherd Is

Melody: Saint Columba 87.87

Music: Trad. Irish Melody
Text: *Psalm 23*, para. by Henry William
Baker, 1821-1877, adapted by
Anthony G. Petti

1

The King of love my shepherd is,
Whose goodness fails me never;
I nothing lack if I am his
And he is mine for ever.

2

Where streams of living water flow,
To rest my soul he leads me;
Where fresh and fertile pastures grow,
With heav'nly food he feeds me.

3

Perverse and foolish I have strayed,
But he with love has sought me,
And on his shoulder gently laid,
And home, rejoicing, brought me.

4

In death's dark vale I fear no ill,
With you, dear Lord, beside me;
Your rod and staff my comfort still,
Your cross will ever guide me.

5

You spread a banquet in my sight,
My head with oil anointing,
And let me taste the sweet delight
From your pure chalice flowing.

6

And so through all my length of days
Your goodness fails me never;
Good Shepherd, may I sing your praise
Within your house for ever.

# Rise Up, O Men of God

Melody: Festal Song S.M.

Music: William H. Walter, 1894
Text: William Pierson Merrill, 1911, alt.

**1**

Rise up, O men of God!
Have done with lesser things,
Give heart, and soul, and mind, and
strength
To serve the King of kings.

**2**

Rise up, O men of God!
His kingdom tarries long:
Bring in the day of brotherhood
And end the night of wrong.

**3**

Rise up, O men of God!
The Church for you does wait:
Sent forth to serve the needs of men,
in Christ our strength is great!

**4**

Lift high the cross of Christ!
Tread where his feet have trod.
As brothers of the Son of man,
Rise up, O men of God!

# 177

# This Is the Feast Day of the Lord's True Witness

Melody: Iste Confessor
11.11.11.5

Music: Angers Church Melody
Text: *Iste Confessor Domini Colentes,*
8th century
Translator: Peter Scagnelli, 1972

**1**

This is the feast day of the Lord's true
witness,
Who on this day received the glory due
him.
Let all creation celebrate his goodness,
Cherish his mem'ry.

**2**

Prudent in judgment, gentle toward his
brothers,
Open, unselfish in the love he offered.
All of his days the Gospel was his wis-
dom,
Christ his true teacher.

**3**

Brother was he to all the world's forgotten;
Lonely and ill, they came to him for
healing.
God gave him power, gifts for man's
salvation:
Love, health, and pardon.

**4**

One, then, in songs of praise we sing
his glory,
Calling to mind the peace and joy God
gave him,
Asking his prayers to help us in life's
battle,
All through the ages.

5   Glory and praise be to our God forever,
Radiant in splendor, awesome in his power,
Guiding creation onward to fulfillment,
One God, Three Persons.

# Now from the Heav'ns Descending

Melody: Aurelia 76.76.D

Music: Samuel S. Wesley, 1810-1876
Text: James Quinn, S.J.

**1**

Now, from the heav'ns descending,
Is seen a glorious light,
The Bride of Christ in splendor,
Arrayed in purest white.
She is the holy City,
Whose radiance is the grace
Of all the saints in glory,
From every time and place.

**2**

This is the hour of gladness
For Bridegroom and for Bride,
The Lamb's great feast is ready,
His Bride is at his side.
How bless'd are those invited
To share his wedding feast:
The least become the greatest,
The greatest are the least.

**3**

He who is throned in heaven
Takes up his dwelling-place
Among his chosen people,
Who see him face to face.
No sound is heard of weeping,
For pain and sorrow cease,
And sin shall reign no longer,
But love and joy and peace.

**4**

See how a new creation
Is brought at last to birth,
A new and glorious heaven,
A new and glorious earth.
Death's power for ever broken,
Its empire swept away,
The promised dawn of glory
Begins its endless day.

# Now Let Us Praise

Melody: Sine Nomine
10.10.10 with Alleluias

Music: Ralph Vaughan Williams,
1872-1958
Text: English para. of the Breviary
Hymn for the Office of a Holy Woman
by Sister Jane Marie Perrot, D.C., alt.

**1**

Now let us praise a woman noble,
    great,
A valiant servant of the God of Hosts;
Her holiness is famed, renowned
    abroad.
Alleluia, alleluia.

**2**

Afire with shafts of holy love she turned
From earthly joys to yearn for those of
    heav'n;
Eternal triumph now her soul's reward!
Alleluia, alleluia.

**3**

Her earthly prison penance kept sub-
    dued;
She fed her soul on pray'r's sweet food
    alone;
Thus did she seek the glory of her
    Spouse.
Alleluia, alleluia.

**4**

All strength and honor, praise and glory
    be
To God the Father, and His only Son,
And Holy Spirit ever Three in One:
Alleluia, alleluia.

## 80

### The Beatitudes

Melody: The Beatitudes
Irregular with Refrain

Music: Enrico Garzilli, 1970
Text: Enrico Garzilli, 1970

1 Blessed are the poor of heart,
Blessed are the merciful,
For they will be blessed upon the
earth.
Blessed are the poor!

2 Blessed are they who suffer,
Blessed are they who are persecuted,
For they shall be the rulers of the
world.
Blessed are the poor!

5 Blessed are they who labor for
peace,
Blessed are they who suffer in war,

For they shall meet the Prince of
Peace.
Blessed are the poor!

3 Blessed are they who hunger and
thirst
For justice and the rights of all,
For they shall eat the meal of the
Lord.
Blessed are the poor!

4 Blessed are they whose hearts are
clean
And blessed are they who keep his
word,
For they have inherited the land.
Blessed are the poor!

## 181

### Blest Are the Pure in Heart

Melody: Franconia S.M.

Music: W. H. Havergal, 1793-1870.
Based on a melody in J. B. Konig's
Harmonischer Lieder-Schatz, Frankfort, 1738
Text: S. Keble, 1792-1866, et al.

1 Blest are the pure in heart,
For they shall see our God:
The secret of the Lord is theirs,
Their soul is Christ's abode.

2 The Lord, who left the heavens
Our life and peace to bring,
To dwell in lowliness with men,
Their pattern and their King:

3 Still to the lowly soul
He doth himself impart,
And for his dwelling and his throne
Chooseth the pure in heart.

4 Lord, we thy presence seek;
May ours this blessing be;
Give us a pure and lowly heart,
A temple fit for thee.

## 182

### O God, Our Help in Ages Past

Melody: Saint Anne C.M.

Music: William Croft, 1708
Text: Isaac Watts, 1674-1748. alt.

1 O God, our help in ages past,
Our hope for years to come,
Our shelter from the stormy blast
And our eternal home.

2 Beneath the shadow of your throne
Your saints have dwelt secure.
Sufficient is your arm alone,
And our defense is sure.

3 Before the hills in order stood,
Or earth received her frame,
From everlasting you are God,
To endless years the same.

4 A thousand ages in your sight
Are like an evening gone,
Short as the watch that ends the
night
Before the rising sun.

5 Time, life an ever-rolling stream,
Bears all its sons away;
They fly forgotten, as a dream
Dies at the opening day.

6 O God, our help in ages past,
Our hope for years to come,
Be now our guide while life shall last,
And our eternal home.

# Who Would True Valor See 183

Melody: Monks Gate
11.11.12.11

Music: Trad. Sussex melody,
adap. by Ralph V. Williams, 1872-1958
Text: John Bunyan, 1628-1688, alt.

1 Who would true valor see,
Let him come hither;
One here will constant be
Come wind, come weather;
There's no discouragement
Shall make him once relent
His first avowed intent
To be a pilgrim.

2 Who so beset him round
With dismal stories,
Do but themselves confound.
His strength the more is.
No lion can him fright,
He'll with a giant fight,
But he will have a right
To be a pilgrim.

3 No power of evil fiend
Can daunt his spirit;
He knows he at the end
Shall life inherit.

Then fancies fly away,
He'll fear not what men say;
He'll labor night and day
To be a pilgrim.

# O Radiant Light, O Sun Divine 184

Melody: Jesu, Dulcis Memoria
(plainchant) L.M.

Music: Gregorian
Text: *Phos Hilaron*, Greek 3rd cent.
Translator: William G. Storey

1 O radiant Light, O sun divine
Of God the Father's deathless face,
O image of the light sublime
That fills the heav'nly dwelling place.

2 Lord Jesus Christ, as daylight fades,
As shine the lights of eventide,
We praise the Father with the Son,
The Spirit blest and with them one.

3 O Son of God, the source of life,
Praise is your due by night and day;
Unsullied lips must raise the strain
Of your proclaimed and splendid name.

# May Flights of Angels Lead You on Your Way 185

Melody: Unde Et Memores
10.10.10.10.10.10

Music: William H. Monk, 1875, alt.
Text: James Quinn, S.J., 1969

May flights of angels lead you on your way
To paradise, and heav'n's eternal day!
May martyrs greet you after death's dark night,
And bid you enter into Zion's light!
May choirs of angels sing you to your rest
With once poor Laz'rus, now for ever blest!

663

# INDICES

# INDEX OF PSALMS

# INDEX OF CANTICLES

# GENERAL INDEX OF HYMNS

# ACKNOWLEDGMENTS

The International Committee on English in the Liturgy, Inc. is grateful to the following for permission to reproduce copyright material:

*HYMNS*

ACTA Foundation, Chicago, 60613: no. 59, © 1967.

Ampleforth Trustees: nos. 27 and 148.

The Benedictine Foundation of the State of Vermont: no. 139, © 1971.

Benedictine Nuns of Stanbrook Abbey: nos. 29, 76, 83, 150 and 156 from *Stanbrook Abbey Hymnal.*

Geoffrey Chapman Publishers, London: nos. 5, 12, 15, 21, 41, 42, 51, 125, 159, 178 & 185, © James Quinn, S.J., from *New Hymns for All Seasons.*

Church Pension Fund of the Protestant Episcopal Church: nos. 46 & 69.

J. Curwen & Sons, Ltd., London: no. 14, used by permission of G. Schirmer, Inc.

John Dunn: no. 160.

Editors of *Praise the Lord,* © 1972 by Geoffrey Chapman, London: no. 85.

Faber Music Ltd.: nos. 18, 22, 28, 30, 35, 50, 58, 72, 87, 92, 99, 108, 110, 111, 115, 116, 117, 129, 135, 138, 142, 153, 154 & 175 reprinted from *New Catholic Hymnal.*

B. Feldman & Company: no. 16.

Fides Publishers, Inc. Notre Dame, Indiana: nos. 52 & 184, © 1973, from *Morning Praise and Evensong.*

Enrico Garzilli and F.T.T.W.L.: nos. 44, 106 & 180, © 1970, from *For To Those Who Love God.*

G.I.A. Publications, Inc. 7404 S. Mason Ave., Chicago, Illinois 60638: nos. 40, © 1969, reprinted from *Worship* and 114, © 1970.

Helicon Press, Baltimore: no. 64 © 1975, reprinted from *The Catholic Liturgy Book,* nos. 169 & 177, © 1975.

David Higham Associates, Ltd., agent for Eleanor Farjeon: no. 4, © Eleanor Farjeon from *The Children's Bells* (Oxford University Press).

Gabriel Huck: no. 63.

J. R. Hughes: nos. 36 & 86.

Hymns Ancient and Modern Ltd., Suffolk, England: no. 163.

Hymn Society of America: no. 24, © 1959, from *Fifteen Christian Education Hymns.*

Jerome Leaman: no. 34.

McLaughlin & Reilly: no. 91, © 1964, from *Hymns for use at Holy Mass,* and no. 179 from *Charity Sings* © 1967 by McLaughlin & Reilly; copyright assigned 1972 to A. P. Schmidt Co., Evanston, Illinois.

Earnest Merrill: no 176.

Methodist Publishing House, London: no. 7 from *Hymns and Songs.*

Mount Saint Bernard Abbey: no. 2.

National Office of the Apostleship of Prayer and of the Eucharistic Crusade, Dindigul — 620004, India: no. 136.

North American Liturgy Resources, Phoenix: nos. 66 & 113, © 1970.

Oxford University Press: nos. 89, 122 & 172 from the *English Hymnal,* nos. 25, 39 & 144 from *Enlarged Songs of Praise* and nos. 17 & 37.

Search Press Ltd, Ldn: nos. 102, 147 and 170 (*The Westminster Hymnal*)

Stephen Somerville: nos. 78 & 93, © 1971 by Stephen Somerville.

Stainer & Bell Ltd.: no. 38. © 1972, from *Pilgrim Praise* by Fred Kaan.

West Malling Abbey: no. 48.

World Library Publications, Inc., 2145 Central Parkway, Cincinnati: nos. 3, 11, 55, 68, 90, 98, 107, 130, 161, 162, 164 & 167, © 1965, from *Biblical Hymns and Psalms, Volume I* by Lucien Deiss, C.S.Sp.; nos. 79 & 128, © 1970, from *Biblical Hymns and Psalms, Volume II* by Lucien Deiss, C.S.Sp.; nos. 80 & 144, © 1964, 1966, no. 62. © 1965, and no. 60, © 1966 from *Peoples Mass Book;* no. 137, © 1955, 1961, nos. 65, 95, 124 & 158 © 1955, 1966, nos. 82, 96 & 104, © 1964, from *Peoples Mass Book,* 1971; nos. 33 and 166, © 1965, and no. 57, © 1968.